CW00970081

PELICAN BOOKS

INCOME DISTRIBUTION

Jan Pen holds the chair of economics at
Groningen University, the Netherlands. Born
in 1921, he was educated in Amsterdam.
From 1947 to 1956 he was Director of
General Economic Policy at the Ministry of
Economic Affairs; and from 1960 to 1967
Visiting Professor of Macro-economics at the
Free University of Brussels. He is a Fellow of
the Royal Netherlands Academy of Sciences.
His previous books are *The Wage Rate under
Collective Bargaining* (1959), *Modern Econo-
mics* (Pelican, 1965), *Harmony and Conflict in
Modern Society* (1966), and *A Primer on Inter-
national Trade* (1967).

JAN PEN

Income Distribution

PENGUIN BOOKS

Penguin Books Ltd, Harmondsworth, Middlesex, England
Penguin Books Inc., 7110 Ambassador Road, Baltimore, Maryland 21207, U.S.A.
Penguin Books Australia Ltd, Ringwood, Victoria, Australia
Penguin Books Canada Ltd, 41 Steelcase Road West, Markham,
Ontario, Canada

First published by Allen Lane The Penguin Press 1971
(This was the first publication of *Income Distribution*,
written in Dutch, and translated by Trevor S. Preston)
Published in Pelican Books 1974

Made and printed in Great Britain by
Cox & Wyman Ltd, London, Reading and Fakenham
Set in Monotype Times

FOR JUDITH
*who supplied, in a continuous
domestic debate, a good deal
of the inputs*

Contents

CONTENTS

CHAPTER I

The Many Faces of Income Distribution

1. *Facts, Theories, Value Judgements*

THE purpose of this book is to survey the facts, theories and value judgements of income distribution. It is difficult to imagine a more controversial subject. The inequality of incomes has been debated for centuries without passions waning or a clear picture emerging. The facts are the subject of differences of opinion, the theories are many and often conflicting, and above all people fail to agree on just what a proper or fair income distribution should be. Everybody knows that incomes are unequally distributed, but everybody has his own ideas about the causes of this and about the steps that would lead to an improvement. Come to that, some think that there has been far too much of a levelling. The differences of opinion are partly the product of opposing interests: many people feel that others receive unjustifiably high incomes, that others cause inflation with their wage demands or their increased profits, or even that other people's incomes are entirely misplaced (interest!). The debate has generated more heat than light. But in addition it cannot be denied that the cooler, theoretical approaches differ greatly, and that, in particular, forms the subject of this book.

Economics does not give a clear-cut and single answer to the question of what really determines the distribution of incomes. One of the reasons for this is that 'income distribution' may mean different things; for instance, distribution among persons, or among social groups or among labour or capital. The nature of the theoretical approach is radically different, depending on the subject. In the one case – that of distribution among a large number of persons – it is logical that we should look for statistical regularities and explanations and this brings us almost automatically to chance and its very specific and sometimes odd laws.

7

In another case it seems more fruitful to apply the typically economic mode of thought, in which the value of a commodity, a unit of labour or a unit of capital is explained by its scarcity. The latter approach is found in the explanation of the height of wages and interest; there, 'supply and demand' is the magic formula with which economists solve the matter. And we set about things in yet another way when we try to explain total income of labour or capital as a whole. We then fall back on modern macro-economics, where things are quite different from what they are in micro-economics, which applies to small units in economic life. Take as an example of the difference in reasoning: if John Williams, a lorry-driver, gets a 10% rise, he is 10% better off (apart from PAYE); but if all workers in a country get a money wage increase of 10% prices will rise, so that income distribution changes less than one might think at first sight. If all income recipients – workers, shopkeepers, businessmen, rentiers – get 10% more money, the distribution does not change at all; a simple truth, but one that is often forgotten. This difference between micro-economics and macro-economics confuses many people, and one of the intentions of this book is to blow some of the smokescreen away.

It goes without saying that facts and theoretical explanations must be kept separate. And yet, in popular discussions, they are often intermingled, and in the process a number of persistent misunderstandings also occur. Take as three examples: many people (and in particular many wage-earners) believe that the inflation that has been going on since the war has harmed real wages. In other words, they believe that prices rise more quickly than wages. This is not correct, except in a few exceptional cases, and then only for brief periods. Calculated over a number of years, money wages in all modern countries rise more strongly than prices; this results in a real wage increase of several per cent a year. That process has already been going on for a century or more, and inflation has not interrupted it. On the contrary, the price increase in most countries is accompanied by an accelerated growth in production (unfortunately not in the United Kingdom) from which almost everyone benefits. This is a fact that can be established by statistical observation – which does not even need to be very exact. Closer inspection reveals a shift in distributive shares;

but capitalists, not workers, are the victim of this. Now some commentators apparently ignore this, and indulge in bitter reflections on the harm suffered by their own share, reflections based on non-existent facts. Come to that, inflation gives almost everyone the feeling that he is lagging behind – behind his neighbour, his boss, behind prices, behind what he wants. A real lag occurs only among small groups: rentiers, pensioners, scattered small businessmen. Before debating possible causes of income differentials, agreement must first be reached on such facts; otherwise rational discussion is out of the question.

A second misunderstanding prevails among the middle classes: teachers, doctors, senior civil servants. They often think that their incomes are around the middle, in the sense that about as many people earn more as earn less. We are not concerned here, any more than we just were, with a subtle difference of opinion about the facts, but with a common prejudice: people overrate the number of the very wealthy. In reality even some secondary school teachers are among the top 5% of income recipients in Britain (1969), and most doctors among the top one per cent. I once asked a medical specialist, who is probably among the top 0·3% of the income pyramid, which part of the population he thought were above him. He considered the question and answered: 20%. Such gross misconceptions do not contribute towards a cool intellectual climate.

A third misunderstanding, or rather a misleading simplification, is that there are only two kinds of income recipients: low-paid workers and rich capitalists. This is a less popular idea, for casual observation shows us that there are small businessmen, such as publicans, and working members of the middle classes, such as dentists – two occupations with which everyone comes into contact. The dichotomy between labour and capital is a favourite subject of theoreticians, like left-wing intellectuals and neoclassical students of macro-distribution (see Chapter V). Nor is it correct that workers receive income only from wages and capitalists income only from capital. In other words, it is misleading to think that workers and capitalists form two completely separate groups. There are many people in paid employment who also own a few shares, although these are often the people with the higher wages and salaries. Yet the opposite view is even further from the truth: that our society has become a 'people's capitalism', in which every worker has managed to save a little capital and industry is owned by practically everybody. Once again the facts are just not like that. There are few figures to hand about the amount of savings held by workers, but they suffice to show that the expression 'people's capitalism' is nothing but empty propaganda. A study for the Wider Share Ownership Council reveals that more than one-third of British shop-floor workers own less than £50, and only 16% have over £500 in savings. Only 7% of the adult British population own any shares.* The top 1% of the people – that is, the well-to-do, the rich and the very rich – own, in most countries, about 30% of total personal wealth.† This figure points to tremendous inequality but, on the other hand, it shows that 70% of personal wealth is owned by people who should not be depicted as very wealthy. It is not true that 'the nation's wealth is owned by a small group of capitalists', for the really rich constitute only a fraction of the top 1%. Nor is there any truth in the assertion that 'the wealthy capitalist' is nowadays somewhat of a historical figure.‡ Millionaires are still alive and kicking, and it takes a good deal of ignorance to assert the opposite. It seems that in this field you can get away with almost any kind of nonsense.

A further source of confusion lies in overrating the share of profits in the national income. Many people feel that this share is about 50% or even more. Actually the figure is about 20%, and this still includes remunerations for work (lawyers, small businessmen, farmers). Moreover, generous helpings of income accrue not to natural persons, but to legal persons. In particular the limited liability companies pocket a large part of total profits. It is tempting to compare these profits with workers' wages. However,

---

* *Sharing the Profits*, two studies made for the Wider Share Ownership Council, 1968.

† An often quoted figure for Britain, i.e. 43%, is even higher. It was estimated by H. F. Lydall and D. G. Tipping ('The Distribution of Personal Wealth in Britain', *Bulletin of the Oxford University Institute of Statistics*, 1961). I have reason to believe that 43% is too high (see p. 278).

‡ Made by Lord Shawcross and Maurice Macmillan in their Foreword to *Sharing the Profits*.

this is comparing cows and apples. For the companies' profits are passed on to natural persons: shareholders, management and the board of directors, executives and sometimes all the employees. The distribution of profits depends on institutional circumstances, which may work out in quite different ways. If broad profit-sharing schemes are the rule for all employees, the personal distribution is naturally different from the usual case in which the management and the directors award themselves liberal bonuses. The spread in shareholding also influences the ultimate distribution of income among individuals. For the purpose of understanding personal distribution it is rather meaningless to set the profits of these collective bodies against the wage of the individual worker.

Differences of opinion about facts and contrasting ideas on the most effective theoretical explanation are only two of the three sources of confused discussion. The value judgements give the most trouble. Thoughts differ about what ought to be. Many people have ideas about a just income distribution, which of course is fine, but these ideas sometimes trip them up when trying to explain the existing state of affairs. It usually makes a difference whether you want to explain a phenomenon or pass ethical judgement on it; and yet the two are often confused, with the result that both the explanation and the judgement may suffer. It is not so very long ago that some considered it inadmissible to explain wages in terms of supply and demand, the argument being that human labour ought not to be bought and sold like a commodity. (In the same way doctors ought not to be able to investigate the causes of tuberculosis – after all, bacteria should not exist!) Nowadays this blend of moral condemnation and causal explanation is outmoded, at least among economists. However, there is now a tendency towards the other extreme, as they try to banish the whole ethical side of economics. This chaste attitude is cutting us off from a whole area of explanation of reality – that is to say in all those cases where evaluations are the causes of observed facts. Now that is exactly the case in income distribution. For some incomes – mainly top incomes – reflect a social value system, and we can understand them only if we know the standards that lie behind them. I shall repeatedly come back to this point.

Thus, unlike most economists, I am of the opinion that it is quite relevant to discuss the justness and the moral correctness of income distribution. Consequently, this occurs below, though in a separate section (Chapter VII, 1). That does not mean to say that a coercive system of normative rules acceptable to everyone emerges; rather, I shall confine myself to a survey of the existing ideas and some comments on them. It is for everyone to decide how he applies his criteria and to make up his own mind, but some discussion of these criteria is not taboo. On the contrary, I feel that precisely the economist, who after all is used to pondering problems of distribution, can make his contribution to this ethical discussion, and I also feel that he must have some understanding of social value systems if he is not to adopt an uncomprehending attitude towards some particularly interesting income relations.

The primary intention of this book is to supply information on the many varying approaches to income distribution. Although facts are indispensable and I shall not shy from discussing evaluations, the stress lies on the ways of explanation, i.e. on theory. We shall see that in this field too there is an enormous diversity.

2. *Income Creation and Income Distribution*

The term income distribution is really a misleading one.* It suggests that first a total income is created which is then distributed among people by some official body or other. That is, in fact, the procedure in a family, although in that case as well the distributing authority is not so easy to point to. Indeed, much the same thing can happen in small units of production, for instance a kibbutz. But distribution works differently in a country as a whole. There income is created in production; the four factors of production – labour, capital, land and entrepreneurs – collaborate in a firm to bring about a product. In the course of that process a large number of things happen simultaneously; one of them is that incomes are paid out. In other words, income is created and

---

* Except when we interpret it in the sense that statisticians do; they speak of a frequency distribution. For this purpose a mass is divided into a number of size classes; the frequency distribution indicates how densely these classes are populated. See below, Chapter III, 2.

distributed at one go. Income distribution is from the very start the outcome of an intricate economic complex.

It is worth while establishing this simple truth. For this stresses that there is no central office that regulates distribution; after all, production takes place in thousands and thousands of firms, and in non-profit organizations too, such as government services (a school is also a productive unit). From that decentralized process there emerges a certain pattern of distribution for which no single person, or group, or official body is responsible. Of course groups, especially government agencies, can consciously influence distribution, and that happens on a large scale, but in the first instance income relations are a by-product of a much more comprehensive economic process. It is as well to make a distinction between primary income distribution, which comes about in production, and secondary income distribution, which ultimately occurs after the government has levied taxes and paid out subsidies, after social security contributions have been deducted and benefit has been paid out on account of illness, disability, unemployment, children, old age, and so on. Between the primary and secondary income distributions are the income transfers. The latter are deliberately organized by institutions that are responsible for them. Criticism of the income transfers is criticism of a deliberate policy. Criticism of primary income distribution is criticism of a system, a mechanism, a process. True, conscious influencing again occurs in this context: unions try to have wages raised, salaries are deliberately set at certain levels, agricultural organizations want higher incomes for farmers (and the government helps them by supporting the prices of agricultural produce), profits are increased by cartel agreements and reduced by government intervention; but nevertheless this is much more diffuse. Blind forces predominate, and that truth is brought out when we recall that incomes are created in production.

And moreover we would do well to bear in mind the intimate relation between income creation and income distribution, because that is what makes clear the real basis of most people's income. It is in principle the contribution that they make to production. This is the basic idea of the neo-classical distribution theory: the factors of production are remunerated in accordance with the

13

value that they add to the social product. It is an idea, of course, which provokes many questions: how is that contribution determined? Is it not true to say that in fact nobody can be dispensed with in production? How is the total value of the product created by the blending of all the productive contributions broken down again? These questions will of course be discussed; but the connexion between production and distribution of the income remains an elementary fact that has to be faced.

When we speak of productive contributions – and that will happen a good many times from now on – we must not think of labour alone. Capital also contributes to production. This is occasionally overlooked by those who find that the capitalist is not entitled to his income acquired without working. Whether he is in fact an exploiter or not is something that we shall not consider here – that is another question. But it is a fact that the result of production can be tremendously enhanced by capital, i.e. machinery, bridges, roads, telephone lines, schools, hospitals. Indeed, the production per man (labour productivity) depends much more on the amount of capital per worker than on the degree of effort displayed by the latter. And so it goes without saying that the factor of production known as capital receives remuneration. Of course, that does not prove that capital has to be in private hands and even less that that number of hands has to be so small. One could imagine capital as the property of workers' co-operatives, of institutions of public utility, of the state or of 'the people'; those are political questions. But that capital increases production, and thus under a system of free markets commands a price, is a cold fact, and an understandable one too. In the past there has been a great deal of most esoteric writing about the deeper essence of capital (a shadow of this will be found in Chapter IV, 5) and that is amusing as long as we do not allow it to confuse us and do not lose sight of the simple fact that scarce, productive capital can command a price on the market.

3. *Three Problems*

In order to arrange the many theories about income distribution in some kind of order, a distinction is usually made between three main problems. This distinction largely determines the theoretical approach (and the set-up of this book), and is made between personal distribution, functional distribution (also called 'the prices of productive contributions' or 'factor prices') and distributive shares.

Personal distribution (or: the 'size distribution of incomes') relates to individual persons and their income. The *way in which* that income was acquired often remains in the background. What matters is how much someone earns, not so much whether that income consists of wage, interest, profit, pension or whatever. And further special attention is paid to income recipients as a collective body, in which regular patterns are sought. While therefore this approach is concerned in the first instance with individuals, they are regarded as countless little components of a mass. The word *mass* has a specific significance here: it is a term from statistics, used to designate the total of the phenomenon under investigation (a synonym is population). And in fact the theory of personal distribution is closely bound up with statistical analysis, which is applicable to everything where large numbers occur: rats, or marbles in a vase, or income recipients. This part of the theory of income determination therefore has a specific method. The investigator begins by so arranging the individuals and their incomes that a reasonably clear picture forms; that can be done in a variety of ways, with which we shall concern ourselves later. He then sets out to find statistical 'laws'; Italian and French statisticians in particular have done a great deal of work on this subject, which is discussed in Chapter VI. They play with concepts that have a lot to do with the anonymous workings of chance, which leads to surprising formulas and viewpoints. Finally, if this approach is to make sense, an explanation must be sought for the regular patterns found. This technique determines the character of the theory of personal distribution. The odd thing is that the individuals who formed the initial starting point tend to vanish from view; they become nameless atoms, subject to random forces. A drawback of this method, at least for the purposes of this book, is that it is rather mathematical and that the laws that it finds are of a somewhat mysterious nature. Sometimes it is believed that an iron law has been found, but what it actually represents is difficult to say. Yet attempts at economic interpretation have been made that are susceptible to a simple explanation, which will therefore be attempted below. One of the characteristics of this field of research is that there are a disturbing number of divergent theories.

Quite a different atmosphere prevails in *functional distribution*. Here we are no longer concerned with individuals and their individual incomes, but with factors of production: labour, capital, land and something else that may perhaps best be called 'entrepreneurial activity'. The theory examines how these factors of production are remunerated. It is primarily concerned with the price of a *unit* of labour, a *unit* of capital, a *unit* of land, and being therefore an extension of price theory (see next paragraph) it is sometimes called the theory of factor prices. That determines its character. Some are not satisfied with that character – they do not recognize income distribution in this approach. Thus E. Cannan spoke of 'pseudo-distribution' and A. Mitra criticized 'the tyranny of mechanistic per unit analysis'.* That seems exaggerated to me – an explanation of the basic forces that determine the wage rate and the interest rate is useful and necessary. However, it is true that this extension of supply and demand analysis does not give the whole picture.

Price theory, which looks at the interaction of supply and demand, is an old and well-thought-out chapter of economics; once upon a time it was more or less the central doctrine, and though that has changed through the advent of modern macro-economics, price determination still occupies many a page in the textbooks. The theories on that subject are fairly homogeneous. There are shades of meaning rather than differences of opinion. Economists make universal use of supply and demand curves to determine price levels, and the same procedure is followed for income distribution. The wage rate is determined by the supply of, and demand for, labour. The interest rate is determined by the supply of, and demand for, capital. This can be read in any textbook of economics; it is the best-known part of distribution theory.

And yet complications arise when we apply price theory to

* E. Cannan, 'Division of Income', *Quarterly Journal of Economics*, 1905. A. Mitra, *The Share of Wages in National Income*, 1954.

labour and capital. These relate in the first place to the influence of power. Some observers would rather think in terms of the power structure than in those of the forces of the market. The high incomes of top executives can in fact be understood only if we bear in mind that they are in a position in which they can fix their own remuneration. Supply and demand do not take us far here, nor does the concept 'productive contribution', dear to the hearts of economists. Here 'power' is a more enlightening term than the forces of the market. And perhaps something of the same kind applies to wages fixed by collective bargaining. A form of power is also operative there – it is concentrated in the part played by the unions. They influence wage determination, but opinions differ – also among economists – as to how and to what extent. This is a matter which will concern us later (Chapter IV, 4).

In the second place some, including myself, have the feeling that wage determination in particular is subordinate to social value judgements. True, that is not at variance with supply and demand, and yet it is something on which many economics textbooks remain silent. The economists' curves have something deterministic about them, so that we are in danger of forgetting that wages and salaries sometimes express social status more than productivity. That, too, is something to consider further.

In the third place supply and demand analysis begins to present difficulties as soon as we switch from relatively small parts of an economy to very large markets, as for instance the whole labour market. These difficulties arise because national income is influenced by wage determination on a large labour market; in that case micro-economic reasonings are often highly misleading. While micro-economics suits our purposes very well for wage determination in one branch of industry (in that case national income may, by definition, be taken as given), we need macro-economics for determining the wage level in a whole country. A higher wage means not only higher costs, thus reducing the profit; it also means more purchasing power and more sales, thus increasing the profit. The wage-profit-wage spiral influences distribution, and that cannot be grasped by the pure theory of supply and demand. Micro-wage theory may even be misleading because particular wage rates move together: there is a 'wage structure'.

Interest determination is really in all cases a macro-economic problem, because the capital market is a 'large' market. Capital is mobile, as a result of which the 'submarkets' for various kinds of loans are interconnected. Moreover, a part is played by the creation of money by the banks, a matter that obviously belongs in macro-economics: it influences the rate of interest, the price level and national income. And so we cannot say that we have brought functional distribution within the grasp of the theory by constantly murmuring the magic formula 'supply and demand'. There is more to it, as we shall see.

The *theory of distributive shares* (which incidentally some authors call 'functional distribution'; I would argue against doing so) attempts to explain the share of the total national income that each factor of production receives. It inquires into the percentage that labour receives of the whole, and also into the shares of interest, rent and profit. Now individual income recipients disappear beyond the horizon. This is of course pure macro-economics, and in this area we see the most varied approaches. Most textbooks tend to pass lightly over this subject – the many publications on it are of a specialist nature.* The approach now prevailing is the neo-classical theory, which offers countless intellectual and practical advantages, and of which I am a cautious supporter. It explains the income of a factor of production by the contribution that this factor makes to production, which in itself is a simple and attractive idea. Moreover, this leads to a close synthesis between production theory and distribution theory, from which both can gain. Furthermore, the neo-classical theory of distributive shares fits in well with the theory of functional distribution – that may seem a self-evident truth, but a number of competing approaches, such as the Keynesian, lack that connexion entirely (in particular N. Kaldor's theory on the share of labour – about which I will have quite a few bad things to say – has no contact at all with the usual wage theory). And finally it is an advantage that the neo-classical theory lends itself to particularly graceful conclusions

* The theory of distributive shares, inspired by D. Ricardo (see p. 42), faded into the background in the nineteenth century, especially under the influence of marginalism (see p. 77). The great advocate of a renaissance was E. Cannan in his article cited above.

and elegant formulas. Precisely in this field interesting work has been done in recent decades, which has also led to practical results. For instance, the neo-classical theory has recently rendered understandable one of the most paradoxical phenomena of our day, viz. the fact that a society which requires for its production a steadily increasing amount of capital per worker gives the providers of that capital a steadily decreasing share of national income. We shall of course come back to this.

While the division of this book is largely based on the distinction between personal distribution, functional distribution and distributive shares, and I therefore consider this tripartition important, this does not mean to say that the three problems are independent of each other. They are evidently three aspects of one and the same reality, and so interwoven in some way or the other.* But this weft and warp is not in all respects simple.

The connexion between personal and functional distribution is in the first instance obvious: if the amounts of factor of production that every individual has to offer are given, then the factor prices determine how the income will be divided among the individuals. But the matter is complicated by the fact that interaction may occur between quantities and prices. A high income leads to savings, and so wealth is born, which in turn leads to high incomes again. Moreover, the average interest on considerable wealth may be higher than on small investments, because the very well-off investor can take more risks, can get better information and can exercise more power over the firms in which he has invested his money. Evidently the forces that determine personal income are cumulative, and there we have right away a reason for the inequality. This accumulation incidentally also operates in the

* It is therefore strange that they are often kept quite apart in the literature. There are books that deal entirely with distributive shares, without referring to personal distribution. Examples: the otherwise very interesting collection *The Behavior of Income Shares*, 1964, the report of a meeting held in New York (*Studies in Income and Wealth, A Report of the National Bureau of Economic Research*). Also E. Scheele, *Einkommensverteilung und Wirtschaftswachstum*, 1965. Conversely, numerous essays on personal distribution have been written as if there were no theory of price determination, and a link between personal distribution and distributive shares is hardly ever established in them.

direction of low incomes – poverty breeds poverty, for instance because someone who is down and out is obliged to accept the first job that comes along, even if it is badly paid. Here too there is an interaction of quantities and prices, and here too there are forces that pull incomes further apart.

The link between factor prices and distributive shares is much more puzzling. At first sight you might say: if wages rise, the workers get a larger part of national income. However, viewed more closely this is not necessarily true. It might very well be that forcing up wages causes employment to drop – and then the end-result is no longer so certain. There is a theory, bound up with the production function of Cobb-Douglas (a subject that will be further discussed in Chapter V), which states that forcing up wages creates exactly so much unemployment that the share of labour remains constant. In other words, if this were correct there would not be the slightest connexion between factor prices and income shares. The latter would be determined quite differently. I do not say that I believe this – in fact I believe that the 'naïve' idea is correct, viz. that wage increases lead to a larger share of labour. But this apparently simple opinion needs solid support, for it is anything but self-evident among economists.

The connexion between distributive shares and personal distribution is also anything but unambiguous. It is true that the very wealthy acquire their income almost entirely from capital (or from profits tied up with the possession of capital) so that a drop in capital's share in national income makes the personal distribution less lopsided. But on the other hand some people with low incomes are worse off. Small rentiers often have less income than the average person in paid employment; they are the victims of inflation and in this respect the wage push makes the distribution less uniform. These are annoying complications, but we cannot avoid them.

The relations between our three main problems are evidently complex. This makes it impossible to put forward quick and clear-cut theories. My ideal is one fully integrated theory of the prices of productive factors, distributive shares and personal distribution, but the reader will become aware of the fact that economics has not got as far as that. The three issues will stay rather detached from each other. Yet I will try to build at least a few bridges between them, and even this is pretty unusual. Economists seldom point to the undesirability of the apartheid between the three problems. They certainly do not put enough effort into trying to eliminate it.

4. *The Set-up of this Book*

I have long hesitated as to what should come first and what last. Personal distribution is the phenomenon that requires the ultimate explanation, and functional distribution is mainly a way to understand personal distribution. In this sense the pricing of productive factors and the theory of distributive shares can lay claim to a preceding treatment. On the other hand, personal distribution supplies us with the facts of life: income figures of the poor, the middle classes, the rich. Facts go before their explanations. This is why most textbooks start by giving an impression of personal distribution (but they leave it almost unexplained). I follow this example: in Chapter III the facts of income inequality are presented in a preliminary way. This is quite a problem in itself: how to arrange a chaotic mass of information in an orderly manner. I have opted to start from what I call a Parade of Dwarfs, which is a somewhat unusual way of presentation; after that come more traditional graphs (the frequency distribution and the Lorenz curve). In Chapter IV we proceed to the explanation of factor prices – this is basic stuff. Distributive shares naturally follow in Chapter V. Then we return to personal distribution, and more in particular to the description of statistical regularities and their explanation. The set-up has the advantage that in Chapters IV, V and VI the reader will meet increasingly difficult and intriguing material. Chapter VII is about ethical norms for income distribution and about policies for decreasing inequality; it deals with less technical matters.

Our three problems cover a good deal of the theory of income distribution, but not all of it. There is also *sectoral* distribution (which part of the national income goes to agriculture, to banking, to exporters, to the textile industry, to the government?) and *geographical* distribution (why is Northern Ireland poor? Why is inequality between nations even greater than between individual persons?). The simple reason for leaving these questions out of consideration is that books may become too fat.

I am, in this volume, addressing myself to three groups of readers: in the first place to students of the various social sciences, who find the literature on income distribution rather frightening. There are so many publications in this field, and most of them are so specialized, that many students suffer from an *embarras du choix*. Now one book more does not reduce the quantity of literature, but I have tried to give a survey of the existing theories, which may save the reader some trouble. On the other hand, I have tried to prevent the book from becoming too difficult – that is necessary above all for the third group of readers, the general public, a group insisting on comprehensibility. I have also tried to avoid the riding of hobbyhorses; this book is characterized by a lack of originality. It is mainstream economics, written from a slightly detached viewpoint; now and again I speak of economists as of a strange tribe with an exotic folklore, and they deserve to be so treated. The trend of the book is rather sceptical yet I have attempted to retain the best aspects of various forms of explanation. This eclectic approach incidentally means that no ambitious synthesis has been attempted between the many differing theories. The present state of the science does not permit of this. Attempts at building large models covering every facet of income distribution have so far led only to ingenious mental exercises – unfortunately so ingenious that almost everyone is in danger of losing the thread.*

The second group to whom I am addressing myself is that of my fellow-economists. Some of them do not need me – I mean those who have closely followed the work of Solow, who have understood the celebrated article by Champernowne (Chapter VI, 1; unfortunately, I cannot say that I did) or who work with distribution statistics all day long. And yet I would ask these specialists to read the section on Kaldor's theory – true, it is the least pleasant

* This is different in other fields. Keynesian economics lends itself better to model-building.

of the whole book, but it is just too ridiculous that this nonsensical theory is still incessantly praised, elaborated and presented at conferences. This waste of time and effort can end only if the vanguard cooperates and it is high time for that.

But there are so many economists who are not specialists. They know the state of the theory from the textbooks of ten years ago – and that is an inadequate basis. For in the last decade distribution theory has changed rather considerably, notably through the new attention that the production function has been given. Moreover, the textbooks are very incomplete. As a rule they deal quite well with the prices of the factors of production, but pass over personal distribution almost entirely. Pareto's Law sometimes gets a passing nod, but that of Gibrat (which is nevertheless more realistic) hardly ever. The numerous attempts to explain these statistical regularities will be sought in vain in the ordinary textbook, and as a result many economists have not made their acquaintance. These theories are to be found in articles published in journals that are difficult to get hold of. The same applies, to some extent, to the explanation of distributive shares; once again there are plenty of articles on this subject, and particularly fascinating specialized collections – but the textbooks are sketchy or worse on this point.* There is reason, therefore, for a separate survey, which is meant at the same time to brush up old knowledge.

I have tried to give the three parts – factor prices, distributive shares, and personal distribution – the same depth of treatment, and that is what makes the book different from the textbooks and many other publications. This intention dictates the set-up: the three parts each get a chapter to themselves. Chapter IV, which

* P. A. Samuelson's well-known book (*Economics, An Introductory Analysis*) does discuss the distributive shares, but under economic growth. My experience is that most students have difficulty in keeping these two topics apart. R. G. Lipsey and P. O. Steiner devote in their *Economics* – an excellent book, often regarded as the rival to Samuelson – *one* page of text to distributive shares (plus a table, pp. 421–3) where they explain that economics really does not yet understand anything about this subject. This agnosticism does not do justice to the recent quantitative research, and it lays the stress wrongly; the very weak theories of Kalecki and Kaldor are mentioned, but nothing is said about the work of the neo-classical writers. Worse still, Lipsey and Steiner say: 'We cannot deal at all with this important class of problems' (p. 422).

deals with the prices of productive contributions, is not dissimilar from what appears in every textbook (except that I dissociate myself from the all too economic explanation of the wage structure and also consider the social value judgements). It is Chapter V (on income shares) and VI (on personal distribution) that present information lacking in many books. Not in the advanced and highly technical kind; but this book tries to be simple and as non-technical as possible.

I owe that to the third group of readers, my favourite public: the interested laymen and laywomen. I dislike the expression, because it suggests a sharp distinction between the expert author and the non-expert reader. One cannot draw such clear-cut lines in economics. Of course Robert Solow, who is a top man in neo-classical theory, is rather different from the housewife who reads this book out of curiosity about a subject that arouses her indignation from time to time, but Kenneth Boulding is also a great economist, and yet his ideas about income distribution are none too good.* I could go on listing intelligent experts who have slipped up on distribution theory, but it is not my intention to undermine faith in economics. I just want to say that a certain modesty befits we economists. We are indeed qualified to counter some popular misunderstandings, such as 'price increases make everybody poorer', but we cannot convince the public if we adopt a superior attitude, make economics appear more mysterious than is strictly necessary, or forget that the 'man in the street' has often had sound ideas which economists have wrongly dismissed as nonsense (the strongest example is the classical view that there was no such thing as general overproduction – this was still being maintained in the middle of the Thirties!). Moreover, the 'man in the street' is a non-existent fiction: he may be someone who is not interested in economics (but who, for instance by his training in engineering, would have no difficulty in quickly grasping the

* His theory is unfolded in *A Reconstruction of Economics*, 1950 (2nd edition 1962). It is an unsuccessful attempt to derive the distributive shares from a number of accounting identities. The present book will not further discuss this failure, since there is no point in flogging a dead horse (that is the difference with Kaldor's theory – that horse is still trotting around). A criticism is to be found in W. Kerber. *Die Verteilungstheorie von Kenneth E. Boulding*, 1966.

essence of production functions); he may also be someone who has been led by dissatisfaction to adopt all kinds of unreal ideas (such as real wages are continuously falling, or the share of labour in national income is continuously falling). He may also be a politician who is daily confronted with the political aspects of inequality and would like to know what economists have to say about it. A two-class division of economists and laymen is just as misleading as that between workers and capitalists.

And yet my favourite public causes me a few awkward problems. It is so easy to lapse into technical language. The factors of production (labour, capital, land, entrepreneurial activity) are words that are easily written, but does everyone know what they mean? Now a glossary can help, and one is consequently appended. What is more serious, because it is more difficult to avoid, is the mathematical stumbling-block. Many a housewife with whom I should like to discuss income distribution may be daunted by $Q = F(L,K)$, and even more so by $\partial Q/\partial L$. And yet the production function and the marginal product of labour are essential for grasping reality; they can also be translated into words, but this does not make them any easier.

It is therefore as well briefly to explain here how far exactly the mathematics in this book goes. The concept of a function, and more particularly the production function, is essential and will be explained as clearly as I can manage in Chapter IV. The derivatives of the latter function (the partial derivatives: variable capital is added to constant labour, or vice versa) are likewise essential – and explained. Further, *elasticities* are very important. By these the economist means the relative (= percentage) change in a variable that is the result of a change of 1% in another variable. The best-known example is the elasticity of demand introduced by A. Marshall around 1900: increase the price by 1% and see by how much the quantity demanded decreases. If that is e%, the elasticity of demand is e.

In this book various elasticities occur. Pareto's Law has one: take an imaginary income, see how many people earn at least that income, and then raise it by 1%. The number of people now falls by α%. This α keeps on returning, whatever income level one has in mind, and that is then the 'law' (see Chapter VI, 1). In Chapter IV supply and demand elasticities (of labour and capital) come to the fore. Moreover, the elasticity of substitution puts in an appearance there: increase the relation between wage and interest by 1%, and see how the quantitative relation K/L reacts. If this reaction is $\sigma\%$, then the elasticity of substitution is σ. This variable pops up again in Chapter V, where it plays a particularly strategic role. To make matters difficult, a further elasticity appears on the scene in that chapter, which is rather like marginal productivity: let the amount of labour increase by 1%, and see how much production increases as a result of this. If this is $\alpha\%$, we call the elasticity of production in respect of labour α. The same goes for capital; here too we can define an elasticity of production in respect of capital. These magnitudes are strategic variables in the determination of income shares.

While the elasticities are important to the explanation of factor prices and to income shares, in Chapter VI, where we are concerned with personal distribution, we encounter logarithms.* These are powers of a base number (usually the number 10). The logarithm of 100 is 2, that of 1,000 is 3, that of 10 is one and that of 50 is 1·6990 (my son looked the last one up in logarithm tables). There is some point in looking at the logarithms of individual incomes instead of looking at the incomes themselves. A man who earns £1,000 gets the number 3, a man who earns £10,000 gets the number 4 and so on. Gibrat's Law (Chapter VI, 2) is based on this curious manner of presentation, and some insight into these logarithms is therefore essential in order to follow Chapter VI fully. I am aware that this is an almost insuperable difficulty for many readers. For me too, come to that; for if I try to reproduce logarithmic laws in words, and this is what I do, the mathematically trained readers will think me childish. If I do not do so, other readers will not understand me. That's what comes of trying to write for a wide public. But my general advice is: don't let equations put you off. They seem more difficult than they are, and I too

---

*Elasticities and logarithms are, by the way, related to one another. If $Y = X^a$, then a is the elasticity of Y in respect of X and at the same time the logarithm of Y is equal to a times the logarithm of X. This truth may come in handy when we are discussing the Cobb-Douglas function and the Solow function (Chapter V 5).

am a layman in mathematics. The latter may be a consolation to some readers.

One of the general conclusions of almost every chapter of this book is that there are too many theories for explaining the given facts. We do not yet have available measurements, tests or other techniques to tell us which is *the* theory. The reader may therefore choose, if he wants to, although I do guide him to some extent in a given direction (that of the neo-classical theory, but within that theory there are again a number of shades of difference). That freedom of choice naturally is much greater when we are concerned with standards and norms; opinions differ as to what is the most fair or the most desirable income distribution. We can hardly prescribe to another what criteria he must apply, although such prescriptions are dished out daily and on a large scale. In this respect, too, reality has many faces. And with regard to the political measures that can change the distribution, one opinion is certainly not automatically better than another. Differences in political taste cannot simply be abolished, and a good thing too. But ethical prescriptions and political measures can be compared, commented on, discussed; this is done in Chapter VII. That will be a disappointing account for those who think that the distribution can be radically changed at will. Intervention is possible, but the old situation tends to restore itself. A great deal of pressure has to be put on income distribution if it is to be really and substantially changed.

CHAPTER II

Dull Warnings

1. *Statistical Matters*

THE last thing I want to do is to bore the reader. The best way of spreading dullness is to nag about the difficulties of the concept of income, about statistical imperfections, about the little we know of the facts. Yet honesty compels me to make a few of these dull and negative remarks.* There is no escaping the fact that you can come across the strangest opinions about income distribution that are the result of careless juggling with figures. Hence this itemized list.

(a) *Income in cash and in kind.* This is an old matter from the textbooks, in which you often encounter the farmer eating his own potatoes or the butler who is given board and lodging in his employer's home. But much more interesting are the facilities that employees of firms get. The company car that is also used for private purposes. For the top executives: the company plane. Generous expense accounts. Hospitality to business connexions, business friends, relatives and friends at company expense. The country house available for that purpose. All the firm's clerical and technical services are also privately available to the top executives. Neither managers of large firms nor their wives ever have to renew their passports themselves or queue for tickets or for anything else. As someone moves higher up the firm, these privileges increase, and if we forget to include them we find an income distribution that is less unequal than in reality. According as the large, well-organized concern occupies a more important place in society, the number of people profiting from these privileges grows, and a counterforce is created against the levelling-out of

* A sharp critic of the too easy acceptance of the official figures of the Board of Inland Revenue is R. M. Titmuss (*Income Distribution and Social Change*, 1962). He leaves hardly anything standing of our factual knowledge. A useful but discouraging book.

distribution. But since this particularly relates to the top 1% of income recipients, and they earn very large sums anyway, the quantitative effect is perhaps not very large, relatively speaking. (The social effect, on the other hand, *is*.)

(b) *Income and wealth*. Separating these two seems easier than it is. If a person receives an income in cash only, there is no problem; what he saves is added to his wealth. The interest on it is of course income again. But what if the market value of the investments rises? We could debate at length whether that is income or not. The chief criterion is its spendability. Does someone who spends the enhanced market value of his securities on a holiday lose financial ground compared with the situation before his shares rose in value? Has he eaten into his wealth? Answers may differ. I can imagine somebody saying that a rise in share prices is not income but wealth if in the meantime *all* prices of investments and capital goods have risen, because if the investor should wish to convert his securities into capital goods he would have to pay more. This is quite obvious in the event of a person saving to buy a house and holding shares until such time as he has built up the money required. If the price of the shares rises equally with that of the house, then spending the enhanced value of the shares is manifestly a loss; he will have to save further to pay for the house. In this case a rise in share values is not income. But if someone's specific investment portfolio increases in value and the prices of other securities and capital goods remain the same (or rise less), spendable income has been created.

The latter case often occurs in practice when employees of a large firm are paid not in money but in shares. They frequently acquire them for a song. Here we clearly have a supplementation of money income, which may assume considerable proportions. Neither the tax authorities nor the statisticians are consistent in recognizing this income, and so a distortion of the picture again occurs in favour of senior executives of large firms. Here too we easily underestimate the skewness of the distribution.

These special increases in wealth, which may be put on a par with incomes, play statistics false in all those cases in which profits are accumulated in a business firm. A considerable percentage of corporate profits is retained. To which persons must these savings be considered as accruing? Probably to the shareholders, but in our present methods of calculation this does not happen, even if the rise in value of the business is reflected in the market price of its shares. According to the statisticians this is wealth, not income. Reality is even more obscured if one or more people own a firm. Retained profits ought certainly to be counted as their income, but this does not happen; come to that, the extent of this accumulation is not always capable of exact estimation, even by insiders. This means that there are wealthy people who do not even approximately know what their income was over a given year, let alone that statistics could reveal it to outsiders.

(c) *Income and pension.* We see more or less the same distortion of the picture in the pension schemes for managers in which the firm pays the premium. There is a tax gain from replacing someone's last salary increases in his career by a well-devised Top Hat pension scheme. Here too there is more skewness than appears at first sight.

Private persons can also shift income towards the future (or towards their heirs) provided that they are rich enough to have expert advisers. Various forms of settlement (trusts, covenants) are very much the vogue, and in Britain in particular the tax authorities view these benevolently.* In this way chunks of income disappear from those who earn them; they pop up again in the bank accounts of others. The net result is a sham levelling. Incidentally, the pension question does not only occur at the top of the income pyramid. The firms also pay (compulsory) premiums for their workers. These contributions to social security may or may not be included when statistics are being drawn up. Some statisticians include them; others do not. This makes a difference of a few per cent in the figures found for the distributive shares. In the U.K. these premiums form about 5% of the wage sum; that makes a difference of 3·5 percentage points in the share of labour.†

* Titmuss says (p. 70): 'the United Kingdom is remarkable in the Western world for the generous legal opportunities it allows for the alienation of income by means of irrevocable covenants'.

† cf. C. H. Feinstein, 'Changes in the Distribution of the National

(d) *Tax evasion and avoidance*. Much – not all – of our knowledge of distribution stems from tax figures, and they have their own peculiarities. The reader will already have suspected that not everyone tells the tax inspector everything about his income. The distorted picture that results from this fraud operates above all to the advantage of individual businessmen. In addition there are countless legal methods of avoiding tax. In Britain these are above all the voluntary gifts,* which may border closely on fraud. In the United States they include exemptions for interest on state and local bonds, and the fantastic allowance for the depletion of natural resources. And finally, beyond the reach of the tax authorities are all incomes lying below the exemption level – some 20% of income recipients earn too little to receive an assessment, and they do not occur in the fiscal statistics. True, there are other ways of tracking down these incomes: wage statistics, social security, and so on. The total profits that some entrepreneurs deftly whisk out of reach of the tax people can also be estimated for some purposes (the distributive shares) in another way; National Bookkeeping is rather helpful for this purpose. But this still does not give us these incomes on an individual basis, and evasion remains a difficult matter when we try to ascertain the facts of personal distribution.

(e) *Individual and family income*. Incomes are as a rule earned by individuals – only in the case of family businesses, such as farms, cafés, small shops, can one say that the family is the earning unit. There is thus something to be said for considering the individual. But prosperity is more dependent on the total family income, and we usually have prosperity in the back of our minds when we look at statistics. The indications that individual and family income give of prosperity may be completely contradictory. This is particularly evident from the case of the wife working for money. Perhaps she does so mornings only, or for a few days a week – in that case statistics records a low income, and the superficial ob-

---

Income in the U.K. since 1860', *The Distribution of the National Income* p. 119.

*G. S. A. Wheatcroft, *The Taxation of Gifts and Settlements*, 1958.

server is inclined to see this as an indication of an unsatisfactory or even scandalous situation.* The frequency distribution of income displays a number of minimum incomes on the low side, and that gives great inequality. But if we look at family income, the state of affairs is more cheerful: the wife is supplementing her husband's normal income, which perhaps also gives her a feeling of independence. She works as long as she pleases and can indulge in a change of job from time to time. Viewed socially, her situation is perhaps more pleasant than that of a bread-winner with a good salary but tied to his job.

We see the same thing with young people's wages. In the statistics of individual incomes they display a distortion towards the low side. But this is not necessarily coupled with poverty. Large families with a few working children sometimes see a quick rise in prosperity, though one which is often of short duration: after a time the children leave home. The young people themselves do not necessarily feel poor or unhappy with their relatively low incomes either; the skewness of the distribution is therefore rather meaningless. Statistics gets into even greater difficulties if the young people have temporary jobs (a paper round, working for a month to pay for a holiday). Calculated over the whole year these are of course starvation wages. With the increasing independence of young people and the greater tendency to travel such temporary jobs are becoming more and more fashionable, especially among schoolchildren and students. As a result, statistics on an individual basis is beginning to look too pessimistic. But many income figures are modelled on the family.

To escape the heterogeneity of income recipients, some authors have recourse to a somewhat artificial approach. They leave out everyone who works part-time, or even all women and juveniles. The one who goes the furthest in this, H. Lydall, considers only what he calls the Standard Distribution: 'Male adults, in all occupations, in all industries except farming, in all areas, working full-time and for the full period'.† This Standard Distribution is a

* To my mind the situation is scandalous indeed in so far as she receives less money per hour than a man would get for the same work; but that is another matter.
† *The Structure of Earnings*, 1968, p. 60.

good subject for theoretical explanation – which is what Lydall has in mind – but of course it presents a peculiar picture of reality. If we leave women and farmers out of consideration, why not domestic staff, sweet-shop assistants or foresters?

(f) *Ages*. Beside the question of families, that of ages is of independent significance. For incomes are registered to be compared with one another – comparison is the purpose of every study in this field. And it is the question whether that is permissible with incomes of persons of differing age. Imagine a country in which age is venerated. Young people have to work for very low wages that increase with the years. Anyone who has reached the age of forty is entitled to a fair-sized income; from then on it rises quickly. People aged seventy and eighty are very rich, and every centenarian earns £100,000. In such a society there would be a skew income distribution, but the conclusions drawn from it regarding fairness, social structure or economic mechanisms would be quite different from those in a society where age is irrelevant to income.

Now in reality such as we know it age is in fact a criterion, though in weakened form. In this respect there are great differences between occupations. A bench hand who is on his full adult wage and knows his job backwards has only a slight chance of wage increases other than those resulting from the general growth of productivity. He has no career in front of him. Junior executives do have; they are marked out as senior executives, though not all of them make it. Young barristers usually earn little; their income grows with the years. Accountants, economists and engineers display differences in income within their professions that are closely correlated with age. This is probably most strongly the case with heirs; although it does happen that babies are born rich by inheritance or by the provisions of trust funds, most potential heirs have to wait a long time before they can step into dead men's shoes. Often they remain potential heirs until well into middle age. The long wait is sometimes alleviated by arrangements *inter vivos*, but this does not affect the principle that wealthy heirs are often well advanced in years. The opposite, a negative correlation between income and age, is rare: professional footballers and members of successful beat groups are examples.

33

The age group displaying the greatest differences in income is that of the pensioners. Most people have to take a sharp drop in income when they retire. This does not happen to the very rich, the possessors of really big wealth. As they collect more interest and dividends than they can spend, they get richer as they grow older.

The complications that advancing age entails – also for our subject – can hardly be circumvented. A standard distribution might also be envisaged here: we convert the actual income structure into the one which would pertain if everyone was of the same age. But this is a fanciful operation to perform, and I know of no attempts in that direction. Usually personal distribution is taken as it is, and it is accepted that the age of income recipients is one of the many factors determining income structure. This is not entirely satisfactory, but the same may be said of all the points mentioned in this section.

Neglecting the age structure becomes entirely unsatisfactory and completely misleading if the distribution is compared over periods in which the number of old or young people has greatly increased – for instance, a comparison between now and before the war. Today there are many more old people, and young people with a job on the side. If they were still as badly paid as in 1938, the share of the lowest 20% of income recipients in national income would have dropped sharply. Since this is not so, it suggests a greater equality of distribution. It is on this point that some pessimistic views of the development of inequality fall down.*

(g) *Economics and statistics.* It is a familiar complaint of economists that statistics fails to supply the very data that they need. An instance is the concept of rent in the very special meaning attached to it by some theoreticians: an income that is not required to make the recipient do his daily work.† No wonder the statistics tell us nothing about this; this surplus income can be measured only by asking the income recipients penetrating questions ('for which minimum income would you be prepared to do your present work?') which could easily be misunderstood and could lead to vague or irritated answers.

* Chapter III, 3.
† See for this Chapter III, 3.

A better example of the gap between empirical data and economic questioning is presented by the desire to divide income into that from work and that from capital, even if in fact it is earned as one undivided income. A doctor's fee is partly a payment for work (even if the man is not in the paid employment of anyone), partly a payment for capital (medical equipment, car) and partly profit (the difference between proceeds and costs). Now there are economists who want to split national income into only two parts: income from work and income from capital. They come to grief with that doctor, and statistics cannot help much either. This puzzle can be solved in various ways (none of them very satisfactory); Chapter V, 1, tells more about this.

These were sombre remarks. But one can be too sombre; as we shall see, it is possible to outline a number of the main aspects of distribution, though often very roughly. I would not like to convey the impression that all statistics are worthless, all conclusions suspect, all theories unfounded;* but it is as well to bear in mind that we are reasoning on the strength of what are often shaky empirical data. This reservation assumes more importance when we compare periods in which the population structure (e.g. the number of old people) has changed.

2. Social Groups

I can imagine some readers not being satisfied with the nature of the questions raised above. Suppose that we presently succeed – I believe that I can promise the reader that – in grasping the market and power mechanisms that regulate wages, rent, interest and profits, that we find a few elegant formulas that represent the shares of the factors of production in national income, and that we discern some regular patterns in personal distribution. What have we got then? We then know a number of 'laws' – Hicks's Law, Pareto's Law, Gibrat's Law – abstract conclusions that

---

*Titmuss goes just a little too far in this direction for me. Here is an American voice: 'The income figures are surprisingly accurate and complete. The methods used to compile them are sound.' (H. P. Miller, *Rich Man, Poor Man*, 1964, p. 14. This is a useful and very clear book that abounds with figures for the United States.)

convey a theoretical impression and make no allowance for the full reality of social life. Although I have the feeling that we should be careful about speaking disdainfully of abstract theory (for every form of thought entails abstraction), and I also feel that sentimental exclamations about the full life obscure rather than elucidate the world, I still think that in this case there is something to it. For the concepts that economics preferably uses have little in common with the categories that are called 'social', and that is abundantly clear in the field of income distribution. In the case of personal distribution we see colourless individuals that are swallowed up in the masses, and the neo-classical theory pays more attention to dead things than to living people. When it speaks of groups of income recipients it lumps together people who would be surprised to find themselves in the same group.

The best example of this potential surprise is supplied by labour. This means the people who work on the basis of a contract of employment. Anybody who works for someone else is an employee, and it is this collectivity that we have in mind when we speak of wages and the share of labour. That is to say, we have placed under a common denominator the farm hand, the bookkeeper, the doctor's assistant, the Principal at the ministry, the charlady and the managing director of a limited company. It is not automatically pointless to consider such a heterogeneous group, but doubts about its utility are understandable. And the same applies to the concept 'entrepreneurs'; into this category come the smallholder, the grocer, the portrait painter, Robert Maxwell, the prostitute, the self-employed doctor and the banker (providing he owns the bank himself). Anyone who regards income distribution as a social phenomenon will see little good in such a classification and will try to establish one of his own. This gives another face to the theory of income distribution.

The pioneers in this field are Marchal and Lecaillon.* Their theory is sometimes called 'sociological' – a word that gives many people a feeling of warmth, of sympathetic human relations and

*J. Marchal and J. Lecaillon, *La répartition du revenu national*, 1958. Further: J. Lecaillon, 'Changes in the Distribution of Income in the French Economy', in: *The Distribution of the National Income*, ed. by J. Marchal and B. Ducas, 1968.

deeper understanding, but irritates most economists. Marchal and Lecaillon divide income recipients into the following groups: (i) non-independent persons (with as subdivision: manual workers in agriculture, manual workers in industry; domestic servants; foremen; junior managerial staff); (ii) independent persons in industry and trade (subdivided into: legal persons, such as limited companies;* managers; individual entrepreneurs; free professions), (iii) independent farmers, (iv) capital-holders (subdivided into agricultural landowners; urban landowners; private capital-holders; banks), (v) recipients of transferred incomes (subdivided into three groups: children, old people, the sick; unemployed, students, armed forces; the clergy). I have given this list to show the difficulties it encounters. Its aim – to get a grip on the social groups – may be laudable, but its effect summons up a good deal of criticism.

In the first place it is assumed that the groups in fact are distinct and separate; however, this is evidently not realistic. Many private capital-holders are at the same time entrepreneur, or manager, or they practise a free profession. Among the agricultural landowners one naturally finds farmers. In the second place a really social homogeneity of the groups is not achieved in this way. For instance, it is odd that unemployed and students are put into the same group, and the category 'individual entrepreneurs' still contains birds of a very different social feather (bankers and small shopkeepers). The free professions cover wealthy surgeons and impecunious sculptors, who have little in common either economically or socially. In the third place, under (ii) and (iv) legal persons, viz. limited companies and the banks (whatever their legal form may be), are put on a par with natural persons, which tends to be confusing.

However, the greatest difficulty with the theory of Marchal and Lecaillon lies not in their classification, for that could be improved. The trouble is, what they have to offer is not a genuine theory but a collection of figures furnished with some comments. Thus in France (1956) farmers received 10% of national income, agricultural workers nearly 2%, industrial and commercial entrepreneurs 16%, managers and the free professions 7%, junior

*I object to this. See p. 11 above.

management 6%, 'salaried employees' 6%, industrial workers 21%, domestic staff over 1%, and inactive persons 10%, while about 15% of national income went to institutions and firms.* This gives some idea about income structure, but it does not mean that we have a cohesive and clear theory. The facts are not explained.

We do not, alas, have a 'sociological' explanation of distribution, such as many instinctively desire. And that is not surprising, either, for as a rule the social group is not homogeneous in respect of the mechanics of income creation. Take for instance the members of some fashionable club in a not too large town. They may very well form a homogeneous group as regards way of life, status and position, views on society, politics, and so on. It is even conceivable that their incomes are fairly close together. But the *explanation* of those incomes may be entirely different. Their numbers may include civil servants, whose remuneration is subject to Parliamentary control, and rentiers, who are dependent on the blind workings of the capital market and on the vicissitudes of far-off, unknown firms. There may be an entrepreneur among them whose income depends on the sales of a brand-new product that gives him a lead over his competitors, and another entrepreneur whose family business produces an old, well-known brand of something or the other (such as whisky or tweed); the one stands to gain by rapid technical change, the other certainly does not. The doctor likes to see his patients stay alive, given the fluctuating state of health and sickness; the solicitor may have to rely on the death of wealthy capital-holders stricken in years. It is naïve to think that the members of the club have interests in common (except that they would all gain from cuts in income tax) or that their incomes could be understood by means of one simple explanatory principle, such as 'social power'. It is the naïve thought that enters the mind of a person who walks past the club and is not allowed in. But this does not make society any the clearer.

This criticism does not mean to impose a taboo on the consideration of social factors. On the contrary, I believe that social stratification and the differences in environment quite definitely set their stamp on distribution, and that the political ideas of

* Lecaillon, p. 57.

powerful people – ideas on hierarchy, authority, excellence – are relevant. Economics does in fact tend to neglect a few important matters. But that does not mean to say that we must radically abandon the economic explanation; we must supplement it. And this has to be done in at least two places.

Firstly, we should be constantly aware of the inequality of opportunity. This is not only a question of money; children from poor families can get a scholarship to go to university. It is rather a question of upbringing – which begins in the cradle – of the constant guiding of a person's development, of the gentle but incessant prodding in the direction of a future profession. Ambitions are nurtured at a very early age, and ambition is perhaps the most important personal quality that makes someone climb the social ladder. It makes a difference whether a boy wants to be a policeman or whether, like Churchill, he takes it for granted that he will play a leading role in politics. Of course innate talent is not immaterial to such a career, but innate and gradually developed qualities are strangely interwoven. Existing differences between small children are further stressed by their schools and by society. This is a subtle process involving all kinds of social conventions: language, for instance (of course especially in Britain; some regional accents are in order, common urban ones are not), the kind of friends one has, one's hobbies, table manners, and so on. Everyone knows that a process of democratization is going on, that the gaps between the classes are shrinking, that the mass media are working in this direction – but in most countries there is just as little doubt about the fact that social stratification is still tangibly present, that differences between schools accentuate differences in family background, that sons and daughters of graduates get university places more easily than other young people, and that one's social acceptability plays a big part when applying for a job. Economists are not ignorant of these facts; they take them as given, and therefore do not stress them. That may give economic theory an overly innocent outlook.

The social structure operates in another way as well, and this is often overlooked by economics (more than the inequality of opportunity). I mean the fact that some incomes do not express marginal productivity as much as social status. A secondary-school teacher may earn more than a primary-school teacher, and that has little to do with marginal productivity. Incidentally, it is impossible to express the latter in numerical terms – economics has little to say about it that is illuminating. Nor can one maintain that secondary-school teachers are so much scarcer than primary-school teachers, although scarcity may not be automatically excluded as an explanation. But in my opinion what counts is that society feels that a secondary-school teacher *ought* to earn more. He is further up the ladder, and the number of rungs can be measured by the difference in income. This is a social evaluation. The Civil Service hierarchy is reflected by the salary scales, and the top incomes in business are set by what the top executives themselves consider right and proper. This explanatory principle does not apply solely to wages and salaries; it also operates in other areas, such as the fees of lawyers and doctors, although in these cases market conditions naturally cut across it. The interplay of the market and social convention is not an easy thing to disentangle, but one thing is certain, namely that the latter has a considerable effect on income distribution.

This is an important point, among other things because it reveals that the income structure is definitely susceptible to influencing via people's mentality. Hard-boiled economists, who firmly believe in the laws of the market, deny this. They think solely in terms of scarcity, which makes their view of the world deterministic and undermines their confidence in an incomes policy. Now I do not claim that social conventions are easier to bend than supply and demand conditions, but all the same it is useful to know that, via an influencing of mentality, i.e. via a less hierarchically conceived structure, we could arrive at a greater equality of incomes – assuming that we really wanted to.

It is on these two points – the inequality of opportunity and the social conventions as determinants of the structure of remuneration – that the social factors strategically influence income distribution. In addition it is of course true what many young critics of this society claim: that the whole framework of society, and all its institutions (such as private property, the pursuit of profit, the presence of giant undertakings, the vertical or authoritarian structure of all large organizations, the desire of almost everyone to consume more, the way we build our cities) is indissolubly bound up with inequality, and therefore with differences in income. In that special sense every theory of income distribution must be a 'social' theory: it starts from a society as it really is. We may dislike the greed, the authoritarian institutions, the inequality. That need not stop us from having things to say about that society; I repeat what I said on p. 8 that we must not confuse facts, explanations of those facts and value judgements. But I immediately added that some facts can only be explained by value judgements – and that relates precisely to those incomes of civil servants, secondary-school teachers, army officers, doctors, lawyers and so forth. It also relates to the more fundamental arrangements of our society: to education, the balance of public and private power. Norms make themselves visible in a world influenced by people. In that deeper sense any theory of income distribution should be social and political.

3. *Other Countries, Other Voices*

Our problem has faces enough if we merely consider the situation in the modern Western world; the complications increase if we try to understand income distribution in other societies, for instance in a developing African country, where there is hardly such a thing as national income, in an Asian country with an intense shortage of land or in a Latin American country where a small developed industrial sector and a large, poverty-stricken, overpopulated agricultural sector occur side by side. The grim situations in those countries are only distantly related to ours, and in popular discussion disastrous confusion quite often occurs because critics of our industrial society suddenly switch to Latin America and, from the misery there, derive arguments for condemning the 'structures' (that is the critic's word) of capitalist society in general. A general theory of income distribution applicable to all countries and times is perhaps feasible, but it would be highly abstract. I would prefer to adapt the theory to the local situation, and that can be done too; there are variants enough within economics. This is the right moment to remind the reader that the history of economic thought has yielded two

venerable theories relating to other situations than prevail in
our present Western society. They are linked with the names of
David Ricardo and Karl Marx, and they may not be absent from a
survey of distribution theories.

Ricardo analysed the England of around 1800. Industry was
beginning to put in an appearance, but the country was still mainly
agricultural. Much of national income was earned in farming,
and a large part of this income went in turn to the big landowners.
The population increased, productivity in agriculture rose and
farmers were obliged to leave the land. Overpopulation threatened.
Tenant farmers were in poor straits; they had just enough left
to stay alive, and the same applied to workers in paid employment.
A minimum wage level – the cornerstone of Ricardo's reasoning –
held the overpopulation in check to some extent. In Ricardo's
view the increasing population would lead to increasingly poor
land being put to use. The rent of land depends on the difference
in productivity between plots, for the price of wheat is determined
by the amount of labour required on the worst land. On the better
land farming is possible with lower labour costs, and the difference
in costs on the better land does not remain in the farmer's hands
but is ceded to the landowner. Now if the population increases
and the farmers are driven to steadily worse land, the total rental
increases as a result. Wheat and thus bread become more expensive; this must be compensated for by increases in the money
wage because the workers have already been forced down to the
minimum standard of living. Capitalists must pay this higher
wage, and are therefore the ultimate victims of the development
predicted by Ricardo. A shift occurs in income distribution to the
benefit of the landowners and to the detriment of profits. This will
check industrial development, because the landowners spend their
money on frivolous luxuries, while the capitalists build factories.
Ricardo consequently foresees stagnation and growing misery.
His theory of wage, rent and profit is integrated with a theory
of economic development; it is a grandiose system, in which
everything drops neatly into place.*

* But distribution occupies a central position in Ricardo's thought. In his
much-quoted letter to Thomas Malthus he wrote: 'Political Economy you
think is an enquiry into the nature and causes of wealth. I think it should

The reader will note that Ricardo's prediction did not work out. The share of agricultural rent in national income, in those days a score or more per cent, has dropped in Britain to a fraction of 1%. Come to that, agriculture does not contribute more than around 5% to national income. Industrial development has not been nipped in the bud by lack of financing. In other words, it has all worked out quite differently, and the distribution theory did not tally either. For wages did not stay frozen at the subsistence minimum; they gradually increased according as labour productivity grew. Labour shared in the increasing production because it became scarce and improved in quality. As regards modern industrial countries, Ricardo's view is purely of historical significance, and then only to the extent that it pointed to a possibility that did not eventuate. But this does not alter the fact that things might have had a different outcome, and that there are countries in the world where the Ricardian situation means not an imaginary but a real danger. This requires a combination of overpopulation, large landowners and an incipient, shaky, industrial development. In some developing countries situations occur that are somewhat reminiscent of Ricardo's pessimistic view, and this should be borne in mind when we presently, speaking about Western Europe and the United States, arrive at quite a different view from Ricardo's.

The same applies to Marxism. In many respects, this view resembles that of Ricardo. Here too we have a minimum standard of living for the workers. Here too an increase of the share possessed by a group that really serves no useful purpose with that money. But now the villains of the piece are the industrial capitalists and not, as with Ricardo, the landed gentry. The capitalists accumulate the surplus value (that is the part of national income that does not accrue to the workers). This surplus value becomes steadily larger and the exploitation of the working masses therefore grows. The capitalists invest the surplus value in increasing productive capacity, but, since the purchasing power of the people lags behind production, this capacity can no longer be used. The

rather be called an enquiry into the laws which determine the division of the produce of industry among the classes who concur in its formation' (*Works of David Ricardo*, ed. by P. Sraffa and M. H. Dobb, Vol. VII, p. 278).

situation deteriorates further because the new machines force out labour; unemployment increases and purchasing power drops still further. The capitalists compete with ever-growing ferocity for the shrinking market; as a result profits begin to fall too. Unlike the situation depicted by Ricardo, here the entrepreneurs are not faced with a shortage of financing but with a shortage of markets. The small entrepreneurs are reduced to poverty. Only the big concerns remain, and the concentration in business grows steadily. Through all these causes income distribution becomes more and more unequal; as the inequality grows the market crisis intensifies, until the system collapses in a revolution.

Like Ricardo, Marx gives a grandiose summary of the capitalistic development process, which leads to the doom and downfall of the system. In reality capitalism has not adhered to the development outlined by Marx. Among other things, this is because the behaviour of wages has been different; the standard of living of the workers has not remained constant. Real wages have risen about 300% since the middle of the last century. Some Marxists have endeavoured to save the Marxist prediction by arguing that, for all that, the share of labour has dropped (or, in other words, the exploitation has increased), but that has not happened either; since the days of Marx the share of labour has risen in Western Europe and the United States. The personal distribution has not become more unequal, but on the contrary has levelled out somewhat. There is no question of a permanent shortage of markets through permanent overinvestments. True, in the Thirties the market for practically all goods and services was too small, but that was not the result of Marxist overinvestment but of the opposite. Too small investments lead to a depression. It has proved that such a depression does not last for ever. Since 1945 the Western world has not been plagued by a structural shortage of purchasing power, but rather by the opposite: the market is constantly a wide one, so that prices and wages rise. Growth has not been retarded but accelerated. The economic predictions of Marx – with the exception of the one regarding the increasing concentration of firms – have not worked out at all, and in this respect too his theory displays a striking similarity to that of Ricardo.

Nevertheless, the sombre Marxist view of income relations is not pure nonsense. Such a development may occur, namely if increasing overpopulation and a low level of training of labour are accompanied by highly capital-intensive forms of production. The latter go with high profits, modern top salaries and modern comfort. In this special situation islands of wealth occur in an impoverished country; the contrast between rich and poor is sharply demonstrated, and then the danger of too small a market is also present. If this Marxist trend is joined by the Ricardian circumstance of predominant big landowners, a fatal combination of social forces results.

This combination is more or less visible in Latin America. Yet it is dubious whether even in those countries the nineteenth-century theories may be applied without amendment. Complications occur there that Marx did not foresee. Some wages do in fact increase – industry has no difficulty in being generous relative to agriculture, and that creates tensions between workers, a completely un-Marxist idea. Nor do these countries suffer from excessive accumulation or too many factories; on the contrary, it is the smallness of the modern sector which starves the people without work, and keeps the average productivity of the total labour force low. That again is the opposite of Marx's theory. It is the dualistic economy and the agricultural backwardness that determine the wretched state of Latin America, not modern industry. Industry gets the blame for the miserable conditions because it holds a mirror of higher incomes up to the people while – needless to say – it profits from the poverty in that its own average wage level is low. The picture is further obscured by the galloping inflation, by dealers who exploit agriculture, and by corrupt governments. In brief, there is misery aplenty; too much for a simple theory and too much for the simple Marxist categories.

One thing that is certain is that these sombre views do not hold good for the modern industrial society. It is perhaps as well to put down in black and white once again why that is so, and at the same time to show where the difference lies between the old classical theories of Ricardo and the neo-classical view. These theories agree to the extent that they start from a complete use of the productive forces of a country, and disregard awkward phenomena such as depressions and inflationary processes (the analysis of which is undertaken by Keynesian theory). Classical thought, old and new, can therefore concentrate on what happens on the markets for various goods and factors of production within a balanced whole. These markets regulate on the one hand the nature of the assortment of goods to be produced (economists call this *allocation*) and on the other hand the income distribution. Allocation and income distribution are both a matter of markets and prices.

The older classical theory usually took a gloomy view of the effect of these markets. (Even Adam Smith, with his harmony of the invisible hand, is not an exception to the rule.) The pessimistic prediction made by Ricardo is a good example of the general approach. This was why economics acquired the title of 'the dismal science'. Neo-classical thought, on the other hand, often goes to the other extreme: the markets everywhere assure a smooth and harmonious outcome of the economic process, and that may lead not only to too cheerful a view of allocation and economic growth, but also to an exaggerated optimism and determinism regarding distribution.

The principal difference between Ricardo and the neo-classicists lies in the attitude towards wages. Ricardo assumed a minimum wage level; the standard of living of the workers would not be capable of improvement. The neo-classical view takes the more realistic point of view that wages rise along with (marginal) productivity. That this happens is attributable above all to the market mechanism, which reflects the scarcity situation. Since Ricardo labour, and particularly skilled labour, has become scarce, and that is reflected by modern economics.

There are further differences between the old and the new classical thought. Ricardo explains wages, rent and entrepreneur's profit (including interest) in different ways. Wages follow from the minimum cost of living. Rent is determined by differences in productivity between plots of land, and profit is what remains. These are three different explanatory principles. The neo-classical reasoning, on the other hand, treats labour, capital and land in exactly the same way: that of marginal productivity. Only profit requires separate treatment (of which the neo-classical theory makes heavy weather, by the way). The uniformity of the modern explanatory principles may be regarded as intellectual progress.

The purpose of this section was to show that Ricardo and Marx are of only historical significance – they are the spiritual fathers of the venerable misconceptions which in their turn have had so fruitful an effect on distribution theory. There have been more of these fruitful misunderstandings, for instance that the share of labour in national income is an iron constant. That myth, too, has provoked considerable discussion. See for this Chapter V, 1. And I also required this section to explain that Asia, Africa, Latin America and even Spain and Portugal, with their big landowners and their low average incomes, will not be discussed in this book. The reader desirous of knowing more about income distribution in those countries may be referred elsewhere.*

*For instance, the four interesting and highly informative essays in the collection *The Distribution of National Income* (ed. by J. Marchal and B. Duclos, 1968), by M. Negreponti-Delevanis, E. Gannagé, R. Gendarme and P. Okigbo. Some of my comments on the situation in Latin America are taken from this work. Gendarme further points to the enormous influence that races may have on income. In Madagascar Indians and Chinese head the list. If their income is put at 100%, the French follow at 85%, the Réunion Islanders at 30% and the Malagasies at 2%. The autochthonous race is right at the bottom of the pile. The official colonizers (the French) come off second best to the Indians and Chinese. Incidentally, the essays repeatedly show how wrong it is to lump the underdeveloped countries together. Africa is not Asia, and Latin America is something else again. The causes of the low productivity and poverty are everywhere different.

Some Facts to be Explained

1. *A Parade of Dwarfs* (*and a few Giants*)

BEFORE we embark on theoretical reflections we must have a survey of the facts of distribution. The aim of this chapter is to give a provisional and rough impression of these facts. It brings us up against the problem of presentation. Suppose that we know exactly how much each individual of the mass of income recipients earns. In reality that is not so, but thanks to the work of pioneers like S. Kuznets in the United States and A. L. Bowley in the United Kingdom, and through the availability of tax data, quite a lot of figures are nevertheless known. The question is how to marshal this enormous quantity of material. This should preferably be done in such a way that the presentation really tells us something. A chaotic mountain of detached figures or a tiring series of tables must be transformed into a coherent, manageable whole. That can be done in a variety of ways. Some graphical methods, such as frequency distribution and the Lorenz curve, are described next, and in Chapter VI a number of formulas are discussed (such as Pareto's Law and Gibrat's Law) whose ambition is to summarize the whole material in one go.

In this section we are concerned with a first impression. For this purpose we shall organize a parade in which everyone takes part who gets money. We could give all the marchers a sign to hold stating his or her pay, but it is more spectacular if we make everyone's size proportionate to his income. To achieve that we call in Procrustes, a cruel host whose custom it was to adapt the height of his guests to the size of the bed in the guest room. We shall ask him to stretch or to contract every income recipient in such a way that his height corresponds to his income. The average income recipient gets the average height. Anyone who earns more than average becomes taller; anyone who earns less than average shrinks (let's hope that the proportions of the victims, and their health, remain intact). The average income is computed by adding all incomes together and dividing by the number of income recipients. Taxes are not deducted (see Chapter VII, 8 for this), but social benefit, family allowances, pensions, etc., are thrown in. We can therefore see by looking at people what they earn.

It is worth mentioning that in this procedure we consider individual incomes. We ignore wealth, and we concern ourselves with *individual* remuneration. This is not the most decisive criterion of prosperity; usually family incomes are more important. We shall presently come across tiny women, but before we pity them we must bear in mind that perhaps they have a husband who is also earning, so that the wife merely supplements the family income. And young girls are as a rule reduced to pygmies without being bowed down by that; they live with their parents and earn plenty of pocket-money. (Unfortunately, other young girls must live on their wages and rent expensive rooms, and some women have to support families and really ought to earn more and not less than men.) Old people are sometimes small without this troubling them overly; but fathers of large families who have been stretched to more than average height by Procrustes may be financially pinched to a considerable degree. The smallest of all are schoolchildren and students, who work for money for a few months a year; on an annual basis that income is minuscule, but that does not affect their enjoyment of life. These restrictions disappear from sight in our approach. We observe only tall and short human beings. Before passing judgement on their prosperity we ought to know more about them, but we are not attempting that.

The procession is now forming up; just as when a school marches in from the playground, the smallest ones are in the van. The parade moves on at uniform speed in such a way that it is past in one hour, which means that the marchers are going to have to move in double-quick time. They *flash* past. You and I, two persons of average height,* watch the strange spectacle. What do we see?

In the first seconds a remarkable thing already happens. If we have superhuman powers of observation (and why shouldn't we confer them upon ourselves?) we see a number of people of

---

*I'm just assuming. I can hardly know your income; mine is far above the Dutch average.

negative height passing. On closer inspection they prove to be businessmen who have suffered losses and whose capital is reduced. They are not necessarily short people. In fact, right in the front we spot a few very tall men, with their feet on the ground and their heads deep in the earth. The first one may be as tall as ten yards – he must be rich to indulge in that kind of thing. It's an unhealthy way of carrying on, and most of them don't keep it up long. This vanguard is not so small in number either; we live in a rough world, where many are attracted by the successes of private enterprise which, however, pass them by. A third to half of all retail businesses close down within two years of their start* – and all this mortality is not without losses.

After this tragi-comic opening we see tiny gnomes pass by, the size of a matchstick, a cigarette. We think we see among them housewives who have worked a short time for some money and so have not got anything like an annual income, schoolboys with a paper round and once again a few entrepreneurs who didn't make it (though without their having applied for National Assistance). It takes perhaps five minutes for them to pass. We should bear in mind that those who have no income and don't want one either – children, non-working housewives – are not taking part in the parade at all.

Suddenly we see an increase by leaps and bounds. The people passing by are still very small ones – about three feet – but they are noticeably taller than their predecessors. They form a heterogeneous group; they include some young people, especially girls who work regularly in factories, but above all people who are not in paid employment: very many old-age pensioners without other means of support, some divorced women without alimony, people with a physical handicap. Among them are owners of shops doing poor trade. They supply the smooth transitions. And we see artists – they may include geniuses, but the public does not understand their work and the market does not reward their capacities. Unemployed persons also belong to this heterogeneous company, but only in so far as they received a low wage while they were working (otherwise they would be coming later). Some members

* The figure applies to the United States. See P. A. Samuelson, *Economics*, 1964, 6th edition, p. 78.

SOME FACTS TO BE EXPLAINED

of this group receive National Assistance. It takes them at least five or six minutes to pass by.

After them – the parade has been going on for about ten minutes – come the ordinary workers about whom there is nothing out of the ordinary except that they are in the lowest-paid jobs. Dustmen, Underground ticket collectors, some miners. The unskilled clerks march in front of the unskilled manual workers. Precisely among these lower-paid categories each group applies the principle of ladies first – particularly in Britain equal pay is far from being a reality. We now also see large numbers of coloured persons. These groups take their time to pass; we have ample opportunity to observe them at our leisure. It takes almost fifteen minutes before the passing marchers reach a height of substantially more than four feet. For you and me this is a disturbing sight; fifteen minutes is a long time to keep seeing small people pass by who barely reach to our midriff. More than a third of them are women, dwarf-like human beings. In embarrassment we avert our gaze and look in the direction of the approaching parade to catch sight at long last of normal people.

But a new surprise awaits us here. *We keep on seeing dwarfs.* Of course they gradually become a little taller, but it's a slow process. They include masses of workers, just ordinary people with not inconsiderable technical knowledge, but shorties. After we have waited another ten minutes small people approach who reach to our collar-bones. We see skilled industrial workers, people with considerable training. Office workers, respectable persons so to see. We know that the parade will last an hour, and perhaps we expected that after half-an-hour we would be able to look the marchers straight in the eye, but that is not so. We are still looking down on the tops of their heads, and even in the distance we do not yet see any obvious improvement. The height is growing with tantalizing slowness, and forty-five minutes have gone by before we see people of our own size arriving. To be somewhat more exact: about twelve minutes before the end the average income recipients pass by.

We are of course interested as to who they are. Now, they prove to include teachers, executive-class civil servants, clerical workers, older N.C.O.'s, grown grey in the services. Of course we also encounter shopkeepers, together with sales representatives and insurance agents (a number of *them* do not come along until later). This group also includes people in overalls and rubber boots and with callouses on their hands; they are a number of foremen, superintendents and technicians, and a few farmers.

After the average income recipients have passed, the scene changes rather quickly. The marchers' height grows; six minutes later we see the arrival of the top ten per cent, a group that will turn up again repeatedly in the following pages. The first to arrive are around six feet six inches, but to our surprise we see that they are still people with modest jobs. Headmasters, Assistant Principals and Principals. (Our parade is being held in Britain; in other countries the exact order is sometimes a little different, but the picture is the same.) University graduates, but most of them are very young. Small contractors who lend a hand themselves. Seamen too. And once again farmers; in Britain their income is higher than the national average (in this respect this country differs from the United States and from all countries of Continental Europe!). Again office staff, department heads, but certainly not yet genuine top executives. They are people who had never thought that they belonged to the top ten per cent.

In the last few minutes giants suddenly loom up. A lawyer, not exceptionally successful: eighteen feet tall. A colonel, also of much the same height. Engineers who work for nationalized industries. The first doctors come into sight, seven to eight yards, the first accountants. There is still one minute to go, and now we see towering fellows. University professors, nine yards, senior officers of large concerns, ten yards, a Permanent Secretary thirteen yards tall, and an even taller High Court judge; a few accountants, eye surgeons and surgeons of twenty yards or more. This category also includes managers of nationalized concerns; the Chairman of the National Coal Board is likewise a good twenty yards.

During the last seconds the scene is dominated by colossal figures: people like tower flats. Most of them prove to be businessmen, managers of large firms and holders of many directorships, and also film stars and a few members of the Royal Family. There prove to be towers and towers, and we cannot describe them all. To mention a few examples of persons whose salaries have been published: we note, with due respect, Prince Philip, sixty yards (too short to play polo), and the senior managing director of Shell, David Barran, who measures more than twice as much.

Now these giants are still people with salaries (the interest on their wealth makes them still taller – how much so we do not know), and the yard is still a practical measure of their height. But the rear of the parade is brought up by a few participants who are measured in miles. Indeed, they are figures whose height we cannot even estimate: their heads disappear into the clouds and probably they themselves do not even know how tall they are. Most of them are men of venerable age, but they also include women; these are as a rule younger, and we even think that we can see a few babies and adolescents. (Their ranks include Tom Jones; nearly a mile high.) These super-rich people are almost all heirs, and the tallest of them have managed to multiply their inheritance. The last man, whose back we can still see long after the parade has passed by, is John Paul Getty (though as a rule we have not invited American guests, Getty lives for much of his time in Britain and is an Oxford B.A.). At the time of writing he is almost 80 years old and made his money in oil. Few know what he earns (perhaps nobody does); his fortune is estimated at 1,000 to 1,500 million dollars. His height is inconceivable: at least ten miles, and perhaps twice as much.

Suddenly the parade is gone – the income recipients disappear from sight and leave the spectators behind them with mixed feelings. We have watched a dramatic spectacle, full of unexpected scenes.* It is worth while summarizing a few of our impressions.

(a) A striking fact is that we have to wait so long for the average income recipient. The reason lies in the fact that a number of

---

* Honesty compels me to admit that I have intensified the effect because spectators usually pay attention not only to height but also to width of shoulders, size of chest and volume. In our case they should not do so, because a person's volume increases with the third power of his height. You and I must therefore consider only the distance between soles and crown, and ignore the frightening effect of volume. If you think that we are asking too much of our capacity for abstraction, we ought to ask Procrustes *not* to leave the proportions intact; a thirteen-yard general then acquires a very weedy figure, and the gnomes look like soup plates. Getty becomes as thin as gossamer, relatively speaking.

colossal people are bringing up the rear. Not only do they attract the attention of the spectator so much, but they also raise the average; it shifts to well above the great mass of income recipients. For that reason by far the greater part of the parade consists of small men and women, not to say dwarfs. If we were to exclude from the parade those who bring up the rear, say during the last minute, the average height – that is to say your height and mine – would drop considerably. Those remaining in the parade would not become any taller as a result, but the impression would be removed that we have organized a parade of dwarfs. After just over half-an-hour we would already be able to look the marchers in the eye. People desirous of assessing income distribution should bear such things in mind.

Incidentally, we could also have brought the height of the participants closer to the average if we had considered family income instead of individual incomes. That would have removed many women and young people from the procession; their husbands and fathers would have grown taller and many dwarfs would have risen to almost average height. The marchers of the first five minutes would almost all have remained at home. The parade would have been less colourful and less dramatic. A few giants might have grown still taller: wealthy people who have set fortunes aside for their wives and children.

(b) The end of the parade makes a shattering impression. The marchers' height increases with incredible speed in the last minutes, and above all *within* the last minute. It therefore makes a great deal of difference whether we watch the marchers of the last minute (the top 1·7%) or whether we consider those of the last seconds. There is not just a great difference in height: the last minute starts with six yards or so, and the last second we see people of five to ten miles; but there is also difference in the nature of income. A member of the top 1·7% need not necessarily be fabulously rich. He may be wealthy, but this fortune is not essential. His top income may consist in a salary: a senior civil servant, a professor, a manager. It may also be a professional income, earned with the hands: the surgeon. These people have such generous incomes that they can save. This of course breeds wealth, and we consequently see that the top 1% almost always have some wealth in reserve. But this is not a *sine qua non* for their high incomes – the interest is nice to have, but this 'private income' is not essential to their position in the parade.

That is where they differ from the participants of the last seconds. They may also have salaries, but at the same time they are immensely rich. In their case the salary is often subordinate. Their main income consists of interest and profit (these two components of personal income cannot always be sharply distinguished from one another. Their source is different, and consequently we shall at all times keep profit and interest apart in this book. But when the dividend reaches the income recipient it sometimes begins to look like interest). The top fortunes are not only a welcome supplementation to income from work – the capital is the essential basis of the economic position of the financial giants. Their wealth is not always invested in a wide portfolio of shares – it is often deliberately invested in their own firms, in which they have a say.* Considerable misunderstanding occurs through confusion of these two groups – the last minute and the last seconds – though it is of course true that there are smooth transitions between them. The top 1% (and even the top 10%!) are too often identified with the very wealthy capitalists. The latter group is tiny.†

The question is how these enormous fortunes are accumulated. The answer is a straightforward one: the source is always formed by profits. You can save a modest little capital from a salary, and so become well-to-do, but if you really want to build up a huge

---

*Needless to say, considerable attention has been drawn to the significance of wealth to inequality. This was done with great emphasis by H. Dalton, *Some Aspects of the Inequality of Income in Modern Communities*, 1920. Incidentally, it is not so easy to state exactly which part of the inequality is caused by wealth distribution. That requires sophisticated quantitative methods. See below, p. 64.

†Anyone desirous of getting to know this group's American counterpart should read the informative book by F. Lundberg, *The Rich and the Super-Rich*, 1968. He tells us who the rich are, how they acquired their money, how they spend it, how they solve their tax problems, their relations with politics, arts and science and with each other. No such book exists for Britain. Although I have some criticism of Lundberg's view (see pp. 274 and 277 below), I can strongly recommend the reading of his 1,000-page paperback.

fortune you cannot leave it at that. (It is of course easier to inherit the money, but that passes over the manner in which the testator came by the money.) Savings from wage and salary may form a springboard, but ultimately the aspiring Croesus will have to rely on the rewards of entrepreneurship. The best thing is to have the disposal of a good, brand-new product (with the necessary patents) and to start producing it with drive. You might come a financial cropper, but you might bring it off. The survivors cross a threshold after which their profits accumulate, and so the lucky ones join the rear ranks of our parade.

The process of getting rich sometimes goes faster than you might think. It does not always take generations; the list of the enormously wealthy is growing. The theory that it is impossible to become colossally wealthy nowadays and that the big fortunes are at least a generation old is unrealistic. A well-known example in support of the contrary is that of Dr Edwin H. Land, who invented the sixty-second camera in the Forties. At first the public did not see much in it, but took a second look and found this way of photography attractive after all. Incidentally, Dr Land has many other optical inventions to his name. In 1968 he was number 4 on *Fortune*'s list of the Super-Rich, that is to say behind J. Paul Getty (oil), Howard Hughes (aircraft, among other things) and H. L. Hunt (oil), but ahead of the old families like the Duponts, the Fords, the Mellons and the Rockefellers. Land's fortune is estimated at $500 to 1,000 million. Chester Carlson is another example of an inventor (Xerography; he started as a lawyer!); he is said to be worth $150 to 200 million. According to *Fortune* there were 153 people in the United States with a net worth of above $100 million in 1968 (including wealth held by spouses, minor children, trusts and foundations). A third of these 153 were not yet really wealthy ten years before. Of course the big heirs with the familiar names are still to be found on the list of 153. They have been displaced from top position by the *nouveaux riches*, but they're keeping their end up very nicely.*

(c) The head of the procession naturally also deserves closer attention. We must make a distinction between the part-time workers and casual earners on the side on the one hand and the

* *Fortune* (May 1968), 'America's Centimillionaires'.

shocking social emergency cases on the other. Recently more has become known about the latter group: the cumulative processes operating at the bottom end of income distribution have been brought to light in particular by M. Harrington in his book on the American poor (see Chapter VI, 4). This group is of importance to social policy (minimum wages, social security, tax exemption limit, negative income tax). Some are inclined to make this very group the principal objective of distribution policy, and I heartily agree. In my opinion they form a more urgent problem than the very rich.

(d) Also of interest is the great difference in predictability and determinateness of the incomes. People are marching in our parade whose earnings we know within narrow limits. That applies to all wage-earners whose incomes are laid down in collective agreements, to civil servants, to many other salary-earners: a good 80% of the population. But the fact that someone is called a rentier or capitalist (depending on the observer's preference) tells us nothing at all about his place in income structure. He may scrape together a small income from interest, just enough to supplement his pension slightly; he may also belong at the end of the procession. We already know much more about him if he tells us how great his wealth is – then his income can be predicted within certain limits.

But this predictability does not apply to profits. The man who lives on profit may pop up anywhere in the procession. Even further information on the size of a person's business is no criterion of his income. Firstly because there are flourishing and highly profitable small businesses that place their owners in the last minute of the parade, and there are large firms that make a loss. In the second place because the distribution of a firm's profit may differ so greatly. Three brothers may each pocket one-third of the profit made by the family business, but that may also be arranged quite differently. The very large firm has again a wider variation in its arrangements: shareholders, top executives and staff may share in the profit in accordance with different criteria. And then there are profits whose volume it is difficult to estimate. If a wealthy shipowner wants to know how much he earns and how that income is made up, he has to ask his accountant. We, as inquisitive outsiders, certainly cannot find out. It is profit that often escapes our understanding and at the same time creates the tremendous inequality.

(e) Our procession has the attractive property that we can see and recognize the participants. We saw men with boots on and dirty hands, respectable gentlemen with briefcases, striking figures and ordinary ones. We saw with our own eyes the richest man in the world. We saw great numbers of very small women, an appalling sight. The other side to this dramatic effect is that our procession is an imaginary one. It is not the custom to organize such shows, and they would in any case meet with opposition from the participants, if only because of the preliminary treatment by Procrustes.*

In a highly watered-down form we can achieve something similar by a graph that hurts no-one. (Incidentally, this graph is about as rare as the parade – I've never yet seen it in a book or an article.) On the horizontal axis of this graph (Fig. 1) minutes are plotted, and on the vertical the height of the income recipients. The curve illustrates the dwarf-like nature of most people; the average is indicated by the arrow. The recognizability of the individuals has now disappeared. Nor does the graph lend itself to accurate reading-off, because the right-hand part rises so steeply that small inequalities in the drawing lead to great differences in income. The last millimetre comprises, on a reduced scale, a top manager of a good 100 yards and the super-rich capitalist of 10 miles. The vertical axis ought in fact to be well over two hundred yards long. Is this perhaps why the graph does not appear in the books?

And yet this drawing suggests one of the most striking properties of income structure: the huge inequality illustrated by the right-hand part of the curve. Other drawings conceal this property. In the next section we shall encounter the frequency distribution, a curve that is very usual in statistics; the income classes are

---

*On paper the operation is painless but it is not performed either. The transformation of incomes into heights is not to be found in the books, with, as far as I know, only one exception: a casual remark by Mrs Barbara Wootton (*The Social Foundations of Wage Policy*, 1955, p. 18). I have never come across the parade in economic literature.

plotted horizontally and the number of income recipients in every bracket vertically. As we shall see, this presentation is useful and stimulating, but it spirits away the very rich. All the same, the frequency distribution also shows reality. The Lorenz curve, yet another technique, shows us the same facts through yet other eyes, so that yet other properties strike us. This illustrates my argument that income distribution (and even the narrower subject of *personal* income distribution) has many different faces. It depends on the

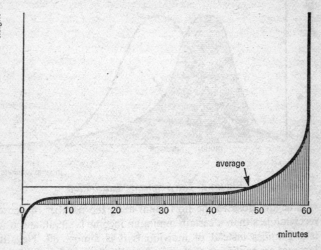

Figure 1. *A parade*

temperament, the intellectual structure and the political preference of the reader which face he recognizes best. If I may speak for myself, I am rather struck by the presentation in this section. The inequality that emerges from it colours my view of the problem.

2. *The Frequency Distribution*

We have now obtained a provisional impression of personal distribution by watching a parade formed by many dwarfs and a few giants. Their height represented their income. This dramatic method of presenting the facts is not to be found in economics

59

or statistics textbooks. They stress another manner of putting forward the same data: the frequency distribution. Income brackets are plotted horizontally and the number of income recipients falling into such a bracket vertically. Fig. 2 shows the curve.

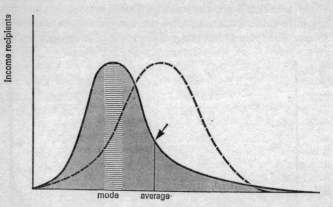

Figure 2. *The frequency distribution*

It begins close to the horizontal axis; the number of people receiving less than a certain minimum income is small, and if we take families instead of individuals it is almost nil. Negative incomes are to the left of the vertical axis; they are barely visible: there are too few of them. After the social minimum income – the amount of National Assistance – the curve climbs steeply, then bends to the right. It quite soon reaches a peak; the income bracket for which this is the case is called the *mode*. Here most people are thus to be found, and these are mainly workers. From then on the curve falls. The downward gradient is less steep than the upward one. Moreover, the downward gradient gradually begins to flatten out; seen from above, it is concave. There is even almost a visible kink in the curve. To the right of this kink, close to the horizontal axis, there is a very gently falling part that gradually ends in a kind of thin tail. Here the well-to-do are to be found, and further on the rich. In the drawing only part of this tail is shown; it goes no further than something over twice the average income, and at that level you are far from rich. How far the tail continues to the right in reality depends on how high the highest income is. The last part almost coincides with the horizontal axis, and as a result we cannot properly see how far the curve goes to the right. The richest people can be drawn into a frequency distribution, but they do not catch the eye. Only by making the curve a broad one – which is not really permitted! – are the super-rich made to stand out. One single man – Paul Getty – can extend the curve very far to the right. If we had shown the whole line, the page would have had to have been at least a hundred yards wide – an unusual size for a book, even if we were to use Playboy-type gatefolds. No wonder that most textbooks simply give up. And yet it is this tail that, according to some, wags the economic dog.

A number of remarkable differences from the parade method of presentation are evident right away. When we were watching the parade of income recipients we were still seeing, in principle, individuals; these are now swallowed up in the masses. In both cases rising incomes passed in review from left to right, but while in the parade the height of the income was vertically visible, we see here the frequency with which the income occurs plotted as the vertical variable. As a result the participation of very wealthy people in a parade has a most dramatic effect – we saw at the end of the procession top managers of 100 yards and more passing by, and a few seconds later capitalists ten miles high – while these people are barely noticed in the frequency distribution approach. The parade ends with a bang, the frequency distribution with a whimper. True, the different methods of presentation show exactly the same facts, but they do so in so different a way that divergent properties of those facts come to the fore. Part of the difference of opinion about income distribution is explained by this pheno-menon. Two people observing the same facts can nevertheless notice entirely different things!

One of the first things that catches the eye about this curve is that it has one peak. That seems self-evident, but it is not so. Some mass phenomena are so distributed that we see two peaks. One could imagine that in a certain country two classes of income recipients are kept apart, with the colour of their skin as the criterion. We then see on the left a dark curve and on the right a white curve, each with its own peak. Another such bipartition is men and women – sex also influences income. The fact that we find a single-peaked curve in Western Europe and the United States already suggests to some extent that there are no strictly segregated groups of income recipients and that the well-known split into workers and capitalists does not dominate the picture either. There are smooth transitions between 'rich' and 'poor', even though the differences are tremendous.

The inequality of incomes is, it is true, expressed by the frequency distribution in a less shocking way than by the parade of dwarfs, but it nevertheless becomes visible. Especially in the sense that the curve is skew. It rises steeply on the left and falls gently on the right. Moreover the arithmetic average (shown by the arrow) lies to the right of the mode. This asymmetry is in part simple to explain: the curve is cut off on the left-hand side, which means that society will not accept extreme poverty. In primitive communities the poorest of all disappear through hunger and disease; in present-day society their number is reduced by social provisions. The poorest of all are pushed somewhat to the right. On the right-hand side, by the high incomes, we allow a free run-out to exist (the figures are before income tax). Hence the asymmetry.

However, this does not dispose of the skewness. It has deeper causes than just the existence of a social minimum. In the following pages we shall encounter numerous forces that create the right-hand tail and as it were shoot individuals to the right of the graph. The explanation of this ballistics is an essential part of the theory of income structure.

The skewness is obvious.* The curve therefore has the great advantage that it invites us to make a comparison with another form of the distribution curve, very well known from statistics, namely the *normal* distribution or probability curve. This is symmetrical (average and mode coincide, the tails are of equal

---

*It applies to all overall income distributions, but not to the pay structure of certain groups. For manual workers the distribution is much more symmetrical, as demonstrated by H. Staehle ('Ability, Wages and Incomes', *Review of Economic Studies*, 1943) and H. P. Miller (*Income of the American People*, 1955).

length on either side) and further satisfies very special properties that are described by a sharply determined equation.* To look at, it is a kind of bell – the dotted line on Fig. 2. A normal distribution of this kind, often called a Gaussian curve after the man who discovered it, comes into being when a large number of independent forces are operating on a phenomenon. Throw a bag of marbles into a shuffleboard (a book has been placed under one end, so that the marbles will roll), let their path be influenced by a large number of nails hammered into the board, and in the sections a probability curve will form, viewed from above.

Now it so happens that the normal distribution holds good for a large number of measurable qualities of human beings. This was discovered by the Belgian statistician L. A. J. Quetelet more than a century ago. The height of soldiers, for instance, is described by the typical bell shape. Perhaps the same applies to human intelligence, at least at a very early age (but that has never been measured). Incomes, on the other hand, describe an entirely different curve. And yet in a certain sense incomes too are 'qualities' of people. This obviously contains a problem which the dotted line in Fig 2 emphasizes.

The drawing suggests a number of interesting things, of which the most technical is a method for reproducing and analysing inequality. A primitive criterion is the breadth of variation: the difference between the highest and the lowest income. A person earning a top salary gets 100 times as much as the lowest wage-earner, and a millionaire a still larger amount. This criterion is primitive because the position of an occasional top dog is decisive for this difference, and the criterion says nothing about what goes on between ordinary people. This becomes somewhat clearer if we consider the difference between the arithmetic average of all incomes and the mode (the income at which the curve displays a peak). Statisticians also divide this difference by the standard

---

* It is pointless to write down this equation here, because the statisticians already know it and it frightens the others off. But it is nevertheless a nice touch that π occurs in it (the ratio between the circumference and the radius of a circle), the number e (the base number of the mysterious natural logarithms) and the standard deviation of the frequency distribution (see below). How strangely everything is bound up together!

deviation (see below), and call the result the Pearsonian coefficient of skewness. This quantity characterizes the asymmetry of the distribution; with the Gaussian curve this quantity is nil. In income distribution the skewness is positive, i.e. the average is higher than the mode (that is why the average man was such a long time appearing in the parade).

The *spread* of incomes is characterized by various numbers, of which the standard deviation is the best known. This is the square root of the arithmetic average of the squares of the deviations from the arithmetic average of all incomes. This sounds more complicated than it is; statisticians work a lot with the number and they are quite happy with it. According as the standard deviation is smaller, incomes are closer to the average, which points to less of an inequality. Instead of the standard deviation its square is sometimes used, known as the variance. (A clear distinction must be made between spread and skewness, which together reproduce inequality; the diagram teaches us that without difficulty.) Income distribution is in addition often characterized with the aid of other coefficients, such as the a of Pareto or the percentage of the total income earned by the top 10%. These criteria will be discussed below.

The statistical concepts outlined here with extreme brevity may serve to track down the causes of inequality and to correct over-evocative theories. For instance, it can be investigated what part of the variance is caused by capital-holding. We saw above that the super-high incomes (the top within the top 1%) are always connected with huge fortunes. But it would be overhasty to deduce from this that capital is the great source of inequality in general – that ignores the differences between unskilled labourer and expensive lawyer: quantification is obviously urgent here. This has been attempted by W. H. Somermeyer.* For a fairly typical distribution curve (the Netherlands in the Fifties) he finds that one quarter of the variance must be ascribed to capital and three quarters to labour. The significance of capital for the *general* picture of inequality can therefore easily be exaggerated. Here too we again see that everything depends on how we look at the facts:

* *Inkomensongelijkheid: een analyse van spreiding en scheefheid van inkomensverdelingen in Nederland* (with English summary), 1965.

the one is fascinated by the incomes of a few top dogs, the other by an overall curve.

Back to the discrepancy between the normal distribution and the actual income structure. It follows from this discrepancy that income inequality cannot be explained in a simple and direct fashion from the inequality of people. This refutes a well-known apologia. People – and in particular people with ample incomes – say: 'No wonder that incomes are unequally distributed. After all, human beings aren't alike – some can run faster than others, or think faster, or play better tennis. It's quite natural that incomes reflect these differences.' Such a reasoning, which often entails a value judgement (the normal distribution is regarded as 'natural' and therefore just) opposes the statement: 'Rich people are poor people with money.' Rich people are special and exceptional in more than one respect.* It is refuted by a glance at the actual income structure.

But only the simple, naïve variant of this reasoning is refuted. For it is quite feasible to reconcile the normal distribution of human qualities with the skew distribution of incomes. To do that we have to make a call on more complicated relations between probability distribution and income distribution than the naïve reasoning establishes. Such more advanced relations have therefore been put forward by various observers, and they are discussed in Chapter VI. These observers hit upon the idea as a result of the (apparent) contradiction between the two curves.

Perhaps this is the right moment to mention one single theory that can eliminate the contradiction between the probability curve and the income curve. This amounts to our assuming that among young children intelligence is still normally distributed, i.e. in accordance with a probability curve. But as the child grows up, environmental influences make themselves felt. A child with better-off parents usually gets a better upbringing. In the family circle the child already hears about things that prepare him for society, i.e.

---

* Some authors, like A. L. Bowley ('The National Income of the U.K. in 1924', *Economica*, 1933), have propounded the theory that incomes would have been normally distributed *if* all persons had been brought up in the same environment, possessed no wealth, were paid piece rates, displayed the same industry, etc.

for the better jobs. And so a differentiation occurs which in the near future will be continued at school. Children of richer parents suddenly prove to be more intelligent – their environment entails that. They consequently pass more easily through the school system. As a result they also have a better chance of going to university, and there the basis is laid for a number of top incomes. And then of course there are the inherited fortunes that give the richer children a lead. Social stratification sets its stamp on a person's development. What began as a normal distribution gradually becomes a skew distribution through the influence of society. (By the way, there is an uncertain factor in all this, and that is ambition. A doctor's son often has the ambition to become a doctor – and he usually succeeds. But children from the slums often have a grim determination to escape poverty. And they sometimes succeed as well.)

The theory of the chances of upward mobility distorted by society explains part of the asymmetry of the income curve. It is discussed again below. Come to that, it is a view on which discussion is not closed, and agreement is not to be expected either for the time being. It is bound up with the eternal debate on 'nature' and 'nurture', hereditary talent and environmental influence. These two groups of influences can hardly be distinguished quantitatively, among other things because intelligence cannot be measured until the child is a few years old. And by then the environment has already had the time to make itself felt.* But nobody denies that the theory that considers milieu important contains a good deal of truth. The problem is above all to compare the effect of the distorting forces with other forces that will be discussed below.

We thus find that the frequency distribution can give us ideas, and that is a splendid property of such a dead diagram. But this graphical representation has definite disadvantages too. For instance, there is little point in filling in absolute numbers on the axes; for the absolute incomes change every year through economic growth and the steady inflation. The curve shifts constantly to the

---

* It is sometimes said that heredity is 75% responsible and environment 25%, but the empirical support for this proposition is not strong. See H. Lydall, *The Structure of Earnings*, 1968, p. 75.

right without the income relations having to change at all. (The fact that economic growth *can* change the curve, and in a systematic fashion, is discussed in Chapter VI.) A related drawback is that the frequency distributions of different countries and times cannot easily be compared. You are always faced with the choice of the units in which the incomes are expressed; it is not automatically possible to superimpose the curves. The latter is permissible only after some manipulation, but all kinds of problems can creep in there. In this respect the frequency distribution differs greatly from the Lorenz curve to be discussed below, which is detached from the choice of monetary units and renders immediate comparison between different distributions possible.

And further it is not easy to derive from the frequency distribution how much of the total overall income accrues to a given bracket. Vertically we see only numbers of people – to get total money incomes of a group they have to be multiplied by the average incomes. Speaking in geometric terms, for this purpose we have to know the total area under the curve and the slice that is cut out of this area by the income bracket in question. Now this information can of course be obtained from the figure (or from a matching table), but it is not immediately apparent. In that respect too the Lorenz curve is at an advantage. It is discussed in the following section.

Finally, the frequency distribution has the property already mentioned of distracting attention from the very rich. Some will welcome this property of the curve, others will certainly not. In the literature it is seldom pointed out that this disappearing trick occurs. One thing that is certain is that anyone who is fascinated by the giants had better watch our parade, read F. Lundberg's *The Rich and the Super-Rich*, or consider the technique that we are now going to describe.

3. *The Lorenz Curve*

In 1905 the American statistician M. O. Lorenz devised a diagram which is now the one most used to depict income distribution.* It is

* 'Method of Measuring the Concentration of Wealth', *Quarterly Publications of the American Statistical Association*, 1905.

stimulating and provocative, and it has further advantages. On the horizontal axis the numbers of income recipients are plotted, though not in absolute terms but in cumulative percentages. As a rule we do not take individuals but families. At point 20 we have the lowest 20% of the number of families, at point 50, 50%, and by the end we have had them all. The vertical axis shows the share

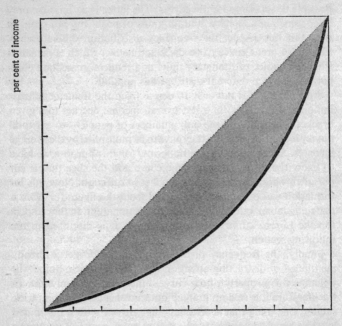

Figure 3. *Lorenz curve*

in total income going with each of the percentages. Both axes are equally long; the figure is enclosed in a square. The curve gives the relation between the percentage of the income recipients and the percentage of income. With the diagonal it forms a kind of banana, as shown in Fig 3.

Now we can count from below to above (for instance, the bottom

SOME FACTS TO BE EXPLAINED

30% of people get 8% of income) or from above to below (the top 30% receive 60% of income). In between there is somewhere a group likewise of 30%, who receive exactly 30% of the income; these are therefore, to a certain extent, middle groups. The figure does not allow of reading off the latter figure exactly, but we can more or less localize the average income recipient; at that point the curve runs parallel to the diagonal of the square. That happens right of centre. Should the curve completely coincide with the diagonal, this would point to absolute equality of all incomes. The extreme inequality, i.e. a situation in which one person gets his hands on the whole national income, is reproduced by the coincidence of the curve with the bottom axis and the right-hand vertical axis. The more the line curves, the greater the inequality.

This method of presenting the facts has its advantages. As opposed to the frequency curve, the lines for different countries and different times can be superimposed. Usually it can then be seen at once whether the incomes are more or less unequally distributed in the one case. Usually, not always, because for this simple way of comparison the curves may not intersect. As a rule they do not, but it could conceivably happen, and in that case it cannot be seen at a glance which distribution is more uniform. We then have to take refuge in some criterion or the other.

We can use as such the relation between the shaded area of the banana and the area of the half-square. This is the Gini Concentration Ratio. It can be located between 0 (everybody gets the same) and 1 (one person gets everything). In actual fact this variable usually lies well below 0·5; for the United States (1946) a ratio of 0·41 was calculated and for Britain 0·39.* It is not a very usual criterion.

It is preferred to consider the share that this or that group gets of income. For this the top 10% (also known as the top decile) are chosen, or the top 1% (the top percentile), or the bottom 20%. Owing to the fact that we are relatively free in that choice, there is scope for discussion (and for talking at cross-purposes). The one observer is after all more fascinated by what happens in the

* I. B. Kravis, 'The Structure of Income', *Some Quantitative Essays*, 1962.

highest regions, while the other observes the underdogs. In this way the one may find that income distribution really does not change in the course of time, while the other can assert the opposite. It is just a matter of which facet is considered most important.

The Lorenz curve therefore does not give completely unambiguous answers to all the questions that we could ask, but usually it proves satisfactory. It presents the information in a clear and provocative fashion. The inequality is rendered visible, as in the following examples.

In most countries the top 10% get a percentage of around 30. Although even between the developed countries there are differences – the top 10% get more in the United States than in Britain, viz. 29% as against 28%* – not too much importance must be attached to this; there are international differences in statistical counting (see the chapter on the dull warnings!). The high share of the top 10% group attracts attention everywhere. However, one must not make a mistake about the nature of these income recipients; the impression is easily created that these are wealthy people, but we have seen that this is not so. Teachers, executive-class civil servants, supervisory technical personnel; if they have sufficient years of service and in addition have had a little luck they already belong to the top 10%. The Lorenz curve conceals this information; one cannot read from it where the limits of the groups lie. This method of presentation even contains a slight invitation to deception: top 10% sounds as if we are concerned with a small élite of the very rich or at least well-to-do, but that is not so. 'Top' suggests much more than it actually contains, and in addition the association with upper ten must be avoided, because in the latter case the word per cent is missing – and that makes quite a difference.

The top 1% do in fact form an income élite. The latter's share is relatively high in most countries: it lies around 10%. In the United Kingdom and the United States it is somewhat lower: 8%. When we were watching the parade we established that within this group too the inequality is enormous. Greater than within the population

*See H. Lydall and J. B. Lansing, 'A Comparison of the Distribution of Personal Income and Wealth in the United States and Great Britain', *American Economic Review*, 1959.

as a whole. The top 1% includes senior civil servants, professional people and so on, who like to regard themselves as modest, hard-working members of the middle classes; but the multimillionaires also belong to this top, of course, and if we were to draw a Lorenz curve confined to this group we would certainly find a strong curvature.

The small incomes also stand out in the Lorenz curve. The small share of the bottom 20% of the families is brought to our attention by this presentation. In Britain they receive $7\frac{1}{2}$% and in the United States 5% of national income. Various books have been devoted to their position, of which the most gripping is M. Harrington's *The Other America* (1962). The book caused a considerable uproar. He calculates that a quarter of the population of the United States lives below the poverty line. But such figures were known long before Harrington wrote his book. The glaring contrast between 20% and 5% means that the lowest group has on average a quarter of the average income. That can be read from the Lorenz curve, and these curves have been regularly published since 1905. What is new about Harrington's book is therefore not the figures but the lively description of the processes that keep the poor poor (we shall of course be coming back to this).

The Lorenz diagram can in addition be useful in comparing the income relations within certain occupations or professions. For instance, it is obvious that the remuneration structure within the group of the civil servants is more uniform than within the group of the lawyers. However, it is not clear in advance what the situation is with the medical profession; are the incomes of the doctors more or less levelled out than those of the lawyers? Even if all individual data were available in their full exactitude, the answer would not be immediately clear on account of this mass of figures, but the Lorenz curve gives unambiguous information: for the United States at least the lawyers' curve lies outside the doctors'. That of the army officers, as may be expected, is again a good deal flatter.*

The one country displays more inequality than the other. Comparisons are hampered by differences in statistical observation and classification, and the conclusions can only be very approximate

* See P. A. Samuelson, *Economics*. 1964, 6th edition, p. 120.

ones. And yet Lorenz's technique suggests that Sweden is a relatively egalitarian country: the top 10%, just as in Britain, get 28%, and the top 1% get 6% (in Britain 8%). Western Germany has a very unequal distribution: the top 10% have 41%, the top 1% nearly 20%. This country stands out. France, where the top 10% get nearly 37% and the top 1% about 10%, is another country of inequality.*

Furthermore, it cannot be denied that underdeveloped, mainly agricultural countries yield more inequality than modern industrial states. The share of the top 10% is higher in India (about 40%), Ceylon (ditto), Mexico (nearly 50%), Colombia (ditto)† than in the United States and Western Europe (usually below 30%). Western Germany, with its 41%, shows up as an underdeveloped country. Of interest is the position of Israel, in part a superdeveloped country but with a low average income, where the Government and the unions have for some time deliberately pursued pronounced levelling; the top 10% get roughly 25% of the total.‡

More important than international comparison is an investigation of the development in time, i.e. the question of the continuing levelling process. There is a difference of opinion about this; some – they are usually not professional economists – feel that economic growth and technical development lead to greater inequality; others claim the opposite. There is no doubt that the latter opinion is correct. We can draw a whole battery of curves for a given country, each with its own year. § The younger curves lie closer to the diagonal than the older ones. True, this does not always apply to *all* parts of *all* lines. For Britain in particular we see rather a number of points of intersection occurring in the bottom part, which means that within the lower incomes both a

* Source: *Incomes in Post-War Europe* (United Nations), 1967, Table 6.10.

† E. Gannagé, 'The Distribution of Income in Underdeveloped Countries', *The Distribution of the National Income*, 1968. However, Gannagé's figures are old (c. 1950) and not very exact owing to the well-known differences in tax legislation.

‡ The figure is uncertain. It relates to the urban population. See *Statistical Abstract of Israel*, 1968, p. 166.

§ See for instance W. Krelle, *Verteilungstheorie*, 1962, p. 286 *et seq.* R. Bentzel, *Inkomstfördelungen*, 1952, p. 101.

greater and a lesser degree of equality has occurred. Anyone who takes a close look sees all kinds of subtleties and complications, but in broad outline the picture is one of a gradually decreasing inequality. This is quite evident for the United States, for (Western) Germany, for Sweden and for the Netherlands. As regards Britain, the top 1% were still getting $12\frac{1}{2}$% in 1938, as against 8% now.

The opinion that the Lorenz curve is becoming flatter is fairly general among economists and statisticians, but all the same it is not shared by everyone. The most prominent critic is G. Kolko.* He considers it meaningless that the top decile in 1910 still got 34% in that year whereas they now get no more than 29%; in his opinion these figures are unreliable as a result of tax evasion, incomes in kind, etc. The imperfections of the statistics are also underlined by others; Kolko is not alone in that. More interesting is what he says about the share of the lowest 20% in the income of the United States. Since the beginning of the century this has declined, as is also borne out by the official statistics. In 1910 the lowest 10% of American families were still getting 3·4% of national income; by 1959 this had shrunk to 1·1%. The lowest but one decile received a share that fell in the same period from 4·9% to 2·9%. The bottom 20% thus saw their share decline from 8·3% in 1910 to 4% in 1959. (All this is before taxes.) Kolko concludes from this that the prosperous American society has become tougher towards its poor, and that seems all the more paradoxical because between 1910 and today the social security system has been expanded.

The explanation of the paradox lies in two phenomena. In the first place: formerly there were relatively fewer old people, because they died before they grew old. These aged persons form a substantial part of the recipients of low incomes. If, therefore, nothing had changed with regard to income structure, the share

* *Wealth and Power in America, An Analysis of Social Class and Income Distribution*, 1962. Another dissenter (but a much more cautious one) is H. P. Miller (*Rich Man, Poor Man*, 1964) who takes the position that the narrowing of income differentials was limited to the Thirties and the Forties; since 1950 the figures for the United States have shown no appreciable change.

of the lowest 20% would decrease. This is what Kolko finds, but he does not realize, or at least does not say, that a changed demographic structure leads to this contracted share. He makes it look as if the harshness of modern capitalism is on the increase, and that is not necessarily so: the ageing of the population explains the figures. But there is a second phenomenon that is even more important. At the beginning of the century countless old people, unemployed, handicapped, had no official incomes at all. As a result they did not appear in the statistics. Through the present social provisions they get at least something, and now they are counted among the others. Consequently the number of persons with minimum incomes has grown, and the illusion is created that their position has become relatively worse, while the opposite is true. Kolko's pessimism is based in part on this misunderstanding. Which shows that the Lorenz curve, like all other methods, is tricky – before you know it you're making mistakes.* And particularly the lowest deciles are unreliable, because there fiscal data are deficient; the exemption level lets us down. It is better not to draw too many conclusions from the statistics on these lowest groups and instead to consider the curve as a whole.

In the course of time this becomes flatter. But this is not to say that the growth of income and technical progress automatically cause the inequality to decrease. A number of super-rich owe their incomes to rapid expansion and the profits that are the fruit of technical progress. Furthermore, it is certainly true that among the bottom 20% there are people who have been left behind by the general rise in incomes and inflation: small businessmen, farmers, casual workers. For the United States at any rate it is true to say that the social provisions are far from watertight. It is definitely not so that progress automatically communicates itself to the lowest groups. They may even become the victims of the technical development from which others profit; this happens in particular to older employees.† Here too we see that there are more things between heaven and earth with regard to distribution than emerge from all too wide generalizations. A general, though

* Kolko's argument that the rich evade tax is of course correct. But it hardly explains the drop in the share of the top 10% from 34 to 29%.
† See for this my *Harmony and Conflict in Modern Society*, 1966.

moderate, tendency towards equalization is in operation – but not all the poor profit from it. The Lorenz curve encourages the use of expressions like 'bottom 20%', but it may not lead us to forget that this group comprises individuals of varying interests.

A further use that we can make of the Lorenz curve is for estimating the influence of taxation. In all modern countries income tax is progressive. The levelling that this brings about can be depicted by the curvature of the line. It then proves less than many, in their fear of the Inland Revenue, believe. The curve flattens out only slightly. The top 10% get nearly 30% before tax, and after tax 26%. The top 1% are dealt with only slightly more firmly: income tax reduces their income from 8 to about 6%. That is encouraging (or disappointing), when we bear in mind that the marginal rate increases to no less than 90%. According to Kravis (see his publication mentioned on page 69) the Gini Ratio for Britain in the early fifties was 0·39 before tax and 0·34 after tax. Evidently the Lorenz curve does not record the fiscal blood-letting in a dramatic way.* This is another indication that the same facts can be imparted in quite a different way.

We thus see that the Lorenz curve is a particularly interesting and effective way of presenting some aspects. But it has its funny little ways, and it does not invite much theoretical depth. (In the latter respect it differs from the frequency distribution.) It is no easy task to discover regularities in the curve. It has sometimes been believed that the curve displays a certain symmetry, and indeed in most countries the bottom 20% get roughly 5% of income, while the top 5% get about 20% of income. But this symmetry is inaccurate; come to that, the average lies right of centre. Nor can an interesting philosophy be derived from the curve. For theories that dig deeper other arrangements of the statistical material prove more stimulating. This will be discussed in Chapter VI.

* Or perhaps the blood-letting itself is less dramatic than some believe it is. See below, Chapter VII, 8.

CHAPTER IV

Prices of Productive Contributions

1. *Unscrambling the Results of Production*

THE theory of functional distribution seeks to explain the 'factor prices', the expression that economists use when they mean the wage for a unit of a given kind of labour, the interest on certain forms of credit, the rent of a given acre of land. As we have already seen, the keyword for this explanation is marginal productivity. (Another key expression that incidentally amounts to the same thing is 'derived demand'; I shall have more to say about this in the next section.) These concepts form the groundwork of the traditional theory to be found in every textbook. It is firmly founded in the theory of production. The basic idea is that a factor of production receives as much income as corresponds to its contribution to production. This idea contains a tempting normative association: if a unit of labour or a unit of capital gets what that unit has contributed towards the result, everything is ethically in order. But that ethical judgement must be avoided. We shall see later that marginal productivity may be on a strained footing with the justness of income distribution – for the time being we shall leave the ethical side out of consideration.

Economists have long suspected that distribution does in fact depend on the productive contributions made by the factors of production. This basic idea is found in J. B. Say, the French classical economist of around 1800. But in those days economists came up against an almost insuperable difficulty. *All* the factors of production are needed to make a given product. Labour without the aid of capital goods yields practically nothing; capital without the aid of labour nothing at all. True, without human intervention nature creates animals, plants and minerals, but before these are any use to us *production* is necessary: labour and capital must make the product in the right form and at the right place. And not only are the three factors of production essential as a whole, but specific kinds of labour are often essential too. If the gateman does not open the factory gate, production will be in a bad way. And therefore, on the strength of the productivity theory, he can claim the whole product. Or not? That was the question puzzling nineteenth-century economists, which they were unable to solve at first. The problem is known as that of imputation. It can also be called: how to unscramble the separate contributions of the factors of production.

The riddle of imputation was solved about a century ago by the marginalistic thought originating from Vienna and, as regards income distribution, applied above all by the American J. B. Clark.* Marginalistic thought means that small additions of a variable to a basic quantity are considered. Let us assume that a certain amount of capital is already available to a firm; consequently, there is a building, and machines are running. There is also a given labour force in that firm. Next we examine how much extra product results from the addition of one extra worker. That extra product is called the marginal product of labour. In the same way, the marginal product of capital is defined as the extra amount of product resulting from the addition of one unit of capital to the existing equipment. Now the theory of marginal productivity entails that the wage rate is equal to the marginal product of labour and the interest rate equal to the marginal product of capital. The equality is brought about by the entrepreneur, who is out for profit, for he will continue to add labour as long as the marginal product is higher than the wage and to add capital as long as the marginal productivity of capital is higher than interest. There are catches in this reasoning, but this is the idea.

The idea, as already mentioned above, can be defined more accurately by means of the *production function*, a concept which occupies a central place in classical thought. It is implicit in the work of Ricardo and other nineteenth-century economists; one of the first to write down the function was the Swede K. Wicksell.† The concept really came into its own after the pioneer publication

---

* *The Distribution of Wealth*, 1899.
† *Finanztheoretische Untersuchungen*, 1896.

by C. W. Cobb and P. H. Douglas, *A Theory of Production*,* in 1928. Their work is further discussed in Chapter V.†

Call the amount of product Q, the amount of labour L and the stock of capital goods K. (At this stage land is still being regarded as capital – in a later section this is no longer so – and for the time being nothing will be said about the entrepreneur and his profit.)

Now obviously Q becomes larger according as more labour and capital are used. The production function (F) describes how much larger. It assumes that a certain value of L and a certain value of K are matched by a certain value of Q. In other words, Q depends on the two variables L and K, and on the production function itself, and on nothing else than these three things. The function is written $Q = F(L,K)$. It is a technical relation, which is usually taken as given in economics. It may refer to one single firm, to a branch of industry or to a country as a whole.

Let us see what this function could do for us. The most obvious application relates to economic growth. At a given production function we know how much extra production will appear if we make the quantity of labour or the quantity of capital, or both, increase in a given way. If we wish to understand the historical development of production we can therefore call on the production function. Unfortunately, it then proves to have a serious shortcoming: the function has not remained stable, as a function ought to do. In the course of time it has shifted, in the sense that a considerable increase in production has occurred that cannot be explained by increases of L and K. This shift in the production function which was discovered in 1956 by M. Abramowitz‡ and others, is called 'technical progress' – an expression which of course does not explain exactly what happened. The discovery of the unexplained 'Abramowitz Residual' has not made the production function superfluous, but its importance to economic growth longer-term has proved more complex than economists

* *American Economic Review, Papers and Proceedings*, 1928.

† Anyone desirous of reading a stimulating introduction to the production function may be referred to the first six chapters of M. Brown, *On the Theory and Measurement of Technological Change*, 1966.

‡ 'Resource and Output Trends in the U.S. since 1870', *American Economic Review, Papers and Proceedings*, 1956.

once believed. Investigations are now everywhere being made into the precise nature of the residual, and to that extent it may be said that the concept of the production function, precisely because of its shortcomings, has given the impetus to new research and to new views. Education, technology, innovation and communication prove to be stronger motive forces of economic growth than capital formation and population growth. These recent views are also of importance to income distribution; we shall come back to them (Chapter VII, 6).

However, there is a much more direct connexion between the production function and distribution theory. From the relation $Q = F(L,K)$ we can derive by how much Q increases if we increase L but not K by one unit. The interest in Q which results is then called a derivative (or a differential quotient) of the production function, a well-known concept from differential calculus. This derivative is written as $\partial Q/\partial L$, in which the symbol ∂ indicates that a slight increase has taken place in the variable that immediately follows it, while the variable K has remained constant. The economic term for $\partial Q/\partial L$ is the marginal product of labour. If, conversely, we were to keep the quantity of labour constant and to add a unit of capital, the production would increase by $\partial Q/\partial K$, the marginal product of capital. This too is a (partial) derivative of the production function.

Now these two marginal productivities (of labour and capital) prove to play a decisive part in the neo-classical theory of distribution. The marginal product of labour determines the wage; the marginal product of capital determines the interest rate. This is by no means the whole story (for in that case there would have been no need to write this book), but it certainly states one of the main principles of neo-classical thought.

It is not difficult to state why this principle applies. The entrepreneur organizes production. It is not foolish to assume that he combines labour and capital in a proportion that is as advantageous as possible to him. Now if the wage that he has to pay to every worker is lower than the extra product that an extra worker supplies, it is to the entrepreneur's advantage to engage that worker. As long as the marginal productivity of capital is higher than the interest rate, he will want to get hold of more capital. Perhaps the entrepreneur does not succeed in exactly achieving the optimum relations in his production process – complications occur that we shall have to consider further – but nevertheless there is a constant force at work pursuing an equality of the remuneration of the factors of production and the marginal productivities.

This simple truth, propagated by J. B. Clark, is important. To start with, it supplies a synthesis between the production theory and the distribution theory. This is fortunate, because much research has been done in recent years precisely into the production function. This research can be coordinated with that on income distribution. The quantitative results can check each other. The synthesis gives solidarity and consistency to thinking on distribution, especially on distributive shares.

Unfortunately, this consistency does not go so far that the neo-classical distribution theory is the be-all and end-all. In the first place, it has hardly found application in the field of personal distribution; this problem, rightly or wrongly, remains detached from the main body of economics, and as a rule is approached by quite other methods: those of theoretical statistics and probability theory. In the second place the neo-classical theory is rather at a loss as regards the remuneration of the entrepreneurs, while profits form some 20% of national income. That is most certainly another point that has to be considered. Then the problem of power is solved by the neo-classical theory in a very specific and rather narrow way. It is assumed that all economic power is fragmented, and really ceases to exist, as a result of perfect competition. But perfect competition does not explain discrimination between men and women, between races and between social classes; it does not make it clear why top executives earn as much as they do and why unions can push up wages. The neo-classical theory glances off these points. And finally, in addition to the neo-classical theory, there are a number of rival macro-theories that deserve to be discussed separately. They relate above all to the circular flow of incomes and expenditure, and they can help us to understand short-term movements in distribution. The Keynesian theory in particular helps us to grasp the influence exerted by inflation and deflation on distribution. This does not alter the fact that in my opinion the neo-classical way of thought is the pivot on which distribution theory turns.

This statement may surprise some readers who know me from earlier publications (e.g. *Modern Economics*, 1965) as a Keynesian, while they have learnt at the same time that Keynesian theory and neo-classical theory are poor bedfellows. I owe them an explanation, which amounts to the fact that Keynesian theory is in fact superior for answering certain questions, but not others. If we want to know how large the national money income will turn out to be, what total consumption will be, what will happen to investments, tax proceeds, the surplus or the deficit on the budget and the balance of payments, to inflation and deflation, then we call in Keynesian theory. It tries to show what each component of expenditure depends on, and how expenditures influence one another. Consumption leads to more demand for capital goods, and this in turn creates income and thus consumption. For such processes classical thought is of little help to us. But if we ask questions about economic growth and income distribution we have to fall back on neo-classical thought.* It shows how productive capacity grows by the addition of labour and capital, and it relates to the way in which labour and capital are combined. As stated, the central position is occupied by the production function. A complete theory of economic life must of course compromise neo-classical relations (production theory) and neo-Keynesian relations (expenditure theory), but in this book we are more interested in the classical half of the system.

So the production function represents a way of looking at production that has obvious advantages. One of the venerable laws of production, originating from Ricardo, can be handily formulated in this way: the law of diminishing returns. This implies that subsequent additions to a factor of production do yield extra product, but a successively smaller amount. To put it

---

* However, I should add that precisely the neo-classical theory of growth has variants that are ingenious but unfeasible. They consider an equilibrium between L, K and Q that proceeds in time in a flexible yet compelling fashion – the State of Steady Growth. This equilibrium growth path is completely predetermined by utterly simple quantities, particularly the rate of population growth. The increase in the stock of capital adapts itself to the rate of Steady Growth. This mental construction has a fascinating effect which causes some economists to forget that reality displays jerky growth. This is also connected with income distribution. See Chapter V where W. Krelle is discussed.

technically, if the fraction K/L increases, the marginal product of capital decreases. This is an essential point for the explanation of income distribution. When we saw the entrepreneur at work pursuing his maximum profit, we assumed that he continues engaging extra labour as long as the marginal product is higher than the wage. He stops as soon as the two are equal; we have therefore implied that the additions cause the marginal product to drop. If that is not so, the reasoning does not tally, and in that sense distribution theory is based on Ricardo's old law.*

The production function has a further useful property. It shows that labour and capital can replace one another. In other words, the entrepreneur is usually faced with the choice of achieving a certain volume of production in different ways: with more or with less capital. There are various conceivable technical processes, and even once the entrepreneur has fitted out a given factory (and therefore opted for a given technique) some variation is still imaginable. The latter is essential. If the relation between labour and capital were fully fixed – as many people think it is – the traditional distribution theory would collapse. For if the relation between L and K is fixed, the marginal product of both is zero. An addition of a unit of labour, with equipment constant, yields nothing, any more than an extra amount of capital, without the addition of labour, would. In such a case the wage would also be zero, and the interest. That is of course nonsense; in fact a wage rate and an interest rate come about even with fixed relations between L and K, but the marginal productivity theory is no longer suitable for explaining them. Recourse must then be had to other principles, and they do exist,† but they have not been in-

* It should be commented that Ricardo himself had another wage theory: overpopulation forces wages down to the subsistence minimum. In Ricardo's thought the marginal product does not yet occur as an explicit mental instrument.

† The oldest is that of F. von Wieser, *Theorie der gesellschaftlichen Wirtschaft*, 1924. It amounts to the simultaneous solution of a set of equations that relate the value of the inputs to the value of the outputs for every branch of industry. With two factors of production and two branches of industry the set of equations is determinate. We shall return to this in the following chapter.

cluded in the mainstream of distribution theory. And so marginal productivity remains the watchword.

The possibility of substitution between labour and capital will later prove to be of great importance, especially for the distributive shares, but also for the power of the unions. The reader will be able to appreciate that. If substitution goes easily, i.e. if the entrepreneur has a wide choice between various combinations of L and K, a wage increase will lead to a reduction in the demand for labour. This is a strategic matter for the unions, but even without such pressure on wages the ease of substitution plays an essential part in the process of distribution. This option of the entrepreneur has been summarized in one variable: the elasticity of substitution, whose symbol is σ. We shall use it when we have to understand the declining share of capital in national income.

This elasticity of substitution may be understood as follows. The entrepreneur will proceed to replace labour by capital if the wage rate rises in respect of the interest rate. This is evident from what I said above about the maximization of profit; another way of explaining it is to say that a person, whether producer or consumer, will try to be more economical with things that have become more expensive. In other words: if the price relation between L and K shifts, the relation K/L will shift, but in the opposite direction. The elasticity of substitution σ shows by definition the percentage by which the fraction K/L changes if the price relation between the two production factors changes by 1%. In other words, if wages are pushed up by 1%, and the interest rate remains the same, the fraction K/L will increase by σ%. The definition comes from J. R. Hicks, and it is worth while remembering it. Not for nothing is the book in which σ was presented to the world called *The Theory of Wages* (1932).

The condition for the marginal productivity theory may now be formulated as follows: the elasticity of substitution may not be equal to zero, for then the marginal products are also zero. On the other hand, the possibility of substitution may not be infinitely great; that would mean that if there were a slight increase in the price of labour (for instance by a new collective agreement), all labour would be expelled from production forthwith. This is, of course, a not very realistic case. A particularly interesting possibility is the case where $\sigma = 1$. This means that forcing up wages by 1% at a given level of interest leads to a 1% reduction in employment. It is a possibility which we shall presently encounter when discussing distributive shares; it has long occupied the minds of economists. It cannot be stated in advance what the real situation is; it depends greatly on the branch of industry that we have in mind. Perhaps the reader already senses that the value of σ might be of importance to wage increases in a branch of industry, and that is in fact what some recent investigations have shown. We shall be coming back to this.

Incidentally, the marginal productivity theory is not based solely on a reasonable value of the elasticity of substitution. There are further conditions. One of them is self-evident: the entrepreneurs must behave more or less as maximizers of profit. If they do not do so, and calmly maintain small employment while the marginal product of labour lies above the wage, something is wrong. It is not necessary for every entrepreneur to be able to find the exact point of equilibrium; some will overshoot the equality of wage and marginal product, others will remain below it. However, the trend is towards equality. In this sense the theory gives only a rough approximation of equality, but as such it is probably not bad.

However, there are still a few catches. One of them, which has given rise to quite some controversial argument, is the following. Suppose that labour is remunerated in accordance with the marginal product, as Clark says, and that capital is remunerated in accordance with *its* marginal product. Assume that there are only two factors of production and that we forget about profit for the moment. Would it then be true to say that the whole income from production has been exactly divided up? Or can it happen that the remuneration of labour in accordance with the marginal productivity leaves too little for capital, or vice versa? This question is known as the 'adding-up difficulty'. Mathematicians will be able to translate it into their own language without difficulty; they will then see the solution at once. Whether remuneration in accordance with marginal productivity does or does not exactly exhaust the total product depends on the mathematical form of the production function. If this satisfies the requirement that multiplication of the amounts of labour and capital (i.e. of both) by an arbitrary factor c likewise causes the amount of product to increase by a factor c, everything works out nicely. Then (wage rate times the amount of labour) plus (interest rate times the amount of capital) equals the total proceeds of production. Economists call this case constant returns to scale. Mathematicians say that in that case the production function is homogeneously linear, and they invoke the name of Euler, but we'll leave that to them. The practical question is whether constant returns to scale do or do not occur in reality: once again, that differs entirely for the different branches of industry. In the grand total of a country as a whole these differences more or less cancel each other out, but discrepancies can occur between branches of industry. At some places there will not be enough income to remunerate everyone in accordance with his marginal productivity, at other places something will be left. That too shows that the marginal productivity theory gives only a rough approximation of reality.

And that approximate nature of the marginal productivity theory is underlined from another angle too. Entrepreneurs do not know the marginal productivities of the various inputs so well. Incidentally, that is the first objection put forward by entrepreneurs when I try to explain the theory to them. They say: 'Look, you're telling me that I perform mental processes and calculations that I don't perform and in fact couldn't perform if I wanted to, because I don't know the production function. Your whole distribution theory is something you've made up. It's all very ingenious, but there's no rhyme or reason to it.' The economists answer this argument with a rather mystic explanation of the unconscious wisdom of human reactions, or by pointing to the invisible hand of competition. They tend to say that entrepreneurs are out for maximum profit and that, though the charting of this course is surrounded by great uncertainty and ignorance, competition exerts constant forces that keep the entrepreneur more or less on target. That target is described by the marginal productivity theory. This theory of the deeper, unconscious forces finds some backing from the fact that there are many entrepreneurs who operate independently of one another. The one will make a 'mistake' in the one direction, the other in the other direction. The one will engage more labour than tallies with marginal productivity, because he is keen on expansion; he is a 'thruster'. The other entrepreneur prefers to play it safe; he signs up too few workers, or perhaps he is a 'sleeper', who does not realize what chances of profit the market offers him. Perhaps these discrepancies cancel each other out. The hard struggle for survival keeps the discrepancies within bounds; the entrepreneur who gets right off course is destroyed by the market. Competition achieves a relation between K and L at which the marginal productivity theory more or less applies.

I should like to accept this view, though by way of a rough approximation. Through the use of differential quotients economists sometimes convey the impression of a misleading precision. We need that apparent exactitude to keep our mind on the rails, but we must not fall victim to it. This is especially so in the cases where the marginal product is an utterly vague variable. There are numerous inputs into production in which the connexion with the outputs is so indirect, and the qualitative differences so great and at the same time so uncertain, that marginal productivity no longer forms a guideline. This applies in the first place to executive and staff work; this naturally influences the productive result, and even to a major degree, but the exact nature of this relation can hardly be established, neither in advance nor after the event. Consequently, these remunerations are fixed in another way: social conventions, the power structure, considerations of prestige and status play a much larger part than marginal productivity. And that also holds good for the remuneration of people not working in industry: of teachers, for instance (what is the marginal productivity of a contribution to the knowledge of economics?) and of doctors (what is the marginal productivity of a human life?). There are sectors in which other laws apply than the derivatives of the production function. Economists often forget this, and it leads to a somewhat different, less deterministic view of the structure of remuneration. But this does not alter the fact that I consider marginal productivity a plausible starting point for the explanation of most incomes.

However, one point still remains in the above that is puzzling and that plays many a student of these matters false. The whole story is based on the fact that, thanks to the entrepreneur, an equality occurs of marginal product of labour and wage and of marginal product of capital and interest. But the technique of this equalization is that the entrepreneur adapts his relation K/L to a wage rate *given* for him and a *given* interest rate. That is also how things happen in real life. Most entrepreneurs do not fix wages; these are given from outside. A firm must be huge to follow an active wages policy, and then usually in the higher echelons of salary-earners only. Even a giant concern cannot fix the interest rate, because the capital market is too large for that. In other words, the prices of the production factors may be equal to the marginal productivities (though with certain ifs and buts, and only approximately) – but that in no way explains those prices. And in fact the theory that we have described is not a complete one. It gives only half the picture. The marginal productivity theory supplies us with the explanation of the demand side of the markets for factors of production. Opposed to this is the supply side – the price follows from the collision between the two. Let us further consider this matter.

2. *Derived Demand and Semi-Autonomous Supply*

The most frequent and by no means the worst answer to the question of how wages, interest and rents of land are determined runs: by supply and demand. Of course, this too has to be qualified, and the reader must not be made to feel that I am trying to push two theories at the same time: that of marginal productivity and that of supply and demand. But first we must have a clear picture of the market mechanism, and for that purpose I should like to lay some emphasis on the fact that economists employ the concepts of supply and demand rather differently from common usage. The word 'demand' makes most people think of an *amount* of goods, or an *amount* of labour, or an *amount* of capital that is desired on the market. Economists, on the other hand, have a more refined concept in mind, viz. a *demand function*. They mean by this the connexion between the various amounts of a good (it may also be labour, or capital) that would be demanded at different prices of that good. In other words: not one amount and one price, but all possible *conceivable* amounts and corresponding *conceivable* prices. The demand function is shown by a curve, which is reproduced here as Fig. 4; on the horizontal axis stand the quantities, and on the vertical axis the prices, of a given good (or labour, or capital). The demand curve has been drawn as a continuous line; the broken line is a supply curve, of which more presently. The demand runs from the upper left to the lower right, which is obvious because more is demanded at a lower price than at a higher one. The curve need not be straight; as a rule it usually drops somewhat more quickly at the beginning than at the end.

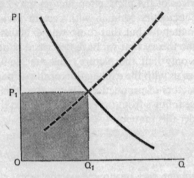

Figure 4. *Demand and supply curves*

It represents how those with a demand react to the price; this reaction can be shown by a number, and that number will play an important part in what follows. This is the elasticity of demand, defined as the percentage increase in the quantity demanded resulting from a price reduction of 1%. When the elasticity of demand is low – for instance one tenth – price variations have little influence on the quantity demanded. In that case the curve is more or less vertical; demand is inelastic. If it is flat, the elasticity is high, for instance 10; the demand is elastic.* The reader will

*A complication: the elasticity usually differs from point to point; in that case it is not correct to say that a curve has one elasticity. Contrary to what some students believe, even straight demand lines have different elasticities in different points, unless they stand vertical (elasticity is zero) or be horizontal (elasticity is infinite).

already appreciate that the position of these curves is particularly important to income distribution; an elastic demand for a factor of production entails that no pressure can be exerted to increase the price. The quantity demanded would drop strongly as a result of forcing up the price. A high elasticity of demand implies powerlessness of the suppliers.

The economists were not wrong to introduce the demand curve and elasticity into their world of thought. (This was done above all under the influence of A. Marshall, at the end of the previous century.) These instruments increase the productivity of thought, and therefore we must forgive the inventors of these concepts for the fact that at first sight they have made matters somewhat more complicated. An unfortunate circumstance is that the quantity demanded is plotted horizontally, while we usually regard this as a function of the price. This is confusing, because everyone who works with graphs plots the independent variable horizontally and then sees what happens vertically. That is why people with a feeling for logic but without training in economics so often get mixed up when they have to do with demand elasticities. They would really prefer to turn the demand curve ninety degrees and hold it before a mirror, but I do not recommend this. The reader is invited to follow the custom of the economists and to plot the price vertically and the quantity horizontally.

As may be expected, a demand curve is confronted with a supply curve; this shows the reaction of the quantity offered to the price. The curve (the broken line in the figure) runs from the lower left to the upper right, and if it is elastic it lies rather flat; if it is inelastic it is upright. Completely inelastic means that the quantity supplied does not change if the price works out higher or lower. This position may be unpleasant for and injurious to the supplier of a factor of production, for then he is at the mercy of those with the demand. Power and impotence are reflected by the supply and demand elasticities, and it is therefore justifiable that a book on income distribution lingers a moment on these fundamental economic concepts.

Supply and demand (in the sense of two curves) together determine the equilibrium price. This is reproduced by the point of intersection; that is the only market situation in which the supplied and the demanded quantities are equal. In the figure, price OP_1 clears the market; the amount of turnover is OQ_1. At a lower price (wage rate, interest rate) more is demanded than is supplied; this excess demand will usually force prices up. Conversely, too high a price will lead to excess supply, and this pushes the price back down again. This mechanism is not a faultless one; on the labour market in particular scarcity and unemployment can exist for a long time without wages adjusting and this rigidity will certainly engage our attention later. But in broad outline competition attends to movements in the direction of the point of intersection. This is the main theme of the theory of price determination, which may be found in every economics textbook.

We must now work that theory out somewhat further for the factors of production. We then run up against the fact that labour, capital and land are not demanded for their own sake. What people ultimately want are consumer goods. Labour, capital, and land can demand a price only to the extent that they assist in the production of consumer goods. Their value is a derived value, and the demand is a derived demand. The theory of income distribution usually starts from the various demand curves for consumer articles; these are given. From this demand curve the demand curves for productive factors must be derived. How do we do that?

The key to the answer lies in the preceding section. Every separate entrepreneur can derive from the demand curve for his product and the production function given for him how much he wants to pay for his marginal worker. According as he engages more labour the marginal product will be lower, and moreover this marginal product will sometimes bring a lower price on the market (because the demand curve usually drops from the upper left to the right. The entrepreneur notices this only if his sales are large enough in comparison with the total market. If he is a small man in a large market this price effect does not operate; that is the case of perfect competition). From the interplay of the law of diminishing returns and the declining trend of the demand curve for end-product a curve can be deduced that shows the marginal value of the product of the last worker. This is the demand curve for labour as it proceeds from the individual firm; it is identical with the marginal revenue product curve. It shows how much labour an entrepreneur will engage at a given wage rate.

The demand for labour of a certain specified kind can be found by adding together the demand curves of various firms for this special kind of labour. Economics textbooks warn against a complication that occurs in this addition, consisting in the fact that the location of the individual demand curves is not independent of the prices of the factors of production that ultimately eventuate. One may not construct a demand curve for labour without bearing in mind that this depends on the interest rate, for the relation between wage rate and interest rate determines which optimum relation between L and K the entrepreneurs will choose. The unpleasant fact occurs that the location of the demand curve for labour cannot be determined until we know what interest rate will emerge, but this also applies to the demand curve for capital, and therefore to the rate of interest. This in turn depends indirectly on the wage rate. This is a good example of how everything depends on everything else in economics – economists speak of general interdependence – but it is not something that we need to dwell on here. (The point returns when we are considering the inflationary spiral – it is of great practical importance there.)

By now it will have become more or less clear how the demand curve for a factor of production is derived from that for end-products. One thing that is certain is that the concept of marginal productivity plays a part in this. In that sense there is no contrast between the theory of marginal productivity and the theory of supply and demand. The former is part of the latter. The above reasoning helps us to understand on what the elasticity of the demand for a specific productive contribution depends. We have seen that this elasticity is important, because it is directly tied up with problems of power and impotence. The factors that determine the elasticity of demand (let us say for labour, but it can also be capital or land) may be divided into the following groups.

(a) The elasticity of the demand for end-product. If the ultimate buyers are insensitive to price increases, wages can be forced up and passed on in the final price without the total volume of production decreasing. The elasticities of the demand for the various end-products differ rather, although most values lie between 0·5 and 1·5. It is important to the worker to choose the branch of industry with the low elasticity – assuming that he knows this (but he doesn't. Often economists don't either.)

(b) The profit in the branch of industry. This can be exceptionally high, for instance because there are obstacles in the path of new firms entering or because strong suppliers keep the price up. Wage increases can then be paid for from the profit and the elasticity of the demand for labour is low.

(c) The ratio of the productive factor in the price of the end-product. This varies strongly. On average the share of labour in the cost price is about 60%. But in oil refining it is only 30%, and in some labour-intensive services it comes close to 100%. According as the ratio is smaller, a wage increase has a smaller effect on the amount of labour demanded. If we do not consider labour as a whole as against the other factors of production, but specific kinds of labour, the ratio may of course assume much smaller values again. An old-fashioned example: the work of a locksmith is a small part of the inputs required to build a house, and that makes the demand for locksmith labour inelastic.

(d) The elasticity of substitution. Even though the demand for end-product is inelastic, the demand for labour may still be elastic. In that case the volume of production is not affected by a wage increase, but the ratio between capital and labour shifts; the same volume of production is achieved with a smaller amount of labour. The higher the elasticity of substitution in a certain branch of industry or for a certain kind of labour, the higher the elasticity of demand and the smaller the possibility of an upward wage pressure.

(e) The connexion between factor prices. Sometimes the wages for specific kinds of labour move hand in hand. This occurs if there is a traditionally strong relation between the wages of various kinds of workers, for instance on the strength of a sense of justice. And sometimes the profit margin goes up as well. Such a relation makes the elasticity of demand smaller or, to put it another way, in this way there is less reason for substitutions between the various inputs. Macro-economically this connexion plays a big part, for – as we shall see – money wages, interest and rent of land have a tendency to climb upwards on each other's shoulders. This is particularly the case in an inflationary process. That is one of the reasons (not the only one) why the elasticity of the demand for factors of production is so much smaller macro-economically than the micro-economic one. It can quite easily become zero, which means that the amounts demanded no longer react to prices. This is a marginal case that does not so often occur in micro-economic situations.

These five points explain the elasticity of the demand for the various kinds of labour – an important matter for income relations. But we must bear in mind that this reasoning is *static*, i.e. it assumes that the curves themselves remain stationary. When we think about the possibility of influencing incomes, that is to say when we discuss the unions presently, we must also think about *shifts* in the curves, and in particular a shift of the demand curve to the right. This takes place under the influence of the growth of productivity and technical progress, and the dynamics of the wage structure originates in this way. More about that in Section 4.

The above gives a general theory of the derived demand, which can be applied to three of the four factors of production: to labour, capital, and land. Not to the entrepreneurs' remuneration – this calls for a separate explanation. Labour, capital and land are therefore treated more or less equally by this reasoning. But this uniformity is lost as soon as we start to discuss the supply side of the market. There most varied forces operate. The supply of labour is a matter of human talents, of education and choice of occupation. Here a decisive role is played by environment, social stratification, the educational system. The supply of capital is determined by quite different things. Behind it stands saving, something in which economists have always been highly interested, and bank credit. The supply curve of savings is a tricky subject, if only because right from the outset it is of a macro-economic nature, so that we become entangled in the theory of the circulation of incomes and expenditures. The supply of land, on the other hand, is a much simpler matter; sometimes it is assumed for convenience's sake that the amount supplied is fixed by natural circumstances, so that the supply curve is a vertical. For some regions this is more or less true, for others it is not (the Netherlands has been largely made by human hands) and in the course of time the acreage available will decrease (road-building and so on). As a first approach a very inelastic supply line is a usable standpoint for land.

This much is certain: that the various factors of production call for a separate treatment, especially on the supply side. The theory of distribution has a slight tendency to assume supply as autonomously given, and although personally I am not too much in favour of that, the following reflections will clearly be more fleeting as we try to look behind the supply curves.

3. *The Wage Structure: Marginal Product, Social Norms, Education*

On purely theoretical grounds I could easily get out of this section. The wage structure in a country is explained by constructing a supply and a demand curve for every kind of work, every skill, i.e. for every submarket. There are an enormous number of submarkets: per branch of industry, per region, per trade, per skill; separate submarkets for men and women, juveniles and adults. Wage determination depends on both the supply side and the demand side. There is mobility and substitution between submarkets, but not to an unlimited extent. Some groups of workers compete, others are separated by barriers: the social stratification, the differences in schooling, divide people into non-competing groups. But in principle there is a series of markets, each with its own curves, and that's that. Wage structure has been explained.

But that would leave the reader with several questions unanswered. In the first place, is it really true that these curves make everything clear? Precisely where the wage structure is concerned, human feelings play a part: wage relations are regarded as just or unjust, there are traditional differentials – is all that nonsense, or has it been boiled down in the curves? And what about education? If it is true that part of somebody's salary may be considered as a return of the investment in 'human capital', the wage structure might be explained in this way. And there is a second group of questions: unions concern themselves rather vigorously with the wage structure; we have heard nothing about that so far. Does this mean that I regard it as unimportant, or has allowance been made in some way or the other for a sense of justice and the presence of unions? And thirdly, we see in practice a narrowing of a number of differentials – is there something more to say about that? Is it perhaps connected with the growth of productivity, about which nothing has been said so far, or is it a matter of a slowly proceeding social change? These three groups of questions impose themselves, and they will be answered below.

But before we do that, a number of distinctions have to be made. Wage differentials may vary in their nature. To begin with, there is the difference between rates and earnings. Rates are what are laid down in collective wage agreements: so much per hour for such and such work. Earnings are the worker's wage income; this sum naturally is higher if the worker is more highly classified, but also if he does more overtime, for instance. Earnings generally rise more than rates; the difference is called 'wage drift'. It includes shifts between occupations, upgrading, changes in overtime, changes in piece-rate earnings and specific wage settlements at the enterprise level, in excess of the collective agreements. This is a matter that causes statisticians a great deal of trouble,* and which of the two has to be considered depends on the problem. We are talking here about factor prices, and in that connexion basic rates are perhaps more important than earnings (where personal distribution is concerned, the opposite applies).

Next we must make a distinction between horizontal and vertical wage differentials. The latter category refers to the relation between a colonel and a lieutenant, a foreman and a skilled worker, a sister and a nurse. Horizontal wage differentials occur between branches of industry: a lorry-driver gets more for the same work in one branch of industry than another. These horizontal differences prove to be very stubborn; it is anything but true that the mobility of labour wipes them out quickly. This section is concerned with the vertical wage structure, which is the more interesting; in the next section elements of horizontal wage differentiation are also discussed.

---

* In the early Sixties conventional rates rose in Britain by about 4·6% per year; earnings rose by 6·3%. This resulted in a wage drift of 1·7%. Estimates by C. T. Saunders in *The Labour Market and Inflation*, 1968, p. 15.

Then there are major regional wage differentials. A well-known example is the North–South differential in the United States, which is roughly 20%. This will not be dealt with at all – suffice it to say that in my opinion it is mainly determined economically, and so can be explained by supply and demand relations (unlike vertical wage structure, where quite different forces also operate).

Finally, there are considerable wage differences between men and women, between ages and between races. These will be briefly discussed in this section; they have an appreciable effect on personal distribution, and are a source of injustice and frustration. Marginal productivity is only very partly capable of explaining them.

The most important question that we have to answer is to what extent the vertical wage structure can be explained by the theory described in the preceding section – a demand curve, derived from the demand for end-products, that is intersected by a supply curve – or whether something quite different plays a part, namely the fact that people have ideas about what is correct and fair with regard to wages. There is no doubt that people have these ideas, and that they often act accordingly. That is, they protest, they exert pressure on union officials, and sometimes they sit at bargaining tables or they even set wages. Ideas have hands and feet. Nor is it to be doubted that most economists, or let me say the authors of textbooks, have the greatest difficulty with this fact. Usually they react to these things by shrugging their shoulders and saying that in the long run supply and demand or, in other words, scarcity, are decisive. Feelings of justice may cause temporary aberrations from the economically founded pattern, they may delay or accelerate adjustments, they may be troublesome, but no more than that. The wage structure is based on supply and demand, and the marginal productivity curves ultimately set the tone for that. Cynical practitioners of economic science will add that what people call fair and just is nothing more than the reality to which they are accustomed, with a small margin for the improvement of their own position at the expense of that of another. Scarcity relations dominate not only wages but also our lofty ideas about good and evil.

This is not my opinion. For in some cases marginal productivity is a vague idea, which leaves room for wage and salary movements that may be most considerable. So large, in fact, that the whole economic reasoning drowns in it. Take for instance the relation between the salary of a primary-school teacher and that of a secondary-school teacher: a ticklish matter in almost every country. The concept of marginal productivity breaks down here. Of course these teaching professions contribute to the welfare, and so to the total product of a country, but nobody is able to estimate this quantitatively. It cannot be denied that there are supply and demand relations, nor that they influence the salary relation. We must grant the pure economists that. But the point is that the shape of these two curves is under the influence of what people consider right and proper. The supply curve depends on the feelings of potential teachers in the two categories. If the secondary-school teachers consider their salaries too low, they will do their best to find work elsewhere. This is normal, and is not in conflict with the traditional theory, although the elasticity of the supply curve can be greatly increased by emotions. But such considerations also operate on the demand side, and that is not so easy to reconcile with economic theory. The demand curve for both groups of teachers, i.e. the salary policy and the recruiting policy of the educational authorities, is a political matter. It is not marginal productivity but views on what is right and fair that are decisive here. The moneys that may be spent are the result of a budgetary process. Higher salaries will usually lead to higher sums being voted; the elasticity of demand approaches zero, which means that considerations of supply determine remuneration. The supply and demand diagram itself is under the influence of normative views of all parties concerned. This creates considerable room; the policy-makers have a good deal of freedom to fix remuneration.

This situation is characteristic of the Civil Service. The marginal productivity of a civil servant in the Treasury is a vague concept – many a person who takes a dim view of the activities of officialdom will laugh bitterly when he hears productivity mentioned in this context. Of course economists have tried to bring these activities, too, within their grasp. It is not inconceivable to apply a kind of cost-benefit analysis to government work, but the social utility of these activities is much too vague to be of any use in salary policy; cost-benefit analysis is used in appraising large projects such as dykes, roads, the canalization of rivers and the like. The marginal productivity of civil servants is not calculated in that way. Since the government employs about one-fifth of all labour, a large sector has been created in which supply and demand are partly determined by ideas about what is an equitable salary structure. The most significant example of this is the salary relation between two officers – say a lieutenant and a colonel. This relation definitely expresses something, but not the marginal productivity. It is the quantitative translation of a hierarchy seen through the eyes of status and prestige.

But that is by no means all. In the higher echelons of private enterprise, too, the derived demand is much more a wide band than a sharp line. It is difficult to say of many jobs how much they contribute to the result of production, and the mystique of the market, which states that silent forces will attend to an 'economic' valuation, is not credible. A good top manager is of great value to a firm – but how much? He has to judge this for himself, within the value system of the managerial group, and that creates a pleasant margin for awarding himself a salary. A tremendous income is a sign of excellent abilities, and what is more pleasing than to deck oneself out with that sign? Even if the managers' remuneration is regarded as a criterion of the responsibility they bear, a figure with a lot of noughts is a reason for self-respect. Moreover, with these top salaries loyalty is bought – loyalty of the executives towards the firm and, sometimes, towards the small group of powerful financiers who control some companies. This loyalty is an expensive article.

And what is the value of a doctor to his patient? The whole medical sector is difficult to reconcile with marginal productivity. The demand curve is practically vertical, and the supply curve is dominated by ideas – doctors' ideas, mainly. Similar situations occur with lawyers, accountants, architects. I do not mean that salary scales in business or the professions are arbitrary or can be changed at will; I mean that they express something else than the economics textbooks tell us. That something else is the social ranking as it is seen by society or at least by that part of society that has a say in this. It is norms, evaluations, that form the foundation of part of the wage differentials (and that is why it is so misplaced for economists to stand aloof so frequently from discussions on those norms and values). The wage structure reflects the fact that the better people are better and the ordinary man ordinary. They lend force to master-man relations. Authority finds support in an income structure.*

These social conventions are also largely responsible for the difference in pay between men and women, between adults and juveniles and between whites and people with skins of a colour to which whites object. It is of course true that women are sometimes less productive (to the extent that they are temporarily employed, marry, have children), that juveniles have still something to learn, and that Negroes, through racial discrimination, are forced in large numbers into jobs in which whites cannot develop either. But, apart from these differences in productivity, wage differentials remain that reflect the social fact that women, juveniles and Negroes are regarded as second-class citizens.

These remarks do not make an explanation of the wage structure any the simpler. For I do not claim that the theory of the preceding section – an explanation of derived demand from marginal productivity – is nonsense. It makes sense for a large number of incomes. Practice shows a complicated interplay of two kinds of evaluation mechanisms: the 'economic' value of a factor of production as a reflection of the value of an end-product, and the status value of an occupation or profession on the strength of its place in the social hierarchy. These mechanisms intersect one another. As a rule the status value prevails according as one rises in the wage structure, but among manual workers, too, conventions are at work; especially in Britain! People compare their wages and they often have strong feelings about the proper pay structure. 'Comparability' has become one of the keywords of wage policy.

* Formally, this approach may be reconciled with supply and demand analysis by assuming that the supply curve is horizontal at a level determined by the value judgements of the policy-makers. But this leaves the supply function even more in the air than it already is. Is the curve in the short run vertical because the number of workers is fixed? Or is it in the short run horizontal because the value judgement is fixed? I do not recommend this kind of sham integration of the two approaches.

(We will meet this point in Chapter VII when we discuss the possibilities of influencing income distribution.)

Conversely, in the higher echelons too the forces of scarcity and the market operate. Salaries of tax inspectors are influenced by the salaries of tax consultants working privately or for business firms, and a kind of marginal productivity is certainly present there – indeed, a very high one. Engineers with the Ministry of Works compete with engineers in business, and there something can definitely be sensed of a measurable marginal contribution. The wage structure is the result of a network of two groups of forces which is not easy to disentangle. It is not even easy to establish whether the income of one given income recipient – let us say an electrician or a dentist of the National Health Service – is determined by 'economic' forces or by the system of social values. I maintain that the electrician's income is more susceptible to analysis by the supply and demand diagram and that the dentist finds his income determined more by what those who have a say in such things think is proper – but in both cases there is a mix of forces that cannot easily be unscrambled.*

Nor does this exhaust the complications. By introducing a social system of norms we have laid ourselves open to the question: *whose* norms? People have their own views on the right income distribution; they do not always run parallel. A colonel perhaps has a different view of the discrepancy in pay between colonels and lieutenants from a lieutenant. The same goes for adults and juveniles (come to that, colonels occasionally regard lieutenants as young people; in the military and official an age hierarchy is discounted). Views may differ on the 'right' wage relations between skilled craftsmen, office workers and unskilled labourers. In a pluralistic society there is a mass of norms that can easily conflict

* The idea that social values influence the wage structure is of course no invention of mine. It is defended by Mrs Barbara Wootton (*The Social Foundations of Wage Policy*, 1955) who argues that supply and demand explain nothing at all – a somewhat extreme view. The notion of social values is also reflected in many publications by experts like H. A. Clegg ('The Scope of Fair Wage Comparisons', The *Journal of Industrial Economics*, 1961), H. Lydall, K. G. J. C. Knowles and many others. But in economics textbooks marginal productivity predominates, and social norms are seldom mentioned.

with one another. Somewhere a consensus must be found that allows of decisions; that consensus comes about in a complicated process of consultation, pressure, opinion-shaping. There are rational methods of approach conceivable, with which we shall be concerning ourselves (job evaluation), but they are not universally accepted. Official reports (by the National Board on Prices and Incomes or other solemn bodies) play a part, but so do newspapers, television – in short, we are busy shifting the determinants of the wage structure to an area about which science has so far been able to tell us little that is lucid. For our understanding of income structure we are at the mercy of sociologists, socio-psychologists, experts on mass opinion, and that is a dreadful thought for economists. Here there are no curves that intersect, no elasticities, no diamond-hard derivatives of the production function, but indeterminate views on what people feel and think.

And, on top of that, we also have to consider power. For public opinion on the wage structure only makes its effect felt in the facts if certain decision-makers put these evaluations into practical application. Competition also operates in the system of social values, but this is not so anonymous that the decision-makers have no freedom of movement. Who is it that takes the decisions on wage and salary relations? All we can do is roughly distinguish a number of groups.

First, the government as an employer. The economic indeterminateness of salaries is particularly applicable in the public sector, and there it is not too difficult to show which bodies are pulling the strings. The salary policy of these bodies influences remuneration in the private sector, and vice versa. In every modern country there are ministerial departments that concern themselves with official salary relations. In Britain the Treasury does this. Its work is reflected in the salary scales for the various grades.

Second, the big firms, and more particularly their personnel departments. They use evaluation systems which will be discussed later (Chapter VII, 2). An interesting point is that the very high incomes of senior officials and top managers are practically fixed by themselves. The part of the total concern income that they receive is so small that the shareholders suffer hardly any financial harm from ample salary increases for the top group. The only guideline operating here is what these people themselves regard as a proper reward for their own super-capacities. That in turn depends on what their colleagues, their fellow club members, their wives and their better selves consider proper. There is plenty of play in those opinions – between £5,000 and £50,000 a year, and sometimes the sky's the limit.

Third, the unions. They too are in the force field that determines wages. True, they have no influence on the higher salaries (though that could change if labour gets a say in management – a desire strongly felt on the Continent), but they do influence the great mass of wages. There is reason to examine their position separately. That will be done in the next section.

Fourth, the government again, but now in its official role of custodian of the common good (and not as an employer). This raises many issues which will be dealt with in Chapter VII.

So far we have met two kinds of forces that bear on the wage structure: marginal productivity and the social norms. But there is a third group of forces, and this gives rise to a third theory. This theory is that remunerations from work depend on the education that a person has received. This approach likes to see education as an investment in human capital. An increasing number of authors are seeking the explanation of vertical income differentials in this direction.*

In its strictest form this view amounts to education and training being regarded as a rational investment on which individuals take rational decisions. They equate the marginal rate of return on the investment in their own productive capabilities to the marginal cost of obtaining funds to finance this investment. This exact variant has been worked out by G. S. Becker.† It excels in intelligence, but its drawback is that it represents the choice of profession too much as cool calculation; in reality many 'irrational' factors are involved in this kind of decision, especially tradition.

---

* A few names: T. W. Schulz, who is probably the father of the concept of 'human capital' (see his *Investment in Human Capital*, 1971); H. P. Miller; B. A. Weisbrod; E. F. Denison. The most consistent adherent of this theory is probably G. S. Becker, whose work is discussed below.

† *Human Capital and the Personal Distribution of Income: An Analytical Approach*, W. S. Woytinsky Lecture No. 1, 1967.

This does not alter the fact that the vertical pay structure proves largely to be correlated with differences in education. E. F. Denison found for the United States that 60% of the wage and salary differentials between high school and college graduates can be ascribed to training. M. Blaug finds a similar result for the United Kingdom.* Although these calculations are necessarily rough ones, they do give an undeniable indication of the significance of education. It would be an exaggeration to claim that the income structure is completely dominated by education, but it is certainly a factor that we must bear in mind, especially when we discuss methods of improving income distribution in Chapter VII.

Meanwhile this section has shown us that there is no unique formula for the wage structure. Marginal productivity does not explain everything, nor do social norms, nor does education. Taken together, the three of them do perhaps present a picture, with regard to which we must bear in mind that they influence one another reciprocally.

4. The Trade Union and the Dynamics of Wages

The role of the unions is a controversial one. There are workers and union officials who believe that every wage increase that takes place is extorted in a hard struggle by the union, but that is hardly credible. At the other end of the spectrum we find a number of economists who deny that the unions can ever do anything more than organize meetings, nurture a sense of solidarity and collect contributions. And further these critics point out that the unions often substantially lower wages because they harm productivity. (Britain offers arresting examples: a whole container port near London that is not used – the ships go to Rotterdam.) As regards the effectiveness of the unions, the saying 'so many men, so many opinions' holds good. The statisticians ought to act as referees, but they have their own difficulties to contend with. Indeed, they do find higher wages in the strongly unionized branches of in-

* E. F. Denison, *The Residual Factor and Economic Growth*, Organization for Economic Development and Co-operation, 1964. M. Blaug, 'The Private and the Social Returns on Investment in Education: Some Results for Great Britain', in: *Journal of Human Resources*, Summer 1967.

dustry, but that does not prove much, because the largest numbers of skilled workers are found in such firms, and as a rule the latter are larger, which favours productivity and thus wages. In the United States, since the Thirties, the wages of agricultural workers and of very low-skilled personnel – domestic staff – have been raised by far the most, and those are weakly organized sectors. There is no doubt that the law of scarcity operates among domestic staff in particular – all this being in accordance with the simple principles explained in section 2 of this chapter. A union can utilize a rapidly rising labour productivity to conclude fine collective agreements, but the higher wages might also have eventuated in any case, under the influence of the market. The statistical material is not easy to interpret. Let us look at the theory instead.

This does not present an unambiguous picture either. The economist who has the supply and demand curve in mind (the reader who does not might perhaps have a look at p. 88) reasons in the following way, which leaves the union little scope. The equilibrium wage lies at the point of intersection of a supply and a demand curve. This intersection determines the fundamental scarcity of labour, and it is hardly possible for the union to shift the curves. Perhaps the union can do something about limiting the supply – countering immigration, fixing the number of apprentices – but that does not achieve much. A more rational policy is to raise productivity, as a result of which the demand curve moves to the north-east, but some unions are more inclined to do the opposite. They are scared that the increased productivity will lead to unemployment, or to stepping-up of the rate of work, or to both, and this fear restrains the rise in productivity and thus in wage rather than it fosters it. What therefore remains is the direct wage increase, achieved by collective bargaining. In this process the unions manage to force the wage up by threatening to strike – an actual strike is usually unnecessary – and in this way the collective agreement comes about.

In this pessimistic reasoning the union's success seems better than it is, however. For there are two possibilities. Either the wage lies at the equilibrium level, and then the whole action has little point. Or the wage lies above it – but in that case the quantity demanded is less than the quantity supplied, and that leads to excess supply, or in plain English unemployment. That is the bitter alternative: the union is superfluous, or it creates unemployment. This is not a reasoning that is music to the ears of union leaders.

There are of course counter-arguments. The simplest is that profits must absorb the wage increase. Yes, certainly they must, according to union officials, but that does not mean to say that they always do. It is not improbable that the employer passes on the wage increase in prices, as a result of which, according to the static theory, the quantity of end-product demanded, and thus employment, drops. And even if profits really absorb the wage increase, this could easily lead to a decline in employment. The entrepreneur would get rid of marginal workers. Conclusion: the static theory is not the friend of the union man. It does not help him to escape the elasticity of the demand for labour.

There lies the second counter-argument: the traditional theory is misleadingly static. The textbooks and their graphs of supply and demand mask the fact that collective wage agreements come about once a year, or once in every two years, whilst in the meantime the curves do not stay put. The marginal productivity of labour increases slowly but surely under the influence of new and better machinery, technological progress, increased know-how; and the demand curve for labour therefore shifts slowly but steadily to the right. This pushes the equilibrium wage rate upwards, but the conventional wage rate, as it is laid down in the collective wage agreement, does not reflect this increase. It may occur that earnings go up because some workers are paid on a productivity basis, or that wages are increased in excess of the conventional rates. The shop steward may classify workers in higher brackets and award higher rates, and this too leads to a semi-automatic increase in labour income. This is called wage drift; it causes some shifting of the actual level of earnings in the meantime. But as a rule the wage drift is smaller than the increase in labour productivity. At the end of the contract period, when the new agreement has to be negotiated, the conventional rates will usually be too low in an equilibrium sense; and what the trade union can do is push the wage rate up to the new intersection of supply and demand. In other words: the trade union sees to it that the workers get the benefits of increased productivity. In this view the union's wage policy does not create unemployment; on the other hand, the union cannot claim to improve the worker's situation in excess of what the market will bear. This policy of shifting the conventional wage rate to its supply and demand equilibrium level is a rather modest one.

There are additional dynamic arguments. The demand curve for labour may be pretty inelastic in the very short run. If wages are pushed up profits may suffer at first. Employment does not decrease. This creates a breathing space, in which things may change and the demand curve for labour may shift to the right. For instance, some union officials believe that lazy businessmen may be stimulated into more aggressive selling, modernization of their plants, weeding out unnecessary office costs and so on. If this optimism is warranted the higher wage rate is justified by higher productivity. (It is, however, difficult to see how this increased efficiency can come about without hurting employment.) The breathing space opens still another possibility: other wages may also rise in the interim. That is an important point, for this brings us from the micro-economic forcing-up of wages to the macro-economic forcing-up of wages; from the macro-economic point of view the demand for labour is much more inelastic (this is further explained in section 8 of this chapter. It amounts to the fact that wages are not only costs, but also incomes, so that higher wages lead to a shift to the right of all demand curves). And then there is also the argument, derived from the preceding section, that a number of wages and salaries are not so much the reflection of an equilibrium between supply and demand as an expression of the social hierarchy. In many of these cases a higher salary will simply lead to proportionately larger incomes. If the Principals in the Civil Service are given a rise, the demand does not decline, but more money is earmarked for them. The same applies to senior executives in business. Here the demand elasticities are low, and moreover the connexion between the various wages ensures that this or that kind of work does not price itself out of the market.

Such reasonings suggest that the union has some scope for pushing through its own ideas and achieving its own objectives.

What do these objectives look like? And more in particular, is the union put off and restricted in its wage policy by a reduction in employment?

This too has been philosophized on at length without too clear-cut results. Two schools are or were opposed: that of J. T. Dunlop* and that of A. M. Ross.‡ The former, entirely in accordance with the principles of the economic textbooks, wishes to regard the union as a 'maximizing unit', whose aim is to make a target variable as large as possible. This target variable may be the wage rate, or the total wage bill (the elasticity of demand therefore being taken into account – if the elasticity is greater than one, a higher wage rate leads to a lower wage bill!), or the total wage bill plus unemployment benefit, or still other variants. Minimization of unemployment may also be envisaged. Such reasonings have the advantage that they can be expressed in curves; here too the marginalistic approach leads to exact results, at least on paper.

Against this is the view of Ross, who believes on the one hand that the union official lacks the information for following so exact a policy (very little is known about the elasticities, everything is a matter of trial and error) but on the other hand also that Dunlop subscribes to too rationalistic a picture of the objectives. In reality, Ross says, the union is not a maximizer of some quantitative variable or the other, but a political body aiming at institutional survival and growth. Pressure is exerted on it from all sides, and the reconciliation of the various pressures is the task of the officials. Mechanical applications of the principle of maximization can only lead us astray.

Of course, Ross's view leaves much more scope for understanding the unions' behaviour. It is more flexible. The difficulty is that it is also much more vague than Dunlop's exact view. The number of groups exerting pressure on the unions is large, and their wishes are contradictory. The members want higher wages, the entrepreneurs do not, the public has on the one hand an active dislike of wage inflation but is of the opinion that its own wage or its own salary never leads to inflation, the government tries to keep the unions within the bounds of what is economically possible –

* *Wage Determination under Trade Unions*, 1944.
† *Trade Union Wage Policy*, 1948.

often interpreted as the rise of productivity – and the executives of the unions themselves are satisfied if, after a hard day's bargaining, they can pick up their briefcases and go home with more than the entrepreneurs wanted to give. Victory is a fine feeling, not only for the executives themselves but also for the members and for everyone who is on the side of organized labour. The 'reconciliation of pressures' mentioned by Ross amounts as a rule to a permanent wage struggle, in which the unions try to get what they can, gently or somewhat harder – that depends on the mood.

But an awkward difficulty occurs here. Such a policy of more and more offers the best chance of success in branches of industry with a labour demand curve shifting rapidly to the right. The dynamics of the branch of industry is probably more important than the static elasticity of demand discussed in section 2. Under the influence of progressive technology and the increasing amount of capital per worker, the average national product per worker increases annually by 2 to 4% (that depends on the country). Within a country there are again considerable differences. Some branches of industry (chemicals, energy) are growing fast: 10% or more per year. Others are almost stationary. If the unions exploit these differences in growth rate they scrape the barrel, and for a moment it seems as if the members will appreciate that; but the result would be that the wage structure could be badly distorted. Horizontal pay differentials would occur, with the rapidly growing branches of industry as pacemakers and the sluggishly developing branches as grumbling stragglers.

Predictably, opinions may differ about the appreciation of these horizontal wage differentials. Some economists are inclined to say: fine, the more the merrier. High wages in the rapidly growing, productive branches of industry attract labour and ensure that the factors of production are used where they are most efficiently employed. The mobility of labour increases the productivity of a country. Others view the argument sceptically: they suggest that the rapidly growing branches of industry perhaps do not need so much labour; there the labour productivity rises on occasion as quickly as production, so that employment remains roughly the same. Sometimes employment in the growth sectors drops, as in prosperous oil refining, where tremendous increases in production are achieved with fewer and fewer people. The sceptics also say that pay differentials do not form the greatest incentive for mobility, but that quite different motives enter into play in the choice of occupation: the attraction of a line of business, the influence of the environment, the social rules of the game. Strongly horizontal wage differentials are not urgent in this reasoning, and they have the disadvantage that they are in conflict with the principle of equal pay for equal work.

And that is in fact a point that the unions have to bear in mind. It is considered unjust when workers doing comparable work receive greatly differing wages. The distortion of traditional 'relativities' can lead to criticism of the unions – and it is a form of criticism that in the unions' interest deserves more than routine attention from the officials. For it comes from within the union, and must therefore be taken seriously by the leaders of the unions. Tension between unions does not foster institutional survival and growth. This is all the more cogent if the unions are organized in federations or congresses as is now the case in all modern countries. The interest of the federation entails that a certain equilibrium is maintained between the unions and that too strong horizontal pay differentials are avoided. And that can mean in turn that the unions are somewhat inhibited in their wage policy in the rapidly growing sectors. Incidentally, it also means that in the lagging branches of industry wages are demanded that are really too high. Too high in the sense that they lead to cost increases and force the wage level above the static market equilibrium. In such cases the union definitely tends to increase wages.

From theoretical reflection back to the facts. The question is how the dynamics of productivity and the pressure of the unions have in fact influenced the wage structure. Let us first consider the horizontal wage differentials. Then the conclusion of practically all students of the British wage pattern is that this has remained fairly stable over a longish period. There is nothing to be seen of a considerable lead by the rapidly growing branches of industry, nor of a pronounced lag by the others. (Note that we are concerned with horizontal differences; presently, when we are concerned with vertical differences, we shall see a clear trend.) This might suggest that the unions have in fact heeded the cry for equal pay; that they have tried to avoid the pay structure being distorted between skills of comparable levels. 'Comparability' seems to be a strong force in wage determination. But the cause may equally well be sought elsewhere: in economic forces. An ingenious explanation of the relative stability of the horizontal wage structure has been given by H. A. Turner and D. A. S. Jackson.* They have analysed many statistics for various countries and have come to the conclusion that two variables explain the wage increases per branch of industry: the growth of labour productivity in that branch of industry and the elasticity of substitution between labour and capital. The latter variable has a negative effect: if substitution goes more easily the wage increase is checked, this being entirely in conformity with section 2 above. Now the interesting discovery made by Turner and Jackson is that the rise in productivity and the elasticity of substitution are correlated. Sectors with a rapid growth are usually at the same time sectors with an easy substitution of labour by capital. The two variables therefore compensate one another, hence the stability in the horizontal wage differentials. It is a theory that definitely does not have the last word, but we can see from it that the stability of the pay structure does not prove the irrelevance of supply and demand. A more positive conclusion: the efforts of the unions to control the horizontal wage structure are backed by the forces of the market.

We have been discussing the development, or rather the lack of development, of the horizontal relativities. The vertical wage structure appeals more to the imagination. The vertical differentials display their own dynamics, and there is a clear trend in this; there is a tendency going on for the gaps to shrink. This has in any case been prevalent since the beginning of the century (with the exception of certain trades and certain periods, such as the first half of the Thirties). The longest row of figures relates to the building trade, and there the differential between skilled and unskilled labour has obviously become much less. The same applies to

* 'On the Stability of Wage Differences and Productivity-Based Wage Policies: An International Analysis', *British Journal of Industrial Relations*, 1968.

industrial workers. If we consider the white-collar workers, the picture is somewhat more complicated. The 'middle groups', that is to say the senior office workers, have seen the gap between their remuneration and that of industrial workers shrink. The lower white-collar workers have lagged behind; their salaries did not rise as much as the wages of industrial workers, and because they were often worse off anyway we do not see here the shrinking of a vertical differential, but a growth in it. In this sense, inequality is increasing. But at the top of the salary scales there has been a good deal of levelling going on. Most senior business executives and top managers saw their relative position worsened in comparison with lower echelons. This is contrary to what many people believe. (The point is taken up below, p. 279.) What we in fact see is a greater overall equality between wage-earners.* This occurs in practically all modern countries, and certainly in Britain and the United States, Sweden and Western Germany. An exception was Japan, with its pronounced economic growth; this country long displayed a constant vertical wage pattern, but in recent decades this seems to have been changing too, and the skill differentials are becoming narrower. It is a trend in the modern industrial world, and the question is how it must be explained.

This brings us up against a problem referred to earlier, viz. how two groups of factors interact: scarcity relations (supply and demand) and the symbolics of the social hierarchy. There is no doubt that much of the reduction of the vertical wage differentials, especially among manual workers, is the result of changed supply and demand relations, but further up the salary scales social evaluations also play a part. Moreover, the sharp contrast between manual work and brain work, between blue collars and white collars, is fading. The number of occupations and gradations of skills is rapidly growing. This results in a blurring of pay scales, which in itself already influences the opinions of people on just and unjust wages; if occupations smoothly merge into one another, it is difficult to regard society as vertically divided into a number of separate classes that have to stay separate from one another

---

*cf., D. J. Robertson, *The Economics of Wages*, 1961; H. Lydall, *The Structure of Earnings*, 1968, and the work cited there of researchers such as H. Ober, H. P. Miller and others.

through obvious income differentials. It is clear that all these causes are operating; unfortunately, their mix is unknown. Some consolation may be found in the fact that these forces are working in the same direction.

Behind the changed scarcity relations there is certainly a supply factor too: a tremendous expansion of training and education is going on. Now in itself that conveys little about remuneration differentials. For modern industrial society does train many more persons but at the same time *demands* a tremendous number of skilled people. The net result is difficult to predict; it cannot be said in advance whether the more highly skilled labour will become more or less scarce through economic growth. But the facts of income distribution do suggest that the shortage of highly skilled labour has decreased rather than increased. I cannot put it more cautiously than that.

It is probable that, in addition to the influence of increased education, a certain influence of the union is also active. Industrial workers have made up some of their arrears on the white-collar workers – and that is perhaps partly attributable to the fact that large groups of factory-workers are better organized and that their unions have followed a more aggressive wage policy. Some insiders venture a quantitative impression: Albert Rees, speaking about the United States, says that one-third of the unions have increased the wages of their members by 15 or 20%, another third by 5 or 10%, and the rest not at all.*

And then there are the minimum wages. Besides their direct effect, which in itself entails a levelling process, they make their effect felt upwards in the wage structure, and in this way secondary effects come about. We may not expect that nothing will change as regards the incomes located just above; in that case the wage relations at the bottom would be distorted by the minimum wage, and that would lead to protests. The other extreme is also improbable: the whole wage structure goes up, like a ladder lifted from the bottom. In the latter case there would be no point to the minimum wage, for besides wages prices would also adjust. In fact the ladder is telescoped a little from below; the wages in the lower echelons come somewhat closer together.

* *Wage Inflation*, 1957.

This does not exhaust the causes of the reduced vertical differentials. Reference is often made to inflation: price increases lead to wage increases, and labour sometimes gets compensation in the form of wage rounds that tend to be the same for all wages in absolute size. This kind of narrowing of differentials occurred in the Fifties, and it will happen above all when the government concerns itself with wage determination. But it must be added that such a policy cannot be maintained if it is not supported by deeper forces, since proportional increases in earnings seem the most obvious pattern of economic growth.

A shift in the social system of norms could be regarded as one of those deeper forces. Vertical wage and salary differentials are nowadays regarded more critically than formerly, and in the above I have tried to convince the reader that these evaluations could influence the actual course of affairs. It would have been impossible to reduce the gap between industrial workers and the middle groups if this had not been accepted. The authorities that fix official salaries, the personnel departments of the large firms and the unions need not have accepted the levelling; it was within their power to pull the vertical wage structure apart. Perhaps the word 'accept' is too weak, and these bodies played an active part in a certain levelling. A definite opinion is not possible in the present state of our knowledge, but this hypothesis cannot be rejected automatically.

The above shows that the facts of wage structure can be explained by various views. For the first time we see something which we shall increasingly encounter later in this book: an observed phenomenon suffers from an excess of explanations, and we cannot select the most exact theory. It is already becoming evident that our ideas still have room for improvement.

5. *The Interest Rate: Apparent Problems and Real Problems*

Interest is the price paid for the use of capital, and by capital we now mean funds for financing. In production theory we understand by capital the stock of capital goods, such as machinery, buildings, supplies of raw materials. The two concepts – monetary capital and physical capital – must be distinguished, but quantitatively they are the same. Funds for financing are tied up in capital goods (and also in debtors, but these cancel each other out from a macro-economic point of view).

Interest usually puts in an appearance as a percentage for the borrowing of money, for instance 6% a year, while the loan must be repaid after a certain time; but even if somebody uses his own capital, and makes a profit in that way, a distinction can be made between the interest and the actual profit. The reason why interest exists lies in the productivity of physical capital. Experience shows that production can be enormously increased by the use of machinery; even if we allow for the labour required to make such a machine, the production detour via the engineering industry is still remunerative. Capital therefore results in a net increase in productivity, and consequently the entrepreneur can increase his profit. But to pay for these physical capital goods finance is required: monetary capital. These funds are scarce and therefore are not available free of charge. The interest charged reflects this scarcity.

There has long been a great deal of philosophizing about interest. In this process most people had the idea in the back of their minds that there was something immoral about it. In no other field of economics were causal analysis and moral judgement so intermingled. Aristotle thought that money was infertile; he probably had in mind loans for purposes of consumption. Medieval schoolmen stuck fast at the idea that money does not litter, although it is quite evidently incorrect. They regarded interest as usury. But capital, in the sense of finance for physical capital goods, quite definitely bears fruit – once the depreciation and all other costs are paid, a net productivity remains.

In this technical sense interest is not a specific aspect of capitalist society either (unlike profit, which will be discussed later). If the State is the owner of the capital goods a net productivity likewise occurs, which in that case is of course pocketed by the State. Under the capitalist system the interest largely accrues to private persons, but that is not essential to the phenomenon of interest. It is incidentally the reason why we are considering it here.

Anybody is quite entitled to regard the collection of interest by private persons as wrong or unethical (more about that later).

But this does not imply that he has to repudiate net productivity; this is a fact, and moreover a fortunate one, for without that productivity the incomes of all of us (also and in particular wage income!) would be in a bad way. He may think that there is something dirty about the capital market, but this does not imply that he should be led to invent mysterious and complicated theories. And yet mystery and complication are the characteristics of the older capital theory.* That is fostered by some genuine entanglements – the banks play a part in this respect, and so does money; somebody once said that there are three main causes of insanity: women, ambition and the study of monetary affairs. Opinions may differ about women and ambition, but monetary theory has indeed yielded abstruse dogmata. This is not the proper place to discuss them; but we shall, of course, take the activities of the banks into consideration.

Many of the old differences of opinion about interest have now been cleared up. The heroic battle between three schools – interest is determined by productivity, by savings, by liquidity preference – has now been more or less settled. There is general agreement that productivity, and savings, and liquidity preference all play a part, and their interplay can best be understood by starting from the simple little graph on p. 88. The basis of the demand curve is formed by marginal productivity. For entrepreneurs are prepared to pay interest for exactly the same reason as they pay wages – they need scarce factors of production to make an end-product. The marginal productivity is lower according as the amount of capital used in production is larger; that follows from the form of the production function. The law of diminishing returns applies

---

*A highly obscure view is that held by nineteenth-century classical authors to the effect that wages are paid out of capital. In fact they are paid, like interest, out of the proceeds of the product. A confusing figure is also Roscher's fisherman, so called after the German economist W. Roscher (1850). The man first fishes by hand, which yields disappointing catches; try it yourself sometime. Then he makes a net, but during that time he cannot fish, and he must therefore first save a stock of fish. His productivity increases as a result of the net. So far so good. But then Roscher starts to call the stock of fish capital, which of course does not help to make matters clear. The net is a capital good, the fish are there to be eaten. The idea that capital is 'really' postponed consumption was current for a long time.

here, just as with labour. This demand curve therefore does not differ essentially from the demand for labour.

The supply of loanable funds is fed by savings – households (and also business firms) do not consume their whole income, but accumulate part of it for investment purposes. By investing they give up the liquidity. Originally they had their savings in the form of money, so that they could still do with it what they wanted; this freedom of spending is called liquidity. The lender surrenders this freedom, and if he did not receive any interest he would not do so. In this sense interest is therefore a reward both for saving (by the lender, or by the forefathers from whom he inherited the capital), and also for surrendering the liquidity. Saving and parting with liquidity lie behind the supply curve. But interest can also be traced back to the productivity of the capital goods; without this there would be no demand for monetary capital, or at least much less. The point of intersection of the supply and demand curve determines the level of interest; all the determinant elements fall neatly into place.

As stated, there are complications (where does economics *not* present complications?). Some of the demand for capital comes from households (so, come to that, does some of the demand for labour); evidently private persons who want to build a house, buy a car or acquire a washing machine are also prepared to pay a price for the means of financing. More obscure is the fact that the government asks for capital, and not only to finance a port or a canal, but also to cover a deficit in the budget. The how and why of borrowing for current expenditure is a complicated matter, connected with the regulation of the circular flow of incomes and expenditure – a subject from modern Keynesian economics, about which I fortunately need say nothing here, since there are other useful books on the subject.* But one thing that is certain is that borrowing by the government causes interest to land at a higher level than it would otherwise have reached, and that therefore influences the distribution of income.

Against this is the fact that there are other suppliers of capital than private savers. Much of the saving is done in the form of

* Modestly recommended: J. Pen, *Modern Economics*, Pelican Books, 1965.

retained profits by firms; this is a kind of advance levy on the income that the shareholders receive. Incidentally, as a rule these savings do not flow over the open capital market; they remain in the firm in which they were made, where they are invested in the firm's expansion. Nevertheless, these savings lower the interest rate, for otherwise these means of financing would have had to have been found on the open capital market. Then part of the savings comes from pension funds, insurance companies and social security funds. To some extent these savings are obligatory ones, that is to say they are imposed by law on employees, who have to pay a compulsory contribution. This legal obligation also makes the interest rate lower than it would have been.

Somewhat more difficult to grasp is a third source of financing: the supply of credit by the banks. The remarkable thing about this is that this increase in loanable funds has not come about through saving, but through the creation of money. Banks do in fact possess the ability to make new money out of nothing – an activity that is based on a claim on a bank being accepted by the public as a means of payment. This money-creating ability has already inspired many reflections, which do not interest us particularly here; the main thing is that interest becomes lower as a result. It is pushed below the level – sometimes called the 'natural' level – at which it would have landed if the supply of capital had been exclusively savings. A banking system that operates well thus influences income distribution, namely in the sense that the average income of the capitalist is somewhat reduced by it. Some critics of capitalism, who view the banks with suspicion, would never have thought it!

The above whole of additional supply and demand components can be summarized in the usual graph (p. 88). Normally a separate supply curve is drawn for the creation of money, but that is not necessary. However, the reader must bear in mind that one single graph for the whole capital market really entails a pretty far-reaching simplification. Lending and borrowing assume different forms: some credits are short-term, it often being left to the borrower to decide how much use he makes of the credit (a bank overdraft). The shortest and most flexible credit is call money between banks and financial institutions. Other credits, such as debenture loans, last longer, and have specified dates of repayment. Some credits are furnished against security or are covered by a mortgage; this makes a difference to the lender's risk and thus to the interest rate. And then there is the important type of financing in which capital is transferred without the obligation to repay it: participation in a firm, for instance in the form of shares. In that case, too, one can to a certain extent speak of interest, although its rate is not fixed in advance, and it is not easily separated from profits. All these submarkets have their own peculiarities, their own risks and their own interest rate. In other words, there is a structure of interest rates, just as there is a wage structure. The interest on short-term credits (this is also called the money market) is in principle lower than that on long-term ones (the capital market), which is understandable, since in the latter case the lender has to wait longer for repayment and meanwhile runs the risk of a rise in the price of goods, which reduces his purchasing power. The lower interest on short-term credit is hidden from view because the additional costs are much higher, and the banks earn more on the short-term transactions. The most expensive is consumer credit, especially in the form of hire-purchase credit. The one interest rate is sometimes three times as high as the other, but the submarkets are nevertheless connected. Capital is fairly mobile, and the various interest rates move in more or less the same direction.

And therefore for our purposes it is no great mistake to speak of one capital market, although we must bear in mind that some investors – usually the small ones – can profit only from a relatively low interest rate. They traditionally buy bonds, and that is not the best of choices, especially in times of inflation. If interest rises, the market value of these bonds drops, and if the prices of consumer goods increase, this strikes another blow at the bondholders. The rich investor, who can stand to run more of a risk, buys shares, and these are better proof against inflation. And the really rich invest in firms which they own and control – that may lead to very high incomes, partly profits, partly interest. These are also points to bear in mind, but for the rest we shall regard the capital market as one big macro-economic whole.*

* There is in addition a rival method for analysing the creation of interest.

118

There has been much to do in economics about the way in which the supplied and the demanded amounts of loanable funds react to interest. We are thus concerned here with what we have called above the elasticities of supply and demand; these are important for understanding the height of the interest rate.

The major part of the demand is exercised by business. It is evidently a derived demand, and the money productivity of capital plays a part. The demand curve falls away to the right; at lower rates of interest more is demanded than at higher ones. And yet it has been asserted on occasion that the reaction of the demanded amount of funds to interest is a weak one. The costs of loans are often only a small part of the total costs, the more so if the financing is done mainly by ploughing back profits (on which incidentally interest must also be calculated, though the firm gets this interest back as income). Investment projects are always risky; the risk margin makes the exact level of the interest rate less important. The capital must be earned back within a limited number of years – say ten or so – and over that period the burden of interest is, of course, lighter than over very long periods. The latter occur in house-building, and there the elasticity of the demand for capital is naturally greater. Generally speaking, too, the government's demand for financing is not very elastic; if the Chancellor of the

---

This does not start from two flows of capital – a supplied and a demanded flow – that encounter one another on the capital market over a certain period, but from the total stock of assets existing in a national economy at a given moment. These assets are divided into a number of main groups, such as physical capital goods, shares, bonds, bills and cash stocks. The basic idea behind this interest theory is that all these assets are owned by somebody; the various interest rates must be such that people want to own the whole stock. The investors achieve their optimum by portfolio selection – the catchword of this analysis. Given the properties of the various assets and the preferences of the various individuals, there is an interest structure that keeps the total stock of assets exactly in place. If the interest structure is different, the assets shift; they change hands just as long as is required for everything to be back in its right place again. This approach lends itself in particular to an explanation of the interrelationship of the interest rates. Nor is it in opposition to the usual supply and demand analysis, but may be converted into this. The one economist prefers the flow-of-loanable-funds analysis, the other the theory of portfolio selection, just as the one investor prefers shares and the other bonds.

Exchequer has a budgetary deficit for whatsoever reason he just has to borrow money, whether the interest is high or low. All in all, the elasticity of demand must not be pictured as too high.

Much the same applies to supply. Some comes from private persons who simply earn more than they can spend – they are interested in the interest rate because it helps them to determine their income, but its level does not influence their savings. Matters are different with small savers, but in their case an unexpected negative effect occurs: a man who saves to attain a given income from interest will achieve his aim sooner at a higher rate of interest than a lower one! Incidentally, the latter is rather a curiosity than a real cause of the inelasticity of supply. What is more important is that pension funds and insurance companies accumulate tremendous wealth that they have to invest. They prefer a high interest rate to a low one, but even at a low rate they still have to offer the funds on the market. Liquidity costs them income. They can briefly postpone investment if they expect a rise in the rate – and that may influence the market, so that the rate does in fact go up – but in the long run these institutions are obliged to part with their money, high interest rate or low.

The above seems rather inconclusive. Both the supply of and the demand for capital are rather inelastic; that means to say that the traditional curves tell us little about the exact height of the interest rate. Of course it continues to be true that scarcity determines interest, but it is difficult to predict how intense that scarcity will prove to be. And then it should be borne in mind that the principal complication behind these two curves has not yet been discussed.

It is this: in a modern country, with a well-organized capital market (and where the hoarding or exporting of savings is an exception), the position of the capital demand curve tends to influence the position of the supply curve. This torpedoes every simple long-run theory of interest. The meaning of this at first sight obscure statement is as follows. If entrepreneurs decide to invest more and thus order more capital goods, they create an income for the producers of those capital goods. The engineering industry pays more wages and more profits; these accrue to the income recipients, who will save part. Another part is devoted to consumption, and that increases incomes in the consumer goods industry. The investments have an 'income effect'. A multiplier acts on the primary impulse; national income grows, and as a result so do savings. The capital supply curve shifts to the right. You can also put it this way (the Keynesian formulation): investments summon up their own savings. Now one may never derive from this reasoning that there will never be a shortage of capital, or that capital is not scarce and so cannot command a price. In a growing economy there is more demand for funds for financing than supply; the multiplier does not change that at all. But it is true that long-term movements of the demand curve to the right will be followed by shifts in the supply curve in the same direction. That is a macro-economic relation which makes the rate of interest much less determinate than might appear from the elementary diagram on p. 88.

It is impossible to say *a priori* where all this will lead to in practice. Perhaps the reader now thinks: anything can happen to the interest rate, nothing is certain, the wildest fluctuations are probable. But then he is in for a surprise. For the result of all this theoretical indeterminateness is: relative stability, and in any case a remarkable constancy of the interest rate over very long periods. While every possible economic variable steadily grows – production, consumption, wages – the interest rate remains more or less the same. This is the great riddle of the interest rate.

Please note that I do not claim that the interest rate is rigid. On the contrary, it is highly sensitive to all kinds of influences. The conditions on the capital market are a quick pointer to what is going on in a country; that applies in particular to the stock exchange. The prices on this security market are inversely proportional to the interest rate; if the price rises this means a drop in the interest rate, and vice versa. Everybody knows that such fluctuations are like ripples in a pool of water. But the net result of all these influences on the interest rate is nevertheless most limited. Interest rises and falls, but within fairly narrow limits.

While I write this, we are going through a period of very high interest. The rate for quality bonds has climbed above 8% per annum. Some of this is due to inflation: anyone who lends his money for a period of some length wants compensation for the depreciation of money. That partly explains the excessively high interest rates of the present day. The real interest rate is quite a bit lower – well below 5%, and perhaps not much higher than three. Just after the war, the percentage in Britain was three – Hugh Dalton tried to push it below three, but did not succeed. In the Thirties, 3 or $3\frac{1}{2}\%$ was likewise a usual level. If we go even further back, into the nineteenth century, we find similar percentages. Although there is nothing sacrosanct about the figure three, it does seem a good figure for roughly expressing the level of interest over long periods, with a certain rise in recent decades.* Come to that, it doesn't matter much what figure is chosen – if one compares what has meanwhile happened to wages.

For in the course of time money wages have risen. They are now four times what they were before the war. But in the Twenties they were already several times as high as in the nineteenth century. The level of money wages is at present at least ten times what it was then. In the light of this, it is more or less irrelevant whether we start from a 'normal' level of 3 or 5% when considering interest. The main thing is that interest roughly hovered around the same level, while wages steadily rose.

Real incomes – the goods that one can buy for one's money income – have, of course, risen much less than money wages; the wage increase was accompanied by a price increase, but as a rule there remained a real wage increase every year. Nowadays this is three or so per cent per annum in most countries; it may be somewhat less, or also more – that depends on economic growth. In former times the real annual wage increase was lower, around $1\frac{1}{2}$ or 2% per annum, and there were also occasional lean years of recession, like the hungry Thirties. But the trend is clear: a steady increase. Conversely, the trend of real interest (interest rate divided by price index) is a steady decline. Not until the end of the Sixties did this change. Nowadays one buys much less for 8% of a hundred thousand guilders than for 3% of a hundred thousand guilders a century ago. That is the long-run result of the interplay

* cf., F. W. Paish, *Long-term and Short-term Interest Rates in the U.K.*, 1966. Between 1875 and 1913 the percentage fluctuated between 2·26 and 3·40 (table on p. 52).

of supply and demand on the capital market, and that result is rather enigmatic. It is not the fact that interest exists that is puzzling, nor its monetary aspect, nor the wonders of roundabout production, nor the burning question whether money breeds money or not; these are all apparent problems. The real mystery lies in the fact that the rate of interest fluctuates around a relatively trendless level, and that in a world where everything, and certainly incomes and prices, goes up and up.

Attempts have been made to find a conclusive explanation of that phenomenon. The supply and demand diagram does not elucidate matters sufficiently. For in the course of time the two curves have shifted to the right, whereby increases in demand have brought about increases in supply via the investment – income creation – saving nexus. The relative inelasticity of supply and demand suggests that the interest rate may be a conventional variable determined by what the market, i.e. the human collectivity, thinks it ought to be. In this sense the interest rate would rather resemble some salaries, which also reflect a social evaluation. But this hypothesis, applied to interest, is a rather dubious one and it does not make it clear why the percentage is so constant.

An explanation has also been sought in a kind of Ricardian mechanism.* In Ricardo the real wage was constant because population growth forced it down to the subsistence minimum. If the wage level were to rise somewhat above this rock-bottom level, people would breed like rabbits (and the death rate would improve). This additional supply attended to restoration of the old minimum. Now it might be thought that capitalists react like Ricardian workers. If the interest rate rises slightly above the conventional level, capitalists begin to accumulate like crazy, and interest returns briskly to the minimum. If the percentage were to become too low, the supply of capital would be choked off, and interest would rise again. The drawback of this point of view is that it seems to start from a completely elastic supply; I thought that in the above I had made it plain that substantial sections of the supply of savings are precisely inelastic, certainly in a

---

*T. Scitovsky, 'A Survey of Some Theories of Income Distribution', in *The Behavior of Income Shares* (Studies in Income and Wealth, Vol. 27), 1964. Scitovsky ascribes this theory to, among others, N. Kaldor.

modern society with its institutional investors and its retained profits.

A more fruitful approach is that via marginal productivity. The rate of interest is more or less stable because marginal productivity is more or less stable. Of course, this begs the question why that marginal productivity behaves in such a way. That comes about through the continual accumulation. The amount of capital per worker (in symbols K/L) grows steadily in the course of time. In accordance with the law of diminishing returns this ought to force down the real interest rate. Deducing in this way, we would expect a downward trend – and in actual fact we ought to be surprised that the interest rate has not in fact fallen much further! Indeed, some economists have occasionally suspected that the interest rate would fall practically to zero as a result of the constant rise in the fraction K/L. Keynes in particular wrote very evocatively on this point. He predicted a situation of an absolute plethora of capital, coupled with a very high level of prosperity. This is known as the Euthanasia of the Rentier.

However, matters have not yet reached that stage. The Keynesian prediction was doubtless influenced by the particular situation of the Thirties, in which the interest rate was in fact very low for a time. The capital demand curve had been shifted to the left by the Depression, and come to that so had the supply curve, but the result was nevertheless an apparent and paradoxical plenitude of savings on the capital market. Since then both curves have resumed their trend to the right. The demand curve has shifted as a result of technical progress. Accumulation and the law of diminishing returns force down the interest rate; technical progress counters this process. Viewed in this way, the relative constancy is the net effect of two opposed forces. The result is rather a chance one; matters might also have turned out differently.

Meanwhile the capitalist is alive and well, although he has clearly slipped back in respect of the wage-earner. The Euthanasia of the Rentier is not yet upon us. If we want to define his position in society more exactly than has happened in this chapter, we must consider the share of capital in national income. For real wage and real interest are difficult to compare directly.* The theory

* They have different dimensions. Wage is a sum of money per physical

of distributive shares must further elucidate this matter. That will be done in the next chapter.

6. *Rent of Land: What's so Special?*

It will have struck the reader that rents of land have been treated rather carelessly in the above. Sometimes they are forgotten, and on other occasions they are included among the proceeds of capital. Rent of land also resembles interest; in both cases money has been invested and there is a return on it. But while interest is the price of a money loan that is repaid, rent of land is the price paid for the use of land. Land does not wear out. The latter will be contradicted by every farmer, but it should be borne in mind that, in the footsteps of Ricardo, what economists mean by 'land' is the 'original and indestructible powers of the soil'. What does wear out is the capital component of land, and indeed land and capital are closely interwoven in practice. As regards farming: artificial fertilizer, drainpipes, reallocation of holdings, land reclamation. And, as regards urban land: the building of streets, sewerage, numerous cables and pipes – the virgin soil can barely be recognized except as a solid substance that serves to bear people and buildings. However, this substratum has its own problems, and also the incomes that proceed from it give rise to a number of peculiarities.

Rent of land stirs the imagination. Consequently, most people overestimate its importance. Its percentage in national income is much lower than many believe who see extensive landed property before them and who know that many pay rent for their house. The percentage is actually unbelievably low – for agricultural rents below 1%, for urban rents not more than 2% of national income. This was not always the case; furthermore, underdeveloped

---

unit of work. Interest is a percentage of a sum of money. That also plays us false when we correct for price increases. As regards the wage, correction is straightforward: real wage is money wage divided by price level, and the percentage *rise* in the real wage is equal to the increase in money wage less the price increase. Matters are different with interest; there we take the percentage of interest over a period (say a year) and deduct the price increase (over that same year) to find the real interest rate. Note: not to find the *increase* in real interest! The comparison is a tricky one.

countries, which suffer from a large agricultural sector, have to contend with high land rent figures.

Rent of land derives its special place in the textbooks from the grandiose theory developed by D. Ricardo at the beginning of the nineteenth century, and which has been discussed above (Chapter II, 3). It amounts to the fact that population growth and shortage of land will force up the share of land rent, as a result of which no money will be left for the financing of industry. Ricardo predicted stagnation of economic growth, but this prediction did not work out, nor has the increase in the share of rent of land occurred. The very low value of the present share of rent of land is in fact something that would surprise nineteenth-century observers; they might suspect that landowners were not prepared to rent out any more land for such a low remuneration, but this fear would be misplaced. There is in fact a clear shortage of land at many places, and especially in the cities this may lead to high prices and rents. This situation is not without its problems, but it is nothing like Ricardo's prediction. The share of the rent of land in national income will intensively engage our attention in the following chapter.

By the way, the person of the landowner is also the subject of much popular misconception. He tends to be regarded as a member of the peerage, owning huge tracts of landed property, inhabiting a castle and living in great style – a romantic conception, which in Britain at least can boast of a historical tradition, but which overlooks the fact that many a landowner is a small rentier, or an ex-farmer who leases out his farm after he has retired. The rent must then finance his old age. Furthermore, much land is owned by institutional investors – faceless bodies, behind which the interests of very different investors are concealed. Moreover, a considerable part of the land (differing from country to country) is used by the owner himself, as a result of which he as it were pays the rent to himself; this is sometimes called implicit rent. In other words, landowners are a mixed bunch.

So to see, there seems to be little reason for a special theory of land rent. The demand for land is largely a derived demand; somebody is prepared to pay rent because he wishes to grow the corn that will, he hopes, make him a profit. From the demand curve for corn the demand curve for land can be derived. Marginal productivity gives a helping hand in this. Someone who wishes to make chemical products exercises a derived demand for land. The demand for living space also leads to a demand for land, because so far houses have not been able to float in the air. Also important is the continual expansion of roads, airfields, etc. Up to now there has been little reason to differentiate land from labour and capital. On the supply side we see a clear inelasticity: despite reclamation and sporadic poldering the total amount supplied is fairly constant. It is this inelasticity that has given the economists all kinds of ideas, and these are reflected in separate chapters of the textbooks.

For what is the case? If the supply is completely inelastic, the position of the demand curve determines the rent. Land is worth what those demanding it offer, and the suppliers are completely powerless. This is at variance with many popular ideas about the relative power of owner and tenant, and this contradiction is quite understandable. The landowner may be at the mercy of the market mechanism, but that is to his advantage when land is scarce and the demand high. He can calmly let the shortage make itself felt in his income, and he does well for himself in the process. Only when the market situation turns against him is his impotence evident. The latter is occurring in some parts of France, where people are leaving for the cities and the demand is disappearing. Since the land can hardly be taken to Paris, it becomes almost worthless.

Land rent is therefore dependent on demand, and in this very special sense it is a residue. The landowner gets what remains. It is tempting to say: what remains after other factors of production have had their share. But take care. The latter may also be said of interest, if necessary of wages, and certainly of profits. A residue is what enters into consideration last, and that depends on the whims of whoever is doing the considering. However, it is not true to say that the farmer can make the level of his land rent simply depend on what he spends on the other factors of production. If he were to try that, the landowner, backed by the market mechanism, would soon be up in arms.

The question of whether land rent is a residue or not has been haunting discussions since the beginning of the last century.

Ricardo was right when he wrote: corn is not high because a rent is paid, but a rent is paid because corn is high. But that 'right' must be interpreted solely in the sense of inelastic supply curves that are confronted with a derived demand. If the latter is at a high level because the end-product is expensive, a high land rent results from the market; that rent is not a cause but a consequence. However, one may not deduce from that that the rent for the individual farmer is not a part of the costs. Not a single farmer would believe that, and rightly so. He simply has to pay for the land, as for labour and for capital.

Incidentally, this discussion of the residual nature of land rent has put the economists on the track of a phenomenon, not without importance to our subject, known as economic surplus. The basic idea is that the market mechanism steers the factors of production towards the most remunerative application. A metal worker who can earn more elsewhere does not remain in his present job, and capital moves to the uses with the highest profit. There is general mobility, which ought to be able to lead to optimum efficiency. But there are also units of factors of production that are paid more than is necessary just to keep them where they are. I would be prepared to do my present work – the teaching of students – for half the salary I get. The other half, which is not required to keep me in my job, is called economic surplus (of course, I usefully employ that extra money, and perhaps I wouldn't like to be without it either – the definition of surplus refers only to what is in excess of what is required to keep a factor of production where it is). A person's income breaks down into two parts: the costs, also called alternative costs or opportunity costs, and the surplus.

This 'superfluous' income was first clearly seen with reference to land. Since in that case the total supply is inelastic, the total income from land rent may be regarded as surplus. However, this applies only if we consider the total. If land has various possible uses, and it generally has, a relatively low land rent for the one use will lead to something different being done with the land. If houses yield too small a derived demand for land, and car parks a higher one, the property standing on it will be demolished and car parks will appear. (In this way optimum allocation fosters the decay of the cities.)

In the same way, surplus can also be discovered in the other factors of production. Capital put into a given machine stays tied up in that machine until the latter has worn out. As long as that capital has not been released by depreciation it earns surplus; there are no alternative costs. Workers who are tied to the firm through occupying houses owned by that firm earn a surplus income. This surplus concept can further be useful for understanding certain processes, especially with regard to the passing-on of taxes; it has no ethical implications. Nobody has ever claimed that somebody's surplus income may simply be taken away from him. Only, if someone (for instance the Inland Revenue) were nevertheless to perform that operation, the victim would not react by looking for another job. That is why it is sometimes claimed that taxes are passed on until they encounter a surplus. In this view, the recipients of surplus always come off badly. This point is taken up in Chapter VII, 8.

An additional complication is that many authors have given this surplus concept the name of 'rent' or 'economic rent'. One might almost think that this terminology has been deliberately chosen to confuse us, for many of the rents of land and of houses are not surplus incomes if there are adequate possibilities of alternative use.

An important practical problem is, in conclusion, the relation between the rentals of various pieces of land. This is analogous to that of the wage structure and the structure of interest rates: there is something like land rent structure. This is of course governed by the quality of the land, not only the type of land and its fertility being important, but above all its location too. There are excellent pieces of farmland in the world that are worthless owing to their eccentric location, and conversely there are plots that no farmer can do anything with, but which strategically overlook a beautiful landscape and are suitable for a hotel or an expensive house. And one square yard in Bond Street is of high value, derived from the demand for expensive goods.

This land rent structure does not yield many difficulties in theory – supply and demand regulate matters in a natural fashion. The problems arise when we start to consider the share of land rent in national income. The spectacular drop in that fraction summons up questions. But that is a matter which will concern us later (see Chapter V, 7).

7. *Profits: the Troublesome Category*

Profits motivate production by firms. They are therefore an essential element of what is called capitalism – which makes it all the stranger that the distribution theory has so much difficulty with these incomes. The usual analysis, in which a derived demand curve is confronted with a supply curve of a factor of production, does not apply here. The concept 'marginal productivity' is not applied as a rule to the activities of entrepreneurs. Worse still, this factor of production – initiating and organizing production, taking decisions on the nature of the product, the amount, the method of production, the investment in capital goods, the engagement of labour, the bearing of risk – does not occur in the usual production function, which sees production as dependent on labour, capital and possibly land. In many macro-economic studies the entrepreneur seems to have been forgotten. The neo-classical theory has trouble not only with the volume but even with the *presence* of profit – the latter is often reasoned out of existence by styling it a temporary residue, or assuming that competition will cause it to disappear. A 'normal' profit is occasionally counted among costs, because these are said to be necessary to keep entrepreneurs at their work. These are the alternative costs of entrepreneurship, and that is all very well theoretically, but how exactly this normal profit must be separated from surplus profit is not always clear. For theoretical economics profits are an awkward affair.

Practically oriented minds who are daily concerned with profits – bookkeepers, accountants, business economists, and the entrepreneurs themselves – have their own problems. It is not difficult to define profit as the difference between proceeds and costs, but what exactly are costs? Strictly speaking, the entrepreneur's own work must be included among them, and the interest on the firm's own wealth. This can be estimated. But how much has to be written off? How must price increases of stocks and machinery be dealt with? This growth in wealth remains tied up in the firm; that may not be regarded as profit, though some (the Inland

Revenue) think differently about it. How much must be reserved for technical innovation if we are to speak of genuine profit? Profit has also been defined as what a firm can spend without eating into its capital, or without impairing its future earning capacity – but that calls for a look into the uncertain future, at the competitive strength of the firm in comparison with that of others. Profit is not a clear-cut concept for practical use, although people seem to manage.

It is also of importance to our view of profits that we do not only consider business firms. A person who works on his own account – like a doctor, lawyer or painter – does not receive any wage income. He is not in the employment of anyone. Professionals of this kind receive total proceeds, deduct the costs incurred and what remains is, economically speaking, profit. Many a doctor would object to being described as a profit-maker, but all the same his income can best be understood as the difference between proceeds and costs, the result of a series of decisions that he takes independently. He operates in a market. On the other hand, there is also something to be said for regarding at least a part of his income as remuneration for work; included among the costs is a calculated wage that he pays himself. Similarly, part of the income is interest on capital invested in medical equipment and so on. The division between wage, interest and profit causes in the case of doctors and lawyers similar problems to those in the case of small farmers and grocers, only in the former case it is more arbitrary; for the 'income from work' part differing figures can be entered. The division is rather artificial, and perhaps there is something to be said for counting the whole income simply as profit.

To give an impression of the size of the problem: the profit of concerns, plus the net income of self-employed businessmen and members of the free professions, is about 20% of national income. If one wants, one can allocate about half of that to work. The 'pure' profit is then 10% of national income. A further part of that is 'normal' profit, in the sense of a remuneration for the entrepreneurial activity which is necessary to continue running the business at the same level. It is difficult to say exactly how large this fraction is. Furthermore, taxes are paid from the profit. At most

5% of national income remains in the form of genuine super-profits, i.e. residues of a surplus nature. This numerical example is only an approximate one, but it gives an order of size that may be disappointing to those who regard profit as a substantial and use-less category of income, which ought to be transferred to others or suppressed.

It is this pure profit that we have to explain. It is not difficult to point to a number of explanatory principles, although this enumeration does not in itself give us a real theory. The causes of profit are usually listed as follows.

(a) *Reimbursement for risk*. The combining of means of production into a rather rigid whole anticipates a market demand, but this may prove disappointing. Then losses are suffered which are all the greater according as the equipment is more specialized. In every form of society this uncertainty must be accepted, although in our modern mobile society it is greater than in a static one determined by traditions. The risk is not borne by the entre-preneurs alone; the workers, too, can share in losses in painful fashion. And yet they are better insured than the entrepreneurial capitalists, for if the firm suffers a loss, the latter see their invest-ments drop in value and nobody absorbs this drop for them.

The risk must therefore be built in in advance if entrepreneurial activity is not to stagnate. Some risks (fire, loss of profits through a stoppage) can be insured against, but this is not the case with the typical uncertainty of the market. If the proceeds of production turn out favourably, part of the profit is pocketed, which may be regarded as compensation for accepting the uncertainty.

Losses are not only a theoretical possibility or an insignificant phenomenon. Among small shopkeepers the risk of failure is terribly high. An American figure: one-third to one-half of all retail businesses are discontinued within two years.* This is accompanied by a great deal of distress, but it does not seem to put the newcomers off. They are attracted by the hope of profit and that is, in a certain sense, the cause of the losses.

(b) *Differences in efficiency*. Some firms produce at a lower cost

*P. A. Samuelson, *Economics*, 1964, 6th edition, p. 78.

than others. The price is adjusted in such a way that less efficient firms also take part. The cost differentials can easily be of the order of size of one to two – a tremendous possibility of profit for the better-organized firms. It has sometimes been postulated that it is precisely the large firms that have a lead in costs, so that it is in fact the cost level of the smaller firms that determines the price. This is then the 'mixed oligopoly', which is advantageous for the large firms in more than one sense. They make profits, invest these in their own firm and in this way increase their lead in efficiency. Profits engender profits.

(c) *Differences in the nature of the product.* Even within relatively homogeneous branches of industry differences still occur in product innovation. The firm which has a lead here, and makes something that appeals particularly to the public, can earn enormous profits. This relates to the first producers of transistor radios, the first self-service businesses, the Beatles; it covers fashion designers like Mary Quant, and a number of chemical and pharmaceutical industries. Innovation is the watchword of competition, and in this area the interests of the vanguard of producers and that of the consumers usually coincide. The man whose name is always mentioned in a discussion of innovation is J. Schumpeter; half a century ago he already depicted the entrepreneur as the motivator of progress, the dynamic organizer of new combinations of factors of production, the man who ensures that the technical ingenuity of the engineers is converted into economic reality and who is rewarded for his efforts by large profits. Note: technical progress creates profits in *some* firms. In other firms, which suddenly discover that their product is outmoded, losses occur.

Now the rate of technical progress is not a constant datum. Everybody knows that technical acceleration is now going on: more and more inventions are appearing, and they are being applied more quickly. It is not certain, but at any rate probable, that the total of profits is rising as a result. This is not noticeable in statistics – the share of profit is fairly stable – but that may be due to the other factors cutting across the picture. For instance, it is possible that rapid technical progress at the same time stimulates competition. The exact mechanism is obscure.

(d) *Differences in location*. The producer who is close to the market or favourably situated on a road or waterway saves costs or develops more quickly than his competitors. However, the resultant profits can be taken away from him by the landowner; profit is transformed into land rent and thus into costs. In actual fact this transformation does not always happen; factories stand on their own land, and they remain there as the agglomeration of consumers spreads or rail traffic is intensified. And yet there is something to be said for regarding extra profits made in this way as costs that are comparable to interest on the firm's own capital. This is a theoretically correct view; but in practice it is not always easy to make the separation between implicit land rent and pure profit. In statistics, for instance, we don't even try.

(e) *Monopoly profits*. This is the harmful side of profits, and critics of capitalism often see only this side of the matter. The real monopolist – the one and only supplier in a branch of industry – is rare, but in many cases a breath of monopoly pervades competition. One brand is not the same as another – economists call that product differentiation, and as a result an element of power creeps into the market that yields an extra profit for the supplier. He can fix his own price, which is impossible under perfect competition, and perhaps he extends his volume of production a little less than he would otherwise have done. In some cases this limitation of production is an obvious danger: contrived scarcity leads to profit for a small group, and to harm for the public.

For this effect a quantitative yardstick has been devised by A. P. Lerner: the degree of monopoly. It is assumed that in perfect competition the price equals the marginal costs; by the latter we mean the costs that are caused by the expansion of production by one unit. These costs rise as production expands; the optimum volume of production (the maximum profit) lies at the point where the entrepreneur, at a given price, makes no more profit on his last unit. The price p then reflects the scarcity of productive factors. In monopolistic competition the price is higher than the marginal costs m. The difference, $p - m$, expressed as a fraction of the price, is the degree of monopoly. Thus $\dfrac{p - m}{p}$. This fraction is 0 in the case of $p = m$, i.e. under perfect competition; if m is very small it may lie in the neighbourhood of 1, but that is improbable. Values of 0·5 or 0·8 are not inconceivable; the average will not be higher than 0·3.

The degree of monopoly has a scholarly look to it, but on closer inspection this variable does not differ so much from what a businessman calls his gross profit margin (only this is an average, and not a marginal variable). Everyone will accept at once that this figure is of importance to the size of profit. In some theories, especially that of M. Kalecki on distributive shares, the degree of monopoly occupies a central position; it is the only determinant of the level of profits. Now this seems exaggerated to me. For one of the difficulties with this concept is that it is so hard to use macro-economically. The marginal costs lie at a different level per firm; efficient firms have a lower cost curve than inefficient ones. Now if the efficient firms make extra profits, this is caused, as we saw above, by a bonus on having a lead. If we use the macro-economic degree of monopoly, the danger threatens that we shall ascribe part of the profit that has been made as a result of differences in efficiency to the existence of monopoloid situations. This, of course, distorts the causes of income distribution. The degree of monopoly must therefore be handled with care – a vague formulation, which amounts to the fact that often we are at a loss what to do with it. This discussion is shifted to the following chapter when income shares are concerned.

(f) *Windfall profits in a branch of industry.* These are the result of sudden shifts in demand. The most pleasant example is presented by the sudden crazes that all at once provide high revenues. For instance, the hula hoop brought in plenty of money for the manufacturers of plastic tubing (which is used in the building trade), and something similar is going on at the moment with the kangaroo ball, a large plastic ball with a handle on it, on which one can sit and hop along like the marsupial from which it takes its name – an amusing business, also for the spectators. These are extreme examples. But gradual shifts in demand are going on all the time; the quick entrepreneur anticipates them, and consequently it is not possible to make a sharp distinction between the bonus for taking a lead, the bonus for taking a risk and windfall profits. Come to that, one often finds a monopolistic element in the situation too; precisely when the increase in demand occurs quickly there is no time for new suppliers to rush into the market.

(g) *General windfall profits*. These are the product of rapid increases in expenditure, costs lagging behind; in other words, of the inflationary process. Not every inflation leads to a swelling of profits. In recent decades in particular wages have tended to take the lead in the inflationary spiral, and then profits sometimes have difficulty in maintaining themselves. This is called a cost push. Opposed to it is the demand pull: in this form of inflation the increase in demand is in the van, and then one sees profits increase. Especially if losses were suffered beforehand through excess capacity, the influence of increases in demand on the general level of profits will be substantial and will considerably affect income distribution. That is the reason why the share of profits in the national income goes up in times of recovery from a depression.

The two forms – cost push and demand pull – may incidentally occur simultaneously, or alternate; often it is not easy to say which came first, the chicken or the egg, and the exact behaviour of profits in a complicated inflationary process is therefore not easy to predict. Much depends on the branch of industry – a labour-intensive production process has more trouble from inflationary wage increases than an automated branch of industry. But, speaking macro-economically, one can say that rapid growth, a high level of expenditure, a slight, lasting inflation are good for profits, and a depression extremely bad.

In the above, seven elements of profit have been listed. The reader may wonder whether as a result a quite decent profit theory has not been outlined, and whether it is true that profits form an income category that is so difficult to pin down. My answer is that seven is a fine number, and that the classification a-b-c-d-e-f-g looks nice and clear, but that the concepts used are not particularly sharp in a quantitative respect. They are not operational, like marginal productivity, they overlap, and they are not easy to mould into a systematic model. An exception is the degree of monopoly, but unfortunately that is the most vulnerable and misleading concept of the whole lot.

Illustrative of our lack of insight is the discussion around the passive nature of profits. The usual view, especially among entrepreneurs, is that profit is a residual quantity. Once the forces of the market are spent, the entrepreneur finds out what his profit is – or his loss. He can do his best to produce efficiently, to choose the right products, to apply the latest inventions quickly, to advertise his product strikingly, to motivate his employees as ingeniously as possible, but these are all indirect methods. In this view there is no direct approach to fixing profit.

Opposed to this view is that in which profit is programmed in advance. The entrepreneurs do not wait and see what fate will bring them; they make a plan and carry it out. Of course, some uncertainties remain, but modern technology reduces these to a minimum. The uncertainty is marginal, and the main thing is profit control. American business economists speak of profit engineering, and this is redolent of a spirit of energy and drive. In this view the large firms dominate both supply and demand. Many large contracts are concluded on a cost-plus basis, and that applies in particular to the lucrative dealings with the government. The demand of the large mass of scattered consumers is also programmed and manipulated. The customer is no longer always right; advertising, the dictates of technical progress, autonomous economic growth, these are the new arbiters. Supply is primary, demand follows. Prices and profits are not passive quantities, but the instruments of a monopoloid business management.

This reasoning, which may be found among various critics of capitalism (usually of neo-Marxist stripe), is also defended by J. K. Galbraith, who has put all his eloquence into it. He speaks of the Revised Sequence: formerly the entrepreneur just had to wait to see what the consumers would decide and at the end of the year he saw the results in his profit and loss account; but this sequence is the wrong way round. The market is put out of the picture; business dominates, aided by the State, with which it is tightly interwoven. This is the theme of *The New Industrial State* (1967).*

* Unlike the neo-Marxists, Galbraith does not conclude that power is concentrated in the hands of a few industrial and commercial managers.

137

What worries me as an economist is that the two views of profit can calmly subsist side by side. We have no exact method for deciding who is right. Of course, in the case of perfect competition profit is a residue, we can reason that – but Galbraith claims that competition no longer works, and has been replaced by planning. Now I am personally convinced that Galbraith paints a highly distorted picture of reality, that he exaggerates the power of the big concerns over the buying public to the point of ridicule, that the programming of profits is tried and in some cases also succeeds, but that it is often touch and go. However, if someone wants to adhere to Galbraith's point of view he can do so without my being able to convince him of the contrary with forceful arguments. I can point out that government contracts without risk form only a small part of total sales (they are of course important in the aircraft industry); I can adduce that Galbraith cheerfully confuses profit and profit margin: many entrepreneurs fix prices and thus profit margins, but whether that ultimately results in total profit also depends on the development of the market and of costs, and they do not have control of these. I could give examples of fierce struggle between industrial and commercial giants for the market: cars, oil companies, department stores, newspapers, shipbuilders, with as result substantial movements of profits, the sudden appearance of losses. I could point out that the planned profit margin and the certain turnover are more likely to be found in the sector of the free professions than in that of the concerns. All this culminates in the conclusion that Galbraith and his fellow-spirits uncritically repeat the contemporary tales about the manipulated consumer and programmed sales, while businessmen themselves have a much more realistic and therefore more anxious view of their sales. Finally, I might adduce that Galbraith is probably impelled more by a tendency towards grandiose and original conceptions than by a sense of reality; but the point is that the reader is free to continue to look sceptical, with the idea in the back of his mind that I am in the grip of the System, and he may disregard all sober

---

He stresses the widespread character of responsibility; the Technostructure in which the decisions are taken is a large and diffuse group, in which the lower echelons are also widely represented.

arguments. It is not a question of my having to be proved right; the trouble is that two views of profit can exist side by side, without economics being able, as arbiter, to pass unambiguous judgement on the strength of facts visible to all. This casts an unfavourable light on our knowledge of the factors that determine profit; it shows us that gripping fairy-tales can live on stubbornly.

However, the specific obscurities of profit are not confined to the causes and bases of profit. Some confusion may also arise over the question: who gets his hands on the profits in the end? A few inconclusive words on that subject.

As regards the incomes of independent businessmen and practitioners of the free professions, there is no problem: they draw the profits themselves. The difficulty lies in the profits of limited liability companies, roughly 10% of national income. A considerable part of these profits is not paid out, but retained in the firm. In fact dividend payments form the smallest portion; American investigations speak of about 20% of the total gross corporate profits or, if we consider profit after deduction of tax, over half.* These proportions differ in accordance with the general state of the economy; in bad years the shock is absorbed by the reserves, so that the percentage of dividend payments is at a somewhat higher level.

What influence do these retained profits have on personal income distribution? It is best to allocate them to the shareholders. But that calls for calculations that cause the statistician grey hairs. He works on a basis of tax data, and tax legislation does not require of the shareholders that they work out and declare the net value of the firms in which they participate as small shareholders. That would be asking too much of them. The price of shares on the stock exchange is the characteristic fiscal datum, and the relation between the net book value of a company and the market price of its shares is distant and sometimes weak. As a result, retained profits tend to be rather in the air when we speak about personal distribution.

A relatively modest part of the company's profits goes to managers, directors and usually also to a few senior executives in

* C. L. Schulze, 'Short-Run Movements of Income Shares' in the collection *The Behavior of Income Shares* mentioned above (p. 19).

the form of bonuses. Although this is only a small percentage, it gives rise to very high and sometimes grotesque incomes for a very limited number of persons. This explains part of the fantastic skewness of income distribution. It is as well to bear in mind that this inequality is determined institutionally. The division of profits by a company can be arranged in a variety of ways; if so desired, the whole personnel can be allowed to share in the profit, or the bonuses of top executives can be greatly restricted. True, this does not result in a spectacular improvement of prosperity for large groups of the population – that is impossible, since so limited a part of national income is concerned – but in this way the top incomes could be reduced, thus eliminating the offence and irritation they cause the lower-paid sections of the community.

The question of the division of profits among shareholders and others is thrown into relief by the huge differences in earning capacity between the companies. This beats everything that our society has to offer in the way of inequality – a fact that remains too much in the background in some textbooks of economics. Economists often leave it to journalists to draw attention to this, as a result of which their observations easily acquire too innocent and naïve a character. A student can wade through learned books on distribution, and above all functional distribution, without it striking him that a tiny percentage of the corporations earn the lion's share of the profits. An illustrative figure: the top 0·5 *per cent* of the American corporations pocket roughly half of the total corporate profits.* This is an essential characteristic of modern capitalism, and it imparts something fascinating to profits as a category of income. It sets its stamp on personal distribution, and we shall encounter that fact again.

8. *Macro-economics of Demand and Supply*

Up to now we have been viewing income distribution mainly in a micro-economic light. That means to say that we have investi-

* It is not difficult to find out this figure. Just take the *Statistical Abstracts of the United States*, for instance those for 1968, and turn to table 698. For Britain the share of the top $\frac{1}{2}\%$ is somewhat lower; I guess about 35 or 40 % (Calculated from the *Report of the Commissioners of Her Majesty's Inland Revenue for the year ended 31st March 1968*, Table III.)

gated the price determination of the factors of production (and profit) on the assumption that the 'Great Variables', such as total production, national income, price level, were constant. The reader will recall that we have not always kept up this micro-economic assumption of a constant national income: the trouble started with interest theory, when attention was drawn to the effect that investments have on national income and thus on savings. This was typical macro-economics, and that is not surprising, either, for the capital market is so large that it does not leave national income untouched. In fact a micro-economic interest theory is not really feasible. Wage determination more rightly allows of analysis in isolation; in its case it is a legitimate assumption that wages are raised in not too large a part of the labour market without national income starting to move. And yet, even with wage determination we were on thin ice, for we have spoken of a wage structure, of wages for special professions that help each other to rise, and of the unions that consider the overall picture of wage 'relativities'. We were therefore dangerously close to the concept of wage level – and that is a macro-economic quantity.

Perhaps the reader thinks: what difference does it make to me, micro or macro – a philosophical distinction, nothing to worry about. That is a wrong idea. One of the salient points of economics is that it does quite definitely make a difference. Theses that are correct for a small part of economic life are incorrect for the whole of it. For instance, if prices rise and Jack Jones gets the same money income, he loses ground. If prices rise, and national income remains constant – whoa, that is wrong, because if all prices rise, national income also rises. For prices are built up from incomes. Another example: if wages rise too much in a branch of industry, the product becomes more expensive and less of it is sold. Employment declines. If *all* wages rise, many things happen at the same time. Perhaps the overall purchasing power increases, and the demand for all products, and thus employment. The macro-reaction is more complex and may work out quite differently from the micro-reaction.

Let us summarize the new elements, I shall mention three, and then briefly discuss them. Note that we are concerned here with functional distribution, and therefore we ask what determines the wage *level*, the *level* of land rents, the profit *per unit of product* (and the interest rate, but that was a macro-variable right from the start). We are therefore not concerned with the *share* of labour, land, etc., in national income. The latter are also macro-problems, but they will be discussed in the following chapter.

The three new elements are as follows.

(a) We must make a distinction between nominal and real variables. For instance between money wage and real wage; the latter relates to the collection of goods that a person can buy for his wage. In micro-economics we may assume the price level to be constant; in macro-economics we must recall that rises in the level of money wages may lead to price increases. Let us nevertheless agree that in this section we shall continue to speak of money incomes; the influence of increases in incomes on the price level is postponed until the following section. After all, wage negotiations are conducted on nominal wages; land rent contracts contain nominal land rents.

(b) If we ponder the elasticity of the supply of and the demand for labour we must take into account macro-effects. The labour demand curve becomes less elastic as a result of increases in purchasing power. Supply, too, displays macro-economic peculiarities. Higher wages for nurses probably induce a large supply, but from the macro-economic point of view such a reaction is improbable; the total labour force hardly depends on the height of wages. Here, too, the elasticity becomes smaller.

(c) We must bear in mind that general wage increases can very well give rise to reactions among other categories of incomes. Perhaps profits become smaller as a result, or perhaps precisely larger. Possibly the rate of interest increases too. In other words, if we enter the field of macro-distribution we run the risk of encountering the inflationary spiral, a kind of abominable snowman. It will be discussed in the next section.

In the present section we are concentrating on the macro-demand for labour, that is to say the reaction of employment to wage increases. This is a controversial matter. The classical school, which dominated economic thought until 1936, was rather heedless of variations in the flow of purchasing power. It did not realize that wage increases would lead to a greater demand for consumer goods. The reason for this short-sightedness lay in the fact that the classical theory was fascinated by equilibria. If all markets are in equilibrium, and moreover national income is exactly enough to buy the national product, incomes and expenditure flow undisturbed along the right track. There is always enough purchasing power; depressions and inflationary processes are in this way excluded from thought. This balanced circulation is said to be brought about by the price mechanism, and more in particular by the operation of the capital market, which equates savings and investment. This is called Say's Law, an important pillar of classical theory. It entails that, from a macro-viewpoint, every supply creates its own demand; national income is determined by production.

In the classical reasoning wage increases therefore lead exclusively to cost increases. The flow of purchasing power does not change as long as Say's Law is applicable. This implies that the burden of higher wages has to be borne primarily by other incomes. More wage means less interest, or land rent, or profit (probably the last in particular). In this reasoning the firms will try to absorb the higher wage costs by engaging less labour and using more machines. Substitution takes place, within a given production. Now if the level of money wages were to be forced up too high, for instance by the unions, this substitution would go further than can be reconciled with the equilibrium on the labour market; unemployment results. The demand for labour is elastic; the elasticity is determined by the five factors that we have listed above in section 2.

In this classical view the supply and demand diagram is therefore also applicable to the labour market as a whole. There is in actual fact no contradiction between the micro and the macro reasoning. The wage level is determined by the point of intersection of the two curves, and the elasticity of demand is large enough to supply a stable equilibrium. An upward wage push punishes itself and is therefore not to be expected as a permanent phenomenon.

This classical reasoning was long challenged by supporters of the purchasing power theory. There are early examples. Well known is the view of Henry Ford, who advocated higher wages because then the workers could buy his cars, which would lead to mass production, lower costs, and still higher sales. Employment increases instead of decreasing. This 'economy of high wages' was very particularly attuned to the rapidly expanding car industry; for a country as a whole it was too optimistic. Moreover, official economics would have nothing to do with it because it was at variance with Say's Law.

This law was set aside in 1936 by J. M. Keynes (*The General Theory of Employment, Interest and Money*). The total flow of purchasing power, or national income, was the great variable that had to be explained, and that gave macro-economics a new start. Keynesian economics had initially the nature of an explanation of the Depression, with unemployment, too small a demand and low wages. Unemployment was explained, not by excessively high wages (as in the classical view), but by underconsumption and underinvestment. Later the theory was extended into a general analysis of incomes and expenditure, which can also explain inflation. In the acceleration of economic thought the theory of the macro-demand for labour was also swept along. No wonder, for in Keynes's theory too this is a derived demand – though not derived from a fixed demand for end-products, but from a demand curve that shifts to the right if national income increases.*

Now wages and salaries are part, and even 70%, of the national income; it may therefore happen that a higher wage level leads to such a shift in the demand for end-products. That is to say, provided that the higher wage level leads to a higher wage bill and provided that this higher wage bill is not completely neutralized by lower profits (land rents and interest usually continue in the ordinary way – they are laid down in long-term contracts). If both conditions have been satisfied, total employment will not react to higher wages, or perhaps will do so in a positive sense. In both cases the classical theory is invalid.

The first condition, i.e. that a higher wage level leads to a higher

* A rather more exact reproduction of Keynesian theory follows in Chapter V, 4.

wage bill, is really circular reasoning, because it amounts to the fact that the elasticity of the demand for labour is less than one. For if an increase in wage level leads to a drop in employment that is less than 1%, the product of wage and employment (that is to say the wage bill) will increase. We are therefore seeking to prove that the elasticity is small, and proving this from a reaction based on a small elasticity!

Of course, it is possible to get out of this. It could be remarked that the reaction of employment to the higher wage takes time. This creates a breathing space in which purchasing power increases somewhat. Precisely during that period the increase in demand can get going; it then has a further cumulative effect and neutralizes the cost effect of the wage increase. If we want to be really optimistic we can add to this that the classical substitution mechanism leads to additional investments, and manufacture of the capital goods again creates income. Thus profits need not decrease as a result of the wage increase. In the circular flow of incomes and expenditure impulses occur which reinforce one another reciprocally and cancel out the negative effect on employment.

This is a precarious logic, full of assumptions regarding lags and elasticities. I can well imagine that the reader is not sold on it. But the facts confirm the assumption that employment is proof against wage increases. This was already confirmed in 1938 by M. Kalecki, who examined the enormous wage increases in France; they had come about after strikes and sit-downs (there's nothing new under the sun). According to the classical theory unemployment, which was already considerable, ought to have increased. Kalecki found that this had not in fact happened. Prices more or less adjusted to wages, the French franc depreciated still further (those were the days of floating rates of exchange), but employment did not fall. The demand for labour proved to be fairly inelastic.*

This is a strategic conclusion. True, it does not mean that the classical theory of the effects of forced wage increases is 100% wrong. One important truth remains: if wages are forced up entrepreneurs will try to replace dear labour by capital. The ratio

* 'The Lesson of the Blum Experiment', *Economic Journal*, 1938.

K/L (the capital intensity) will rise, and we must remember that reaction to understand the movement of distributive shares. But the substitution will not lead to unemployment, because the new investments keep the capital goods industry running, and there additional income is created. This is spent on additional consumer goods, and that leads to new incomes. The income multiplier does its work, and overall demand remains at a high level. Labour is replaced by capital without the total demand for labour being affected.

Thus the wage push – provided that it happens over a wide front – is not an enemy of full employment, although in political circles the opposite is often asserted. This low or even zero elasticity of the overall demand for labour has repeatedly been confirmed since 1938, except in countries whose exports fail to develop further. Wage inflation leads to higher prices and to a spiral which also sweeps along profits and even the interest rate, and as long as exports keep on going the demand for labour remains up to the mark. If exports stagnate, this can be compensated for by devaluation. (Britain objects so strongly to devaluation that it prefers to accept stagnation and deficits on the balance of payments; the inspiration for this strange conduct is mainly national pride. Wage inflation, economic expansion and national prestige are strange bedfellows, but that is not our subject.) Econometric investigations have been performed on this subject that likewise point in the direction of a low elasticity of macro-demand, but even without these sophisticated techniques it has proved since the war that wage inflation is lastingly compatible with full employment. Otherwise, after 25 years of postwar inflation, there would be no employment left.

We now have sufficient ground under our feet to posit that the labour demand curve is fairly steep, and perhaps entirely vertical. Now it so happens that this also applies to the supply curve. Micro-economically speaking this is not so, for in a submarket a higher wage can draw labour away from other sectors. However, the total labour force is hardly under the influence of the wage, and moreover the reactions are contradictory. A higher wage level may tempt some married women into factories or offices, but if their husbands earn more they prefer to stay at home. The net effect is probably a vertical supply curve. Where does that take us?

It takes us where theory does not want to go: to indeterminateness. This too is a point on which I should like to change most economics textbooks somewhat. They do not make it clear enough that the usual supply and demand diagram is not properly usable for the labour market as a whole. For partial markets – London bus-drivers, the steel works in Sheffield – it is an illuminating theoretical instrument, but from the macro-economic point of view it is dubious. For there are three possibilities: either the curves coincide, or the demand curve is to the right (an over-strained labour market) or it is to the left of the vertical supply curve (unemployment). In none of these three cases will the normal forces of the market invoke an equilibrium. The wage level is detached; there is room for institutional and conventional factors. Power gets a free hand. The wage level could be doubled, and even then employment would be unaffected (provided that devaluation took place). Prices and other incomes would adjust, and inflation would sweep like a wave through the whole income structure, but the supply and demand diagram would not make us any the wiser.

The factors determining wages now lie elsewhere. Perhaps the unions would rather not have inflation, and that may put a check on wage demands. Or it may happen that unions are aggressive because they do not share the political ideas of the government. Or dissatisfaction with wage relativities leads to wage claims, now here, then there, and so the whole level goes up. Public opinion will be critical of inflation. The government will try to exert counterpressure in some way or the other. Bargaining takes place in a different environment, and the outcome may depend on political and psychological factors. The strategic forces shift to another field than that of the curves in the textbooks. The step from micro-theory to macro-theory requires a change in our way of thinking.

This is discussed in the following section. There we deal with the current case in which the demand curve for labour coincides with or lies somewhat to the right of the supply curve. The depression, in which demand is to the left of supply, will not be considered.

We are concerned with inflation, and more particularly with the spiral. The question is what result this yields for the factor prices. I should already like to draw your attention to one property of the following observations: marginal productivity, derived demand, the point of intersection of two curves – these no longer enter into it. The atmosphere is quite different from that in micro-economics.

9. *The Inflationary Spiral and Distribution*

Before we seriously examine the level of money incomes, a view must be combated in passing that has little trouble with the problem of the money wage level. This is the monetary view, which is propagated among others by M. Friedman of the University of Chicago. It states that the price level, and also the wage level, is determined by the amount of money in circulation, and by the velocity of circulation of the money. (The latter variable is constant within certain limits. The more refined forms of monetary theory also analyse the determinants of the rate of circulation; the more primitive ones assume it to be approximately constant.) Since the banks and the monetary authorities (the Bank of England) have the amount of money under control, it is also they who determine the wage level. No unions, no spirals, no complicated network of relations – just straightforward one-way traffic running from the money-creating institutions to the wage and price level.

This view must be rejected. Although it is true to say that a certain wage and price level can be maintained only if the matching amount of money is in fact provided, the monetary theory takes too one-sided a view of the causation. If wages are driven up autonomously, and prices go along with them, there is an urgent need for new money, and the banks usually ensure that this becomes available. Of course the Bank of England can put the brakes on, and it does. But practice shows that it dare not go too far with this, for fear of a liquidity crisis. This means that the amount of money (and come to that the rate of circulation too) adjusts to wages and prices rather than the other way round. Of course there is a slight influence of the purely monetary factors on the wage and price level, but this plays a very modest part in the whole interplay. I do not deny that sometimes matters are different; in a

148

galloping inflation the creation of money, caused by a budgetary deficit of a generous government, sometimes heads the field. But in the Western world these are exceptional situations. The normal state of affairs is a steady price increase, rendered possible and supported by an expansion of the stock of money, but not caused by it.

A better theory of the wage level is that of A. W. Phillips,* developed at the end of the Fifties, and since then the subject of much discussion and research. Phillips does not explain the wage level so much as the percentage increase in it. He posits that this annual increase depends on the tension on the labour market. This can be negatively measured by the percentage of unemployment. If this is at a certain value – for instance in the neighbourhood of 3% – money wages rise only moderately, and they stay within the room created by the annual increase in productivity. If unemployment is less, wages rise more quickly. At 6% unemployment no wage increase is to be expected; a slight drop is more likely. Phillips's theory thus establishes a connexion between the wage increase w and unemployment U. The function $w = f(U)$ can be reproduced by a curve that runs from the upper left to the lower right and thus is slightly reminiscent of the demand curve; however, it is quite a different thing.

The curve suggests that there are no other factors involved than the tension on the labour market. (Incidentally, Phillips makes an exception for a rise in import prices.) That is where its strength lies – it is a strong theory, clear, straightforward, evocative – but it is also the source of its weakness. For in fact there is more between heaven and earth than this philosophy would have us believe. The unions may not be as powerful as some proud executive officials or some frightened employers think, but all the same we may not simply ignore their influence on wage level. And profits are also important: if they rise quickly the wages will go along with them.† If productivity rises in a given year by an

* 'The Relation between Unemployment and the Rate of Change in Money Wages in the United Kingdom, 1861–1957', *Economica*, 1958.

† The supporters of the Phillips curve would say that profits are also a function of the tension on the labour market. But that is not necessarily the case – profits are no more uniquely determined than wages.

INCOME DISTRIBUTION

unusually high percentage – for instance 6 or 7%, or even more, as occasionally happens in some countries (Western Germany, Italy, France, the Netherlands) – money wages will tend to climb along with it. The Phillips curve sweeps all these relations under the carpet. Nor does it leave any scope for combating wage inflation in any other way than that of the reduction of tension on the labour market, or even the deliberate creation of unemployment; that has, of course, tended to make it unpopular in political circles.*

There is no doubt that Phillips has put his finger on an important determinant of wage increases. Too high expenditures, greater than the productive capacity can keep up with, lead to price increases, and a tense labour market leads to wage increases. Both go hand in hand. Come to think of it, Phillips' theory fits in very well with modern Keynesian analysis, which tries to explain an inflationary gap (too high expenditures) and then feeds this gap back into a model: the excessive spending, which is greater than the productive capacity, sets the spiral into motion, and this in turn reinforces the inflation. This account is almost identical with that of Phillips, because the tension on the labour market is a criterion of the inflationary gap. Cost push and demand pull are interconnected. We must welcome this analysis. But we may not automatically exclude the possibility of other factors than the inflationary gap being involved. Statistical research into the Phillips curve confirms this proposition; the correlations between w and U are not as high as they ought to be. The curve is not a thin line, but a fairly wide band.

What are these other factors that help to determine the wage level? We have already mentioned some. Price increases can definitely play an independent role. Phillips already pointed out that rising import prices may entail demands for compensation. The same applies to increases in excise duty and purchase tax, although one can dispute the reasonableness of this (an increase in the tax burden, democratically fixed, must be borne by all and should not be compensated for workers alone). Also of great

* In Britain the view that wage inflation must be combated by slight unemployment is known as the Paish theory, after F. W. Paish. Incidentally, there are differences of opinion about the exact content of this doctrine.

PRICES OF PRODUCTIVE CONTRIBUTIONS

importance is the development of productivity; if this rises, we can also expect wage increases. The attitude of the unions is likewise important. Do they try to get all they can, or are they prepared to help damp down the inflationary spiral? These are all contributory causes, but the most important of all is nevertheless another one, namely the reaction of the other incomes. If profits pull themselves up along with wages, and rents and the interest rate also go up, even a small autonomous increase in wage level can start off an escalation that drives up all money incomes.

We can best understand this interdependence of the various categories of incomes by bearing in mind that distributive shares in national income are involved here. There is not a single group that likes the idea of its percentage being forced down as a whole – opposition will develop to this in some way or the other. The matter with which we are concerned here in fact belongs in the next chapter. It is the struggle for the distributive shares. My point of view is that these shares also help to determine the nominal wage level, the nominal profit level, the nominal land rent level and the interest rate (why no level here? Because it is a percentage). I do not claim that this struggle – call it the class struggle – is the only determinant of the structure of incomes; such a slogan might sound fine, but it would be just as one-sided as the monetary theory or the doctrine of the Phillips curve. But it is a fact that the attempts to push up the share of wages contribute towards inflation, and that profits and even the interest rate react to this. This can be illustrated by the following reasoning. A part is played in it by a small equation for the share of labour (we are therefore in fact anticipating Chapter V).

To keep things simple we suppose that there are only two factors of production, labour and capital, and two categories of incomes, wage and a complex entity that we shall call profit (and which therefore also includes interest and land rent). There are no taxes and no imports. The money wage level is W, the amount of labour L, and the wage bill is therefore WL. If we designate national income by Y, the share of labour, represented by the letter λ, is equal to WL/Y. National income can be broken down into two factors: the physical volume of production Q and the price level P. Therefore $\lambda = W/P.L/Q$. Now on closer inspection both W/P and L/Q have a specific meaning. W/P is the real wage level. L/Q is the reciprocal of Q/L, and that is by definition the production per worker, also known as (average) labour productivity. We therefore find that the share of labour is equal to the ratio between the real wage and labour productivity. If the former variable increases more rapidly than the latter, λ rises; a constant share of labour is realized if the real wage level rises as quickly as labour productivity. In that case the money wage level must rise just as quickly as the sum of the price increase and the increase in labour productivity. This conclusion is worth holding on to, and I shall write it again in symbols. The percentage increase in W is called w, and the percentage increase in labour productivity h. If λ is constant, $w = p + h$. Let us assume for the time being that the unions do in fact aim at a constant λ, and are not out to increase their share.*

We thus already have one equation in which w, p and h occur. However, there is a further relation between these two variables, for the price increase finds its origin in income increases. We have only two of these: the wage increase w and the increase in profits (in the broad sense) per unit of product. The latter, the increase in the absolute profit margin, is called z.

The percentage p is therefore built up from w and z. However, it would be incorrect to write $p = w + z$. For in the first place the price increase of the two factors of production must be weighted, namely by their shares in the cost price. In the simple case we have in mind (no taxes, no imported raw materials) these shares coincide with the shares in national income, i.e. λ and $1 - \lambda$. In the second place we must allow for the fact that an increase in money wage, as regards its influence on cost price, can be compensated for by an increase in labour productivity. For this ensures that fewer real units of labour have to be put into a unit of

---

* Some authors assume without more ado: $p = w$. For instance, W. Krelle: 'Evidently, prices move proportionately to the wage rate . . . if there is no over-utilization of capacity, and they rise more if the economy runs into bottle-necks' ('The Laws of Income Distribution in the Short Run and the Long Run', *The Distribution of the National Income*, p. 427). Krelle assumes here either that $h = 0$ (which is unrealistic) or that productivity increases lead to a constant drop in λ (also unrealistic).

product; in this way room is created for an increase in the level of money wages.

Taking this into account, we find the following relation:

$$p = \lambda (w - h) + (1 - \lambda)z$$

and we already had $w = p + h$.

If we combine these two equations, we find $p = z$. Thus prices rise just as quickly as the absolute profit margins per unit of product. This relation will occur if the share of labour and therefore the share of profits as well are to remain constant in national income. It is a plausible result, for $p = z$ means that the relative profit margin, i.e. the relation between the absolute profit margin and the price, is constant. The entrepreneurs let their gross incomes grow along with the movement of prices.

Now $p = z$ does not in itself make the system determinate; we have two equations with three unknowns (p, w, and h). To find out more about inflation and income distribution we need further information. We can use this model in a variety of ways. The most obvious one is to accept the rise in labour productivity as given, let's say 4%. That is a figure that most modern countries more or less achieve (Britain is, unfortunately, an exception). To render the system determinate we have to make some assumption or the other regarding the behaviour of profits. We can then spell out the implications of that assumption and see whether reality offers us anything similar. We shall then find that some assumptions that look plausible at first sight soon lead to absurd results.

To give an extreme example: suppose that the entrepreneurs want a profit margin that rises at the same rate as wages, and that they have a market position that makes this possible. Then $z = w$. That may not seem so silly a starting point, but a glance at our equation shows that it leads to an explosive spiral. For to keep the share of labour constant, we have to have $w = p$ plus 4%, and z would have to be equal to this. But at the same time $z = p$. That is to say, $p = p + 4\%$; the price increase tries to become 4% larger than itself, and that can't be done. If the entrepreneurs pursue this increase in profits, they drive up prices and thus wages, in a manner reminiscent of the sails of a windmill. They will never catch each other up, but in the meantime there will be galloping inflation.

It is unlikely that the entrepreneurs will behave in this way. Perhaps they will prefer to do something else that is predicted by the theory of oligopoly. Oligopoly is a form of market with a limited number of suppliers keeping a close watch on one another. In this process it may happen that none of them dares to reduce his price because they are all frightened of a price war. If productivity rises in such a situation, the price does not become lower (as would happen under perfect competition). There is a good deal of psychology in this explanation. Now suppose that the oligopolists keep the price rigid. In that case the rise in profits corresponds to the rise in labour productivity. Therefore $z = h = 4\%$.

We now get a much more comprehensible result than the one we just had. No explosion, but a fixed rate of the spiral. For not only do we have $z = 4\%$, but also $z = p$. The wage increase exceeds that by 4%. Money wages rise by 8%, profit margins by 4% and prices also by 4%. It may seem as if the share of labour increases in these circumstances, but that is not so. The distribution remains the same, and the creeping inflation proceeds dourly. The numerical example, as regards its order of size, is reminiscent of what many a West European country has displayed in the past years.

This little model shows that the wage increase cannot solely be explained by unemployment percentages. The Phillips curve ignores the reaction of the other incomes – unless we were to assume that this reaction of profits (and land rents and interest) is also exclusively dominated by basic economic facts like the situation on the labour market. The latter is hardly plausible. There is something which is rightly called the entrepreneur's price policy. He has an option, a certain degree of freedom. And the same is true of the union's wage policy. There, too, psychological factors influence decisions.

Up to now our reasoning on the inflationary spiral has covered solely things that might happen. The question now is, what really happens. Is it correct that $p = z$? Is p in fact equal to h? And is it true that the spiral leaves distribution intact, or do shifts meanwhile occur in the relative remunerations?

The hypothesis $p = z$ does tally in general with the facts observed in Western Europe and the United States, but then z has to be regarded as the rise in the *pure* profit margin; interest and land rent must be left out of consideration. These categories of incomes usually rise less than inflation suggests. They act as buffers; as a result the rate of the price increase is checked somewhat. In most countries it is clearly lower than the increase in labour productivity, and in that sense the above model is too pessimistic.

The latter can be seen if the p/h ratio for various countries is calculated. For France and the Netherlands this fraction (over the period 1955–65) was one. All other Continental countries and the United States were lower: between 0·5 and 0·8. Only Britain was higher, with 1·3, which is what the pessimistic model, in which $p = z$, would lead us to expect.*

The buffer effect of land rents and interest has another result: the share of labour in national income is increased by the spiral, and the share of capital and land reduced. Inflation fosters this shift. It would be incorrect to ascribe this movement in distributive shares solely to the wage push: more fundamental forces are operating in the same direction. But the postwar spiral has up to now intensified the tendency, capital receiving an increasingly small share of income. The unions have used the market situation to improve the relative position of labour to some extent; profits have maintained themselves well, and interest and land rent, as a fraction of the total, have shrunk. The deeper mechanism of this shift, which has already been going on for fifty years, will be discussed in the next chapter.

The picture sketched here of the dynamics of income distribution under inflationary conditions is of course a very rough one. If we examine the data of special countries in special periods we see deviations. For instance, for the Sixties in the United States it was not at first true that wages were the pacemakers in the spiral. They rose somewhat less than labour productivity, and the price increase was therefore caused by the other incomes. At that time the share of labour did not increase either; it displayed a slight drop. However, this is an exception, which was cancelled out again at the

* A somewhat more detailed reasoning is to be found in J. Pen, 'Shifting the Blame, or the Innocence of Profits', in: *Inflation, Papers read at the Business Economists' Group Conference at Oxford,* 1968.

end of the Sixties.* Conversely, France and the Netherlands had a more powerful wage push than the other countries; in other words their p/h ratio was very high, viz. one. The United Kingdom had a moderate wage increase, which, however, was too high for the productivity increase; wage costs rose annually over the period 1955–65 by 3·5% on average. The price increase was 3%, which, in agreement with the general picture, points to a slight increase in the share of labour.

If we look more closely, we discover other things. The inflation of the postwar years has, broadly speaking, left profits untouched. But that does not mean to say that all entrepreneurs have had the same experiences with wage and price increases. Some have profited from them; others have been put in a tight spot. These two categories can be roughly distinguished from one another by considering the rise in productivity. Firms with a large increase in labour productivity – in the chemical and energy sectors – had no trouble with the wage push; their costs dropped rather than rose, and at the same time sales increased tremendously. Here the dynamics of the spiral was greeted joyfully. But the labour-intensive sectors with a limited rise in productivity had difficulty in keeping up with the inflation. They had to pay the higher wages, and to maintain profits they were obliged to pass on the higher costs to the consumer. Sometimes that works, sometimes it doesn't. There is no doubt that the turbulence of the wage-price-wage spiral has played havoc among a number of firms. It has increased the risk of business management. Probably the concentration of firms has been accelerated by it. This shift from small business to big industry is not exclusively due to inflation either, but the trend has been stimulated by the spiral.

We thus see that inflation accentuates a number of fundamental shifts in income distribution: perhaps the wage structure is somewhat telescoped by it (see section 4 above), the share of labour becomes greater at the expense of that of capital, large profits increase more than small ones. In each of these cases it is a trend already present that picks up somewhat more speed.

* N. Weinberg, 'The Death of the United States Guideposts', *The Labour Market and Inflation* (Proceedings of a Symposium at the International Institute for Labour Studies in Geneva), 1968.

Once we have established this, we can turn the proposition round. Inflation passes like a huge wave through the structure of income distribution without effecting much fundamental change. It is surprising how well relative incomes manage to maintain themselves. True, a number of small businessmen and further the familiar group of rentiers and pensioners suffer considerable harm. The private pension and the annuity fall in value, though as a rule social security benefits rise with the general income structure. But apart from a number of small groups the various income recipients manage to leapfrog along. The rate of inflation is determined among other things by the greed with which they do this. Although this rate is certainly also determined by 'harder' variables, such as the tension on the labour market, the inflationary gap, competitive conditions in the markets for final products, and the increases in import prices and indirect taxation, the struggle of the pressure groups is a determinant of price increases. Their mentality – aggressiveness versus reserve – makes a difference. That is a conclusion to return to when we talk about incomes policy.

CHAPTER V

Distributive Shares

1. *Miracle and Myth*

DISTRIBUTIVE shares are the province of high theory. The elegant equation, the succinct and surprising relation, the sophisticated econometrics and the formidable model ride high here. Unfortunately hobbyhorses are also ridden; some authors are so charmed by this or that relation that they try to solve the whole problem with it. There are occasional whiffs of rubbish in the air. Since I want to explain what is going on, I shall draw attention to the nonsense too, the more so as it is associated with celebrated names, like that of N. Kaldor. One of the so-called Keynesian theories (which have little to do with J. M. Keynes) is a classic example of how in my opinion economics should *not* be practised.

Besides the small and simple theories illustrating one building block of economic interdependence there are impressive synthetic models, like that of W. Krelle.* In these models everything depends on everything else, and moreover in all kinds of ways. This contains a deep but uncomfortable truth. Many economists – including myself – are rather uneasy with these models, which may be a consolation to the reader. I shall try to say something about general interdependence (in section 9), but I don't guarantee any success.

The inspiration of much theoretical work is the assumption that income shares are constant over long periods. The share of labour – which in the following too will be designated as λ – has long attracted attention, and many authors have believed that it was constant. Investigations by A. L. Bowley† and by E. H. Phelps Brown and P. E. Hart‡ for Britain have made a particular contri-

* *Verteilungstheorie*, 1962.

† A. L. Bowley, *Wages and Incomes since 1860*, 1937.

‡ E. H. Phelps Brown and P. E. Hart, 'The Shares of Wages in National Income', *Economic Journal*, 1952. These authors allow for variations in the share and they even explain them, but their statistics show an almost constant share of wages *for manual labour* over time (39 % in 1870, 42 % in 1924 and the same percentage in 1950).

bution towards this view. The constancy of the share of labour was long regarded as a kind of law. Keynes spoke of 'a bit of a miracle', and J. Schumpeter and Mrs Joan Robinson of 'a mystery'. Various explanations of the mystery have been found – without exception interesting, but strange to the extent that the share of labour is in reality not constant. It fluctuates, and more-over displays a rising trend. Most economists now realize that. True, there are still two schools – the Constants and the Variables – but the former group does not stick its neck out too far and leaves the possibility of certain variations open. It refutes neither the fluctuations nor the trend, but considers these relatively slight. In the words of R. Solow, the motto for the disputed quantity now is: 'How to be Constant Though Variable'.

Now even the moderate difference of opinion about λ is more appearance than fact. Much depends on what our definitions are and what figures we choose. The statistics are uncertain and do not fit in with the ideas of the economists. There are repeated Gordian knots to be cut; the three main ones are the following.

(a) What is to be done about the high salaries and other emolu-ments of top business executives? Some are inclined to count these incomes as wage. After all, they are the product of a contract of employment. Others point out that these incomes include components of profit. A top manager gets a bonus, which is clearly profit, and even a part of his salary reflects profit. The borderline between profit and wage is ill-defined. In addition this view adduces that the concept 'share of labour' loses all sociolo-gical meaning if managing directors of limited liability companies are to be regarded as workers. The share of labour ought to relate to the working classes, not to the typically managerial group of capitalism (the exploiters). In this reasoning top salaries have to be left out of consideration.

One drawback which I see to the latter view is that the borderline between wages and salaries is not a sharp one. Suppose that we don't count the salaries of the managing directors – what about the salaries of the group immediately beneath them? From the socio-logical point of view these are not members of the 'toiling masses' either. And if we exclude these salaries as well, how far down the line do we have to go? Do we want a separate group share for white-collar workers (as advocated by Marchal and Lecaillon*)? In that case we lose the economic ground under our feet, and are left without a theory. And how are we to regard the salaries of civil servants that are somewhat comparable to top incomes in business? The Permanent Secretary and the Assistant Principal receive no profit – must we nevertheless exclude them from labour's share?

I personally prefer to include all incomes from a contract of employment; I am therefore prepared to ignore sociological characteristics. Otherwise, matters become too complicated and too vague. The top dogs are admittedly small in number: the corporate officers, as I. Kravis calls them, receive in the United States about 3% of national income, or something in excess of 4% of the total wage bill.† But the salaries of the lower white-collar echelons are substantial. I should like to take them all together.

The influence of this choice of concepts on the share of labour is obvious. By the inclusion of salaries labour's share naturally becomes greater at a given moment, and above all the development in time is positively influenced. True, large groups of white-collar workers lag behind in income, especially if we consider the periods that comprise the years 1945–60. But their *numbers* are increasing strongly. A century ago the share of salaries was still less than 7% of the income from work; now it is about one quarter.‡ By including salaries in the share of labour the latter rises much more over a period of time than it would otherwise have done. This increase reflects part of the process of upgrading.

(b) What is to be done about the wages and salaries paid by the government? Some say, don't count them, because we're interested in the laws of distribution in free enterprise. Only the private sector, organized for profit, is the right subject for this kind of study. The government, which pays out about 20% of wages, is left out.

* See Chapter II, 2.
† 'Relative Income Shares in Fact and Theory', *American Economic Review*, 1959.
‡ C. H. Feinstein, 'Changes in the Distribution of the National Income in the U.K. since 1860', in: *The Distribution of the National Income*.

This argument is sometimes backed up by statistical considerations. A number of old time series (those of W. I. King, from 1850 to 1900 for the United States), do not make a clear distinction within the government sector between wage income and non-wage income. Even for the present day little is known about the government's stock of capital goods. Write-offs are arbitrary. What is Westminster Hall worth? But as a rule we are fairly well informed about government expenditure, better than we are about the expenditure of the private sector, and anyone who so wishes can make reasonable estimates. There are worse things in a statistician's life.

Many – I would say most – economists consequently take the point of view that the share of wages must be calculated for the economy as a whole. Restriction to the private sector is arbitrary, and originates from a nineteenth-century world of ideas that labels the government as unproductive. Wrongly so, for large lumps of production (education!) are provided by the government. If we exclude that we must also exclude other non-profit-making organizations. All this is unpractical. We are concerned with income distribution as a whole – the government's share in it is substantial, and that is not coincidental. Industry, with its rapidly rising productivity, has an outturn of labour, and these persons are absorbed by the service sector – much of which is government. This development in favour of services influences income distribution, and if we confine ourselves to the private sector we close our eyes to part of this development.

I should like to associate myself with the latter view. What this choice means to the distributive shares is obvious: the government is labour-intensive, and its share in national income is growing. In the last century the government's contribution to national income was 5 to 10%; it is now 20 to 25%. By including the wages and salaries paid by the government we therefore find a growing share of labour more quickly than if we confine ourselves to the private sector.

(c) What is to be done about the profits and the incomes of self-employed persons? Large profits cause no difficulties, but the small businessman and the professional do; their income contains a large degree of remuneration for work. But there is no contract of employment. Three points of view are defensible.

(i) Coarse minds regard the whole income as profit, and do not bother about the fact that it includes a wage for the recipient's own work. (They worry even less about interest on his own capital.) In this way the share of profit becomes too large, strictly speaking. (ii) A more subtle approach prefers to make a split-up, certainly as regards own work. A part of what was first profit is then considered as income from work. This can be done by seeking a comparable individual in paid employment and fixing the salary accordingly. However, a piece of pure profit still remains (from which interest is deducted in appropriate cases). (iii) Others again wish to divide up the *whole* profit and the *whole* income of professionals into labour income and property income. This wish is prompted by a theoretical model with only two factors of production, and a matching production function $Q = F(L,K)$. The complete division into labour income and property income is no easy matter. The income of the self-employed dentist must be chopped into two, and even that of the civil servant.

The supporters of the last method of calculation are sometimes rendered despondent by it. Thus S. Lebergott first argues that income distribution can be theoretically understood by using a two-factor model, and then comes to grief through the unmanageability of the split. He concludes that: 'the entrepreneurial puzzle makes it meaningless to consider trends for any sector where the entrepreneurial share is a great one – agriculture, trade, service'.* This pessimism gets us nowhere. It is not surprising that method (iii) is followed only by statisticians who couple perseverance with daring and a certain lightheartedness. The great pioneers of econometric research, C. W. Cobb and P. H. Douglas, used it successfully; they practised macro-economics in a way which has led to many new insights, but which was not characterized by an excess of reserve and caution. They found a labour share of roughly 75%. A more recent and extremely detailed survey by E. F. Denison† arrives at a labour share of 81·1% for the

* 'Factor Shares in the Long Term: Some Theoretical and Statistical Aspects', in: *The Behavior of Income Shares*, 1964, p. 84.

† *Why Growth Rates Differ*, 1967. An impressive book, full of detailed

United Kingdom and 82·0% for the United States (other countries, such as Italy and Germany, work out somewhat lower: 74%). These figures contain some imputed labour income of unincorporated enterprises and of the free professions.

For most purposes I nevertheless prefer method (i), in which national income is not divided into two shares but into four: wage, profit, interest and land rent. The reason is that these four categories require different explanations. Profit is regarded as the full gross operating income of concerns, businessmen and professionals. That too is not without its problems, but at least it keeps separate what has to be kept economically separate.

The four shares roughly display the following picture for the modern countries. (Roughly, because any pursuit of precision comes up against differences between the various countries which are in part real ones and in part are founded on different definitions and groupings of the figures, for instance those on national income. Consequently, exactitude is not aimed at here.) Labour's share is in the neighbourhood of 70%. For Britain and the United States it is somewhat higher, for France and Belgium somewhat lower. Of the remaining 30%, two-thirds is profits; it goes to small and large firms and to professionals not in paid employment. It is my impression that about half of this income is earned in the big companies, and the other half in the small firms (including the self-employed professionals). There then remains about 10% of national income for the remuneration of capital and land, this figure being somewhat higher for France and Belgium. Land gets no more than a few per cent, and sometimes even less. This, then, is the picture: 70 + 20 + 8 + 2. It is consistent with, though not exactly equal to, figures stated in various other publications.*

calculations on many countries. But I should like to debate with Denison on a number of details – in my opinion he finds much too high figures for the share of non-residential land: 2·9% for the United Kingdom would mean that 60% of agricultural proceeds go to the landlords, and 4·5% for the Netherlands is also highly improbable. 1% is more like it.

*Compare the figures in the collection *The Distribution of the National Income*. B. F. Haley gives 70 − 12 − 18 for the United States, but the last percentage contains not only interest and land rent, but also corporate profits. C. H. Feinstein lists various percentages for the United Kingdom,

INCOME DISTRIBUTION

By way of contrast, let me mention a few figures for primitive countries. According to P. Okigbo,* African countries display a much lower share of labour: 60% in Congo (Brazzaville), lower than 20% in Mali, Ivory Coast, Chad, Niger and Togo. This suggests that there the self-employed person or family is the backbone of the economy. There is consequently nothing 'natural' about the distribution as we see it in the West.

If we adhere to the impressionistic formula $70 + 20 + 8 + 2$ for the present day there is no doubt that the share of labour λ has increased in almost all modern countries since the beginning of the century. For the United States and the United Kingdom the percentage then was 50–60, and it was even lower for Germany. For the Netherlands it was likewise 55%. The rising trend is clear. A more or less constant λ can be found by considering manual workers only (that is a tremendous help in the United Kingdom), by leaving the government out of consideration, by exempting from the calculation special branches of industry (such as agriculture), and the like. But in that way you can prove anything and everything. I do not recommend this.

The theorem of the constant λ was a myth. As is the case with other myths, it has had a stimulating effect; in this case it has not inspired revolutionary action but empirical and theoretical research. In the process the myth disappeared and even the miracle. It is in no way surprising that λ moves somewhat in the short term – against the economic trend; if the total demand increases

---

but in each case only two (capital and labour, the rest being imputed to one of the two). He arrives at a labour share of 74, or 75, or 82, depending on the national income used. Thus these percentages contain a portion of self-employed persons' income. M. Falise works for Belgium with figures in which social security benefit has been included separately; after correction I find $60 + 26 + 14$. A. Jeck swamps us with German figures, but does not use the four-category distribution; labour's share is 65%, then 28% goes from the business firms to the households, over 5% remains in the firms and 2% results from public enterprise and property. These are therefore different criteria again. For the Netherlands the formula $70 + 20 + 8 + 2$ is about right. I am aware that the varying calculations create the impression of statistical fiddling, and that this may undermine confidence in the whole business.

* op. cit., p. 395 et seq.

164

profits as a rule rise the most – and grows in the long term. No wonder, too, that the movement goes very slowly. Even very simple theories can explain this lumbering development (or 'relative constancy'); see for instance the next section.

The increase in the share of labour has not been at the expense of profits. The latter have maintained themselves roughly at 20%. It is, however, probable that within them a shift has occurred to the detriment of small profits of farmers, the shop on the corner, small craftsmen, and to the benefit of the large profits made by concerns. In the course of the industrialization process many small self-employed persons have entered paid employment – this in itself explains part of the growth of λ. The present fifty-fifty division between small profits and large profits was much higher in most countries at the beginning of the century. In those days there were relatively more small businessmen and farmers, and relatively fewer concerns.

The big losers in the historical race are interest and land rents. Their total has shrunk from sometimes above 30% to less than 10%. Land rents have been hit hardest, which of course is connected with the relative decline of agriculture (from nearly 50% of national income in the early days of the nineteenth century to below 10%; in Britain to below 5%!). But the most striking thing is the drop in the share of capital, because it would not be expected. This share was around 20% and has been forced down to less than half. This is a puzzling phenomenon in a society using more and more capital. If people must believe in miracles, here is one, and we shall need a separate theory to explain the phenomenon. The reader may be reassured; the explanation follows.

For some purposes the two-share formula, i.e. work versus property, may be useful; for instance if we want to know the total income of the capitalists, or if we estimate the income share of the top 1% of the population. Instead of 70 + 20 + 8 + 2 we then write something like 80 + 20 (the 20% profits now have been divided up among labour and capital). At the beginning of the century the ratio 80/20 was closer to 60/40. Viewed in this way, too, the shift is striking, and a constant distribution is a fairy-tale.

Before we abandon mythology, a few further warnings. At

first sight we would connect a rising λ with an improved relative position of the workers. This is tempting, but incorrect. For the fraction may rise as the result of circumstances from which the workers have nothing to gain. If small businessmen give up their unprofitable businesses and enter paid employment, a portion of profit is replaced by wage. For Marxists in particular there is something contradictory in this course of events. It is true that Marx predicted the eradication of the small shopkeeper; he would be driven out by the big concern, and this prediction has come true to some extent. But the odd thing is that as a result the share of labour is able to increase – in Marxist terminology the big concerns thus attend to a reduction of exploitation!

We may learn from this that λ is not a good yardstick for measuring the relative position of the workers. There is a better criterion of this: the wage ratio, i.e. the quotient of the average wage level per worker and the average income per income recipient. In most countries this fraction lies around eighty per cent, being somewhat higher in the United Kingdom and the United States. Unlike λ the wage ratio may increase above 100%; that seems to be the case in Japan. Such a high figure indicates that there are a large number of small shops and poor farmers alongside an industrial sector with relatively high wages. The wage ratio tells us little about capitalist exploitation – whatever that may be – and in any case nothing that is clear.

There is another possible misunderstanding. The share of labour is of course influenced by the height of the wage level, in relation to the other incomes – i.e. by the wage ratio. This causal relation is important. But if we don't watch out we shall start to think that this is the only factor that determines λ, and moreover we shall be attaching to an increase in this wage ratio ideas about the effectiveness of unions and so on. Unfortunately, all this is more complicated. The wage level can rise without the wage structure changing – simply because workers transfer from the poorer-paid branch of industry to a better-paid one, thus from agriculture to industry. Improved training also leads to higher average wages without it being necessary to amend collective agreements. Upgrading is a permanent process, and for that reason alone the wage level, the wage ratio and also the share of wages rise; that has nothing to do with union policy, power and the like. And further λ may increase without even the wage ratio changing: the case of small businessmen entering paid employment. If they do so to increase their security and to be rid of the worry of scratching a living together, the share of labour increases while the wage ratio remains constant. (If their new wage is higher than their former income from profit not only the share of labour but also the wage ratio increases.) λ will moreover also increase if the labour-intensive branches of industry grow more quickly than the others. To what extent the latter happens is difficult to say or predict with accuracy; the labour-intensive service sector is a successful grower, but so is the capital-intensive chemical industry. The net effect can be isolated only with econometric methods (see below, section 6).

All this strengthens the desire for a straightforward theory of distributive shares. The challenge is in fact one of an intellectual nature. We must beware of attributing an ethical significance to the share of labour too quickly. It is true that the increase in λ, which, we observe, is explained by a lesser weight of the 'unearned' income. But is it ethically desirable to harm the small saver, for instance by wage inflation? The standards for income distribution lie above all in the field of personal distribution. We have already seen that a shrinking share of capital (together with a strong concentration of wealth distribution) leads to equalization of personal incomes, but this connexion is an indirect one and not everybody will regard it as an excuse for wage inflation.

We *do* enter into an ethical discussion of λ by way of defence, i.e. in discussions with those who claim that capitalism pushes down the share of labour. These are sometimes union leaders, but usually Marxists or uninformed social critics, who want to make it clear to us how rotten society is today. Then we answer: 'You are wrong, labour's share is on the increase'; yet we must remember that this answer is not a conclusive argument regarding the moral acceptability of a free enterprise economy. Anyone who rejects profit and interest, considers capitalism an affront to human dignity, and free enterprise a thoroughly bad thing is entitled to his point of view, and he does not need the theory of the declining share of labour for that. But if he adheres to that

Marxist dogma he contributes to the myth-making and to confused and unclean thought.

The practical relevance of the distributive shares emerges above all from discussions on the nature of capitalism. The following sections will, I hope, demonstrate that. They are not confined to distribution pure and simple, but also deal with the deeper mechanisms of the society in which we live.

2. *A Useful Tautology and Several Theories*

A tautology is always true – so much so that it teaches us little about the recalcitrant world of things. And yet a truism can form a useful starting-point for thought. A good example is offered by the small equation that we met in the preceding chapter. There we wrote the share of labour as the quotient of the real wage level and labour productivity. We shall discuss the utility of this presently, but first something about the correctness of the equation.

Strictly speaking, it does not tally. We found it by dividing the wage bill by national income Y – that is correct by definition. Breaking down the wage bill into the money wage level W and the amount of labour L must also be in order. But the resolution of Y into Q and P contains a complication. For this P is the price aspect of national income; by definition $P = Y/Q$. A little later we do something that does not fit in with this: we call W/P the real wage, and forget that P now suddenly represents the price level of consumer goods. This can change owing to the fact that the import prices increase; in that case Y remains the same and so does Q, but the real wage drops. The same happens if prices rise through an increase in purchase tax. That does not change λ. It is worth while drawing attention to these two cases, since they are of practical importance. We live at a time in which both import prices and indirect taxes rise quite considerably. The workers feel these price increases and put them on a par with those resulting from an increase in profits or interest; the unions ask for compensation. But this compensation changes the distribution in favour of labour. It is a political question whether this is desirable or not – it can be maintained that an increase in the duty on beer must bear on everyone, and not only on the self-employed. One can also adopt another political point of view (for instance by recalling the fact that self-employed persons occasionally pass on taxes to others!). But the fact remains that an increase in purchase tax and import prices leaves the shares in income untouched, and that a wage compensation for these price increases does not.

This already suggests that our little tautology can give us ideas. Come to that, this was something we already knew. In the last chapter we saw that λ = real wage/labour productivity easily leads us to the condition under which λ is constant. In that case money wages must rise percentagewise by the sum of the percentage increase in prices and in labour productivity. This contains a piece of practical advice for a union man who is worried about the share of labour in a growing and inflating economy (whether worrying about λ is advisable is another point – that may be doubted, see the preceding section).

The utility of our tautology extends further. Our quotient suggests that λ moves only slowly. For real wage and labour productivity are forced into parallel paths by numerous forces. For instance, if the (average) productivity rises as a result of technical progress – and it does everywhere – marginal productivity also goes up. In section 2 of Chapter IV we saw that in such a case the derived demand for labour moves to the right, so that wages go up as well. The market attends to that. Come to that, the activity of the unions operates in the same direction. For if productivity rises and the entrepreneurs do not pass this on in the form of a cut in prices, profits grow. That provokes wage demands from the unions. Should competition induce the entrepreneurs to pass on the increase in productivity in the price, the real wage goes up as well. In all these cases productivity and real wage level move in the same direction. Their quotient need not remain constant, as the myth asserts, but a slow movement is nevertheless exactly what one would expect. Violent fluctuations would be more miraculous than a sluggish development. Perhaps the reader is already beginning to understand why I am so taken with the tautology real wage/labour productivity.

There are more reasons: If the national product is Q and the amount of labour L, the number $\delta Q/\delta L$ gives the physical marginal productivity, and in neo-classical theory that is equal to the real wage rate. The (average) labour productivity is Q/L. Therefore:

$$\lambda = L/Q.\delta Q/\delta L.$$

This is *nearly* a tautology (not entirely, for wage is not equal *by definition* to $\delta Q/\delta L$; conditions must be fulfilled, such as the maximization of profit by entrepreneurs and competition in product markets*). In any case it is a magic formula, the basis for the neo-classical theory of income shares and the key to a number of mysterious matters. Isn't it nice that it says here that the share of labour is equal to the ratio between marginal and average productivity of labour? Yes, that certainly is nice, and not only as an unexpected joke. It shows how important the law of diminishing returns is to distribution. Additions to labour with given amounts of capital cause the marginal product of labour to drop. As a result, the marginal productivity is lower than the average. If this law were not to operate, average and marginal productivity of labour could be equal to one another. In that case labour would get the whole of national income. Marx would then get his way through a purely technical relation!

The reasoning can of course also be applied to the share of capital κ. This fraction is equal to the relation between the real interest rate (= the marginal productivity of capital) and the average productivity of capital. The latter variable has been attracting attention lately. For in the course of the years it proves to move only very slowly, so that some regard it as constant.† The latter is definitely exaggerated, but there is a striking difference between the strong, uninterrupted trend of a rising labour productivity and the lack of movement of the average capital productivity. Together with the drop in real interest – caused by a

---

* Perfect competition on the labour market is not a condition. If there are unions that raise the money wage, the entrepreneurs can adjust to this, so that the wage again becomes equal to marginal productivity. True, in that case employment will have decreased in the classical view, but the theory of marginal productivity still applies.

† The famous growth model of Harrod and Domar is based on this hypothesis.

combination of a fairly stable interest rate and rising prices – the drop in κ occurs.* Our tautology puts us on this track.

The subject may be pursued somewhat further. The share of labour $L/Q.\delta Q/\delta L$ may also be written as follows: $\dfrac{\delta Q/Q}{\delta L/L}$. This now states that λ is equal to the ratio between a relative (percentage) change in the national product and the relative (percentage) change in the amount of labour that was the cause of that product. The formula is useful, arresting and elegant. It may be read as follows: increase the amount of labour by 1%. See by how much production increases as a result. Suppose that this is $x\%$. In that case $\lambda = x$. This x is called the elasticity of production in respect of labour, or the labour elasticity of production. We have therefore derived the thesis that *the share of labour in income is equal to the elasticity of production with regard to labour*.

This is the most important proposition of neo-classical theory. It forms the basis for extensive research, which will be discussed below (section 5). The proposition may also be applied to the share of capital κ; there $\kappa = \dfrac{K.\delta Q}{Q.\delta K}$, and that is the elasticity of production with regard to capital.

Now in neo-classical thought there are only two factors of production, so that $\lambda + \kappa = 1$; but the thesis that the share of income is equal to the partial elasticity of the production function can be applied without difficulty to any group within society. The share of carpenters is equal to the elasticity of the national production with respect to carpentry. The share of heavy clay is equal to the elasticity of national production with respect to heavy clay. Only in the case of the entrepreneurs does our formula fail to apply; this factor of production does not appear in the production function as an input. Pure profit does not fit into this story – something else will have to be found for that.

In the above a number of introductory remarks to neo-classical theory have been made. It is as well to realize that this view does not satisfy everyone. Stressing the elasticities of the production

* When W. Krelle, the German scholar, tires of his tremendous models, he takes a breather with this *Einfache Theorie* (Chapter XVIII of *Verteilungstheorie*).

function presupposes that the forces of the market determine distribution. A well-oiled equilibrium mechanism is in operation, which keeps both the ratio K/L (the capital intensity) and economic growth exactly in the right track. The price determination of the factors of production is an anonymous process. The problem of power does not enter the foreground. This is not to the taste of those who regard distribution under capitalism as a matter of exploitation, power and usurpation. And in fact we have to agree with them: the classical distribution pattern may be distorted by monopoly and power, by social conventions and by the actions of pressure groups. That is the germ of truth in the theories of M. Kalecki *et al.* to be discussed in the following section (No. 3).

But there is still more to be said about the classical theory. Its most serious one-sidedness is that it proceeds from a circular flow of incomes and expenditure that is always in equilibrium. Neither overspending (inflation), characterized by rising prices, nor underspending (deflation), characterized by unemployment, occurs in its dictionary. That limits its validity, and this too influences the distribution theory. It is Keynesian analysis that examines the interplay of incomes and expenditure, and variants of this theory have been applied to income distribution. This was done above all by E. Föhl, a German fellow-spirit of J. M. Keynes; his theory relates above all to profits. To that extent it corresponds to the theory of M. Kalecki, but the causal connexions are entirely different. In Kalecki it is monopoly that determines the profit level, and in Föhl the circular flow of purchasing power. Föhl's theory will be discussed in section 4.

Another thing that I don't like about the neo-classical theory – I have already mentioned it – is the way profits are made to disappear. A two-factor model, in which $\lambda + \kappa = 1$, does violence to reality. The criticism by both Kalecki and Föhl ties in with this, but it is not only a matter of monopoly and windfall profits; technical progress also creates entrepreneurial incomes, and we have to take that into account. This pesky cause of shifts in distribution is discussed in section 6.

Finally, neo-classical thought contains one more vulnerable point. It starts from a given demand for end-products that proceeds from a given national income, and derives from this, with the aid of the production function, the factor prices and distributive shares. The way in which people spend their incomes is given. But the difficulty is that this spending depends on the distribution! Rich people buy luxury goods and poor people do not. Now that fact is unimportant as long as all goods come under the same production function, and that is what macro-economics likes to assume (if this assumption were not made, every distribution would be accompanied by a separate production function – a dreadfully complicated state of affairs). But there is a school in distribution theory that does not wish to overlook the fact that rich people save more than poor ones. On this simple fact a closely reasoned distribution theory has been built up by N. Kaldor. Closely reasoned, but funny. This point is likewise dealt with in section 4.

And one school goes even further. It desires to take into account various feedbacks from distribution to production, and it does not hesitate at more than one production function. Rich people buy capital goods, and the production of capital goods may be described by a separate production function. This separate function influences income distribution, and so personal income distribution influences distributive shares. The recognition of this kind of interdependence takes courage and a large model of equations meshing into one another. So noble an endeavour should not be ignored, and so I shall devote a separate section (No. 9) to it. But the subject is really beyond us.

Considering the above, we arrive at four groups of theories: the classical doctrine (to be dealt with in sections 5–8), the power theories (Kalecki *et al.*, in section 3), the circular flow theories (section 4) and the great synthetic models (section 9).

3. *Social Power*

The feeling that power determines distribution is widespread. Unfortunately, it often lacks precision, or the precision is at variance with the elementary facts. The latter is the fate of Marxism.

To Marx capitalist power was identical with ownership of the means of production. The working class owns nothing, and so gets nothing. In other words, the wage is sufficient to keep the worker alive, and 'alive' here may if necessary be interpreted as the socio-cultural minimum. But he does not pluck the fruits of technical progress. The surplus value accrues to the capitalists; exploitation increases, the share of labour falls. The owners of the means of production see their share rise, though this does them little good. They accumulate the surplus value – i.e. everything that the worker does not get – and invest it in capital goods that cannot be used for lack of sales. Through this perverse activity (the inner contradiction of capitalism) depressions and revolutions come about.

In this book we need not concern ourselves with this depression theory, which is a good thing too, for it is an obscure subject, full of doom and false reasoning. It is enough to establish that the increasing exploitation in the Marxist sense does not occur. Real wages keep on rising; they end up far above any minimum, however it is defined. The share of labour is also rising, and the share of capital falling. These empirical facts are not reconcilable with Marxism.

The reaction of the Marxists to the variance between facts and theory is a dual one. Either they try to prove the declining share of labour, or even the declining wage, with statistics – that is the technique of Russian authors like S. P. Figurnow.* Their endeavour calls for compassion rather than respect. More modern Marxists choose the other path and abandon this twisted scholasticism. They pounce on something else, for instance the underdeveloped regions (although there too the theory does not tally too well) or they interpret the exploitation as a psychological phenomenon. This 'alienation', which is likewise said to be brought about by the separation of property and work, goes back to the 'young Marx' and is a much more flexible view than the development of income shares. You can claim anything you like about it, and in the wild events on the campuses of Berkeley and

* According to A. Nove in the *British Journal of Industrial Relations* (February 1963) this author demonstrates that real wages in the United States in 1956 were lower than those in 1939; the workers now spend less of their income on food, and therefore are too poor to eat. Moreover, Figurnow compares *real* wage with *nominal* profit. You can prove anything this way.

Columbia and at the Sorbonne a confirmation can be seen of the Marxist theory. This is an interesting subject for discussion, but not a point that should engage us here. We are concerned with income distribution; the student in revolt considers that a vulgar and materialistic subject. It goes with the consumer society – a terrible thing that paralyses the mind and makes slaves of men. He is at most prepared to talk about the connexion between high incomes and economic and political power, and in that we are prepared to follow him, though only incidentally (see Chapter VII, 1).

An ingenious attempt at specifying the power theory was undertaken in 1939 by M. Kalecki.* Ingenious, because this author does not proceed from a falling share of labour but from a constant one (in accordance with the fashion then prevailing) and yet implies an increasing exploitation. The trick is that the colonial countries that supply the raw materials are brought into the reasoning. Their position becomes steadily worse – that is a form of capitalist exploitation. The workers in the developed countries are parties to this, and they profit from it. In their turn they are harmed by the monopolists, but, as far as the share of labour is concerned, the two forms of capitalist exploitation compensate for one another.

Kalecki's reasoning is based on the concept of degree of monopoly (see above, Chapter IV, 7) thought up by A. P. Lerner.† This variable is defined as the difference between price and marginal costs, expressed as a fraction of the price. It is a yardstick for the price increase resulting from a lack of competition. An entrepreneur need not be a real monopolist to screw up his price above the marginal costs; even the corner greengrocer can do that. Only in the case of perfect competition does it not come off. There the market dictates the price, and the entrepreneur adjusts his volume of production until the marginal costs are equal to the given price.

According to Kalecki, the marginal costs are equal to the average

* M. Kalecki, 'The Distribution of the National Income', in: *Essays in the Theory of Economic Fluctuations*, 1939; *Theory of Economic Dynamics*, 1954.

† A. P. Lerner, 'The Concept of Monopoly and the Measurement of Monopoly Power', *Review of Economic Studies* (1933/34).

variable costs (which considerably simplifies his theory), and consist of two components: wages of manual workers and the costs of raw materials. The salaries of senior employees are regarded as fixed costs by Kalecki. This technical artifice conceals a socio-political idea; these salaries are lumped together with profits, land rents and interest. The white-collar workers are separated from the working class.

The macro-economic degree of monopoly, defined as $\dfrac{P-M}{P}$

(where P is the price level and M the macro-marginal costs), is identical with the share of the non-workers, provided that there exist no separate outlays on raw materials. To find this we multiply numerator and denominator by the volume of production Q.* We then get $\dfrac{Y-MQ}{Y}$, where Y represents national income and MQ the wage bill. In this way the degree of monopoly specifies the power theory of distribution.

On the basis of these formal concepts Kalecki unfolds his view of distribution. He sees an increasing concentration in business: firms are becoming larger and larger, entirely in accordance with the Marxist prediction. The increasing degree of monopoly reflects this trend. A declining share of labour would follow from this were it not that the prices of raw materials are likewise subject to a trend; they fall steadily, the terms of trade between industrial countries and those supplying raw materials shifting to the disadvantage of the latter. As a result the share of labour remains more or less constant.

At first sight this theory† appears plausible. It explains a fact – the constant share of labour – which at the time was accepted as an established one. For the rest it is flexible enough to make it possible to understand other facts too – a slightly increasing share of

---

*If the marginal and the average costs were not the same, this would not have been permitted.

†Which has been formulated even more exactly by R. H. Whitman ('A Note on the Concept of "Degree of Monopoly"', *Economic Journal*, 1941). In his thought the share of labour is equal to $1 - (d + M/Y)$, in which d is the degree of monopoly, M imports of raw materials and Y national income.

labour. In that sense it is not dogmatic. In particular, so it seems, the share of profit is elucidated by it, and that obscure phenomenon can well do with it.

Unfortunately, upon closer examination the Kaleckian theory proves disappointing. We have a presentiment of this when we examine what happens under perfect competition, i.e. in a neo-classical world. Then the formula produces odd results: the degree of monopoly is zero, and the share of labour is 100%. But nevertheless capital remains scarce *and* productive – it is improbable that it would receive no remuneration. Now of course it may be argued that Kalecki's theory was not designed for such a world, but all the same it ought to be able to embrace this borderline case as well.

The difficulty lies in the nature of the degree of monopoly. Kalecki regards this variable as a structural characteristic, i.e. a 'hard' constant, determined by the degree of competition. And it is certainly true that the degree of competition is important. However, there are other forces in operation that likewise influence profits and interest, and which may not be described by words such as 'monopoly' and 'competition'. One such force is the shortage of capital. Another, which is probably highly important, is the existence of cost differentials between firms. If efficient and inefficient firms work side by side, large differential profits may occur. These do not disappear through competition, nor are they determined by the existence of monopolies. Differential profit is a category of income which simply cannot be fitted into Kalecki's system. And, worse still, these bonuses for higher productivity appear in his mind as the consequences of monopoly – a typical example of how to turn wine to water. Boom profits (windfalls) can also increase the profit figure. If necessary, these could be banished from a long-term theory. But that cannot be done with the pursuit of higher wages by unions, elicited by high profits. Kalecki passes over the position of power of the unions – he sees only the power of the capitalists, so that a reduction in the degree of monopoly through countervailing power remains outside the picture.

And in addition to all this, Kalecki has wrongly estimated the influence of the prices of raw materials. In his view the share of

labour increases as the prices of raw materials fall. But A. Mitra*
has shown that in fact the opposite happens, and not surprisingly
either. A rapid drop on the raw materials markets takes place in a
depression, and in such periods turnovers and profits fall more
quickly than the wage bill. This upsets one of the most striking
political features of Kalecki's model – the complicity of the workers
in colonial exploitation.

Finally, the connexion established by Kalecki between industrial concentration and profit margin also seems rather
vulnerable to me. It is a cheap illusion to believe that large concerns help one another furtively. It is easy to describe oligopoly as a
few firms hand in glove with one another. But the reader who is
familiar with the business world knows that the competition
between giant concerns can be particularly fierce, also as regards
prices. Concerns struggle for markets; and in the process they are
not always afraid to lower prices. Sometimes oligopolistic competition leads to unstable market conditions, and prices drop.
It is of course true that the increase in the market share of the giant
concerns also causes their share in the total profit to increase. We
have already seen that the concentration of profits is colossal; in
the United States half of the corporate profits go to half a *per
cent* of the corporations. However, that is not the point; what is at
issue with the degree of monopoly is the profit *margin*. In general
it has not been proved that this is higher for large firms than for
small ones. Small firms sometimes need a higher profit margin
to stay in business, and they often succeed in charging relatively
high prices.

Anyone who wants to be unkind about Kalecki's theory regards
the degree of monopoly as a tautology that confuses us rather than
a structural characteristic. *All* factors that influence profit (*and*
interest, *and* land rent, *and* in Kalecki even the salaries of employees!) meet in this variable. It is a kind of garbage can for
causal factors, and thus explains little. If the share of profit
fluctuates, for whatsoever reason, the degree of monopoly
fluctuates along with it. This does not widen our understanding.

* *The Share of Wages in National Income*, 1954. Mitra himself explains λ
by a series of variables, including some that are difficult to grasp. His theory
is stimulating but would take us too far here.

This strict judgement on Kalecki's analysis hardly seems over-done to me. His intention – seeking a structural variable that explains distribution – is a good one, but he has failed to achieve his objective. Complex reality cannot be squeezed so easily into one variable.

A caricature of Kalecki's theory has been circulated by S. Weintraub.* He asserts that entrepreneurs apply a constant mark-up to wage costs, so that national income works out at k times as high as the wage bill. The constancy of this k is pro-claimed by Weintraub with a fanfare as the 'Law of k' ('probably the most important economic law, in the true sense, that econo-mists have to work with', p. 33). In this way he explains all kinds of things, including of course a constant share of labour. However, it so happens that this k is rather variable. This is evident from Weintraub's own figures (the table on p. 14 of his book gives a variation from $1\cdot87$ to $2\cdot16$, i.e. of 15%, for the period 1929–57), but he quickly skates over these fluctuations. If he had paid at-tention to business practice he would likewise have been able to observe enormous differences in the mark-up between branches of industry; from a few *pro milles* to several hundreds of per cent (pharmaceutical industry). There is no question of a constant mark-up, and shifts in the composition of the national product can influence k (together with numerous other forces). Weintraub's book illustrates the endeavour of the human mind to discover Great Constants, even at places where they do not exist. If we strip his 'theory' of the exaggeration, what remains is that the macro-economic mark-up has displayed a fairly considerable resistance in the course of time. This fact is interesting enough in itself, but it calls for a subtler treatment than that given it by Kalecki and Weintraub. We must be alive to the fact that very many factors influence distribution – this is obscured by the proclamation of simplifications.

This section was, unfortunately, mainly negative, but this does not mean that the problem of power is a nonsensical one. I share the opinion of Kalecki and Weintraub that entrepreneurs who are able to fix prices have as a result some say in distribution. This is

* *A General Theory of the Price Level, Output, Income Distribution and Economic Growth*, 1959. No more and no less.

an essential element in capitalism for which we must make thorough allowance. If, for instance, the unions force wages up, they may expect reactions in prices. It does not stop at the passing-on of these cost increases, with the inflationary wave rolling on – profit incomes themselves rise. The share of profits (including the incomes of professionals) in national income displays a fairly considerable degree of stability at 20% (though within them shifts occur from small to large profits. That reflects the business concentration.) This share of profit does not allow itself to be crushed by a simple show of strength by the unions. That is the core of truth in Kalecki's and Weintraub's view. (Experience suggests that what does allow itself to be crushed is the share of capital.) However, this truth is the result of the divergent forces that were discussed in Chapter IV, 7. Economics has succeeded in describing these forces but not in placing them in one equation, unless circular flow analysis can help. That is a matter for the following section – which unfortunately does not turn out to be very encouraging either.

4. 'Keynesian' Theories

Brief mention has already been made of the penetrating importance of J. M. Keynes's *General Theory of Employment, Interest and Money* (1936) to economic thought. The central position in this theory is occupied by national income Y. In classical economics this variable followed from productive capacity. For this determines the national product Q, and Q determines Y in accordance with the simple relation $Y = QP$. The price level P is filled in via some monetary equation or the other – the amount of money, together with its velocity of circulation, determines the price level. This classical reasoning, in which production is always at its maximum and the circular flow of incomes and expenditure is always in equilibrium, was attacked by Keynes. In his system sales determine national income. They can deviate from productive capacity; this causes underspending or overspending. To track down the variations in sales, aggregate expenditure was split into two components: consumption C and outlays for capital goods I. Sales create income and are also equal to it; this must be so because the macro-economic Profit and Loss Account is always in equilibrium. Thus $Y = C + I$.

Now to determine income it is assumed that C depends on Y (consumption function) and that I is given in some other way; there are many variants for the latter. In the simplest case we have

$$Y = C + I$$
$$C = C_0 + cY$$
$$I = I_0$$

where C_0 and I_0 are given constants, like c (the marginal propensity to consume). These three equations, plus the three given constants, determine Y, C and I. Everything is fixed. In words: national income Y will become so large that it generates exactly as much expenditure $C + I$ as its own size. The value of Y need not tally with that which keeps the productive capacity fully occupied. If we call the latter variable $Y\star$, $Y - Y\star$ may work out positively. This is called the inflationary gap. If it works out negatively it is called the deflationary gap. In the case of inflation ($Y - Y\star > 0$) production is right up against the ceiling of its capacity, and the rise in money income follows from the rise in prices.

This dual connexion between Y and $C + I$ is the heart of Keynesian theory. It can be worked out in all kinds of directions, but the principle is always maintained: expenditure determines income, and income determines expenditure. The result is an equilibrium of circular flow, determining the variables that we are seeking. However, this model does not contain a distribution theory; the latter was added at a later date by Föhl, Kaldor and others.

The simple three-equation set-up is sufficient for understanding the distribution theory of C. Föhl (see below). To grasp Kaldor's distribution theory, Keynesian theory must be somewhat further explained for those not familiar with it. Suppose that I increases; then, in accordance with the first equation, Y increases; in the engineering industry and the building trade new incomes come into being. In accordance with the second equation C consequently increases, and as a result of this so does Y, and as a result of *that* so does *C*. It may perhaps seem as if this multiplier process goes on for ever, but that is not so. For in each period part of the income is unspent. This part is represented by the marginal propensity to save *s*. If we call the additional savings $\triangle S$ (whereby $\triangle S = s\triangle Y$), it can be proved that the increase in *Y* stops as soon as the extra investments $\triangle I$ have summoned up an amount of extra savings $\triangle S$ equal to $\triangle I$. Then the equality $I = S$ applies, and the multiplier has spent itself. The Keynesian view of national income (which was discussed above in connexion with interest theory, Chapter IV, 5) can now also be formulated as follows: *Y* becomes so large that an amount of savings is summoned up such that $I = S$. Since $\triangle S = s\triangle Y$, it is also true to say that $\triangle I = s\triangle Y$, or $\triangle Y = 1/s\triangle I$. The factor $1/s$ is called the multiplier. National income becomes equal to the multiplier times the autonomous expenditure (the purchases of capital goods). This proposition is not at variance with the above formulation: *Y* becomes so large that $C + I$ becomes equal to *Y*. On the contrary, both propositions amount to the same thing; they describe how *Y* is determined by saving (or consuming) and investing. The equilibrium of saving and investment tells us nothing about income distribution, but N. Kaldor has given this Keynesian reasoning a pendant that claims to do this.

But first C. Föhl's theory.* He examines what happens if aggregate expenditure $C + I$ increases at a given productive capacity $Y\star$, i.e. in a Keynesian process of expansion. As long as $Y < Y\star$ there is room in the system; as the demand increases idle

---

* Various publications, including C. Föhl, M. Wegener and L. Kowalski, *Kreislaufanalytische Untersuchung der Vermögensbildung in der Bundesrepublik und die Beeinflussbarkeit ihrer Verteilung*, 1964. Föhl became known in Germany through a kind of Keynesian analysis published more or less simultaneously with the *General Theory* (*Geldschöpfung und Wirtschaftskreislauf*, 1937). In this the fact that *I* is larger than *S* evokes new profits; now if these are invested again they keep on returning to the entrepreneurs. Föhl calls this the *Wiederumlaufsprinzip*; Keynes spoke (in the *Treatise on Money*, 1931) of the Widow's Jug that automatically refills itself again and again. Föhl's automatic return of profits breaks down on the fact that the multiplier summons up extra wage incomes just as much as profits. With the *a priori* that $I - S$ generates only profit we would lead the distribution theory nastily astray. Incidentally, Föhl's point of view in 1964 still somewhat resembles that of 1937.

machines come into operation again, and jobless workers find employment. In the course of this expansionary process, wages will rise somewhat. Profits rise more strongly. Interest is fixed by old contracts and does not rise along with the others. This wage increase is at first less than that of national money income. However, labour costs gradually rise. According as bottlenecks occur on the labour market the wage cost curve rises more sharply.

This can be illustrated by the figure below. On the horizontal axis Q is plotted, the national product or the real national income. On the vertical axis are the income categories LW (wage bill), RK (total interest income) and Z (total profits), and presently also aggregate expenditure $C + I$. The curve LW runs to the upper right, and does so all the steeper according as Q is greater. This does not hold good for interest incomes RK; these are constant at a given capacity, and the curve $RK + LW$ thus runs parallel to LW.

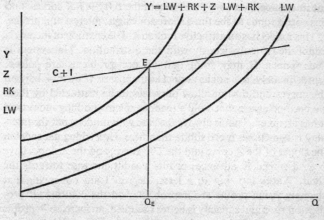

Figure 5.

The most striking trend is that displayed by the curve of profits Z. According to Föhl profit will increase relatively with an increasing utilization of capacity. That lies in the fact that now the less efficient concerns will also start to operate at full strength; the intervals between the individual cost curves grow. We are thus concerned here with bonuses for taking the lead. The curve $LW + RK + Z = Y$ climbs with ever-increasing steepness. The price level, i.e. the relation Y/Q, rises. It can be read from the figure that the share of profit increases towards the right. The absolute volume of RK is constant, but the share of interest becomes smaller towards the right. The share of labour $\dfrac{LW}{Y}$ also becomes smaller.

These three curves represent a series of possibilities, but not a determinate result. The latter requires that the Keynesian point of equilibrium is fixed on curve Y. That is done by inserting a curve $C + I$ showing how expenditure depends on Q. The point of intersection of this expenditure function and Y represents the Keynesian equilibrium E; there the income is so large that it calls forth expenditure that matches that income. The distance EQ_E measures the resultant level of national income; this distance is cut into three pieces by the LW and the $LW + RK$ curves, and this corresponds to the three shares of wages, interest and profits.

This model has an attractive look to it. The creation of income is established simultaneously with the distribution. The system is determinate. It may seem that all our problems are solved. Unfortunately, it is not as perfect as it appears. If we look beyond the curves and do not allow ourselves to be distracted by them we become aware that Föhl's theory explains nothing more than it has assumed. That is always the case with models, but the interplay is sometimes more subtle than here. Everything depends on the slopes of the Z curve and the LW curve, and these slopes have been assumed in advance: profits steadily increase towards the right. Wages too, but to a lesser degree. I am not saying that strongly rising profits are improbable; on the contrary, if production rises and capacity is better occupied, an increase in profits is self-evident. Föhl ascribes this to cost differentials between firms, but there are other, more obvious reasons. If the turnover increases and the fixed costs are fixed (which fixed costs often are), profits rise; every businessman knows that. The losses through excess capacity disappear, and once you're out of the red you're in the black. Come to that, this homely truth has also been verified by clever econometricians. For instance, C. Schulze has established that the profits of corporations in the United States tend to rise by about 1·7% if sales rise by 1%. Moreover, the profits of corporations are more sensitive to fluctuations in sales than the incomes of small firms and of self-employed persons.*

Föhl's reasoning shows us what happens short-term to the share of profit if the economic situation improves. It goes no further than that. It says nothing about long-term developments, nor does it explain why the distribution is what it is. For the LW curve does not have enough of a basis for that. Föhl is so fascinated by profits that he dismisses the money wage level as a determinant force in distributive shares. As a result, even his short-term explanation of profits is not convincing. For big profits bring forth wage increases. It is inadmissible to allow the Y curve to rise, resulting in enormous profits, and then to assume that LW remains quietly where it is! Even with a demand pull – that is the case that Föhl has in mind – wages rise as well after a short time, either via the market mechanism (the Phillips curve!) or via union efforts. In the case of a cost push it is the LW curve that treks north under its own steam, and Föhl's reasoning is not equipped to deal with that case. Schulze, who surrounds his econometrics with all kinds of safeguards, also passes over wage inflation, while this may nevertheless threaten profits. That is also seen in a persistent boom; sales still rise, but profits are here and there put under pressure by wage demands. As a rule they manage to hold their ground, but with difficulty. We find nothing of this in the model.

Föhl has therefore shown us only one side of the coin of the economic situation. This theory is not a general one, but extracts one element – that of the demand pull – from the general inter-relation. What remains is that quick spurts by aggregate demand increase the share of profit; that was also plausible without this theory. This doesn't take us much further. We could make the model more complete by making the wage equation and the profit equation more explicit, and by exactly specifying the variables on which these categories of incomes depend. In the case of wages we might envisage the Phillips curve: the percentage wage increase depends (negatively) on the percentage of unemployment

* 'Short-Run Movements of Income Shares', in: *The Behavior of Income Shares*, 1964.

(see Chapter IV, 8). The latter is directly connected with the deflationary gap $Y^\star - Y$, and it is reasonable to assume that profits are related to this variable. It might therefore seem that we can attach both the wage increase and profits to the same variable $Y^\star - Y$, and that is beginning to look very much like a determinate model. Unfortunately, one link is still missing: the influence of the rise in wages on profits, i.e. the degree in which businessmen succeed in passing on wage increases in prices. We can also include an equation for that, but we shall find little empirical support. Perhaps this passing-on also depends on $Y^\star - Y$: in a deflationary situation profits recover from a wage push with difficulty, in an inflationary situation with ease. All we learn from this is that the passing-on process is crucial to the relation between wages and profits, but we already know that, since we discussed (in Chapter IV, 9) the wage-price-wage spiral. This approach must be supplemented by empirical research into this process. Perhaps one day this will result in a complete and testable model, which explains the short-run behaviour of income shares in inflationary and deflationary situations. So far such a model does not exist.

However, in addition to this approach there is an entirely different one, usually ascribed to N. Kaldor,* and since then imitated and elaborated by many.† The starting-point is the Keynesian equality of I and S, whereby investments, via the multiplier process, create savings. These savings are of course accumulated by the savers; they are at the same time the income recipients. The original Keynesian theory of national income did not need to divide the income recipients into groups, but that is what the distribution theory does. The simplest case is a division into wage-earners and profit recipients (in the wide sense, including interest and land rent). The salient point here is that these two

* 'Alternative Theories of Distribution', *Review of Economic Studies*, 1955/56, and *Essays on Value and Distribution*, 1960. Similar ideas had been put forward at an earlier date by F. Hahn, 'The Share of Wages in the National Income', *Oxford Economic Papers*, 1951.

† For instance, G. Bombach, 'Die verschiedene Ansätze der Verteilungstheorie', in: *Einkommensverteilung und Technischer Fortschritt*, 1959. J. Robinson, *The Accumulation of Capital*, 1956.

groups have a different propensity to save. The workers do not
save much; their propensity to save (marginal and average, which
for the sake of convenience we shall assume to be identical) is s_w.
The capitalists are richer and save more; their propensity to save
is s_z. These two partial propensities to save must yield an average s
in such a way that $S = I$. That can, in the Keynesian view,
happen at every possible level of national income. Kaldor pins
down the equilibrium by taking Y as given, and investments too.
Surprisingly enough, that firmly establishes income distribution.
For now I/Y is given, and so is $S/Y = s$. But, with a given s_w and
s_z, this s comes about only if the share of labour λ has a certain
value; for s is the weighted sum of s_w and s_z, λ and $1 - \lambda$ forming
the weights.

This value of λ is derived as follows. The average propensity to
save $s = \lambda s_w + (1 - \lambda)s_z$. Since $s = I/Y$, $\lambda = \dfrac{s_z - I/Y}{s_z - s_w}$. The share
of labour is therefore uniquely determined by the fraction formed
by the investments of national income and the two partial propensities to save. It seems an elegant theory, complete in itself.
One of its amazing aspects is that so many things do not appear
in it: there are no powerful monopolists, no trade unions, no
production functions, no marginal productivities. We need only
three figures to determine the whole process of income distribution.
Saving and investment do the trick.

To show what we have really been up to, a few numerical
examples may be of assistance. Let us first take the extreme case –
it still haunts the literature – in which the capitalists save their
entire income – they live on air – and the workers consume the
whole wage bill. Suppose that 20% of national income is invested.
The share of labour is then 100% – 20% divided by 1. That makes
λ 80%. This looks realistic. We then take I/Y again as 20%, and
assume that the capitalists save 30% and the workers save 10% of
their income. In that case the numerator of the fraction is 10%,
the denominator is 20% and the share of labour is 50%. That is
a low figure. If the workers were to save only 5% of their income,
the denominator would be 25%, and the share of labour would
be still lower: 40%. The workers could reverse this decline from
50 to 40% by saving more; let us assume that they succeed in

putting 20% aside. In that case the share of labour is forthwith raised to 100%, and the capitalists look foolish. They don't get a single penny.

This last numerical example has been presented not only by way of exercise, but also with the malicious intention of showing up the Achilles' heel of Kaldor's theory. The reader feels, I hope, that there is something wrong here. The world is not like that: workers who, by saving slightly more, manage to reduce profits to nil!

And indeed the story is highly misleading. The algebra is in order, but the structure of the reasoning is false. We have assumed that Y is given (not illogically: how is a *given* income distributed?), and in passing fixed I as an independent quantity. So far so good. But then we assumed the two partial propensities to save as given – and that's where the nonsense started. In this way we have distorted all causalities. We assume that the workers can save more, or less, *without the average propensity to save changing*! The only influence of an increasing s_w is on λ; s remains as it is. That is entirely unnatural.

The self-evident relation is quite different. If the workers proceed to save more (and the capitalists save the same), s increases. That leads to one of two things. Either the additional savings go to the capital market, where they are collected by the entrepreneurs waiting for them. In other words: S increases, and consequently so does I. That is the classical reaction. In that case the fraction I/Y increases, and the Kaldorian reasoning breaks down. Or saving causes total demand to fall, I remains constant, and the multiplier reduces Y; the additional savings have not been invested but have disappeared because the shrunken income has made the public less inclined to save. That is the Keynesian reaction. In that case too I/Y increases. If Kaldor takes I/Y as a constant, and all the same allows the partial propensities to save (or one of them) to vary, he drives us into never-never land.

If it is still required, criticism of Kaldor's theory can take a different approach. Suppose that I/Y increases, for instance because the entrepreneurs are in a more cheerful frame of mind. Suppose also that the partial propensities to save remain the same. The Kaldorian consequence is that the share of profit must increase, so as to keep the average propensity to save at the level of I/Y. The entrepreneurs see their optimism confirmed, and invest the new profits. I/Y increases still further, and so do profits. This is a new version of the Widow's Jug (see p. 182) but in this case not *à la* Föhl (profit causes sales to rise and in this way breeds new profit) but via the propensities to save. This mechanism, too, is improbable – a continuing rise of I/Y has quite different consequences, such as overspending, wage inflation, a wage-price spiral, and these consequences determine income distribution. The Kaldorian theory is silent on this point.

The simple reasoning can be embellished and touched up, but it remains misleading. For instance, the given fraction I/Y, which is the trouble-maker, has occasionally been replaced by a given growth percentage of production. In accordance with a certain equation, which need not concern us here, this growth percentage may be reduced to the quotient of the propensity to save and the capital-output ratio $\dfrac{\triangle K}{\triangle Q}$. If the latter is also given, the propensity to save follows from the growth rate and then the game can begin again. We now have a given growth rate, a given capital-output ratio and two partial propensities to save, and the distribution proceeds relentlessly from these. It sounds intriguing, it is high theory – but unfortunately it is a fallacy. It is astonishing that serious economists, intelligent specialists, brilliant minds – Kaldor satisfies all three of those qualifications – concern themselves with it.* There are of course dissentients,† but their influence is obviously not sufficient to expel this particular model from the learned journals.

* Kaldor's theory has been worked out in yet another direction by L. Kowalski (*Einkommensverwendung, Einkommensverteilung und Vermögensverteilung*, 1967). He makes a distinction not between two groups, but between as many as are desired, all with different propensities to save. The share of each group (artists, hotel-owners, redheads) increases as I/Y increases and the group's propensity to save decreases, if the group receives mainly profit, interest or land rent. If the group receives mainly wage or salary, matters are the other way round.

† J. Tobin has made the whole business look ridiculous ('Towards a General Kaldorian Theory of Distribution'. *Review of Economics and Statistics*, 1960) but it has not helped enough.

The latter exercise has brought us little more than sad surprise and the realization that ultimately the economic variables will have to fit together. When we presently examine the neo-classical view we must bear in mind that income distribution must finally square with saving habits, investments and all that. But this is no comfort to us. Everything depends on everything – a thought that discourages rather than inspires. Let us nevertheless press on towards a theory that offers more to go on.

5. *Neo-Classical Theory*

We have already repeatedly seen that the neo-classical theory derives distribution from the production function $Q = F(L,K)$. In Chapter IV we interpreted this in micro-economic terms; there the individual entrepreneur derived his demand for labour, with the aid of marginal productivity, from the demand for final products. We are now concerned with macro-economics and this makes matters easier (in this special case). We may now assume that the amount of labour and the stock of capital goods are fixed *at a given* moment; L and K are therefore filled in, and out pops Q. This is typical classical thinking: all productive forces are in full use. A follower of Keynes allows for underexpenditure: Q is determined by sales, and may therefore be smaller than had been possible. In that case there is unemployment and excess capacity; Q does not follow from a given L and K, but L and K follow from Q, which depends on $C + I$. But, either way, both in the classical and in the Keynesian case Q, L and K are determinate. The marginal productivities that determine the real wage level and the real interest rate are consequently known, as are the share of labour λ and the share of capital κ; income shares are equal to the elasticities of production in respect of L and K. If we ignore for a moment the unsatisfactory fact that profit is nowhere to be found (because $\lambda + \kappa = 1$), and accept a purely labour-capital model (which is what we shall do in this section), it looks as if we know all we need to know. No unsolved problems remain.

That is, of course, not so. To start with, the solution remains shadowy until we have filled in real numbers. What we need is empirical verification. Now there has been no lack of that. The production function is no longer written as an indeterminate F, but as a specified relation that has been approached statistically.* And further we cannot get away with regarding the production elasticities as constants. They could very well change. There are two possibilities for this: the first is that the elasticities, and with them the distribution, shift if we change the ratio K/L – after all, it has not been said that the elasticities are the same at all points of the production function. This depends on the form of the function, and the empirical research work must therefore clear up this issue forthwith. The second possibility is that the whole function shifts in the course of time. In that case the elasticities could also change, and the neo-classical theory would be confronted with an increase or decrease in the share of labour. The latter – the shift in $F(L,K)$ – is called technical change. It is a tricky problem for both statisticians and theoreticians which will engage our attention separately in the following section.

The empirical research was ushered in by C. W. Cobb and P. H. Douglas;† these two are rightfully spoken of with respect. Their production function has the shape $Q = AL^\alpha K^{1-\alpha}$, known for short as the Cobb-Douglas. In this function A is a fairly unimportant constant which has to do with the choice of the units in which the variables are expressed, but the exponent α, as we shall see, is a strategic variable. The function displays a number of remarkable properties. For instance, it is manifest that production without capital is impossible, since L and K are multiplied by one another. Further, the sum of the exponents α and $1-\alpha$ is equal to

* This is of course easier said than done. The macro-economic measurement of L and K yields almost insurmountable problems. In the case of L must we only count heads, or allow for working hours and the quality of the work done? In the case of K, must we consider the stock of capital goods itself or the use thereof? Must we let old machines, with their low productivity, carry just as much weight as brand-new ones? How do we summarize all these different kinds of labour in one L and all these different machines in one K? How do we arrive at our statistical data? Here, even more than elsewhere, econometricians rush in where you and I would fear to tread. They have to.

† 'A Theory of Production', *American Economic Review, Papers and Proceedings*, 1928; P. H. Douglas, *The Theory of Wages*, 1934; 'Are there Laws of Production?', *American Economic Review*, 1948.

1. That implies that an increase in the scale of production has no influence on productivity; just see what happens if L and K are both multiplied by an arbitrary constant n – in that case Q also becomes n times as large.

The most striking aspect is presented by the exponent α: this proves to be equal to the elasticity of Q in respect of L, i.e. to λ. No wonder that the Cobb-Douglas has become so popular. We can therefore do without those α's (and choose our units in such a way that $A = 1$), and write at once $L^\lambda K^{1-\lambda}$, so that every factor of production is provided with its own share of income as exponent.

(The reader who wants to see it proved that $\alpha = \lambda$ should read this paragraph to the end. Anyone who doesn't care, dislikes differential equations or simply doesn't understand them, is advised to skip the following two lines. Under the Cobb-Douglas the real wage level $\delta Q/\delta L = \alpha A L^{\alpha-1} K^{1-\alpha}$. The elasticity λ is by definition $\delta Q/\delta L . L/Q = \alpha A L^{\alpha-1+1} K^{1-\alpha} Q^{-1} = \alpha$. That's all.)

As if the elegant conclusion that the exponents are direct criteria of the distribution between labour and capital were not enough in itself, the elasticities λ and $1 - \lambda$ are, under the Cobb-Douglas, independent of the ratio K/L, the capital intensity or the amount of capital per worker. However much capital we pump into the production process, income distribution remains the same. In other words: the shares of income are not influenced by capital accumulation. The price relation of the factors of production *does* change with an increasing K/L. Real wages go up and the real rate of interest goes down. The degree of change of these prices can be stated exactly. If the amount of capital per worker increases by 1%, the interest-wage ratio under the Cobb-Douglas drops by 1%. The two variations (i.e. that of R/W and of K/L) compensate one another, so that λ remains the same.

This important property of the Cobb-Douglas can also be formulated in a rather different way, viz. by means of the elasticity of substitution σ. (We have already encountered this useful quantity, viz. when we were considering the micro-reaction of employment to wage increases in Chapter IV, 1. This reaction proved to depend among other things on the ease with which labour and capital can replace one another.) This σ is the elasticity of the function that makes K/L dependent on R/W, the interest-wage ratio. If this latter ratio changes by 1%, the capital intensity changes (in the opposite direction) by $\sigma\%$. In the Cobb-Douglas $\sigma = 1$; this means that the replacement of labour by capital is a smooth process, which encounters no friction. As a consequence, the increasing accumulation is discarded as a determinant of distribution.

The Cobb-Douglas is, of course, ideal for explaining a constant share of labour. It was a godsend. Although its inventors were initially more interested in understanding the rate of growth than distribution, the function fitted perfectly into the then prevailing fashion of an invariable λ. This, and the theoretical elegance of the Cobb-Douglas, explains its tremendous popularity. Numerous econometricians have taken it as a starting point for empirical research. This has broadly confirmed what the investigators had in mind, viz. an unchanging distribution. For the United States Cobb and Douglas estimate λ at roughly 75%, and κ at 25%. Many other investigators found similar results for other countries.

Unfortunately, these results are just too good to be true. The statistical puzzles are enormous, many arbitrary decisions have to be taken and the investigator is lastingly subject to the temptation to accept results that fit into the theory more readily than others. The principal difficulties involved in determining L and K have already been indicated above (p. 191, footnote). And in addition to this, profit is divided into two portions: implicit wage and implicit interest – and there all kinds of considerations can be allowed to prevail that greatly affect the result. On top of that, the division is rather unnatural too; two factors of production can be used in production theory, but in distribution theory at least three income categories are required: profits keep spoiling the two-factor game. It is therefore not surprising that the research work has been under heavy fire.*

* See for instance E. H. Phelps Brown, 'The Meaning of the Fitted Cobb-Douglas Function', *Quarterly Journal of Economics*, 1957; he is of the opinion that econometrics has not yielded a production function but a cost function. The constant technique (the fact that the Cobb-Douglas contains no term that can reflect a general rise in productivity) was also criticized very early on (J. M. Clark, 'Inductive Evidence of Marginal Productivity', *American Economic Review*, 1928). However, something can be done about the latter (see section 6 below).

The Cobb-Douglas became ripe for replacement when belief in the constant λ disappeared. It is remarkable that it was not until 1956 that someone came forward with a new production function and even then in connexion with a somewhat different problem (viz. how balanced growth can be maintained with a fluctuating propensity to save). It was R. M. Solow, one of the most alert economists of our day, who proposed a new relation between inputs and output.* The simplest form of the new function, which we could call the Solow, is $Q = (L^\alpha + K^\alpha)^{1/\alpha}$. The reader who has difficulty with the exponent $1/\alpha$ may like to know that this means that a root, of the power α, is extracted. The function is still somewhat primitive because this α occurs three times; we can make the relationship more general by raising L to the power α, K to the power β, and the binomial $(L^\alpha + K^\beta)$ to the power $1/\gamma$. But perhaps this is something you can do without.

The Solow is like the Cobb-Douglas, yet it is a horse of a different colour. Addition is different from multiplication. Indeed, increase of scale also leaves productivity unaffected here (the Solow, like the Cobb-Douglas, is homogeneously linear), but there are two major differences. The elasticity of substitution σ is not equal to one; to be exact, this strategic variable is equal to $\dfrac{1}{1-\alpha}$. That presents possibilities for changes in income distribution that do not exist if $\sigma = 1$.

In the second place, the elasticity of production is not equal to α, but is described by a somewhat more complicated expression.† This expression is not insensitive to changes in the relation between K and L – in other words, under this Solow function distribution depends on capital accumulation. If more capital is introduced into production, the elasticity of production increases in respect of labour, and so does the share of labour. It will be clear that we have dug up a particularly interesting relation here.

Incidentally, this effect of an increasing capital intensity can be

---

* 'A Contribution to the Theory of Economic Growth', *Quarterly Journal of Economics*, 1956.

† Namely $\dfrac{L^\alpha}{L^\alpha + K^\alpha}$ in respect of labour and $\dfrac{K^\alpha}{L^\alpha + K^\alpha}$ in respect of capital.

additionally and better described by means of the elasticity of substitution. The salient point is whether σ is larger or smaller than one. The reader must keep an eye on the importance of this, for it will appear that this σ determines the development of λ and κ. Intuitively most people assume that $\sigma = 0$. That is to say, they believe that there is only one correct way to build a house, make shoes, produce artificial fertilizer. Or, in other words, they believe that a given type of machine requires a given number of workers. In this view the ratio K/L is dictated by technology. Of course an outmoded technology can be applied, but that is backward. Economists look at this quite differently – this is perhaps the most essential difference between economists and non-economists. Economists believe that K/L is subject to a *choice* by the entrepreneurs; the ratio is determined by the price relation between K and L, and σ expresses this reaction. Now there are also economists (R. Harrod, W. Leontieff) who believe that $\sigma = 0$, but they occupy a rather isolated position. For distribution the point of view of this 'fixed proportions school' is useless anyway, since in that case the marginal productivities are 0. And yet few today would be prepared to go as far as Cobb and Douglas, and assume that $\sigma = 1$. This is above all because if the entrepreneurs wish to replace labour by capital that can be done in particular by buying new machinery. The old capital goods require a fairly fixed amount of labour. But the new machines form only a fraction of the total capital stock in a given year. This points to an elasticity of substitution that is smaller than unity. It cannot be said in advance how large σ will work out at; the econometricians will have to calculate that. For this they require a production function, and the Solow allows of such calculations. Unlike the Cobb-Douglas, it does not force us to believe that $\sigma = 1$; the empirical material is allowed to dictate the result.

And in fact the Solow may be reconciled with very different values of the elasticity of substitution. To illustrate this the reader may recall the equation given above, $\sigma = \dfrac{1}{1-\alpha}$. If σ should take a positive value, then α would be negative. If the absolute value of α is very small, σ approaches unity: the well-oiled case of perfect substitution. But if α is, for instance, -2, the elasticity of substitution becomes 0·33; this is the case that theoretical speculation (the capital stock being more in the nature of 'clay' than of 'putty') makes probable. If $\alpha = -0·8$, σ becomes 0·6; and so on. Now negative values of α may seem perverse but they are possible; they mean that we have to take the reciprocal of the base. Suppose that $\alpha = -\frac{1}{2}$; the Solow takes the shape

$$Q = \cfrac{1}{\left(\cfrac{1}{\sqrt{L}} + \cfrac{1}{\sqrt{K}}\right)^2}$$ and the elasticity of substitution becomes $\frac{2}{3}$.

All these examples suggest a good deal of friction.

For distributive shares this suggestion is a vital one. As J. R. Hicks demonstrated* long ago, a low elasticity of substitution means that the rapidly growing production factor must force itself into the production process at the expense of a relatively strong drop in prices. This drop in prices is by definition greater than the relative rise of the amount. The net effect is that the income share of that fast grower drops. This might be called Hicks's Law. In fact capital is the more rapid grower of the two factors of production – therefore $\sigma < 1$ implies a declining κ.

This connexion can be specified. If K/L increases by 1% (of its own accord) the price relation R/W falls by $1/\sigma\%$. The net effect on κ, expressed as a percentage of κ, yields a fraction $(1-\kappa)(1-1/\sigma)$. This fraction is again an elasticity, namely the elasticity of κ in respect of K/L. It shows what happens to the share of capital if the capital intensity increases by 1%. In the same way the elasticity of λ in respect of K/L is equal to $(1-\lambda)(1-1/\sigma)$.†

These equations illustrate the importance of σ to distribution. If $\sigma = 1$ – as under the Cobb-Douglas – the elasticity of κ is equal to 0, and accumulation does not harm the relative position of the capitalists. If $\sigma = 0$ – the highly improbable case of completely fixed coefficients – the expression $(1-1/\sigma)$ becomes infinite, and a slight increase in K/L causes the share of capital to fall to nil. Somewhere in between lies reality.

* *Theory of Wages*, 1932.
† The author is aware that many readers will find this bit of algebra indigestible. I recommend that they keep in mind the essential truth in Hicks's Law and leave the precise nature of the connexion between K/L and λ aside.

It is therefore of essential importance to know what this σ actually looks like. Much research has gone into this since the Solow was discovered. This has been done on the basis of more complicated functions than $(L^\alpha + K^\alpha)^{1/\alpha}$. What they have in common with this basic variant is that L and K, after having been generously provided with coefficients and exponents, are added together, and that the sum is again adorned with a coefficient and an exponent. They also all have the property that, though σ can assume all kinds of values, it is constant as soon as the function is fixed; in other words, the elasticity of substitution does not change if we let the capital intensity increase. For that reason this family of production functions is sometimes known as Constant Elasticity of Substitution Functions, or CES functions for short. The most fertile of the CES family is the SMAC, called after the initials of its inventors' names.* (I mention these technical expressions so that the reader who overhears a conversation between two econometricians engaged in income distribution research can understand what they are talking about. After reading this book you need not feel out of things.)

Much empirical research has been done on the basis of the SMAC and related functions. The primary purpose was not to find out about distribution, but to explain the growth of production. Information on substitution has been usefully gained as a by-product. It proves that the values found for σ almost always lie under one. A figure that has been produced as a rough international impression is 0·6.†

---

* K. Arrow, H. Chenery, B. Minhas and R. Solow, 'Capital-Labor Substitution and Economic Efficiency', *Review of Economics and Statistics*, 1961. The SMAC has the following appearance: $Q = \gamma\,[\delta K^{-\rho} + (1 - \delta)\,L^{-\rho}]^{-1/\rho}$, in which γ, δ and ρ are constants. For our purpose – acquiring some insight into income distribution – this form is overly complicated.

† See for instance the above-mentioned article on SMAC, and further M. Brown and J. S. deCani, 'Technological Change in the U.S. 1950–1960', *Productivity Measurement Review*, 1962; J. G. M. Hilhorst, 'Measurement of Production Functions in Manufacturing Industries', *Statistical Studies*, 1962. For the Netherlands: unpublished calculations by H. de Haan and S. K. Kuipers. Only Solow himself produces values of $\sigma > 1$ in 'Capital, Labor and Income in Manufacturing' (in the collection *The Behavior of Income Shares*, 1964). The latter results were forthwith subjected to criticism by J. W. Kendrick, wielding a battery of figures which in their turn yield an

That is a figure to remember. Even if we are rather sceptical about the statistical methods that have led to this result, so that we are not prepared to guarantee this exact value of σ, we can still make good use of it. The quantity throws a new light on the mechanics of the society in which we live. It proves that the accumulation of capital is the worker's friend. Not only does labour productivity and thus prosperity increase as a result, but in addition increasing capital intensity leads to an increasing share of labour!

A σ of 0·6 entails that the share of labour grows by about 0·2% for every increase of 1% in capital intensity. Now in a country like the United States the amount of capital per worker has roughly doubled since the beginning of the century. That consequently leads to an increase in the share of labour of 20%. And in fact the rise is of that order of size; λ was 55% in those days, and is now about 70%, i.e. an increase of 23%. We can also consider the pure share of capital, including land rent but excluding profit, which has fallen by about two-thirds since 1900, while the equation yields a drop of about 60%.

Roughly speaking, therefore, the prediction is in agreement with reality. In my numerical examples for the United States the shift in the distributive shares is not entirely explained by Hicks's Law; a residue remains, for which we shall have to find another explanation (and there is one – it is coming shortly). The same applies to Britain, where the increase in λ was about a quarter, and the growth of K/L was less than in the United States. Other authors, notably I. Kravis,* arrive on the basis of figures arranged rather differently at the opposite conclusion: the accumulation theory gives an over-explanation of the shift in distribution. In this case another force operating in the opposite direction must have been active, which has increased the share of capital. And in

average of 0·6 (same collection, p. 141). Incidentally, it is interesting that Solow mentions two special branches of industry (tobacco and instruments, both in the United States), with a very high σ. In these two cases the share of labour has also clearly fallen, so that tallies.

* 'Relative Income Shares in Fact and Theory', *American Economic Review*, 1959. This was a pioneering article; Kravis was the first to revive and apply Hicks's Law.

fact this is our next problem: can we say that the growth of K/L in combination with a low σ is responsible for the trend in distribution, or is it plausible that other mechanisms were additionally at work?

The answer is without doubt: in addition to the accumulation there are other influences. These are not explained by neo-classical theory, and so they have not been previously discussed in this section. I should like to remind the reader of the possibility, discussed in Chapter IV, of wages and salaries being pushed up institutionally. That is done by the unions and by the fact that incomes are determined conventionally and reflect status and prestige rather than marginal productivities. Unions are not so powerful that they can cut right across market relations, and probably prestige salaries are not so far away from what scarcity entails, but in this way an additional wage push can nevertheless occur, which is passed on to the incomes of rentiers. There is no doubt that inflation has made its contribution towards reducing the share of capital. The theory discussed in this section made no allowance for that – it sees wages solely as an expression of the derivative of the production function, i.e. as a product of scarcity. The neo-classical theory must be supplemented by the realization that in practice the wage increase may be autonomously greater than corresponds to the creation of capital. If you like, you can call the wage push social power. As a result W/R is raised above the level corresponding to K/L.

Now this gives a further shift in distributive shares than that which proceeds from capital accumulation. It is perhaps as well to point out that this is not the case with all production functions. Under the Cobb-Douglas the institutional and social forces, even if they raise wages and thus W/R, have no effect on the share of labour. In that case the distribution is determined in a purely technical way. Under the Solow and the SMAC matters are different; there, part of the wage push is compensated for by substitution, but the substitution is not, as under the Cobb-Douglas, perfect, and the power of the engineers over the share of labour is therefore curtailed. The new algebra and the low value of σ have in this respect given us a more realistic view of the world. To be exact: if the wage rate rises autonomously by 1% and interest does not go up along with it, λ increases by $(1-\sigma)\%$, i.e. by 0.4%. A wage push of 10% over a period of ten years (a moderate estimate in inflation-ridden countries) increases the share of labour by a further 4%.

As far as λ is concerned, the accumulation of capital and the autonomous wage increase thus operate in the same direction. This can easily lead to an over-explanation of the shift that has in fact occurred. This suggests a third force that runs counter to these, backing up the relative position of the capitalists.

I. Kravis, in his article mentioned above, has designated technical progress as this force. The idea is as follows. A continual creation of capital harms the share of capital only if the production function remains the same. The increase in demand for labour and capital in that case depends only on the increase in production; no other growth of the demand for capital occurs than that which may be derived from the growth of production. If the supply increases this leads to absorption of the additional capital, but only at the expense of a lower R/W ratio. The situation changes completely if the technique of production develops in such a way that a given volume of production requires relatively more capital. If that happens, it affects distribution. Now this brings us to an entirely new theme: technical change.

6. Technical Progress

Economics has a special obligation with respect to technical change. The latter makes a tremendous contribution towards the growth of the national product – we shall presently see how much – but quite apart from that it is complex and confusing. Everything changes at the same time; new products appear, old ones are made in a new way. As a result of the new methods of production, the quantitative relation between labour and capital changes. Profits are created in the one firm and disappear in the other. New employment comes into being at the one place, while elsewhere employment shrinks. Probably income distribution is also swept along in this general turbulence. But in what direction? It is not difficult to develop a gloomy view of this. Marx already saw technology under capitalism as a cause of intensified class struggle, and automation has given birth to a modern form of disquiet. Conversely, it may also be asserted that we all share in the blessings of technology: by cheaper products, higher incomes, greater prosperity. The task of economics is to systematize the various elements of change, if possible to quantify them, and perhaps to pass judgement on them.

Now it must be said at once that from of old economics has stood aloof from the most striking aspect: the purely technical one. A jet is quite different from a sailing ship, and the dentist's modern drill in no way resembles the dental forceps used by tooth-drawers a century ago. Travellers and patients notice the difference, but economists are silent about it. They think in terms of goods, or of money, or of the satisfaction of wants, and they prefer not to specify the nature of the goods or the nature of satisfaction. In macro-theory – and that is what we are concerned with – they go even further, and summarize all products in Q. This statistical operation yields recalcitrant puzzles, for how must we express differences in quality in index figures? But that is not our worry at the moment.

By compressing the whole output into one number Q we have already lost a part of the bewildering nature of technical change. Q is a most hygienic variable. What interests us now comes more sharply to the fore. Technical change means that the relation between the output and the inputs improves, and in this sense we may safely speak of technical *progress*. This relation has a name: productivity. Labour productivity is Q/L, capital productivity is Q/K. Roughly speaking, more product is supplied by the same amounts of factor of production.

Now not every rise in productivity is caused by technical progress. Labour productivity can rise in quite a different way: by using more capital. Economists long thought that the rise in K/L was the principal reason for increasing prosperity; they were wrong about this (as we shall see), but one thing that is certain is that a greater capital intensity increases the production per worker. But the point is this: if Q/L rises because K/L rises, that is not (or at least not necessarily) technical progress. To grasp this, we can make good use of the production function: $Q = F(L,K)$. This describes one given group of technical possibilities. If L

is constant, and K increases, Q rises (though the law of diminishing returns applies), so that Q/L rises; this happens with constant technology. We do not speak of technical progress until the function itself changes, that is to say when Q increases while L and K remain constant. These two things, increasing capital intensity and shifting production function, must be carefully distinguished from one another, even though they have the same effect: increasing prosperity.*

Why this warning? I hear the reader say. We are pondering income distribution – what difference can a scholastic distinction between two kinds of productivity increase make to us? But this distinction is precisely vital to distributive shares, for an increase in K/L reduces the marginal productivity of capital. This is the reason for the great historical process: the drop in the interest-wage ratio. If the increase in capital intensity is in addition combined with an elasticity of substitution that is smaller than one, the drop in this ratio becomes so great that capital's share drops too. That was the conclusion of the previous section.

In the case of a change in the production function $Q = F(L,K)$ this process need not operate, even if the new technology were to bring about a changed relation between K and L. The law of diminishing returns relates only to changes in the relation between K and L *at a given technology*, not to shifts of F. What influence the latter has on income distribution will have to be arrived at in another way. That way is in principle a simple one – although unfortunately the empirical research is anything but that. This simple answer is given by the neo-classical theory, which considers the elasticities of the production function. One can imagine a general increase in productivity that leaves these elasticities intact. We say that the production function shifts in parallel to itself;

* An arresting point: average prosperity depends on labour productivity, *not* on capital productivity. For the real income per head is Q/N, in which N represents the number of consumers. If N is proportionate to the working population L, Q/N is proportionate to Q/L. This proportionality is not certain, but it is not nonsensical either. However, proportionality of N and K is a senseless idea. Consequently Q/K does not determine prosperity. And a good thing too! For Q/L rises in the course of history, whereas Q/K is practically stationary. (This point is also of importance to distribution; it was discussed in section 1 of this chapter.)

technical progress is *neutral*. It may also be imagined that through the new technology the elasticity of production increases in respect of capital (and the elasticity of production then decreases in respect of labour). Technical change is then capital-using (or: labour-saving) and income distribution shifts in favour of capital. In the converse case technical progress is called labour-using or capital-saving.* These classifications are neat enough. The question is: what happens in practice?

And that is not easy to establish. Reality concerns itself little with the distinction between shifts *past F* and shifts *of F*, and allows changes in K/L at a given technology and shifts in the production function to take place at the same time. A businessman who installs additional machinery often changes his technology of production. Conversely, technical progress is almost always coupled with investments in capital goods; you can't change from coal to oil or from oil to natural gas without first changing the nature of your equipment. Technical change is embodied in capital or, to use another economists' expression: capital is the vehicle of technical progress. That is why shifts past and shifts of the production function are so difficult to disentangle. Here too unscrambling proves to be a stumbling-block for insight into income distribution.

The interlocking nature of substitution (increasing of K/L) and technical progress (increase of Q with K and L constant) naturally vexes the statisticians. On top of all their other worries they have to keep apart two things that in practice go hand in hand. The results of their empirical research become even more uncertain as a result. As long as there was a certain confidence in the Cobb-Douglas there was an inclination to regard technical progress as neutral. That is understandable: economists had just got a firm grip on the constant share of labour, and disturbing influences from technology were regarded as most undesirable.

---

* These definitions are not the only possible ones. There are economists who prefer to follow R. Harrod (*Towards a Dynamic Economics*, 1948. p. 23), and who call technical progress neutral only if the constancy of λ and κ is accompanied by a constant capital-output ratio. I shall gladly leave these complications on one side. Our definition follows J. R. Hicks (*The Theory of Wages*, 1932); one sometimes speaks of Hicks-neutral versus Harrod-neutral.

It was assumed that the Cobb-Douglas shifted gradually in time, but the elasticities λ and κ had above all to remain the same.*

This attitude changed in 1956. The reason lay not only in the introduction of the Solow function in that year; the discovery of the Abramowitz Residual was also important (see below). But the new production function à la Solow was indeed highly significant. For it opens the possibility of a decreasing κ under the influence of a rising K/L. Anyone who sees this possibility is open to shifts in the production function; more than that, he welcomes them. We saw above that a σ of 0·6 has, according to some economists, an exaggerated effect on income distribution; the share of capital is more compressed by accumulation than history shows and we therefore naturally start looking for a counterforce. In that sense the Solow and the SMAC summon up a clear need among economists for non-neutral, capital-using technical progress.

This was consequently found from the empirical material, among others by M. Brown.† In a particularly heroic attempt to quantify the various facets of shifting production functions, he arrived at a predominance of labour-saving (or capital-using) changes. That restrained the increase in λ and the drop in κ. To put it another way, as a result of technical change capital becomes somewhat scarcer. It must, however, be remarked that this effect did not apply to all periods examined by Brown. Surprisingly, since 1938, and therefore also after the war, the labour-using change has prevailed. This is at variance with the tales about the present explosion of automation; it can be explained by the spectacular expansion of the service sector, for this sector is labour-intensive. Brown's study leads us to surmise that before the war capitalists benefited from technical progress. Without this their share would have shrunk even further than it has done now.

---

*That is to say, instead of $L^\lambda K^{1-\lambda}$ one writes $F(t)L^\lambda K^{1-\lambda}$, in which t represents time. It is assumed here that general productivity rises every year, though without the Cobb-Douglas changing its character; λ remains the same. In this spirit: J. Tinbergen, 'On the Theory of the Trend Movement', *Selected Papers*, 1959. The article in question dates from 1942; it would be written today with more reserve.

† *On the Theory and Measurement of Technological Change*, 1966.

After the war matters were reversed: then labour's share was slightly supported by technology. We thus already have three causes now for the postwar increase in the share of labour: the increased capital intensity, the autonomous wage push and labour-using technical progress. It's almost too much of a good thing.

Anyone who likes forecasting does not have his life made any the easier by these opposing forces. It is practically certain that K/L will increase further. But it is uncertain what σ will do. If automation proceeds to prevail in industry σ will decrease, because with a highly computerized production process there is little to be substituted, however far wages rise. If σ drops further, the share of capital will drop further, under the influence of accumulation. But at the same time automation is capital-using, which pushes up κ. Simultaneously a further expansion of the service sector is probable. This is likely to have a somewhat higher σ, which supports the share of capital. But the provision of services requires a relatively large amount of labour, and that reduces the share of capital again. The net result for the future is therefore uncertain.

But we aren't there yet. In 1956, besides the article by Solow, the celebrated contribution by M. Abramowitz on the determinants of growth was published.* This produced quite a shock. Until then economists had tacitly assumed that capital accretion was the great source of progress. A rich country differs from a poor one because it has more capital per worker. In this reasoning saving and investing are the typical activities that increase prosperity, and technology is a subsidiary phenomenon. Essential, but not decisive. Which was why a production function could be postulated which either remained stationary or shifted solely in a steady and neutral manner.

This picture was rudely disturbed by Abramowitz. He calculated that the historical rise in labour productivity is only very partly due – say 15% of it – to an increase in capital intensity. The lion's share comes from something else: more training of the workers, another quality of capital goods, more efficient working methods –

* 'Resource and Output Trends in the U.S. since 1870', *American Economic Review, Papers and Proceedings*, 1956.

in short, technical progress. The Residual that remains of the growth percentages once the influence of K/L has been deducted proves to be no small, negligible quantity; it dominates development.

This view, confirmed by many other investigators, stresses activities quite different from saving and investing. Education, research, communication, the knowledge industry, learning by doing, these unorthodox subjects suddenly come much more to the fore. And that means to say that the economists have to turn their attention elsewhere. They may no longer regard technical progress as something which is given, which falls like manna from heaven, but as a man-made phenomenon that should be systematically examined. And in fact such examination has since started, but this kind of research is still in its infancy. It is busy changing the face of economic science, though that has not yet penetrated to the textbooks.*

Now what does this mean to our subject, income distribution? Well, one conclusion is self-evident: the increase in the share of labour might very well be connected with the obvious increase in the *quality* of labour. Technical progress is embodied not only in better machines, but also in more productive human beings. The labour force of today looks different from that of 1900 – the skills and the training are much higher, and it is only to be expected that this is reflected in remuneration. (But the quality of the stock of capital goods has also improved – a complication which perhaps reduces λ again?) The increased training is sometimes described as investment in human beings, and this expression suggests that in actual fact there is some return on capital in λ. In this way you could even reason the increase in λ out of existence: part of what we regard as income from work is in actual fact remuneration for investments in the human race. I don't find this very helpful, because it implies making capitalists of workers, with their bodies and minds as capital. That is not a notion to be recommended for income distribution, because it blurs the distinction between material wealth and labour – if we start on that we might as well stop talking about distributive shares. But that does not alter the fact

*Two important special publications are: E. Denison, *Why Growth Rates Differ*, 1967, and J. Schmookler, *Invention and Economic Growth*, 1966.

that the increased training tends to increase the share of labour.*

We are now faced with the problem of the over-explanation. Hicks's Law in itself almost gave a satisfactory reason for the shift in distribution, and according to some even over-explains the increase in λ. Then there was the wage push – except that it led to a higher interest rate as well. Perhaps it was only before the war that technical progress supported capital's share; since the war it has perhaps been more on the side of labour's share. And the increased training is operating in the same direction. The riddle of the falling κ has vanished into thin air – we ought to be more surprised that the trend did not continue much further and that the rentier has not been finished off completely.

However, the question: 'what does technical change mean to income distribution?' has not been fully discussed above – far from it. I am afraid that the more exact answer must be: above all it means greater uncertainty for the student of our problem. The neo-classical theory of production, the only decent instrument we have for understanding long-term developments of distributive shares, has trusted that the production function would not do anything silly. A quiet shift is acceptable, and so is a little non-neutral tilt, if necessary. But if it is true that these shifts in F dominate the increase in production, the neo-classical certainties become shaky. It may be true that in the past technical progress has stayed close to neutrality – Brown's research is reassuring in that respect – but nothing guarantees that it will remain so. It may very well be that in the near future changes in λ and κ will occur that cannot be understood from K/L, at a reasonable value of σ (say something between 0·6 and 1). If κ were to rise suddenly – after falling for half a century – we would have the explanation to hand: capital-using technical progress. But that answer is unsatisfactory as long as we do not know exactly what is going on, and what exactly determines technology. Here we are at the limits of economic science – limits delineated by question-marks.

Nor is this all. Neo-classical theory is useful for explaining the share of labour and that of capital in the narrower sense – it has

---

* As mentioned before (p. 102), the strategic importance of education is strongly defended by G. S. Becker, who also explains the pay structure by this kind of investment.

little grip on profits. That is not so bad as long as we can place profits within the grasp of the theory in another way, i.e. if we can regard them as the reflection of a monopoly situation, that is to say if Kalecki had fully explained them by means of his structural degree of monopoly. And it is not so bad as regards the increase in profit resulting from the demand pull; this too can be understood by economics. But the point is that the size of the pure profit probably depends above all on technical progress. For if production were to take place year in, year out by the same methods, and if exactly the same goods were made time after time, competition would fine down the profit. Even the slowest entrepreneur would gradually manage to force his costs down to the level of his competitors. That is thus the neo-classical equilibrium; all 'profit' is really wage or interest, and pure profits do not exist. Technical progress disturbs this serene picture. It drives production up and separates the quick from the slow. It creates a lead for the one and pushes the other out of the market. Each new product creates profits and losses, each new method creates differences in productivity. These rarely remain unthreatened – competitors imitate, the unions stand by to demand their part – nor do they always come into being at the same places. These differential profits pop up now here, then there. How large they exactly are is not known; probably they are less than 10% of national income. But it is the most dynamic part that originates in that way – and our fine neo-classical equations do not apply to it. We have already regretted this (Chapter IV, 7) but there is no harm in doing so once again. We are faced with the fact that economics points to a problem here but is not able to solve it in an intellectually satisfying way. Perhaps this will come some day.

7. *The Opposite Case: Rents*

The theme of the preceding sections was the shift in income. The shift from capital to labour is explained by opposing forces, the main cause being the accumulation of capital under incomplete substitution. Although our conclusions do not excel in firmness – technical progress in particular queers the pitch, and makes our insights rather uncertain – and we had to contend continually with overexplanation, nevertheless a kind of neo-classical view appears that collapses only when we are concerned with profits. The shares of pure interest and wages can be understood.

Now it seems to me instructive to apply this neo-classical theory to land rent as well. Not because this category of income is so important – most people wildly overestimate the importance of land rent – but because this exercise can tell us something about the strength and the weakness of our theoretical approach. It will appear that now a number of points of view have to be turned 180°, and that in particular Hicks's Law has to be applied the other way round. Perhaps this section is very suitable for breeding scepticism, but that can't be helped.

There is hardly any difference of opinion about the facts, at least among statisticians. The Ricardian prediction that landlords would acquire a steadily growing part of production has not worked out. In the agricultural society at the end of the eighteenth century land rent was probably anything up to 30% of national income. At present it is not more than 2%. For the beginning of this century Feinstein* mentions a British percentage of 12, as against 5% for the Sixties. However, this also includes rents of dwellings, and not only of let houses but also of owner-occupied ones. This rent of dwellings is quite different from land rent; it is interest on an augmentable capital good, and we shall presently see why that income may not be mixed with land rent. Kravis† finds similar figures for the United States: a percentage of 16 at the beginning of this century, and 3·4% fifty years later. These figures also include incomes from residential property. They amount to about 60% of the total; by deducting this we retain less than 2% for the actual rent of land.

This small fraction has led in the above to a rather careless treatment. Following in the footsteps of the literature on two-factor models, we have occasionally treated land as if it were capital. In so doing we do not make any great error from the quantitative point of view, the more so because the income shares of capital

---

* C. H. Feinstein, 'Changes in the Distribution of the National Income in the U.K. since 1860', in: *The Distribution of the National Income*.

† I. Kravis, 'Relative Income Shares in Fact and Theory', *American Economic Review*, 1959.

and land move in the same direction. But the mechanics of land rent is quite different from that of interest, and in that sense we must definitely make a distinction.

This statement will immediately be applauded by all who attribute a special and sometimes rather mystical role to land. I do not particularly welcome these supporters. They are the latter-day descendants of the eighteenth-century physiocrats, who believed that all net income derived from nature; in this view the farmers are the only productive class, while workers, merchants and industrialists simply transform and transport the product and thus form the *classe stérile*. That feeling still persists to some extent, among farmers for instance. In addition there is the moral judgement of the followers of Henry George* that the earth belongs to everyone and not to a small group; the landowners wrongly control the fruits of nature. The Georgists consider this the basic fault of society, which they wish to restore by an appropriate levying of taxation. Take the incomes away from the landowners, and all other taxes become superfluous. With this *single tax* the great conflict that keeps society within its spell disappears, poverty is abolished and the way is open to true progress. This theory still has its adherents, likeable and mainly older people, who overlook the fact that land rent forms such a small percentage of national income: that 2% is nothing compared to the present tax percentages, which are around 30. (I do not mean to say that nationalization of land would not be a good thing; on the contrary, it is possible to make a strong plea for the argument that in a civilized society the government must be the owner of land in order to decide on how town and country should be developed. Nobody accepts free enterprise as a sensible arrangement for town and country planning in densely populated regions, and then it is more efficient if the government holds property rights. But that is primarily a different argument from that of income distribution.)

Although the physiocrats, Ricardo and Henry George have few wholehearted adherents, many people are inclined to exaggerate the importance of land rent. That is understandable. A large number of us pay rent for a home, and part of that is reimburse-

* *Progress and Poverty*, 1878.

ment for the land. Urban sites are expensive, and speculators earn nice sums from it. This stirs the imagination, and it (rightly) forms a reason for government intervention. Everyone now and again gets out into the country, and, although it is subject to decay and contraction, it remains an impressive sight. Everyone knows that mankind cannot live without the products of the soil. All our goods contain natural, i.e. agricultural, raw materials. All this makes a figure of 1-2% for the remuneration of land incredible, and yet that is reality. Land is essential, if only because we have to stand, sit and lie on something – but apparently essentials are not always generously rewarded.

The question that occupies us here is how we are to understand the sharp drop in the share of land. It must be borne in mind that the amount of land by means of which private income is acquired is shrinking rather than expanding. Reclamation and drainage attend to some growth, but on the other hand land is made unavailable for the acquisition of income by the construction of roads, airfields, military training grounds, and so on. The net effect is a contraction of acreage. In this respect this factor of production is unique: while the labour force continues to grow steadily and tirelessly, and the stock of capital goods displays an even stronger upward trend, the amount of land gets smaller.

The reader who has not understood the preceding sections will see nothing strange about this. It seems self-evident that a factor of production that as it were is overgrown with increasing capital and people industriously propagating themselves receives a steadily smaller part of the proceeds. Once upon a time there was nature, with a number of people plus a little bit of capital. Now we see capital goods everywhere and we can't move for people – of course nature has lost ground, also in income distribution. That goes without saying.

But it does not go without saying when we recall that we have explained the declining share of capital above in exactly the opposite way. Formerly people had little capital – it was very scarce and managed to get control over a large part of national income. Now the stock of capital goods has grown relatively strongly, K/L has increased and, according to Hicks's Law, that has led to a drop in κ. This reasoning, applied to land, would lead us to expect a growing share of land. The problem of this section is how we are to get out of that dilemma. There are five solutions, not all of which are equally convincing but worth mentioning.

The first, the product of intuition, entails that Hicks's Law applies only between certain limits. It seems just too silly that a factor of production that plays an ever-smaller part in the production process should have an ever-growing share. Common sense tells us that this process stops sometime. If the factor has become tiny, if it approaches nil quantitatively, it is illogical to expect a maximum share. And in fact the equations on p. 196 conceal a moderating effect: according as the share of a factor is smaller, the elasticity of the share in respect of a more intensive use is also smaller. But that just weakens the reaction, it does not turn it round. Our intuition and our common sense will have to get used to the fact that a small factor of production – say one man, or one gram of a raw material – that is difficult to replace and governs the whole result of production can claim a very large share of the income. Under the laws of scarcity this claim will be honoured.

A much better solution is to abandon the low elasticity of substitution. Admittedly, the students of the SMAC function have found a low σ between labour and capital, but that tells us nothing about the σ between land and the other factors of production. If this measure should become greater than one, our dilemma would disappear. Now as far as I know no measurements have been done on this, but a high σ between land and the other inputs is not improbable. Land is in principle essential, but can in many cases be used more intensively if its price rises. That holds good in agriculture, where more people and above all more machines can be used; the intensity of the growing plan depends above on all price relations. If labour is relatively expensive, few people work on the land with large numbers of machines. If the land rent increases, the farmer opts for labour-intensive products. It also applies to urban planning, where high land rents invite labour-intensive and capital-intensive production (expensive shops) and high-rise buildings. The adjustment of these quantitative relations can be discovered by casual observation; it points to a high value of σ. In this case the constant amount of land and the growing amounts of labour and capital entail a declining share of land rent. That is in conformity with Hicks's Law, except that this is now applied upside down.

A third explanation lies in the contraction of farming. That is one of the great trends of economic development: before the Industrial Revolution this sector was responsible for almost half of national income, and that fraction has now shrunk to below 10% (at least in Britain and the United States; in Australia farming still provides one quarter of the income). The outturn of farmers is a painful process; it is usually accompanied by a continual pressure on personal incomes. As a result agricultural rents are also harmed. The contraction of the farming business has freed land for industry – the transition has been possible without all too sharp increases in land rent.

The same phenomenon can also be described in another way, and that gives us a fourth explanation of the lag in the share of rents. The progress of technology has been land-saving to a large degree. (Whilst, on the other hand, the interest rate is supported by a slightly capital-using technology.) According as the farming business was replaced by industry, less land was needed for production. Of course, a factory too has got to stand on something, and land is therefore essential – but the essential amount is much smaller per unit of product than in farming. And within industry too a further contraction of the required amount of land is going on – miniaturization is not confined to the production of transistors. Against this is the fact that the new and fast-growing sectors of production – services – will perhaps be land-using. That certainly applies to recreation; the flourishing of tourism will not fail to entail an upward influence on the share of land rent unless the government does something about it.

That brings us to a fifth force: government policy. Despite high substitution, a shrinking agricultural sector and land-saving technical progress, local situations have always occurred in which the prices and rents of land have increased quickly. Especially in the neighbourhood of urban developments there are windfall gains for landowners in the air which are universally regarded as unfair. Speculation aggravates this. These practices do not remain unnoticed, and lead to government intervention. Moreover, in practically all countries agriculture is subsidized by the Treasury, and the taxpayer does not like to see these subsidies passed on to the landlord; control of agricultural rents is a way of stopping that. This intervention has further reduced the share of land rent. Nothing of this kind has ever happened with capital – on the contrary, monetary policy tends instead in times of inflation to drive up the interest rate.

Considering the above, we may say that our original surprise at the declining share of land was uncalled for. It is plausible that land plays quite a different part in society from that of capital. In both cases the share has shrunk, but the forces that have led to this result are each other's opposite. Hicks's Law produces contrary results, and probably technical progress does as well. If there is any point to this section, it is that it spotlights this asymmetry.

Now this has its drawback. I can imagine that the reader has acquired the uneasy feeling that economics is a glib business capable of explaining everything, and that we can do what we want with neo-classical theory; in that way there is no question of prediction. If the share of land rent had grown before our eyes to monstrous proportions – say 50% of national income – economists would also have been able to explain that. In fact, they would have done – it would have been their natural duty. Explaining what happens – that's what theory is for. We're only too glad if it comes off. In the present state of the science, prediction of income shares is beyond our capabilities.

8. *Three Kinds of Unemployment*

So far we have not discussed unemployment. This is entirely in agreement with the neo-classical view, which assumes that labour and capital are fully utilized. There is never too much of the one or the other: the possibility of substitution attends to that, in combination with the flexibility of the price relation of labour and capital. Nor is there ever too much of both factors of production at the same time: that is attended to by the flow of purchasing power, which in the classical conception is always enough to take the whole product. That is Say's Law. In these circumstances L and K are given, and Q follows from them. The marginal products and the elasticities of production may be derived from the production function, and there we are.

Everyone knows that in reality unemployment can occur, and unused capital, in the sense of idle machines, is also among the possibilities. The failure to utilize factors of production points to a disturbance in the production process, and it is getting to be time that we examined its effect on income shares. We shall see that the self-evident does not always have to be correct – which is characteristic of macro-economics. For instance, it looks as if mass unemployment – say of 25% of the working population, as in the Thirties – will lop large chunks off the share of labour. However, the opposite may occur, even if we leave unemployment benefit out of account (and we shall do that, because in this chapter we are concerned with primary distribution, i.e. with the incomes that are earned in production – transfer incomes are regarded as belonging to personal distribution, not to income shares).

This result, a possible rise of λ in the face of unemployment, seems paradoxical. And in fact the money wage level will suffer from unemployment – that was the basic idea behind the Phillips curve, which was described, not without a certain liking for it, in Chapter IV. Further, it is true by definition that employment is less in the event of unemployment – and it follows from that that the total wage bill is eaten into from two sides. However, it would be premature to decide from this that λ falls, for it may be that national income itself is also smaller. Indeed, that is probable – but will the total have fallen more strongly or less strongly than the wage bill? To answer that question we need something of a theory.

To get a grip on this issue it is useful to make a distinction between three kinds of unemployment, each of which influences distribution in a different way. In the first place unemployment may be the result of a shortage of purchasing power, as brought about by a depression. That is the case analysed by Keynes in 1936. We call that unemployment through deflation.

In the second place unemployment can come about without sales falling short because of the fact that the stock of capital goods is too small. People can't work without machines, and there are not enough of these. This can sometimes be seen to happen in certain regions of a country. Note that this also requires that substitution is imperfect – for otherwise labour, without capital, could start producing on its own account. Under the Cobb-Douglas the case can therefore hardly occur, but it is possible under the modern production functions. We call this unemployment through shortage of capital. (For capital land may also be read here – that brings us to the tragic situation in overpopulated agricultural countries, where poverty and disguised unemployment go hand in hand.)

In the third place the stock of capital goods may be too large, i.e. the opposite of case 2. The work is done by machines, and human beings are no longer required. This is unemployment through expulsion. It is the bogeyman of those who expect an automated world dominated by robots and emptiness, with income distribution distorted in an unprecedented manner. These three cases will be discussed one by one.

(a) *Unemployment through deflation.* Here our little equation can make itself very useful: the share of labour is equal to the relation between real wage rate and labour productivity. It is not entirely certain what the real wage rate will do in the depression, but the most probable state of affairs is that first prices will fall, and then workers will be dismissed and wages cut. Thus the real wage rate per unit will first rise somewhat and then fall again. The net result depends above all on the strength of the unions. Usually some per unit real wage increase remains over the course of the depression.

Meanwhile labour productivity is displaying an opposite trend. If sales and production fall, it takes some time before the workers are given the sack; employment lags somewhat behind production. That implies an initial drop in labour productivity. If the depression persists, more and more workers will be dismissed, and the trend in the growth of productivity picks up again. True, not as quickly as in more prosperous times, for the productivity trend depends on investments in capital goods, and they only tick over during the depression, but experience shows that all the same labour productivity continues to increase.

From the movement of real wage and labour productivity it follows that in the depression λ first increases somewhat, then falls again. But both movements are weak; they are the marginal result of forces that practically neutralize one another. According to the figures of C. H. Feinstein, the share of labour in Britain in the first half of the Thirties rose somewhat above the level of 1925–29, and then fell somewhat less; the final figure was somewhat above the level of the second half of the Twenties.* That more or less typifies it.

Now in this story unemployment does not explicitly appear, and as a result it sounds hardly credible. After all, large numbers were dismissed during the Depression – but we carry on operating with the relation between real wage and labour productivity, and pay no attention to these dismissals.

And yet this is correct. It surprises me every time I think about it, but unemployment does not belong in this equation. Its influence on the share of labour is eliminated by labour productivity: the relation between the two volumes Q and L. Employment has fallen *because* production, and with it national income, declined. If labour productivity is constant, Q and L go down hand in hand; unemployment then occurs *pari passu* with a drop in everyone's real income. In that case the share of labour is determined exclusively by the movements of the real wage rate. And if this is constant as well, λ is constant. Reality differs from this only in a subtle way. I think that this again proves the utility of the small tautological equation whose praises I have sung above, in section 2.

The share of interest (and land rent) in national income is influenced by the depression in a somewhat more tangible fashion than the share of labour. The average capital productivity will be more inclined to fall than rise through the depression, but let's assume that it remains constant. The nominal interest rate for new loans will also drop, but the interest on old contracts will of course not do so. On average, therefore, the lenders do not receive much less than before the depression. That is to say, in real terms they get more, for they profit from the drop in prices. If the real interest rate rises while capital productivity remains the same (and cer-

* C. H. Feinstein, 'Changes in the Distribution of the National Income in the U.K. since 1860'; in: *The Distribution of the National Income.*

tainly while capital productivity falls!) the pure share of capital in national income grows. (That is to say if we keep out of income the drop in market prices of shares and the accompanying losses on the principal.)

Unemployment through deflation is therefore coupled with a constant or slightly increasing share of labour and a growing share of capital. Is that possible? In the classical theory it is not, for there they add up to unity; however, we are not talking about a classical situation, but a depression. It is fitting that we then make allowance for profit, and more particularly for the influence of the depression on it. And then it is immediately clear what happens: it is the share of profit that bears the brunt of the depression. Entrepreneurs' incomes have absorbed the first onslaught and try to pass it on; that fails in the direction of capital, because long-term contracts have been concluded with a fixed rate of interest, and it also fails with regard to labour because money wages more or less keep pace with prices. From a viewpoint of income shares, the entrepreneurs are the losers. Both the drop in sales and the fall in the profit margin bring them losses.

The reasoning applies the other way round to periods of marked expansion. If total demand increases strongly, profits swell the most; we have already seen that before when we were discussing Föhl's theory. The wage bill can more or less keep up as a rule, except when productivity suddenly rises sharply above the trend in one year. Such a spurt almost always reduces the share of labour for the benefit of profits. Later, wage inflation comes along to restore λ to its original level. But all the time κ is under pressure; the rentiers are the victims of the rapid expansion and the matching inflation. The case is symmetrical with that of the depression, and once again unemployment does not stand in the way of this symmetry.

It is true that unemployment through deflation – the case that we have been examining so far – fits badly into neo-classical thought, but all the same it is not so that the characteristic reasoning that circles around the production function is put out of court. A fixed relation continues to exist between inputs and output, even though not all inputs are utilized; marginal productivities can still be pointed to, and the elasticity of production does not lose its meaning. The only difference with full-blown neo-classicism is that the production function is read backwards: Q determines how much L and K are required. It is not L and K that determine Q, but sales $C + I$. If we had wanted to, we could also have analysed this case with the usual instrument of production elasticities. The main reason why we did not do so above is because we needed profits as the third category of income – the elasticities of the production function have no hold on that.

However, the applicability of the neo-classical theory disappears entirely in the following case:

(b) *Unemployment through shortage of capital*. Here we see labour become plentiful, while the stock of capital goods is fully used. It is to be expected that K/L will become as small as the elasticity of substitution permits, in other words that the entrepreneurs will hire all the labour that they can place. For labour is cheap, and K is the limiting factor in production.

Of course it may be asked how it comes that K remains so small and why large sums are not invested to eliminate the acute shortage of capital. The bottleneck may lie in expectations for the future: entrepreneurs see insufficient potential sales in the future (in the *present*, by the way, sales are still going smoothly – if not, we end up in case 'a'). It may also be that the entrepreneurs are rather slow: old industries suffering from hardening of the arteries, as are to be found in some regions. In underdeveloped countries the brake on investments may be of a political nature: entrepreneurs distrust the internal stability and the government, and prefer to send their profits abroad. However that may be, the stock of capital goods is too small and L – perhaps because of too rapid a population growth – is too large.

The neo-classical theory cannot help us further here. After all, it assumes substitutability, and in this case the latter has reached its limit. This implies that additions of labour to the given stock of capital goods yield no further additional product. The marginal product of labour is nil, and according to neo-classical theory wage is also nil. The same goes for labour's share. This is of course out of the question.

We must now escape the neo-classical theory by assuming that wage is determined by something else – for instance by a physical minimum *à la* Ricardo, by social conventions or by collective agreements. It is difficult to say where this wage level lies. It is probably low, but how low we do not know. We had best assume that the wage level is given – which means that we do not know the causes.

And bang goes the distribution theory. The share of labour will doubtless be relatively small, and the share of capital high. Real wage will lag behind average labour productivity, although the latter is not particularly high either, owing to the shortage of capital. Exact equations cannot be found in this way. The case is indeterminate in all directions.

It is in this situation that the competitors of neo-classical distribution theory – power and social theories – raise their heads. Unfortunately they lack an exact formulation, a firm backbone, and consequently they can hardly be quantified or tested. This does not mean to say that social power (especially that of the unions) is irrelevant; on the contrary, if in the event of an abundance of labour and sharply limited capital wages wish to rise above the bare minimum, unions, social conventions and perhaps the government will have to bring that about. In this situation the forces of the market are no friends of the worker. But these findings do not give us a well-defined theory.

This dilemma may be avoided in principle in quite a different way, namely that of disaggregation. This sometimes yields a determinate system. We must then assume that not one product is made, but at least two, and that each production process has its own capital and labour input; call these K_n and L_n, in which n equals 1 or 2. Further, the total money proceeds of each product are given. Call the latter Y_n and assume that no profit is made. Then, for each product, $WL_n + RK_n = Y_n$. Here L_n, K_n and Y_n are given, and we have two unknowns, W and R. We suppose that the wage level and the interest rate are the same in both sectors. These can be solved from the two equations. If we also wish to determine profit, we need three branches of industry and three equations. Since you can put anything down on paper, we can also write down ten branches of industry and ten inputs, with which all prices of the inputs are established. As the amounts of all inputs and outputs are given, this also explains the distributive shares.

This theory was described for the first time in 1924 by F. von Wieser*, who regarded it as the universal solution to the distribution problem. He thought that fixed coefficients formed a more realistic hypothesis than substitution, and therefore had to abandon marginal productivity. This view is logically consistent, but that is all that can be said about it. The extreme disaggregation makes it inoperable, since we do not know the equations for the various products. Moreover, it is assumed that in all sectors fixed relations prevail between labour and capital, and that is really going a little too far, even for the special case of an absolute abundance of labour that we have in mind here.

We therefore do not get much further than that in this special situation the share of labour will be forced down. That certainly helps to explain why λ is so low in some underdeveloped countries.

(c) *Unemployment through expulsion.* This is the opposite of (b). Here capital is not scarce, as in the last case, but in abundant supply. The relation K/L has risen so much that, given the state of Q, there is too little employment left for the working population. Technical development has apparently been labour-saving to an overwhelming extent, and perhaps moreover the population has grown explosively. Machines make the consumer goods and they also make themselves. A small number of human beings keep an eye on this process, control it (let us hope), talk and write about it, but for the rest the robots do the job. Humans no longer work.

This case at present haunts the papers and science fiction. This bogeyman is not a new one – Marx too predicted a world in which the capitalists, as a result of their accumulation, would dismiss more and more workers. Before we consider in further detail the distribution of the income produced by robots and computers it is worth while establishing that the completely automated economy does not resemble ours in the slightest. It is generally whispered and suggested, and in some branches of industry – chemistry – people believe that they can detect the signs of the world of to-

* *Grundriss der Sozialökonomik, Theorie der gesellschaftlichen Wirtschaft,* 1924.

morrow, but I venture to doubt whether machines will really make work superfluous. So far the development has been quite different. It is true that here and there some unemployment has resulted from the introduction of machines and computers. But that has always been the case, since the end of the eighteenth century. Textile workers, miners and farmers and recently clerical workers too have undergone the consequences of technical change in an extremely unpleasant way. This can create nasty situations, especially if redundancy concentrates on special groups: the old, the weak, the coloured. But the unemployment was always rather temporary and rather inconsiderable from the macro-economic point of view. Again and again it was absorbed by a growing aggregate volume of production. Q tended to rise more quickly than Q/L. In fact this expulsion of labour is the basis for progress: the tremendous rise of labour productivity in farming released labour for the development of the manufacturing industry. The increase in Q/L in the factories freed people for the service sector. However painful unemployment was for older workers and for people who continued to live in a depressed area, it was confined to the frictional form, a marginal phenomenon. Broadly speaking, employment increased through the phenomenal rise in production. The labour-intensive services (education, the communications industry, travel) called for more and more people. Moreover working hours have been shortened – a continuous process, which would not have been possible without more extensive mechanization and automation. The almost full employment that is now characteristic of the Western countries is in flagrant contradiction to all the pessimistic predictions of an empty, workless world. And, as we have seen, a drop in the share of labour has not occurred either. People are scarcer than ever, especially if they are well trained and highly skilled.*

Now this is not to say that matters will remain like this. It is conceivable that all the trends observed will reverse, and that we shall presently witness a decline in employment caused by Q/L

* Automation is already creating social problems in sectors, and discriminating against people who are in any case at the bottom end of income distribution. But that is another matter; it relates to personal distribution, not to distributive shares.

continually rising more quickly than Q. Theoretically, a macro-economic production process is conceivable that is reminiscent of the image of the chemical industry today, and even going much further. There is nothing against using our imagination about such production by machines. But we must realize that this society is radically different from ours, and that its institutional arrangements will also be radically different. There is little point in pondering this society in terms of neo-classical theory, which assumes that scarce factors of production are remunerated on a basis of their marginal contributions. If we were to do that, we should have to conclude that in the automated world the average product of labour Q/L would be enormously high (for Q rises, while L has become almost nil), while the marginal product of labour would be practically zero. As a result the share of labour would in fact fall to nil, and the share of capital would be in the neighbourhood of 100%.

However, this conclusion is meaningless, because in such a world wages would be detached from the marginal productivity of labour by institutional arrangements. It is not conceivable that a society would accept a wage rate adjusted to a market mechanism in which labour is completely superabundant. A wage rate equal to zero, or a Marxist wage rate at subsistence minimum, would in any case create a phenomenal deflationary gap – who would consume the product of automated society? Surely not the small group of owners of means of production – they would be physically incapable of all that consumption.

The point of such a fantasy is that it demonstrates the need for institutional change. This can assume three forms: either the ownership of capital is drastically widened, so that the workers can live on their interest. Or – more probably – income distribution will be detached from productive contributions. People will receive a money income on the strength of the fact that they exist, not on the basis of their work. That amounts to generous State benefit for everyone. It will not be difficult to levy taxation: after all, the capitalists earn the whole of national income, and a national income that will be many times what it is today. Taxation will have to rise to, say, 90% of the national income. This amounts to a kind of socialism, and it may be efficient to nationalize the material means of production. Moreover, working hours will be drastically shortened, mock jobs will be created, people will take turns at doing work on a large scale – the small amount of real work will be supplemented by artificial work to spread the income.

Now some of these developments are in fact going on. Social provisions are increasing, the government guarantees minimum incomes independently of a person's contribution to production. The steady shortening of working hours has assumed spectacular forms, and it will certainly continue further. A great deal of work is done that does not seem urgent – in both the private and the official bureaucracies, in the advertising business, in the production of rubbish that nobody really wants – and some see in that a sign of the corruption of capitalism. This is all interesting material for discussion, but the point here is that there has been no mass unemployment through expulsion. Most people have to work hard for their living. The share of labour is not falling, but rising. In this sense it is not labour but capital that is becoming abundant. It is a good thing that we ponder the possible case in which mass redundancy occurs, and that we devise possible arrangements for making it run smoothly if it ever comes – it is not a good thing that we take science fiction fantasies for the real thing.

9. *The World Must Mesh*

Perhaps the reader is gradually longing for a theoretical system fitting neatly together in which everything drops exactly into place: productivity, substitution, changed scarcity, imperfect competition, unions, social conventions, the state of general demand, technical progress, redundancy of labour, increased training, everything. I should like nothing better than to satisfy this wish: a synthesis seems to me a suitable ending to this chapter. But an exact model, in which everything tallies, is wishful thinking. We can, however, use the various ideas side by side and for the one phenomenon call on the aid of the one theory and for the other another theory. In other words, to explain λ and κ we fall back on neo-classical analysis of the fundamental scarcity relations (supplemented by the thesis that when $\sigma < 1$ the unions can increase the share of labour by wage push), for profit on a series of not too sharp insights regarding competition, the state of demand and technical progress, and for land rent on the declining share of agriculture, which of course has pulled the share of land rent down with itself, and also on Hicks's Law when $\sigma > 1$. This does supply a loose-knit overall picture, but not an exact model: no self-contained system of mathematical relations describing reality comprehensively. Not one theory, but eclecticism, and to many that is a dirty word.

There has been no lack of attempts at synthesis. These have been typified as 'unholy marriages',* and there is something in that, for the neo-classical theory suffers from a dominating character. After all, it claims in itself to give a self-contained picture from which only the pure profits stand out. The incomes of General Motors and Yves St Laurent can then be tackled separately. That can if necessary be done by the neo-classical theory of limited competition, but so far that has not yet come forward with much that is convincing.† Unions, social convention, inflation and deflation are difficult to tie in with the marginalism that is the core of neo-classical thought.

And yet this is not the whole story. A real synthesis must even contain more than has been under discussion so far in this chapter. For we have looked at distribution solely from the production side; it is there and on the markets for productive contributions that the incomes come about. We have tacitly assumed that insight into these processes is enough to ponder on, and forget that macro-economics is not satisfied with one-way traffic. Income distribution influences in its turn production, consumption and investments, and price level, and taxes, and foreign trade; and all these in turn influence distribution! In a macro-system all these processes must mesh. There is only one current world, in which all relations are simultaneously realized. This truth has imposed itself on us only once, when Kaldor's theory was under discussion (λ and κ must

* By F. Modigliani, on p. 45, in the collection *The Behavior of Income Shares*, mentioned above on several occasions.

† J. G. M. Hilhorst, *Monopolistic Competition, Technical Progress and Income Distribution*, 1964. Limited competition has been analysed since 1933 by E. H. Chamberlin and his school, but that is micro-economics. In Hilhorst the transition to macro-economics leads to a casuistry that is so nit-picking that the reader is discouraged from reading further.

work out in such a way that $S = I$), and we scornfully disposed of that. It is now time to see just what relations we have lost sight of.

If we were to take this task seriously we would now have to build a tremendous system of equations that fully describes production, i.e. $Q = F(L, K)$, income creation and income spending in accordance with the equation $Y = C + I$ (see section 4 above), and which takes all feedbacks in its stride. Praiseworthy, though not entirely successful, attempts in that direction have been undertaken, among others by W. Krelle in Germany* and D. B. J. Schouten in the Netherlands.† These tremendous batteries of equations (with as their centrepiece economic growth) are, however, so complex that they would require a whole book to themselves. The serious student will just have to wade through the originals. This will be no easy task for him; Krelle has said that his fellow-economists did not understand him,‡ and that does not surprise me at all. I too have the greatest difficulty with his models, and I still regard their obscurity as a drawback. Strategic and non-strategic relations are piled on top of one another, important and unimportant aspects both call for a great deal of attention – the reader tires and is inclined to pack it in. Instead of reproducing these systems I shall take from the general model a number of subrelations concerning the essential feedbacks from distribution to the other quantities. They can perhaps best be given in such a way that we write down the conditions that have to be fulfilled to make the quantities fit together and that we specify the movements that take place if these

---

Verteilungstheorie, 1962. One of Krelle's remarkable propositions is that forces that change the share of labour in the short run work exactly the other way round in the long run. I disagree; to Krelle the 'long run' is the neo-classical path of balanced growth, a highly misleading conception. For instance, an interest rate that has been forced up lowers the share of labour, but inhibits growth, so that the share of labour rises again. Personally I do not believe that interest is all that important to the growth rate of production.

† Together with A. H. J. Kolnaar: *Dynamische macro-economie*, 1967. Schouten too is hypnotized by the neo-classical growth theory, in which all quantities (consumption, investments, production) move in predestined paths.

‡ 'The Laws of Income Distribution in the Short Run and in the Long Run: an Aggregative Model', *The Distribution of National Income*, 1968, p. 413.

conditions are not complied with. As a result the following list of ten points acquires a somewhat normative appearance; these are the norms of economic equilibrium, which sometimes materialize.

(a) Sufficient income must end up with the people with a high propensity to consume (or, in free translation: λ must be high enough) to create a wide and growing market for consumer goods. If not, sales are insufficient and a depression comes about. J. A. Hobson worried about this unfavourable possibility a hundred years ago, and the idea of structural underconsumption also occurs in Marx. In these inflationary times the case hardly seems topical. Should it occur, profit will fall above all, because this reacts more sharply to falling sales than wage does, so that λ increases again. A certain automatism operates in distribution which absorbs a deflationary shock. (Unfortunately, at the same time destabilizing forces are active in other fields; investments in particular are unstable.)

(b) The converse condition is more topical: λ may not become so large that consumption (plus investments, plus government expenditure) becomes greater than productive capacity. For then inflation occurs. As long as this is a pure demand inflation profits will increase and λ shrink; after that a wage push can easily occur that increases λ again. This interplay of the demand pull and the cost push is not automatically stopped. It is the task of the government to keep total spending within bounds by taxation and restriction of government expenditure and to damp down the wage-price-wage spiral, but experience shows that this is sometimes less than a complete success. (In addition, the wage-price-wage spiral can also occur under its own steam, independently of overspending – that is discussed under point (i) below.)

(c) Investments must be high enough to keep growth going. It is difficult to say what requirements this makes of λ. The classical reasoning is that if λ is high, S will be small, and S determines I.*

* It is at least naïve and at most misleading when Krelle simply postulates a curve $q = f(\lambda)$, which reproduces a negative relation (q is the growth rate of production). This does not fit into a rather sophisticated model, and is at variance with experience: the rise in production has accelerated while the share of labour has increased. ('The Laws of Income Distribution in the Short Run and in the Long Run', *The Distribution of National Income*, p. 420.)

Keynesian reasoning arrives at the opposite conclusion: I depends on sales, and so on consumption – the higher λ is, the more demand there is, and the more I, and the finances for this come of their own accord. It is difficult to say what exactly predominates, the classical or the Keynesian reaction. However, it is at all times necessary that pure profit is high enough, for that is what drives expansion. Some authors* assume that forcing up wages reduces profit, but that is not certain; the wage increase can be passed on, and the entrepreneurs can adjust their margins to it. On paper you can cook up anything; experience shows that profit is not easily affected macroeconomically by forcing up λ, not even as a percentage of national income. Micro-economically speaking, an increase in wages will reduce some profits, but other entrepreneurs profit precisely from the greater purchasing power of the wage recipients. The net result proves to be a small one, and the effect of a wage increase on investments is more positive than negative.

(d) The distributive shares may have a feedback to technical progress. It is possible, but we know little about it. Occasional attempts have been made to give such a relation a theoretical foundation, but these attempts are not very convincing. I am thinking of Kaldor's Technical Progress Function,† which couples the growth rate of Q to the growth rate of K, and so arrives at a constant capital-output ratio – a forced construction, which moreover suffers from all the defects of Kaldor's 'Keynesian' theory criticized above. It is conceivable that the feedback operates via the share of pure profit – differential profits are devoted to research, and the research keeps profits up to the mark. This suggests a technological two-equation model of economic growth, by which profits and research expenditure are determined. An interesting idea, but one not verified in practice. There is quite a lot of research still to be done in this field.

(e) Another and quite different relation can be established between C, I, λ and κ. Suppose that the workers buy mainly consumer goods, and the non-workers mainly capital goods, and that these two kinds of goods are produced under different technical conditions; there are consequently two production functions side

* For instance Schouten, *Dynamische macro-economie*, Vol. 1, p. 114.
† 'A Model of Economic Growth', *Economic Journal*, 1957.

by side. Suppose that capital goods require more capital (a high κ) and that the consumer goods industry shows a high λ. Two kinds of relations then exist between C and I on the one hand and λ and κ on the other, and from this a determinate two-sector model can be built up. Such exercises have been performed quite frequently in recent times, and they can lead to particularly ingenious constructions.* Instead of two sectors the national economy can be divided into n sectors, each with its own production function and its own income distribution; the total distribution must then tally with the way in which the income recipients divide their purchases among n goods. I respect this kind of mental gymnastics, but I find one production function difficult enough. I am not convinced of the practical utility of these models – for the relation C/I depends not only on income distribution, but on many other causes, such as technical progress, which operate much more strongly than the relation λ/κ. The n-sector equilibrium models with flexible K/L relations are for the time being just ingenious exercises for advanced economists.

(f) If the tax laws are given, tax yield depends on λ, among other things. It has recently been found that a rapid increase in λ (through wage explosions) has disappointing results for the tax authorities – the tax yield is smaller than might have been expected from the development of national income. As government expenditure does not shrink correspondingly, this leads to budgetary deficits that foment expenditure inflation. This in turn often leads to an increase in profits, so that λ is forced back down again to some extent. There is a slight tendency towards the restoration of equilibrium.

(g) The share of pure capital (i.e. interest) may not become so small that the capitalists are no longer prepared to lend their holdings on the market. This is a prerequisite of the functioning of the capitalist system, but it does not look as if this bottom limit has ever been in sight. The supply of capital is occasionally held

* For instance J. E. Meade, *A Neo-Classical Theory of Economic Growth*, 1961, and *The Growing Economy* (Vol. II of *Principles of Political Economy*), 1968. In the latter book, incidentally, Meade displays a preference for a fixed K/L, which makes matters simpler but does not improve them for distribution theory.

back as a reaction to what is considered too low a level of interest, but this is of short duration, and immediately brings about a rise in interest. There is probably a natural bottom limit to the rate of interest, so that this prerequisite is always complied with, despite rising prices and the drop in the share of pure capital.

(h) The share of land rent may not become so small that land-owners are no longer prepared to make their land available. This cannot happen with an inelastic supply, nor under a 'natural' market mechanism. But government intervention in land rents, which is very widespread, may lead to insufficient investment in land, so that the quality declines.

(i) The income shares must be accepted by the pressure groups. This relates in particular to λ. If everyone, and the unions in particular, tries to increase his share by pushing up the rates of remuneration, the wage-price-wage spiral is inevitable, and as a rule this leads to an increase in λ, pure profit is maintained and the share of pure capital decreases. We have even seen (section 9 of Chapter IV) that the pursuit of a *constant* share of labour, in combination with oligopolistic behaviour on the part of the price-fixers, is enough to lead to a spiral; this applies *a fortiori* to a general struggle for a relatively better position. (It should be added that the dissatisfaction that leads to action, such as strikes, does not always have to be based on knowledge of the figures of distributive shares. Perhaps a union does not have these figures available – perhaps it couldn't care less – and some workers simply consider their pay too low, compared with other wage rates. This kind of dissatisfaction about the pay structure can be so penetrating that not a single value of λ yields stability, and then the chance of a spiral is always present.)

Once the cost push starts, it is difficult to stop; it has no natural equilibrium. As long as expenditure is wide enough, and employment remains full, there is no end in sight. This does not come until the price level becomes too high for the foreign customers and exports stagnate. Profits in the export firms suffer, and this propagates itself further in wages. In the meantime the expansion of production is checked. Before the spiral is suppressed in this way, quite a lot has to happen with regard to stagnation and unemployment; that becomes clear from the Phillips curve (see Chapter IV, 9).

Long before then the government has already devalued the currency, as a result of which exports pick up again; then the spiral can continue. Another potential brake – the amount of money – is equally ineffective. The monetary authorities can put the screws on a little, give the banks strict warnings and act as if they really mean business, but what they cannot do is risk a liquidity crisis; they therefore have to accept the wage and price inflation, muttering their disapproval the while. That is why governments nowadays resort to a direct combating of cost push : incomes policy. We shall come back to that in Chapter VII, 3.

(j) Income distribution must tally with the international division of labour. The neo-classical theory considers the scarcity of the factors of production, and this differs considerably from country to country; labour crosses frontiers with difficulty, capital does so more easily but still imperfectly, and land stays where it is. In a well-known theory attributed to the Swedes E. Hekscher and B. Ohlin, the international trade in products is regarded as a substitute for the international movement of labour, capital and land. As a result trade shifts income distribution. A country that is poor in capital will import goods containing a relatively large amount of capital; this will reduce κ. The United States is a country that is rich in capital; according to the Hekscher-Ohlin doctrine, it will import goods requiring a large amount of labour, and this will reduce λ. If the domestic pressure groups were to counter these imports – for instance by import duties – the overall prosperity would be reduced, but the absolute prosperity of the protected factor of production may be greater than it would have been without protection.

The above ten relations ought to occur in some way or the other in a model that claims to be complete. Such a system is anything but easy to handle. If you ask me whether all this is absolutely necessary, I have to reply: no. An exhaustive treatment is too high an aim in the present state of our knowledge. I would prefer to consider the odd strategic feedback. The most important are perhaps points (d) and (i).

Point (d), the two-way interdependence of pure profit and technical progress, is a structural characteristic of modern society.

Even if we are unaware of the exact quantitative relations, it is not too bold to assume that this interdependence preserves capitalism. Whether you like it or not, it is a point to bear in mind when we presently discuss political problems and the possibilities of changing income distribution. Point (i) relates to the struggle of the pressure groups, with its many feedbacks to incomes and prices. Taken together, points (d) and (i) describe the milieu in which the scarcity relations are translated into income shares; that fundamental process is best understood by the marginal productivity theory on the basis of a Solow function. Hicks's Law shows how the accumulation of capital forces down the share of capital and that of land. But the increase in the share of labour can also be explained in another way: by technical progress, which changes the elasticities of production, and more particularly by the specific form of technical progress which is called investment in human beings. The capital of human skills is now competing with the capital embodied in machines – and that has reduced the income share of the latter. The pressure groups wage battle about the outcome of that competitive process. In fact income distribution is over-explained. Too many theories are chasing the same scanty facts.

If the reader still finds this too complicated he can fall back on the tautology of section 2: the share of labour is equal to the quotient of the real wage rate and labour productivity, and the share of capital is equal to the quotient of interest and capital productivity. True, this does not reveal any causal relations, but by means of this equation one can follow what happens. As a rule the rough-and-ready statistics are present: figures for year after year, and even for quarter after quarter, movements of wage levels, price levels and productivity are quickly available. Journalists, union leaders and politicians can take advantage of the insights that the little tautology provides. If the average money wage rises more percentagewise than the price index plus labour productivity, λ rises (you must, however, take care that the price increase is freed from the influence of taxes and import prices). The opposite occurs if demand rises quickly or productivity displays a quick spurt; then the share of profit increases. If the money wage rises more than the price index plus labour productivity, real wages rise, but λ

drops. If the money wage rises more than labour productivity, wage inflation occurs. In the event of wage inflation λ may rise or fall; we usually see a rise. Anyone who understands these relations can boast of a useful starting point without having made his life complicated by advanced economics.

There is thus choice enough between the theories on distributive shares. The phenomenon is complex, which offers scope for hobby-horses and eclecticism: the knitting together of pieces of different theories. I am a proponent of the latter, but I do not wish to impose this opinion on the reader. Just as long as he does not believe in magic constants that are not constant or in very limited relations that have to unveil all secrets of income distribution. That kind of prejudice leads to intellectual games but hardly to insight into recalcitrant reality.

CHAPTER VI

Personal Distribution

In Chapter III we presented some of the facts of personal distribution. It was shown there that these can be displayed in alternative ways, which draw the observer's attention to different properties of the statistical facts. It is now time for explanations, and obviously we want to use concepts and theories that we have been dealing with in the previous chapters. However the curious point is that the most venerable endeavours to analyse personal distribution show a very different character from the theories of supply and demand, marginal productivity, and so on that we met in the preceding pages. The best example of these different methods, and one of the earliest, is the work of the Italian economist Wilfredo Pareto.

1. *Pareto's Law*

At the end of the last century he studied the income tax data then known. There were figures from various states and times: Prussia, Basle, Britain, Augsburg (in the fifteenth century!), Peru, Perugia, Saxony, Florence. He felt that there was a certain regularity in these curves, which has been known since then as Pareto's Law. This was the first time that income distribution had been subjected to an empirical examination in depth: after Pareto had started the work, a flood of studies followed. Variants and descendants of the law were drawn up and verified. This greatly stimulated insight into distribution. By-products were a new graphical presentation and a criterion, the α of Pareto, which is still used for characterizing the skewness of the distribution.

The basic idea is that there is a fixed relation between a certain income, which we may choose at random, and the number of persons earning *this income or a higher income*. I shall first show the relation in the form of an equation, and then explain it again in words. Let us call the income level y. We can fill in arbitrary figures for this symbol. Call the number of persons earning an income of y or higher N_y. It is clear that N_y decreases as we choose a higher y. The extent to which this happens is shown by Pareto's Law, which runs as follows: $N_y = \dfrac{A}{y^\alpha}$.

Here A is a not particularly important constant; it is concerned with the units in which income is expressed. But α *is* important. It is a constant in the sense that we can vary y and N_y but that their interrelation is always described by the same α. This 'constant of Pareto' is, however, not constant in the sense that Peru, Perugia, Britain and Augsburg display the same α. The larger α is, the more quickly the number of people drops if we choose a higher income, and the smaller the inequality. The law is also often written as $N_y = A.y^{-\alpha}$, which to some readers may appear even more cryptic than the form which we first wrote down. But it can also be put into words, although this is seldom done in the textbooks.

In words Pareto's Law amounts to saying that the number of income recipients earning at least a given income decreases by a fixed *percentage*, if we let that income increase by 1%. This percentage is α. Suppose that we have established that in a given country $\alpha = 2$, then we can state the law as follows: imagine a certain income – the Selected Income Level – and count how many people earn this or a higher income; now perform the same operation with an income that is 1% higher, and the number of income recipients will have become 2% smaller. Whichever Selected Income Level we start with, the same percentage always emerges. The α is therefore a member of the large family of elasticities (see p. 25 above). The law can also be formulated in this way: the elasticity of the number of persons above each Selected Income Level is constant, and therefore independent of the choice of this Selected Income Level.

It goes without saying that Pareto and others attached deep importance to this regularity. It is a surprising discovery, and the idea of a fixed law of nature imposes itself. At first it was thought that the α for various countries and times would be about the same, but that is not so. In poor countries with great inequality we find a figure of 1·5; later research shows that in richer countries with greater equality a value of 2 can be reached, or sometimes a little higher. The figure is used to characterize the degree of levelling; a higher α points to less inequality. In their enthusiasm some authors have attributed to α a decisive importance for great historical events; for instance H. T. Davis* believed that a revolution would break out as soon as α fell below 1·3. This is an over-simplification; revolutions are brought about by more complicated causes.

The relation between the number of people N_y and the Selected Income Level y can of course also be shown in graphical form (see Fig. 6). We then plot y on the horizontal axis and N_y on the vertical. The form of the function suggests that we should preferably take not the numbers themselves but their logarithms; we therefore use double logarithmic paper. Pareto's Law is now reproduced by a straight line, because $\log N_y$ is proportionate to $\log y$. The tangent of the angle which this line makes with the horizontal axis is equal to α. The dotted line represents the average.

I can imagine that many readers find this law a difficult affair. The logarithmic function is not easy to grasp; even many economists have difficulty with it. But the relation between an arbitrary income y and what goes on above it can also be formulated in another way, and then everything becomes a good deal clearer. Some thought is again called for, but the exercise seems worthwhile.

The reader must first try to grasp a reformulation of Pareto's Law devised by C. Gini.† He too starts from a certain income y and from the number of people N_y who earn at least y; but, unlike Pareto, Gini does not consider the relation between N_y and y but makes the matter more complicated in the first instance. He establishes the total income earned by these N_y persons; we call this Y. Gini now establishes a functional connexion between N_y and Y, viz.:

$$N_y = B . Y^\beta.$$

Here too B is a constant connected with the correct choice of units of measurement, while β is a criterion of income distribution.

* *The Analysis of Economic Time Series*, 1941.

† A series of publications from 1912 onwards in Italian, plus a paper for the Cowles Commission of 1935: *On the Measure of Concentration with Special Reference to Income and Wealth*.

Gini found this law empirically, just as Pareto did his; it proved afterwards that the two functions can be transposed into each other. In words Gini's Law is as follows: imagine a certain income, i.e. a Selected Income Level, see how many people earn this income, or more, and how much they together earn in total. Then

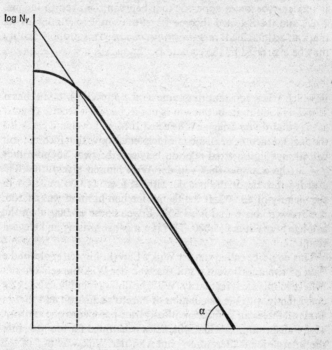

Figure 6. *Pareto line*

lower the Selected Income Level by exactly such an amount that the total income has increased by 1%; consequently, the number of people increases by a fixed percentage (β) which we repeatedly find at every Selected Income Level that we pick.

Gini's equation is hardly less obscure than that of Pareto; Y is no easier to use than y, and if we translate the relation into words there is also a marked increase in the haze surrounding it. But a great step forward was taken by J. van der Wijk* and others. He replaced the variable Y, i.e. the *total* income above a limit y, by the *average* income above a limit y. This is therefore Y/N_y. At first sight this seems to make matters even more complicated. But then it suddenly becomes apparent that between the average income Y/N_y and the Selected Income Level the simplest relation exists that can be imagined: *they are proportionate*. This proportionality may be expressed by the equation

$$\frac{Y}{N_y} = \gamma.y$$

in which γ is a constant (the same as the β of Gini). It still has a scholarly look to it, but now it is not as bad as it seems. What it says is that if you imagine a Selected Income Level and establish the average income of all income recipients above that income, you will always find a fixed relation between the two. Suppose that $\gamma = 3$ (the example that van der Wijk himself gives), then the average income of the people with at least £1,000 must be in the vicinity of £3,000. If the figure one had in mind was £1,500, the average above that is £4,500. If we choose £5,000, then the average above it is £15,000. This is a most surprising and elegant result.

This could be called van der Wijk's Law (he himself spoke of the 'law of averages') were it not that van der Wijk himself did not believe in this fixed regularity. What he did was simply to carry on consistently with the calculation of Pareto's equation and that of Gini; all three can be mathematically transposed into one another. This transposition is a feat which has penetrated far too little into the international literature.† But van der Wijk was not of the opinion that Pareto's equation correctly describes income distribution. Come to that, the weakness of the three relations is also immediately apparent from the equation; if we put the Selected Income Level at nil, the average income would also become nil,

---

* J. van der Wijk, *Inkomens- en vermogensverdeling*, 1939.

† Incidentally a similar equation was developed by C. Bresciani (1910), and it was also used by the British statistician Bowley and others. The equation is known to statisticians. but most economists are not acquainted with it. It does not appear in the usual textbooks.

and that is absurd. Van der Wijk himself was therefore an adherent of another empirical law, the Gibrat distribution, to which we shall return below.

Criticism of Pareto's equation as a *general* law of distribution is now pretty universal. If the variables y and N_y, as described above, are plotted on double logarithmic paper, the result is not an exactly straight line. Only for the high incomes do the empirical data lie close to or on the straight line; for the lower incomes this does not tally very well, and for the lowest incomes it does not work out at all. And we can see this coming, too, because as the levelling process continues we come closer and closer to a kind of line that is different as can be from a straight line, namely two straight lines at right angles to one another. It is an instructive exercise to ponder on this case for a moment: if everyone earns exactly the same we find only one point instead of a straight line. Below the average y there are no people to be found ($N_y = 0$). At the average income we suddenly encounter everybody ($N_y = N$). Pareto's straight line changes into two sections of line at an angle of 90°. Reality gives a reflection – a very faint one – of this. If we reproduce the points found from the empirical data as well as possible by a line, this is not straight; there is a slight curve in it. This is shown as a heavy line in Fig. 6; the curvature gives an exaggerated picture of reality.

On the basis of this curve some investigators, such as Mary J. Bowman,* have sought other appropriate functions; however, these experiments have not yet yielded any results that are theoretically usable. But therewith Pareto's Law has been abandoned for income structure *as a whole*. It applies only to the straight tail of the frequency distribution, i.e. for the higher incomes. For the top 10% it is a usable approach.

The reader may be wondering why we have dwelt so long on supposed regularities which in fact do not completely fit the statistical evidence. The reason is that the efforts of Pareto, Gini and others, though they have not yielded any genuine 'laws', have tremendously stimulated thought processes through their empirical research. In the course of this intellectual process interesting points of view have come to the fore, and an attempt has also been

* 'A Graphical Analysis of Personal Income Distribution in the United States', *American Economic Review*, 1945.

INCOME DISTRIBUTION

made to find the social backgrounds for the empirical findings. As
the first instance of this, reference may be made to the hypothesis
of W. Winkler.*

Winkler attempts to explain a distribution curve displaying
marked skewness to the right, and he is inspired by the mathematical form of Pareto's Law. His starting point is the possibility
of a given person obtaining a higher income. Three cases may be
imagined: the chance of 'improving oneself' is about the same for
all income classes; the further someone climbs the income ladder
the more difficult it becomes to reach the higher rungs; the higher
someone gets the easier it goes. Winkler chose the last possibility,
and shows that this is quite consistent with Pareto's Law. In other
words, he says that towards the top the requirements that society
makes of people become increasingly less. Winkler has thus seized
on an important practical problem. If it were true that society
selects less strictly according as someone has climbed higher up the
social and economic ladder, this would offer an explanation for the
marked inequality. It could even lead to that inequality increasing
in the course of time. In reality this increasing inequality does not
occur, but that is of little significance in itself; it might well be that
selection does in fact become less strict as one climbs higher, but
that other historical forces counter the increasing inequality. As
regards these forces, we might for instance envisage the reduction
of the share of capital in national income. This development has an
equalizing effect and works against a system of forces à la Winkler.

It is easy to imagine the mechanics of such a system. You scratch
my back and I'll scratch yours: the principle is the more rewarding
if the circles in which it is practised are higher. We all know
examples of cases in which it is precisely the better-off who are
offered the lucrative jobs on the side, generous rises on the principle
that someone is considered in view of his already high income to be
of great merit – these are all things that happen. Only, we don't
know how often or with what effects. Quantitative research in this
field is lacking. Winkler has not proved his hypothesis but merely
shown that it is consistent with a Pareto distribution for the higher
incomes.

Other explanatory principles have also proved to be capable of

* W. Winkler, *Grundfragen der Ökonometrie*, 1951.

240

leading to a Pareto distribution. Thus D. G. Champernowne has, in a celebrated but somewhat obscure article,* developed a model in which the incomes are at first distributed at random; in the course of time this changes, namely under the influence of a process that keeps on repeating itself. This process consists in the fact that the incomes vary, every income recipient having the same chance of entering a higher or lower income bracket. These brackets are thought of as proportional, that is to say each income bracket is higher than the one beneath it by the same percentage. This looks rather like Winkler's hypothesis, but it does not go as far. In the case of Winkler society becomes increasingly sympathetic further up the scale; inequality is stimulated progressively. In the case of Champernowne the inequality is stimulated proportionately. Only towards the bottom is there a minimum that may not be exceeded. And yet even with Champernowne a Pareto distribution emerges. This requires among other things that an identical process continues for a considerable length of time. To give a free run to the lapse of time, Champernowne assumes that the incomes are hereditary and so permanent (except that the individual income recipients keep on replacing each other). This is, of course, an unrealistic assumption; it is introduced only to stress the lengthy period of adjustment at the end of which the initial income distribution has finally disappeared. For that is what Champernowne wants to prove: how a stochastic process governed by the laws of probability ultimately leads to the specific distribution that we see in practice. The article is a highly theoretical exercise, more suited to academic connoisseurs than to practical readers. But the conclusion that the laws of probability play a part in distribution is important; it will return time and again in the following pages.

(I called Champernowne's article obscure. That relates not only to the mathematical form but also to the result. If someone's income depends on that income in the preceding period plus a chance variable, one would be more inclined to expect a Gibrat distribution [to be discussed in the following section] than a Pareto distribution. The reason why a Pareto function nevertheless appears in Champernowne's theory lies in a number of subsidiary conditions, and above all in the presence of a bottom limit for

* 'A Model of Income Distribution', *Economic Journal*, 1953.

incomes. There the stochastic process comes up against a brick wall.)

The importance of probability and chance emerges from a third, and very different, theory, that of M. Friedman.* Suppose that society functions like a lottery or a football pool; a popular belief. Everybody buys a ticket or fills a coupon in, but only a few win a prize. This result obviously gives a very skew distribution. The outcome does not necessarily comply with the Pareto equation, but by changing the rules of the football pool in a suitable way we can make it do so.

What Friedman has in mind is, of course, more subtle than a popular belief. In every society there are people who like risk and there are people who don't, just as there are some who like liquorice and some who don't. It would be a good thing if there were arrangements to satisfy these various preferences. Fortunately, private enterprise takes care of this. Private firms sell insurance or run football pools. But these are extreme examples. In fact Friedman sees every business firm in part as such an arrangement. Risk-liking persons set themselves up as entrepreneurs guaranteeing wages to the others. This implies a redistribution of the impact of uncertainty, and it also implies a redistribution of income. The free market reshuffles people and rewards in a kind of optimizing process. Inequality of income may be regarded, says Friedman, in much the same way as the kinds of goods that are produced in a market economy: as a reflection of deliberate choice in accordance with the tastes and preferences of the free members of a free society.

There is obviously a normative judgement associated with this view. Inequality resulting from the free decisions to participate or non-participate in a football pool should not be frowned upon. Friedman is a great believer in the salutary workings of the market place; he wants us to look critically upon all kinds of government intervention in income distribution. (In this quality we shall meet again in Chapter VII, 7.)

The question is to what extent the social processes do in fact

* 'Choice, Chance and the Personal Distribution of Income', *Journal of Political Economy*, 1953. Similar ideas were developed earlier by the Swede K. Wicksell.

resemble a football pool. It is true that in production risks are constantly taken, especially by entrepreneurs. For a number of them this results in a loss, for many a small or moderate profit, and for a very small group high profits. However, the comparison with Bingo or the football pool holds true to only a very limited extent, because it is striking that the same people keep on winning and others never do. In genuine lotteries this would attract the notice of the police. The super-rich do not always run such big risks – they may spread their business interests over many firms. Dangerous risks are often borne precisely by the small businessman, and he consequently often becomes the victim of the competitive process. Moreover, the worker's existence is not free from the chance of things going wrong either, whether he likes it or not. The analogy between insurance and the wage contract seems to me to be of very limited value. Friedman's suggestion is too casual and its normative implications are misleading. Yet it cannot be denied that good and bad luck are important to our subject. This strengthens the idea that the laws of probability influence income distribution, but that hypothesis has to be more closely formulated. That takes place in the following section, which is concerned with logarithmic distribution.

Finally, a fourth explanation of the right-hand tail of the Pareto curve, for which H. Lydall* is responsible. The starting point is that somebody's income corresponds to his place in the social hierarchy. To determine that place Lydall considers the large organizations, and more especially companies. The executives direct persons under them; the more people you have under you, the higher up the ladder you are. The number of immediate subordinates – the span of control – at the various executive levels of the organization is supposed to be same. Under the president come the vice-presidents, and under them general managers, deputy general managers and so on. As the criterion of a person's place in the hierarchy Lydall takes the total income of his immediate subordinates. In this view that sum of money measures a person's responsibility. Now if these suppositions are combined, a distribution emerges that recalls the Pareto curve. Not only has

* *The Structure of Earnings*, 1968. This highly informative book deals only with income from work.

Lydall incorporated this theory in a mathematical model; he has
also verified it empirically. It proves to tally to some extent. He
finds high values for α; these are said to be 3·25 for the United
States, 2·8 to 3·5 for Britain, 2·27 for France and 3·4 for Germany.
The inequality among managers is less than that between income
recipients in general.*

This theory is a good find, because it contains a synthesis of
organization theory – on which the business economists have
written book after book – and the theory of income distribution.
Lydall's Law, to call it such – each Selected Income Level is proportionate to the total of the incomes just below it – ought therefore to apply not only to the pyramidical bureaucracies in the West
but also to those of the Soviet Union, Yugoslavia, etc. And that is
what Lydall suggests. On the other hand, its logic is confined to
bureaucracies – it is concerned with incomes with regard to which
status and prestige are decisive. If the forces of the market are
involved another result may be expected, for it is difficult to see
why supply and demand should yield exactly a price that is proportionate to a person's responsibilities. After all, there are people
in the world with high incomes and hardly any subordinates. A
competent architect, an expert tax consultant and the owner of a
bakery doing good business have much higher incomes than
Lydall's Law predicts.

This gives rise to the question whether we may put the modern
pluriform society on a par with a large pyramidical bureaucracy.
My answer is no. Even within the large organizations we find
experts whose incomes do not tally with the span of control; some
staff officials have only a secretary to order about. But all these
imperfections do not alter the fact that Lydall has put forward an
interesting point of view which can certainly help us to understand
incomes based on social conventions and an accepted hierarchy
rather than on the usual categories of the economists such as
scarcity, marginal productivity and the forces of the market.

* This does not contradict my hypothesis that inequality is tremendous
within the top 1%. Industrial and commercial managers are giants, but the
tiny group of the super-rich leave them far behind.

2. Gibrat's Law

Pareto's Law has its generally recognized weaknesses: it applies only to higher incomes. Another and more fruitful approach to the aggregate empirical material is found in a group of authors of whom R. Gibrat is the best known.* Their starting point is the normal distribution discussed in section 2 of Chapter III. This Gaussian curve is often encountered in nature and among people. True, income distribution does not comply with it; it displays a skew curve. Consequently, Pareto rejected chance as an explanatory principle. But Gibrat and his partisans are not disheartened. For they assume that income distribution (which we can observe) is related to another distribution (which we cannot observe, or not easily), which *is* governed by the laws of chance. Thus ultimately the laws of income should also obey the laws of probability.

The following example may serve to make it clear how the one distribution can determine the other. Suppose that I have accumulated a collection of marbles whose diameter is normally distributed. I put them in a vase (when considering the laws of probability this is what you always do – in real life this is a most unusual method of storage) and I hand the vase to you with the request to see whether the mass does perhaps display regularities. You have no desire to measure the marbles, which is a slippery business; you put them one by one on a weighscale. Then you divide the weights into classes and see how many marbles there are in each class. When you have done this I ask you: 'Well, do we find a normal distribution?' Whereupon you, in all good faith, answer no. No wonder; if the *diameter* is normally distributed, the *weight*, which depends on the third power of the diameter, will yield a skew distribution.

This principle opens spectacular prospects for explaining income distribution. Not only is there a rich variety of factors bound up with income – intelligence; shrewdness; perseverance, adaptability at school, at work or in society; leadership†; ambition – but there

---

* R. Gibrat, *Les inégalités économiques*, 1931.

† On the latter R. H. Tuck bases a social hierarchy which seems rather one-sided to me: *An Essay on the Economic Theory of Rank*, 1954.

are likewise an enormous number of conceivable functions that could describe the relation between income and those other factors. We can take squares, or third powers, or other relations. We could also take logarithms, and it was in this direction that Gibrat looked.

It is the shape of the frequency distribution itself that suggests this. For the tail running off to the right is clearly stretched. That is because the inequality within the top group is much greater than among ordinary people. (We saw this when the last seconds of the parade brought forth such tremendous giants.) Now if we plot on the horizontal axis of the frequency distribution not the incomes themselves but the logarithms of those incomes, the tail to the right is forced back towards the middle.* £100, £1,000 and £10,000 are represented by 2, 3 and 4. The compression creates a distribution that comes closer to the Gaussian curve. Gibrat does something similar. His theory amounts to the fact that it is not the incomes y that are normally distributed but a quantity u, which is a function of y. In the first instance the function has the form $u = a \log y + b$, in which a and b are constants. If u is in fact normally distributed, we call y lognormal. Gibrat's Law thus states that personal distribution is lognormal.

This opens up the path to a large mountain of thought performed by others than economists: lognormal distribution is a well-known chapter of mathematics. It was discovered in 1879 by D. McAlister, and has since then made many investigators enthusiastic. These are the 'log-men'.† The curve can be described by equations, which I shall spare the reader, and it can also be demonstrated by a piece of equipment that was constructed at the beginning of the century by the Dutch astronomer J. C. Kapteyn, also a log-man even then. This thing, which was long kept in the attic of the Genetic Institute of Groningen University (but was disposed of during a clean-out at the beginning of the Sixties) was reminiscent of the prepared shuffleboard of p. 63. Instead of nails there were

---

* For an explanation of what logarithms are, see p. 26.

† 'For your sake am I this patient log-man' says Ferdinand to Miranda (*The Tempest*). The joke is by J. Aitchison and J. A. Brown, themselves logmen, in *The Lognormal Distribution*, 1957. The reader who is interested in the mathematics of the case is referred to this careful study.

wooden blocks in it which looked like toy houses with pointed roofs. When the apparatus stood vertically, the houses were in nine rows above one another. Their characteristic property is that the houses are of unequal width; those more to the right are wider, being in proportion to their distance from the left-hand side of the shuffleboard. If you pour sand from above into the apparatus, the flow is divided by each pointed roof into two equal parts. A grain of sand therefore has an even chance of going to the right. If this chance comes off, the grain ends up among the wider houses. If not, it ends up among narrow houses, and then it falls almost steeply to the bottom. A grain of sand with luck against it is repeatedly pushed to the left, but because it encounters only narrow roofs it does not go very far to the left. The wider roofs (i.e. those more to the right), on the other hand, throw half of the sand in proportion further to the right. As a result a curve is formed in a downward direction which resembles the income distribution curve like two drops of water. I have not been able to perform this operation – as I said, the apparatus has been done away with – but I have seen a photograph,* and it is an odd idea that around 1900 an astronomer inspired by other problems than those of economics, knocked together an apparatus which almost exactly produces the actual statistics of income distribution. (Incidentally, Kapteyn was aware of the relation with economic inequality.)

As mentioned, attention was drawn to the similarity between income distribution and lognormal distribution by Gibrat in particular thirty years after Kapteyn had built his device. Just like Pareto, Gibrat worked empirically, that is to say from figures, not from some theoretical principle. The lognormal distribution proves to describe income structure better than Pareto's Law does. Admittedly, the equation $u = a \log y + b$ has to be changed somewhat, in the sense that we do not take the logarithm of the incomes themselves but of $y - y_o$, in which y_o represents a kind of Ricardian subsistence minimum. In other words, the Gibrat distribution tallies better if we take the freely spendable incomes. And further a slight deviation at the two far ends continues to exist; there are somewhat more people in the vicinity of the poverty line and there are somewhat more super-rich than the lognormal distribution

* In Aitchison and Brown, facing p. 23.

predicts.* The right-hand tail (the top 10%) is better described by
Pareto's Law, which produces a greater inequality than Gibrat's
Law. But in broad outline various investigators find that Gibrat's
Law tallies, and therewith income distribution has been related to
a number of fundamental statistical processes encountered everywhere in nature. The discovery that personal income distribution
is lognormal gives a new view of the underlying factors and has
unleashed a great deal of theoretical work.

The most convincing explanatory principle has been put forward by Gibrat himself. It is the same as the one on which Kapteyn
built his machine: grains of sand that have once moved to the
right have an even chance of being thrown still further to the right.
In economic terms the growth of a person's income is proportionate to that income itself. This stretches the curve to the right; the
number of people in the higher income brackets is spread out over
a wider distance on the horizontal axis. To him that has shall be
given, in accordance with a fixed percentage. Gibrat calls this
l'effet proportionnel. However, the growth of income may not take
place for *every* individual in exact accordance with this pattern; if
everyone's income increases proportionately, a given curve reproduces itself on a bigger scale. There must be a *chance* that a person's
income grows proportionately, and these chances are spread sym-
metrically. The exact condition is that individual incomes grow in
accordance with a factor $(1 + v)$, whereby v has been normally
distributed. The Gibrat distribution is thus the product of a
stochastic process.

For older authors – i.e. in the Thirties – the principle of the
percentage increase was something that had to be further justified.
In fact plausible examples may be thought up of careers proceeding
in accordance with *l'effet proportionnel* (doctors, civil servants) and
this could also be demonstrated in certain cases. In such careers
the existence side by side of different ages is reason enough for a
lognormal distribution. But the percentage increase has a much
more general economic ground which we nowadays all realize. It is
the growth of national income – the daily concern of statesmen,
economists, journalists. If everyone has an equal chance of sharing

* cf. H. Lydall, *The Structure of Earnings*, 1968. He finds the right-hand
tail overoccupied even for salaried persons.

in this growth in accordance with an identical percentage – and that is the simplest if perhaps not the most convincing thing that one may suppose – a Gibrat distribution emerges. For this reason, then, it is not surprising that income distribution is what it is. On the contrary, it is much more the deviations from the lognormal distribution that call for an explanation!

Gibrat's principle has been further worked out by R. S. C. Rutherford.* His springboard is the idea that the age of the income recipients plays a part. In each income period a new intake enters the economic process. Suppose that their 'income power' (that is the u from the equations given above) has been normally distributed upon their arrival on the economic scene; in that case during their career the spread of the curve (measured by the variance) will become greater all the time. If the stochastic process is allowed to continue unchecked, it leads to exploding inequality. But this increasing spread is countered because income recipients do not continue for ever; they are pensioned off and they die. As a result the aggregate curve is kept within limits. Now Rutherford assumes that the number of survivors within each year decreases in accordance with a constant percentage, that the u's for every year are distributed in the same way and that the stochastic process of random shocks always proceeds in the same way. The mathematical elaboration of these hypotheses leads to a distribution that tallies with Gibrat's. The entry and exit of the working population therefore keep income distribution in lognormal equilibrium.

However, exploding inequality can also very well manifest itself if we correlate the growth of individual incomes with the general growth of productivity. For then the newcomers start at a higher level too. This difficulty has been pointed to by M. Kalecki, who also knows a solution for it: he assumes that the spread of the chance variable v from Gibrat's equation is subject to limits. That keeps distribution within bounds.†

From the above the skewness of income distribution comes to the fore as a natural phenomenon that can be understood just as well by astronomers and mathematicians as by social scientists. People are grains of sand in a tray with little wooden houses, these

* 'Income Distribution: a New Model', *Econometrica*, 1955.
† 'On the Gibrat Distribution', *Economica*, 1945.

grains being thrown to the left and to the right. True, we are left with a large number of rich people and also with rather a big group of people at the bottom of the curve, but all the same it tallies rather well. The 'proportional effect' is all we need, and thus distribution is determined. However, before we go into this deterministic side of the matter it must be pointed out that the *effet proportionnel* is not the only possible explanation of a lognormal distribution.

Quite different causalities summoning up the same curve are also conceivable, and one of the most plausible has been put forward by A. D. Roy.* This author assumes that a large number of separate income-acquiring qualities exist, and that these are normally distributed one by one among people; however, their effect on a person's productive capacity, and thus on his income, is described not by addition but by multiplication. Speed gives a person a somewhat higher chance of an income, and so does accuracy; but if someone possesses both talents he has the chance of an income that works out higher through multiplication. If a person's technical ingenuity is 40% above normal and his commercial instinct 20%, his productive capacity, according to this view, is 68% above normal. If we can throw in organizational ability, the art of getting on well with people, and so on, the chance of a high income quickly increases. This multiplication also operates in the direction of low incomes, i.e. for capacities which in themselves each lie below normal: poor health, poor powers of concentration, bad education, have a multiplicative effect independently of one another. That is how the very low incomes come about. Now this relation between properties and incomes tends towards a lognormal distribution.

(For those, and only those, who are acquainted with the basic properties of logarithms *and* want to see proof of Roy's proposition: the distribution of the *sum* of a number of variates, which themselves have independent distributions of a certain but very general kind, tends to normality as the number of these variates is increased. This is called the Central Limit Theorem, a well-known chapter in books on statistics. If we apply this theorem to the

* 'The Distribution of Earnings and Individual Output', *Economic Journal*, 1950.

logarithms of variates, and if we remember that $\log a + \log b = \log ab$, we find that the distribution of the *product* of the variates tends to lognormality.)

This, too, offers us a simple and elegant explanation of Gibrat's Law. It makes no use of the mechanics of Kapteyn's machine; to Roy people are not grains of sand falling down and being directed to the right or to the left. There is no process repeating itself in time. But the explanation of income distribution *is* stochastic: the laws of probability are in operation, statistic regularities are at work which, taken together, produce the lognormal distribution.

The reasoning has its drawbacks. With Roy, as with Gibrat, we are concerned with a hypothesis much more than with a genuine theory, because the multiplicative effect is not rendered plausible independently, i.e. in detachment from the empirically found distribution; we cannot directly measure technical ingenuity, commercial instinct, organizational ability. The starting point does not seem improbable at first sight, but it has not been tested. There is another difficulty, to which Roy himself draws attention. The theory can predict too skew distributions. For if people's separate income-acquiring factors were to be intercorrelated, the effect would be enormous, even though the result remains lognormal. The curve then departs from reality, especially in the sense that we expect more top incomes (from work) than actually exist. If technical talent often goes with a talent for getting on with people, or with ambition, or if the nurturing of one quality by training entails the development of other qualities, income distribution becomes more skew than it is in reality under the influence of the multiplicative effect. The theory then yields an over-explanation of the inequality; the same phenomenon that we kept on encountering earlier when we were considering distributive shares. Now in fact it is not improbable that in the course of the training process such an intercorrelation of income-acquiring qualities does occur. If then an income structure is to appear like the one we know, there must be other, inhibiting factors at work.

These inhibiting factors have been incorporated into a theory by J. Tinbergen.* He too starts from a large number of income-

* 'On the Theory of Income Distribution', *Weltwirtschaftliches Archiv*, 1956.

acquiring qualities that are normally distributed among people, but he does not take into account only the *availability* of these qualities; he also introduces into his model the degree to which these qualities are *desired* by society. A person's income then depends on the tension between requirements and the availability of his qualities. This is a step forward compared with the other theories – the latter suffered from the fact that they left the requirements of society out of consideration. That is really a startling omission, for economics has been explaining the factor prices by supply and demand for a very long time (as became amply evident in Chapter IV). Tinbergen has bridged a gap between the work of empirical investigators and mathematicians (who spoke only of supply) on the one hand and traditional economics on the other. His model leaves open the possibility of some people with very limited talents still acquiring a fair income. Their income-acquiring capacities are weak, but at the same time they are in fairly short supply. And if there is nevertheless a fairly considerable demand for them, the low income is supported by that. This is an extremely important truth, which can be illustrated by the work of road-sweepers, dustmen and charwomen. These people have to be there; demand is inelastic. If they are in short supply the market strengthens their position, whatever their skills and capacities. In the course of technical development it may very well be precisely these low wages that are raised because otherwise the vacant posts cannot be filled, and that has in fact happened in recent decades.

Using Tinbergen's theory one can also explain why the mode of incomes (i.e. those which lie somewhat below the average – the people from our parade who reached to our collarbones) remains relatively low. True, there is considerable demand here but also a large supply, for now we are concerned with ordinary people. Supply and demand force down remuneration. The very high incomes are created when there is an intensive demand for scarce qualities.

Tinbergen's model further amounts to the fact that income distribution as a whole is explained by the sum of a large number of terms, each representing the income distribution for a separate productive quality. These qualities are assumed to have been normally distributed, and Tinbergen shows that a Gibrat distribution appears if the spread of the contributions supplied does not differ from the spread of the contributions demanded. It cannot automatically be said whether the latter is in fact realistic, and Tinbergen therefore rightly urges that further empirical research be made.

Considering the above, we must in the first place conclude that if anything we have too many rather than too few theories. Various hypotheses, which are all plausible, are suitable for explaining the lognormal distribution. The multiplicative effect (Roy), the tension between supply and demand (Tinbergen), the proportional effect (Gibrat) and its variants (Rutherford) all lead, in collaboration with the laws of probability, to the empirically observed income structure. While we know in economics but also in science in general many mysterious phenomena without a theory, we see here a phenomenon (lognormal distribution) under which too many theories can be constructed. That is pleasant to the extent that the investigator can seek out the theory that seems best to him, but all the same it is an unsatisfactory state of affairs that we are unable to point to an explanation as the preferable one. The matter has not yet been concluded, and many investigators can continue to study it.

Another reason for further study is that the theories mentioned all suffer from a certain one-sidedness. They try to introduce one explanatory principle, which of course is elegant but not necessarily realistic. That one explanatory principle – the above theories agree on that – consists in an interplay of chance and something else (multiplicative effect, proportional effect). The laws of probability are reinstated. At first sight the Gibrat distribution, which after all is skew, does not lend itself very well to an explanation by the laws of probability; but the ingenuity of the theoreticians has brought the factor of chance to the fore again via the logarithm. However, in this reasoning – and this is its weakness – no call is made on systematic factors that could upset the laws of probability. We hear nothing said about the power structure, law of inheritance, the concentration of wealth, technical development, the whole social system; an atmosphere of determinism prevails, of grains of sand that are poured into Kapteyn's apparatus. I can imagine that there are people who do not easily accept this. I have difficulty in doing so too, and in the following section I should like to present a number of systematic distortions of chance. These can then serve right away to explain the overpopulation of the far ends – because it is there that the imperfection of Gibrat's Law lies.

Although this section is complicated enough as it is, attention must be drawn in conclusion to an interesting interpretation of the Gibrat distribution by J. van der Wijk.* Independently of Gibrat, he found the equation $u = a \log (y - y_o) + b$, though in a somewhat more complicated form. Van der Wijk started from a very specific interpretation of the variable u; he designates this u as the satisfaction that a person gets from his income. If this designation is correct the lognormal distribution of money incomes entails that the psychic income u is normally distributed among people. The mathematics of the case means that in that case the marginal utility of the income (the extra satisfaction derived from an extra pound) is inversely proportionate to the size of the free income $(y - y_o)$. Van der Wijk is less interested in the causes of income distribution than in the consequences, and these consequences prove to be striking. The idea that the marginal utility of a person's income falls proportionately according as $y - y_o$ is higher proves to fit in with a hypothesis from psychology: the Weber-Fechner Law. If the stimuli which a person undergoes vary in accordance with a geometric series, then according to this law he will experience sensations that vary in accordance with a mathematical series. It is remarkable that this asserted psychic regularity tallies with the facts of the empirically observed income distribution.† And yet van der Wijk's proposition again turns out to be a hypothesis that remains unproven. For up to now it has not proved possible to measure psychic income, and so the proposition that it is distributed normally cannot be tested. This equally applies to a number of further hypotheses that van der Wijk conjures up from his

* *Inkomens- en vermogensverdeling*, 1939.

† Viewed historically, the discovery of lognormal distribution was inspired by the Weber-Fechner Law, i.e. quite detached from income distribution. In 1879 the biologist Francis Galton introduced a paper given before the Royal Society of London, and drawn up by D. McAlister (the first to publish the theory of lognormal distribution). Galton saw the connexion with the Weber-Fechner Law and for this reason recommended McAlister's views.

equations (such as: half the people consider themselves poor; a quarter of them have so much money that they may be called wealthy in the psychic sense, etc.). The interpretation of u as psychic income is mentioned here simply to show what puzzling regularities one can come across if one starts from lognormal distribution. These regularities themselves are perhaps of less importance because they are so speculative. I simply wanted to show that Gibrat's Law is a top hat from which surprising things can be produced – it deserves the further attention of the economics profession.

3. *The Dice are Loaded*

The conclusion from the above is that, though personal incomes do not themselves form a normal curve, they can largely be understood by means of a normal distribution. The forces that lead to the actual distribution have been described by Gibrat, Roy, Tinbergen and others in a way that differed in each case but always assigned a leading role to chance. The processes described are *stochastic*. That raises the question whether things are really like that in our society. Nobody denies the often decisive importance that chance occurrences exert on the course of events – an attack of flu upsets a family's holiday, what would have happened if Napoleon had drowned as a youth, somebody meets his future wife at a party which he attended quite by accident – but that does not imply that we have to tackle the explanation of economic phenomena in that way. It looks for a moment as if we are abandoning every theory of social events.

Now the latter would be a misunderstanding. Large parts of modern science have been constructed precisely on the basis of the laws of probability. In quantum mechanics, for instance, which forms the basis for atomic physics and nuclear physics, observations of probability play an essential part. Modern macroeconomics seeks regularities between variables such as volume of production, employment, wage and share of labour, and does so once again on the basis of the laws of probability. Statistical analysis and thus the whole of econometrics also operates in this way. But chance and probability are not the whole story. In addition there are systematic factors involved. It is the task of science to reveal these, and to do so it uses statistical laws of probability. The latter is quite evident in Roy's theory: there, besides chance, the multiplicative effect is at work; or in Gibrat, where *l'effet proportionnel* leads to the lognormal distribution.

An example of the misconception referred to is the view of A. Loria.* He is a declared opponent of capitalism, and he regards the analysis of income distribution by Pareto, Gini and others simply as an attempt to mask the evil properties of exploitation. According to Loria, capitalist distribution is based on violence, deceit and monopoly, and *therefore* chance may not be called in to help in the explanation. He regards 'theories' proceeding from a normal distribution of human talents as a retrograde step towards a prescientific and superstitious stage of thought. But here he is beside the mark. For one thing, it is simply not true that only violence, deceit and monopoly determine incomes; everybody knows within his own circle examples of people who earn money through their special talents (and if you don't happen to know such successful persons just think of the Beatles – they became millionaires with no more violence than that of electric guitars). But moreover it might very well be that the use of violence and deceit, and also the establishment of monopolies, requires human talents which may in turn be normally distributed. Income distribution among the Cosa Nostra may perhaps be lognormal. I do not say that this is so; all I mean is that there is no contradiction between chance distribution and the acceptance of violence, deceit and monopoly as factors explaining income structure.

And yet awkward questions remain. What we call chance consists in fact in the operation of a large number of minor forces detached from one another. The processes must be of an atomistic nature; they may not be systematically influenced.† Such processes are highly suited for mathematical analysis – it is more or less immaterial whether the scientist is an astronomer, like Kapteyn,

---

* *Theorie der reinen Wirtschaft, Untersuchungen der Gesetze des Einkommens*, 1925.

† This is at variance with what many people believe. Their view is voiced by Anatole France, who said that chance is God acting anonymously; he does not want to sign his name.

or an economist or sociologist. This is an irritating idea for some economists and sociologists (myself included). But should it prove that social mechanics distorts chance, and perhaps in a somewhat more complicated manner than *l'effet proportionnel* of Gibrat – then an economic or sociological theory is required.

In fact reference must be made forthwith to a misleading suggestion emanating from Kapteyn's apparatus. Grains of sand are poured into this and run down. According to Gibrat, this process reproduces the growth of incomes. But in social reality this sometimes happens differently. Rich heirs on occasion are born with an income. They are not poured into a funnel together with the other grains of sand at one and the same place, but they take up their own place – far to the right – immediately. True, this privilege is not at variance with the laws of chance – heirs too are subject to stochastic processes! – but it does cast doubt on whether Kapteyn's apparatus fully describes the process.

The same doubt may also be illustrated by dice which, if all is well, are subject to the laws of chance. They roll over a table, bumping into the surface repeatedly, and the result of these collisions is that all six faces have an equal chance of coming up. This process is seriously upset if someone plants a piece of lead shot in the die; this introduces a system into the rolling that chance does not provide for. Perhaps the dice of income distribution have undergone such a treatment – this is what many vaguely suspect, and not without reason.

There are a number of *a priori* arguments against this suspicion and in favour of the application of the laws of probability to society as we know it. Production takes place in a very large number of firms competing with one another. The market relations between these firms are not frozen; they change according to the skill of the management and the degree to which technical innovations are used. Growth and contraction are under the influence of many external forces; it is not silly to assume that these result in normally spread chances of a fixed percentage increase. New firms keep appearing on the market and old ones disappearing. Something similar applies to the labour market: new generations keep arriving, while the old ones move up. A process of selection is going on in which numerous individuals compete. Their talents differ greatly, and that is a good thing to the extent that society needs very divergent qualities. A violinist must be musical, a sales representative must have the gift of the gab, a driver must be alert; a works manager must be technically minded and be able to get on with people and a general manager must be able to organize (whatever that is). The possessor of daring and commercial talent can become a businessman, with the chance of profit and loss; but the person who opts for security sees many posts in the Civil Service beckoning him. The man of few talents always finds some kind of job that gives him work and a modest income, for modern society still calls for people to perform simple tasks and is prepared to let them share in the rise in general prosperity. A small income may form the springboard for a large one. In this view, society is pluriform and flexible; there is a permanent adjustment going on, as a result of which everyone can grow along with the total. Anyone who fails in one trade or profession usually gets a second chance. Nor is there just one scale of social values; different talents are evaluated in other ways by different people, so that there's always a niche for everyone.* And furthermore luck plays a part: anyone who engages in the right activity at the right time and the right place gets a high income.

This reasoning in no way denies the inequality of human capacities, but it need not run counter to chance distribution. Even the existence of more or less separate social groups (*non-competing groups*) need not be denied; so long as there are *many* of them, they do not disturb the stochastic approach. In the system of permanent competition myriad small forces operate independently of one another, and that is exactly what we call chance. If at the same time everything grows equally, the lognormal distribution comes into being.

* M. W. Reder has pointed out that the social consensus on the preferred capacities leads to increased income differentials. 'There is *the* baseball team that won the World Series, there is *the* heavyweight (boxing) champion, etc. But what about teaching performance? No one knows who is the world's best teacher, and (perhaps) nobody cares.' Hence the poor spread in teachers' salaries. Continuing to reason along these lines, a pluralistic society ought to display smaller income differentials than one with a scale of values strictly and centrally regulated. ('The Size Distribution of Earnings', *The Distribution of the National Income*, 1968.)

But upon closer inspection systematic processes occur that distort this picture of the atomistic, pluralistic, mobile society. They are caused in part by deliberate intervention from above; economic and social policy orders the statistical mass in a way that is not reconcilable with the laws of normal distribution. And on consideration this political intervention forms only a positive reaction to a much more fundamental negative process: the normal distribution is distorted owing to the fact that *cumulative forces* occur in the process of general competition. This cripples chance. It is this cumulation that may be described by the expression: the dice are loaded. What does this disturbance of chance look like?

It differs depending on the group we have in mind. Forces reinforcing one another operate both on the poor – the bottom 20% of income recipients – and on the well-to-do. Let us begin with the latter category.

A male baby is born into a well-to-do environment. His parents (or at any rate his father) thus possess effective income-acquiring qualities. The chance of his inheriting them is, according to the normal distribution, considerable. The family can save; the chance of the child ultimately inheriting some wealth is likewise considerable. Right from the start he is brought up in a milieu that encourages his development. When he goes to school he starts off with certain advantages over his poorer classmates: command of language, fluency, interest. He has a greater chance of better school performance. His parents will collaborate with the teachers. The school performance nurtures ambition and self-confidence – the child knows that he will later climb in society, and gradually comes to take this for granted. He moves up the educational ladder. Even if his talents are not really up to it he gets to university, perhaps with the assistance of private schools, small classes, coaching. Nothing has such a stimulating effect on the intellect as its constant use. Higher education is heavily subsidized by the community. And so a number of factors work together while reinforcing one another. At university he meets young people who help him further with his upbringing, and his friends stand him in good stead in his later career, even without this being a matter of favouritism or dishonesty. He marries a girl from his own circle who will presently be inheriting some money just as he will. Once he is started on his career and he doesn't like his job, he can look for another, and he can afford to take something of a risk – after all, he has some money behind him. This freedom makes him more mobile, and in the long run that increases his income.

This is nothing but an example, though it is perhaps not untypical. I do not claim that all middle-class or upper-class young people conform to this pattern – they may stay behind or drop out, and that can happen in many ways. But what matters is that the chance factors give one another a helping hand and that it all tends to work in one direction. The cumulative forces start at a child's pre-school age and continue to help him in getting on.

A more striking example, from the top 0·1 *pro mille*, and so much more specific. A man with willpower and daring has settled on the American frontier. The time is the last century. His cattle business is going well – the herd is growing quickly, money is being earned and that is being invested in more and more land, which is there for the asking. Personal qualities (which are normally distributed) can give such a business a tremendous expansion, and up to this point everything is as the theories of Roy and Gibrat describe it. But then the land he owns suddenly begins to rise in value. Civilization is advancing. The vanguard of pioneers and adventurers is followed by hordes of energetic, industrious people; what was once prairie becomes urban building land, and its value rockets. The owner is in the fortunate position of being able to keep the choicest stretches of his extensive holdings for himself; investments in stock and land are supplemented by and replaced by investments in hotels, offices, shops. Society provides the cumulative forces that cause his wealth to grow to colossal proportions. And if in addition oil is found here and there – and the chance that oil is found in the land of a large landowner is by definition large – the dollar centimillionaire begins to emerge. Here too a self-reinforcing process, which of course is conditioned by a very special social development in a state like Texas; but this much is certain, that the laws of chance do not adequately describe it (before the reader allows himself to be convinced by this one example that accumulation is the rule, he should recall that No. 4 on the list of America's Super-Rich is the inventor of the Polaroid camera – no speculation in land, no oil, no initial wealth – just a few inventions!).

Unfortunately, cumulative forces also operate at the bottom end of income distribution, and then in a negative sense. M. Harrington has opened our eyes to the many vicious circles to which the economically weak are exposed.* Poverty breeds a special environment and that environment breeds poverty. A sub-culture exists in which other standards than those of official society apply.

The jobless, poor farmers in infertile areas, inhabitants of the city ghettoes – they are handicapped not only by a small income. Poor health, bad food, fourth-rate accommodation are both causes and results of low incomes. Poverty erodes income-earning capacities; special skills that were extant wither and die. Worst of all, ambition and self-respect vanish; paralysing despondency is the worst cumulative factor that can afflict anyone.

Harrington also points to the arrears that children from these environments immediately suffer. Everything works against them at home, the neighbourhood may exert an adverse influence. Their accent is uncouth, their manners deplorable. Their schools are far worse than average. The children at such schools do not encourage one another to become hard-working citizens earning good salaries. The vicious circles begin at birth but continue immediately afterwards. Chance does not get a fair chance.

One of the highly pessimistic aspects of Harrington's theory is that he makes a razor-sharp distinction between the families that keep up with modern society and those who do not make it. On the one hand the hard-working, well-trained, well-adjusted citizens who meet the stringent requirements of modern technology, and on the other the underprivileged, who are pushed back ever further by the advancing technology and bureaucracy. Anyone who once finds himself below the poverty line – and that is the case with 20–25% of the American population! – remains under it and sinks

---

* By a (normally distributed?) chance a namesake has described life in a large company: Alan Harrington, *Life in the Crystal Palace*, 1959. This is an ironical book on the ways of big business seen through the eyes of an employee. Michael Harrington's book is called *The Other America, Poverty in the United States*, 1962.

further into the morass. Harrington regards the subculture of poverty as a separate world from which there is no escape. This closed system is surrounded by prosperity, but the line cannot be crossed. I think that Harrington puts things too sharply (although this has the advantage of giving a clear look at the Achilles' heel of the theories that seek to explain income distribution by the laws of chance). For instance, he does not mention that a poverty-stricken environment breeds certain qualities that may come in handy in a competitive world: cunning, shrewdness, suspicion. Without a doubt financially successful careers have been built on lessons learnt in the hard school of youth in the slums. And Harrington also underestimates the influence of determination to escape poverty. This ambition is less self-evident and therefore more resolute than that of the doctor's son who also wants to become a doctor later. The empirical material, too, does not entirely tally with Harrington's pessimism. If he were right, we ought to find a twin-peak frequency distribution of incomes; each peak represents a separate subculture. The fact that the curve has a single peak argues against Harrington's two-class theory and against the sharp dividing line that separates The Other America from the superabundant society.

Harrington exaggerates; in fact he admits it himself. He does not exaggerate the poverty – that is bad enough as it is – but the *apartheid*. His theory relates too much to the burnt-out poor, and makes insufficient allowance for young people who, though they have to fight against the handicap of their background, are not doomed to lose. Harrington's sombre view does, however, offer a sound counter to the official American view of the Fifties and the early Sixties: the pluralism, the mobility, the equal opportunity, the New Frontier, the Great Society. This optimistic view leaned, among others, on the salutary effects of education, on the idea of Progress, but also on the Horatio Alger Story; it overlooked the cumulative forces of a depressing environment. Even before Harrington wrote his book there were people who described capitalism and in particular American capitalism as a rigid society, with a small ruling class and powerless masses, but anyone who saw it in that light was a Marxist or a foreigner (like Mme Simone de Beauvoir, in *l'Amerique de jour à jour*). They were not believed, if only because they also exaggerated, sometimes to ridiculous lengths. But Harrington has been believed; his motives are not suspect and his ideology is not dogmatic. He does not impute the blame to a small ruling class, but to the vicious circles of the slums and the desolate rural regions; this makes him more convincing. Since Harrington the Administration has created various agencies and instituted a number of programmes for bringing the poor back into society. Their success has not been overwhelming. In the meantime the American Dream has degenerated into a nightmare of violence, and though the situation in the ghettoes is not the only cause of the change in the political and ideological climate, it is certainly a factor that cannot be overlooked.

For all that we, as students of income distribution, are left with a problem. We should like to know how things stand with the vertical mobility of young people coming from the slums; we should like to see empirical material on that point, statistics and coefficients, so that we no longer have to rely on inspiring tales of errand boys who became managing directors or on Harrington's description of the New York Bowery. We want hard facts. And even if we have them we are not there yet – next we want a connexion between these facts of mobility on the one hand and income distribution on the other. Unfortunately, neither of the two forms of information is available to a satisfactory extent.

As regards the first one – material on vertical mobility – the unsatisfactory situation is not immediately evident. For sociologists have in fact performed all kinds of investigations. I may recall the work of G. Thomas for postwar Britain and that of S. M. Lipset and R. Bendix for the United States.* These studies revealed that incredibly high percentages of the top group came from the category of manual workers. In Britain 10% of the managers and the graduate professionals had in an earlier phase of their life belonged to the category of unskilled workers. For the United States one fifth of the professional or semi-professional group had formerly done semi-skilled or unskilled work. This suggests high mobility, in the sense that the persistent, the intelligent, the energetic (or perhaps the fortunate) climb the whole ladder from the bottom to the top.

* G. Thomas, *Labour Mobility in Great Britain 1945–49*, 1953. S. M. Lipset and R. Bendix, *Social Mobility in Industrial Society*, 1959.

This related to the careers of upper-class people who once belonged to the working class. Similar results are available with regard to intergeneration mobility, i.e. opportunities for children. S. M. Miller* has calculated what percentage of the sons of one generation of manual workers succeeded in reaching the income élite. For France this was 1·4%, for Great Britain 0·6% and for Sweden 1·8%. These may seem tiny figures – indeed only relatively few have made the big leap – but the top group is of course much smaller than the bottom strata of income structure. If we put the élite at about 3% of the total population, the chances of the sons of manual workers are definitely more unfavourable than the average chance, but the odds are not prohibitive. The relation between a working-class boy's chance of reaching the top and the normal chance ranges from 20% in Britain to 60% in Sweden. This would suggest unequal opportunities but yet an open society.

All this is useful, though somewhat contradictory, information, but it does not help us to solve the specific problem suggested by Harrington's book: is it true that young or not-so-young people cannot escape the doom of poverty? For these surveys did not state whether or not these successful careerists came from the slums. The fact that a top executive formerly did unskilled work or that his father was a manual labourer tells us something about his personal qualities, it proves that society is not fossilized, that a working-class background can be overcome, but it does not specify the circumstances of his youth. For Harrington does not suggest that *all* manual workers in the United States come within the pull of poverty; he says that only of those who live in the subculture of deprivation and misery. And it is on this very criterion that the usual studies do not enlighten us.

But this lacuna in our knowledge is not the worst one, if only because it could be filled by more research. What is worse is that there is no bridge between the figures on vertical mobility and income distribution. That theoretical bridge has never been built by the economists, because they have a certain contempt for sociology; the sociologists have done nothing about it because they are insufficiently conversant with the problems of theoretical economics. The result is that the absence of this link is not even

* S. M. Miller, 'Comparative Social Mobility', in *Current Sociology*, 1960.

noticed by anyone. Not a single textbook on economics, as far as I know, points out that for an understanding of personal income distribution it is necessary to have an insight into vertical mobility. Even less is it ever specified what the link ought in fact to look like.

I mean this. Suppose that we knew *everything* about the rise (and fall) on the social ladder; that we therefore had available a complete model of the equality and the inequality of opportunity, of the cumulative processes of milieu, of the handicaps of poverty, the privileges of the well-to-do, and so on. Assume that this model has been tested empirically, that all relations have been quantitatively estimated with sufficient reliability. Then the sociologist is content for the moment.

But the economist, who wants to explain the inequality of incomes, is not yet satisfied. For he has to link this sociological model to an economic model à la Gibrat, à la Roy or à la Tinbergen that determines the structure of personal incomes. The synthesis ought to answer questions such as: if the vertical mobility (measured by this or that index) increases by 1%, what will the personal distribution (measured by for instance the Gini Concentration Ratio, the share of the top 10%, or another criterion) do then? How will the income share of the bottom 20% react to changes in mobility? We do not know what this integration of two models ought to look like. Not only has such an exercise never been performed – it has never been asked for yet. To the best of my knowledge there is no research programme directed towards this. Social mobility, or the lack of it, is a matter which economists have so far insufficiently incorporated in their intellectual world. They assume that more career possibilities for everyone lead to a greater equality, and that may be true, but an exact approach is lacking.

It would, of course, be fine if I could fill this gap. But that is not so. I can only point to a loose thread in economic theory. In other words the following remarks on the cumulative processes at the two ends of income distribution are necessarily of an impressionistic character. They are not meant to be exact and quantitative. We remain in the realm of unverifiable opinions and casual empiricism. Once again the conclusion is that our knowledge of economic life greatly needs improvement.

Let us return to the lognormal distribution, which inspired these critical comments on the absence of a bridge between economics and sociology. My examples of society's cumulative processes are not meant as a final criticism of Gibrat's Law. They are, however, meant to contribute towards distrust of the pure workings of chance, and they show why the two outer ends of the frequency distribution contain too many people. The empirically found curve is more strongly occupied at the ends than the lognormal distribution predicts (for the right-hand side we come closer to Pareto's Law than that of Gibrat). This is probably a consequence of systematic relations in our society insufficiently considered by the log-men and the students of stochastic processes.

However, there is more going on than the cumulative processes that make the rich richer and the poor poorer. Otherwise the inequality would grow incessantly, and that is not so. The social order also plays a part; other quite different systematic forces are at work that bring incomes closer together again. These will now be discussed.

4. *The Underdogs: Systematic Influences*

A closer inspection of the bottom end of income structure yields a number of systematic forces that are not explained by the laws of probability any more than the cumulative effect of environment is. However, we shall see that these forces do not all operate in the same direction – some support the position of the lowest-paid groups, others harm it. And we shall also see that these social influences are not only at work in a systematic manner but that they also systematically change in the course of time. The latter provokes a prediction.

The first point is that the ranks of the underdogs – the second and third decile from below* – are so heavily filled by women. Factories and offices discriminate against the weaker sex. The argument that women are less productive and leave their jobs at an earlier age is not always incorrect, but it does not explain the wage differential. There are social conventions, prejudices and taboos at work. They

* The lowest decile of the families consists mainly of non-active members of the population, above all old persons.

266

block or frustrate the chances of promotion. The other sex is crammed into lower-paid jobs. Some figures for the United States: while the American population consists of more women than men, and over a third of the labour force is female, one finds much lower figures in the higher professions: 1% of the engineers are women, 3% of the lawyers, 7% of the doctors. In all Western countries the lower rungs are overcrowded. Women are good enough to become typists or to do undemanding work in the textile industry. Where they do the same work as men, this makes the supply and demand relations in the lower regions less favourable; the disadvantages extend to men working in the same lower-paid occupations. In addition, women get lower pay. In most countries, and Britain is no exception, women's wages are roughly 75% of men's; that is to say, *for the same work*. (If the average incomes of all women are compared with those of all men, a much greater difference is found.) The discrimination is double and that considerably distorts income distribution.

Perhaps this is going to change in the future, resulting in a somewhat more uniform income structure. As far as the United Kingdom is concerned, it is not over-optimistic to hope for a gradual reduction in the taboos. In a number of sectors – Government service, and in particular in education – equal pay is an accepted principle, and the difference in opportunities for advancement is also shrinking there. In business, too, a slight change for the better can be seen. True, Convention No. 100 of the International Labour Organization (1951), which prescribes equal pay, has not been ratified by Britain, and still less complied with, but the fact that this convention exists may point in the right direction. Now, some twenty years later, there is obvious pressure by the T.U.C. to have it ratified. While I write this, Mrs Barbara Castle has announced an Act that will put a stop to discrimination within five years. It is in the interests of the unions to champion women's rights; after all, they have to think about this group of potential members too. But the male workers are not in favour. They, together with the employers who have obvious financial interests at stake, are the reason why discrimination is so persistent. How deeply it is rooted is illustrated by the sad case of male bus drivers going on strike when a woman climbed behind the wheel. Conductresses, all right;

drivers, definitely not. It happened in this England, at the end of the Sixties.*

In fact the wage differential today is much less than it was. Before the war, women in British industry got only half of men's wages; now it is 75%, and the gap will diminish. For the time being society will continue to be dominated by males and their ideas, but these ideas can change, especially if women refuse to put up with them any longer. If they want to, they can exert power – up to now there has not been sufficient will to do so, but this is gradually improving. In this sector progress seems slow but irresistible.

Unfortunately, we cannot say the same thing for sure about racial discrimination. It distorts the distribution in the same way as the unequal treatment of the weaker sex. Negroes not only get the inferior jobs assigned to them, but at the same time this leads to lower wages in the sector concerned (in so far as white men are also employed in these sectors their incomes go down too – grist to the mills of racialists!). Moreover, it occurs that coloured people get lower wages for the same work than white men. This discrimination can be seen – especially in the United States – in sectors where the unions are weak and the collective agreements show gaps. In shipping lower remuneration for non-whites is general; Chinese get half or less of what white seamen earn. Usually a powerful union and a collective agreement that gives good cover can counter unequal pay. According as development goes in the direction of better organized consultation and the legal protection of minorities is improved, it is to be expected that racial prejudice – which, alas, has a long life ahead of it, also and precisely in Britain – will no longer lead to direct wage discrimination. On the strength of this, a certain upward shift in the bottom of the income curve may be expected. But then there still remains the pressure on the low incomes that is the result of overcrowding of the low rungs of

* In the United States, at least formally, there is some legal protection. Title VII of the Civil Rights Act of 1964 forbids employment discrimination on the basis of race, colour, religion, national origin *and sex*. Up to 1969 some 7,500 complaints had been filed with the Equal Employment Opportunity Commission on account of discrimination against women (out of a total of 44,000). Information derived from *Time Magazine*, 21 November, 1969, p. 40.

the social ladder by minority groups.* It takes considerable optimism to expect an obvious improvement here.

A general levelling factor lies in the unions. Historically they developed in most countries among a vanguard of skilled craftsmen, but their influence has spread over the mass of industrial workers. Parallel to this development was a strengthening of the position of the lowest-paid workers. According as the unskilled organize, they ask that their wages be raised in proportion to those of more highly skilled workers. Beside supply and demand 'comparability' enters into the discussion – that is to say, what people consider fair and reasonable. Wage structure remains a tricky problem for the unions – the 'right' remuneration intervals are appraised by those concerned in different ways, and that can give rise to tension within the central organizations. Usually these tensions are relaxed *ad hoc* by giving now the one group and then the other priority in wage increases. It is justifiable to assume that as a result the wage structure is compressed somewhat, certainly in the sense that groups that have genuinely lagged behind because they have the supply and demand situation against them are helped to advance by the unions. To this extent the unions have given some special support to the underdogs, although this support is difficult to quantify. The same naturally applies to the minimum wages instituted by the government, Wage Council procedures and the like. It is to be expected that in this way a number of other stragglers can be assisted in the future, above all by the institution of a general minimum. Some countries have such a legal floor, under which not even the lowest-skilled persons may be placed. In Britain there are only minimum levels per branch of industry, not a general minimum wage level; as a consequence, a (small) number of workers are paid less than the National Assistance benefit (see p. 299 below). In the United States, where there is even more need for it, no such minimum exists either. The introduction of these general wage floors would certainly be an improvement, and it seems that we may expect it in the future.

The most striking influence on the raising of the very lowest incomes is the deliberate intervention in distribution. This has its

* And of course the fact that coloured people have to pay higher prices, especially for living accommodation.

beginnings in the Middle Ages and has gradually developed to what is called in Britain the Welfare State – an expression that arouses too high expectations and thus results in disappointments. We are concerned here with income transfers for the benefit of the people who are out of production (for a shorter or longer period, or for good), such as the sick, the jobless, disabled persons, old people. The Welfare State has therefore little to do with income improvements for the mass of the workers. There is at most some indirect positive influence on wages, because the supply and demand relations are influenced to some minor extent. Old persons are taken out of the market who would otherwise have forced down the wage level in some corners of the labour market, disabled persons do not have to offer their services at disgustingly low pay, and the unemployed do not serve as strike-breakers. However, in direct terms real wages are reduced rather than raised by the social provisions, because the latter have to be paid for. This may happen by contributions or from taxes, and either by the employees or by the employers. In all cases the burden is passed on in the prices so that it ultimately is not clear who bears exactly what burdens. But one thing is certain: the employees pay the greater part themselves, if only because they are by far the greater part of the active population. Extension of social security is always accompanied in the short run by a restriction of the rise in prosperity elsewhere, and that means a smaller real wage increase.

In the years during which new provisions are being introduced, we consequently hear complaints about the poor economic progress of the complainers' own group, and more particularly about the poor increase in real wage. These complaints may lead to wage demands and thus encourage the wage-price spiral. In the general inflationary tumult that continues in this way it can no longer be traced who exactly has suffered a reduction in income. It is probably not the well-off, because they are experts in passing costs on. Perhaps the burden is borne above all by those who are just above the level of those receiving the benefit. And in part a shift takes place of a person's income only in time; he pays while he works and receives benefit if he becomes sick, or old, or disabled.

But fortunately we may be sure that large groups of non-active persons who first lived below the poverty line have now moved to the right in the frequency distribution. To that extent the Welfare State has a direct and obvious levelling effect. This finds expression in the Lorenz curve because the share of the bottom 20%, and above all that of old people, is greater than it would otherwise have been. With $7\frac{1}{2}$% the United Kingdom puts up a better show than the United States with less than 5% – the difference lies partly in the Welfare State, which displays many more gaps in the United States.

In most countries this direct effect will be increased in the years to come, as a result of which the share of the two lowest deciles will increase. Even in countries like Britain, Sweden and the Netherlands, where social security cover is fairly complete, it is to be expected that the level of benefit will rise further. It is not improbable that the amount of money going to the needy will grow more quickly than national income, for the simple reason that this direct form of government intervention is one of the most visible methods of effecting some reduction of inequality. In other countries, notably the United States, large numbers of people who at present are not catered for will be brought into the system.*

We counted four forces that are helping the underdogs and the non-productive groups to acquire additional income and which in the future will probably operate further in the direction of greater equality. Running counter to them are two groups of causes that have worked in the opposite direction and will perhaps continue to do so in the future.

The more sweeping of them is immigration. The Poles, Irish and Italians who entered the United States had to take the lowest-paid jobs at first, forcing down the incomes in these occupations. According as they Americanized, a number of them rose to better positions, but then the following wave of cheap labour rolled in. In cases in which the process of adjustment and promotion are hampered by, among other factors, racial discrimination – as with the Puerto Ricans – the pressure accumulates on the lowest incomes: new waves arrive before the previous ones have flowed on. That may have serious consequences: a lack of mobility may lead to a new proletariat. Britain is now facing this danger; it can be

* The Welfare State and its limitations are again discussed in Chapter VII, 7.

avoided if the immigrants, whatever their ethnic origins, are given fully equal opportunities of training and promotion. Even in that unexpectedly favourable case immigration is making income distribution somewhat more unequal, in the sense that certain low-paid occupations have to contend with an increased supply. This may force down remuneration in these occupations, unless the unions make every effort to get the wages in the sectors concerned raised. (Of course, against this greater inequality, the opposite occurs in the immigrants' country of origin. But in many cases little is noticed of this there, since the surplus of labour and the unemployment in those countries remain a sea of misery.)

In most Continental countries the situation is somewhat easier; for the domestic workers, that is. True, Germany, Switzerland and the Netherlands run their economies on large numbers of foreigners. But these Italians, Spaniards, Turks and Moroccans are engaged only if there is an obvious shortage of labour. They are expensive for the employer, because their stay in the country often involves extra travelling and board and lodging costs. If employment drops, out they go back to their countries. A strong downward pressure on the lowest wages is therefore not to be expected from these victims of the international division of labour.

This could perhaps change in the near future through the application of the E.E.C. Treaty. Within the six member-states free movement of persons will presently be introduced, which may lead to an influx of persons of little training into prosperous regions. What the future development will be in Britain cannot be predicted with exactitude; everything depends on the way in which immigration will be regulated. A humane admission policy will doubtless lead to greater inequality in the country. It will make it more difficult to allow the underdogs, both coloured and white, to share in prosperity. This is an undesirable side-effect which in practice will certainly have an adverse effect on readiness to admit immigrants.

Although not very exact, all this is at least clear as regards the direction of the development of income distribution. The influence of technology is much more obscure. In some industries it creates relatively few jobs at the bottom of the scale of occupations, and automation at the same time pushes people down out of the somewhat higher jobs, especially in the clerical sector. It may be true that as yet no obvious contraction of overall employment is visible – in recent decades technical progress has perhaps tended rather to demand labour (see Chapter V, 6), but this does not mean to say that the occupational structure has remained unchanged. More complicated skills are called for, above all in the service sector, and people with few innate and acquired talents thus have a more difficult time of it. However, it is not an immutable law that technical change leads to greater inequality. For in a number of occupations market relations bring about the opposite: domestic staff, long the worst-paid group, are relatively much better off than before the war. For craft-type work supply and demand have brought about a considerable improvement in remuneration.

A typical illustration is formed by building workers. In an undeveloped country they are at the bottom of the occupational hierarchy, far below office staff. In India a building worker earns only a quarter of the salary of a bank clerk, who often belongs to a higher caste. As economic growth continues, this relation changes. In the West European supply and demand situation the payment of a building worker is about the same as that of a bank clerk; in Sweden it is already higher. In the United States wages in building are almost double those of bank employees. Technical progress and growth have obviously attended to more equality here.

It is quite conceivable that these trends will continue. Repair and maintenance, for instance, are being remunerated better and better; a further increase in prosperity and a further expansion of domestic appliances will continue to push up the once so low wages in this sector. In the welfare sector too – hospitals, old people's homes – an increase in employment is to be expected that requires no great specialized skills but rather a kind heart and a readiness to help. But in industry the opposite is to be expected: more training. The net effect of the changes in technology and social habits will be an adverse one for some economic underdogs and a favourable one for others. In my opinion the net effect cannot be predicted.

The systematic forces mentioned in this section – discrimination, union activity, minimum wages, the indirect effects of the Welfare State, immigration and technical change – run counter to one another. This makes it impossible to generalize quickly on the how and why of income distribution. The most primitive hypothesis is that these influences roughly cancel each other out or, in other words, that they may be described by the laws of chance. The latter is a further argument in favour of lognormal distribution. But this hypothesis is an emergency solution, which can easily conflict with the facts; attractive though it may be from a mathematical point of view, I do not have sufficient trust in it. Blind faith in economic growth and progress seems even weaker to me. To put it mildly, it is uncertain that this automatically communicates itself to all underdogs. The opposite is more likely; in a society that has made technical progress some people of limited capacities have a more difficult life. For government policy that is a point to bear in mind: the position of the untalented and the socially handicapped will need more care, not less.

5. The Top Dogs: Systematic Influences

The rich are getting richer and richer. By constantly repeating this theme, in ever-new variations, every author who can handle a typewriter can create the impression that income inequality is steadily increasing. The colossal fortunes in particular lend themselves to romantic prose. They have a built-in tendency towards vigorous growth which can be described most evocatively. This tendency is patiently fostered and nurtured by the owners of those fortunes. Moreover, according to some authors, these capitalists run things in this world. If you read F. Lundberg's fascinating *The Rich and the Super-Rich* you are easily inclined to believe in a growing share of the top 1% in national income and national wealth. The rich are smart and powerful and unscrupulous. They speculate and manipulate better than ordinary people, they buy politicians and statesmen. Their share of income reflects this power. However, these beliefs do not fit in with the statistically observed facts. Of course, this in no way stops some people from writing compelling books.

The cumulative forces emanating from the big fortunes are indeed self-evident. Capital grows, at compound interest. At 4% a year it doubles in 17 years. This requires that interest is not consumed as income. Now the small rentier has to live on that interest and so, measured in money, he does not become any wealthier. However, with the very big incomes consumptive expenditure may remain relatively low. That is relatively; in absolute terms it is, of course, fantastically high. In this way the super-rich can eat their cake and at the same time have it, and indeed have more of it. Saving attends to itself.

Investment does not – a close watch has to be kept on it, and that is exactly what the rich are supposed to do. There is reason to believe that they make sure that their special investments have higher yields than the social average. They skilfully select the most lucrative projects. For them they engage the best specialists that money can buy. In their own firms, which they fully control, they pay fantastic salaries to those who look after their interests, and so they succeed in allying to themselves a tough and intelligent élite. (In this reasoning the managers of the concerns are not just paid for their skills or their productivity; the high incomes serve to ensure their loyalty towards the real bosses, who remain behind the scenes.) The super-rich get hold of the most expensive legal experts to set up even more advantageous constructions and to help them slip even more often through the meshes of the legal net. Concentrated fiscal intellect is hired to avoid or evade tax legislation. The rich know one another and scratch each other's backs. In their circle everything is geared to getting richer. Politicians are instruments of the industrial, commercial and financial élites – not always by direct corruption, but more by the milder route of interlocking interests – so that the political and judicial superstructures of society, and in particular the tax laws, are how the rich would like them to be. The economic pressure groups are well represented in governments, parliaments and administrative authorities. In particular the military and the industrial top executives form interlocking clusters; there is a lot of profitable business to be done. Through all these arrangements the return on the top fortunes is greater than the average economic growth rate of society, and that is another way of saying that inequality is getting steadily worse.

This theory is a tempting one. However, it is on a strained footing with the facts. It is true that the concentration of wealth is extremely great. That emerges from the Gini coefficient, i.e. the relation between the area of the Lorenz banana and the maximum value of this banana (see p. 68). For British incomes this is 0·34; for holdings of wealth, on the other hand, it is 0·87. According to some serious investigators like Lydall and Tipping, the top 1% of families hold no less than 43% of total private wealth. This is certainly a skew distribution, but it is not true to say that this inequality has increased in the course of time. In the Twenties the top 1% in England and Wales possessed more than 60% of total private wealth. Despite all their tricks and their power, their share has contracted. The same holds good for the United States; at the beginning of the century the top 1% held more than half the wealth, and now the holding is less than a quarter.* Although the exactitude of these figures may be doubted, they do point to an obvious decrease in the concentration of wealth at the top.

The reason probably lies in the influence of inheritance. If capitalists lived for ever, the concentration would doubtless increase. If no wealth were inherited and every generation had to build up its own fortune, the inequality of wealth would be much less than it is now. Between these two extremes lies the world in which we live. In fact inheritance does take place, the number of heirs being greater than the number of testators. Fortunes are broken up. (They are also merged through marriage, but not all rich men marry rich women.) This process of disintegration increases according as those leaving the money reach a greater age – and this is actually a steadily continuing process. In that time they have acquired more grandchildren. This trend could be reversed if the birth rate among the very rich were drastically to decline, or if the disintegration were to be compensated for by selective marriages – money marries money – but there is no convincing proof of this. And then there is the State as heir; death duties are

* Figures for Britain in H. F. Lydall and D. G. Tipping, 'The Distribution of Personal Wealth in Britain', *Bulletin of the Oxford University Institute of Statistics*, 1961. Figures for the United States in R. J. Lampman, 'Changes in the Share of Wealth Held by Top Wealth-Holders, 1922–1956', *Review of Economics and Statistics*, 1959. Lampman is of the opinion that the figure of 51% for the top 1% in the United States is an overestimation. In my turn I feel that 43% is too high for Britain in the Fifties. The American figure is almost 50% lower, and 43% is also difficult to reconcile with an income share of the top 1% of 8%. See below, pp. 278–9.

paid on every estate. True, there are ingenious methods of dodging these – making a gift of one's wealth during one's lifetime, and above all the creation of trust funds – but this evasion has its limits. The tax people take a bite out of the fortune every time one of its holders dies. The final outcome depends on the actual figures and the legal constructions; you can write down numerical examples in which inheritance plus death duties overcomes the cumulative forces of inequality, and you can also do the opposite. The proof of the pudding is in the figures on the actual concentration of wealth, and there we see a decrease. It is much more modest than the plaintive representatives of the rich would have us believe – it is simply not true that all fortunes have been chopped into little pieces and squandered by the community. But the opposite argument – a steadily growing inequality – is also untenable. Evidently systematic forces are operating in the direction of a somewhat greater spread of wealth, though the inequality still continues to be enormous.*

However, the slight trend towards less inequality in wealth is only one side of the matter. Another influence is at work that is causing the share in income of the top 1% to decline: the systematic reduction of the share of capital in national income. We saw in Chapter V that up to now this trend has been unmistakable, and it is surprising that practically all writers on *personal* income distribution leave it out of consideration. In Lundberg's *The Rich and the Super-Rich* you find nothing about it, which shows that economists sometimes have a slight lead on journalists (this is not meant ironically – a perceptive journalist sees things that the learned fail to spot. The newspaperman has an eye for conflict, injustice, dirty tricks, where the economist only surmises algebra). But sophisticated statisticians of personal distribution also often forget that there is also such a thing as a shift in distributive shares. In the meantime the students of distributive shares devise more and more refined models in their particular field.

A numerical example shows the relation. The share of capital plus that of large profits was still around 40% at the beginning of the century. It is now closer to 20%. Let us assume the unrealistic case that the spread of wealth had not become somewhat more

* See for this T. Atkinson, *The Redistribution of Wealth*, 1970.

uniform, and that therefore the top 1% of income recipients still possessed 40% of total wealth. Suppose too that these people had no income from work; they are pure capitalists. In that case the share of this group in national income would have fallen from 40% times 40% = 16% to 20% times 40% = 8%. Or in other words it would have halved. In reality the relative capital income of the top 1% has been further reduced by the decreased concentration of wealth; if we were to adhere to the above figures for Britain, the share of income would drop from 60% times 40% = 24% to 40% times 20% = 8%. This drop from 24% to 8% is no small matter, and one would think that the textbooks and the special studies on income distribution would stress it. They do not.

Now it is true that my numerical example presents events in an exaggerated fashion. For the income of the top 1% does not consist only of income from property. The group also includes working people – managers, senior civil servants, businessmen, professional people. Even some of the super-rich earn incomes from work which may also be very high ones. This counters the drop in their share of income. The percentage of national income that they get works out higher than the 8% mentioned, on account of incomes from work; if half of the top 1% work, and their salaries are on average five times the average income – a highly conservative estimate! – the total income from work and wealth of the top 1% already exceeds 10%, and that is more than we observe in the United Kingdom and the United States, viz. 8%.

Something is wrong here. We can escape this inconsistency by assuming that the very large fortunes are lower in earning power than the small ones, for instance because they consist to a greater extent of country estates, mansions and castles, and also pleasure yachts, all with a low yield, but that is an odd hypothesis, at variance with the high percentage of securities in the great fortunes and also inconsistent with the view that the super-rich are such clever investors. A better way of bringing the British top income share of 8% into line with wealth distribution is to doubt the 43% share of wealth ascribed by Lydall and Tipping to the top 1% of wealth-holders. The latter percentage is improbably high and has a statistically weak basis. For the United States R. J. Lampman found a percentage of 24 for the share of wealth of the top 1%, and that is more consistent with income distribution. Incidentally, it is typical of the fragmentary treatment of this evidence that Lydall and Tipping themselves did not hit on the idea of including in their analysis the consistency of income distribution and wealth distribution. For the time being I shall assume that the concentration of wealth in Britain is less than they state, and that a figure of 25–30% for the top 1% is closer to reality. Of course, it remains a very skew distribution, but it is gradually becoming less skew.*

Despite the uncertainty of the data, the trend is obvious: the reduction of the share of capital, plus the spread in capital holding, has caused the income share of the top people to decline. In addition, there is a third factor involved: it is probable that the incomes *from work* of the top group have levelled out somewhat. They fall under the general rule that salary differentials are gradually shrinking. In some cases this process is backed up by special institutional factors; the introduction of the National Health Service into Britain has brought doctors' salaries more into line with the general salary structure.

Doubt could arise as to whether the levelling does in fact operate with regard to the very high incomes of top executives in business. As mentioned above, the managers of the concerns are in a position to fix their own incomes. The limits are set by what they themselves regard as reasonable, and thus by the general normative climate with regard to income differentials. These incomes reflect the prestige that the top group vests itself with, and perhaps do not obey 'economic' laws too greatly, although allowance must be

* In my opinion the inconsistency lies between 43% and a share of income that the authors themselves put at 6½%, to be found in the article 'The Distribution of Personal Wealth in Britain', *Bulletin of the Oxford University Institute of Statistics*, February 1961. Mr Lydall has pointed out to me that the two groups, top income recipients and top wealth-holders, need not be the same; but at a concentration of wealth of 43% and a capital share of 20% the top group of capitalists automatically becomes the top group of income recipients, and therefore that argument does not mean much. In addition, the income recipients are counted as families and the wealth-holders as adults, which hampers comparability, but it would be most strange if this explained the difference. The whole case shows that these figures have many catches. The American figures are from R. J. Lampman, 'Changes in the Share of Wealth Held by Top Wealth-Holders, 1922–1956', *Review of Economics and Statistics*, 1959.

made for an increased supply (all those Business Schools and Management Courses are not proliferating for nothing). The amount of money concerned is so limited that the shareholders have nothing to gain from thwarting the managers on the matter of their salaries; the marginal productivity cannot be determined; and supply and demand exert little influence because top promotions and appointments take place through co-opting, in which a real market can hardly be distinguished. There is great economic room for allowing normative views to operate.

We could therefore easily imagine that these super-incomes avoid the general levelling process. However, the fragmentary data available do not confirm this supposition. For instance, L. R. Burgess has calculated in his book *Top Executive Pay Package* (1963) that the compensation of the three top managers of each of the 25 largest manufacturing corporations in the United States has come closer to that of the remaining personnel. From 1929 to 1958 the average income of the three bosses increased by over 60%; the general wage increase over that period was about 250%. This is before income tax has struck. And in addition the remuneration at the highest levels was also compressed internally: in 1929 the average income relation between the top levels of the organization was 182–100–77; by 1958 the differentials had shrunk to 145–100–103. The remuneration includes stock options and deferred compensations and pensions, but not expense accounts and fringe benefits.* If this indication is representative, there is also salary levelling going on in the top regions, which may perhaps be explained by the changes in ethical and sociological climate. Evidently something is happening to top circle norms and value judgements too. Anti-egalitarians will sadly conclude that the detestable spirit of drab sameness has also eaten into our business leaders. Left-wing critics of the system will be surprised. Evolutionary egalitarians will derive some slight satisfaction from these figures. (I recommend the latter point of view.)

---

* The exact figures are not in Burgess but in R. Goode, *The Individual Income Tax*, 1964, p. 272. Similar figures for Britain are to be found in G. Routh, *Occupation and Pay in Great Britain 1906–1960*, 1965. Between 1935 and 1955 higher professional incomes fell from almost four times the average to less than three times the average.

But before we get too optimistic about these reduced differentials we must bear in mind that stubborn counterforces are also at work. These are to be found in profits. Reference has already been made above (at the end of section 7 of Chapter IV) to the fantastic inequality in the distribution of profits among companies. The top 0·5 per cent of corporations in the United States get about half of company profits, and in the United Kingdom 30 to 40%. There are no indications that these proportions are changing trendwise. An élite of active financiers profits from this marked concentration. These are the people with the big share portfolios, the club of the super-rich. It is highly probable that this small group is capable of escaping the egalitarian tendencies in society. The passive wealth-holders are the sufferers from the decline of capital's share; the active owners are probably able to avoid the levelling trend. True, they suffer from death duties – that point is further discussed below in Chapter VII, 8 – but the structural development of capitalism does not work to their disadvantage.

Profits tax is not a cure-all against this. For the companies are very handy at passing on the burden to their customers. Some observers, such as F. Lundberg, assume that the large concerns have all their taxes paid by the consumer. More cautious investigators, such as M. Kryzaniak and R. A. Musgrave,* arrive at a figure of 40%. The most probable percentages are a subject of controversy among economists, but one thing that is certain is that the profits tax rates (in most countries a little below 50%) are no criterion of income transfer. A substantial part of this tax is borne by the public in general.

The direction of income development at the top is further complicated by technical progress. As regards this, our conclusions must be just as hesitant as those concerning the lowest incomes. The introduction of new products and production processes is accelerating; this creates high incomes for some entrepreneurs, large and small, and losses for other entrepreneurs. Income shifts occur whose net effect on the incomes of the top 1% is difficult to predict. However, a number of systematic forces can be pointed to.

The most encouraging aspect is that some newcomers get a chance. In section 1 of Chapter III it has already been pointed out

* *The Shifting of the Corporation Tax*, 1963.

that at least two persons from the list of American dollar centi-millionaires (Land and Carlson) owe their super-fortunes to their own inventions. At a somewhat more modest, though not a less spectacular level technology can also help people, who have had absolutely nothing to do with the inventions, to acquire high incomes suddenly. The entertainment industry offers conspicuous examples of this. Through the improved communications techniques (plus the build-up of the film and record companies) a number of men and women whose acting ability, musical gifts or physical attraction are above average have acquired incomes that are disproportionately higher than what corresponds to these qualities. Liz Taylor, who without technical development would probably not have got far from the mode of income distribution, has now, if you will pardon the imagery, been catapulted into the right-hand tail of the frequency curve. In the parade of Chapter III she was (in some years) a tower one hundred yards in height.

This example illustrates what rapid careers are possible in modern society, and how difficult it is to analyse what exactly is going on in the heterogeneous group of the top incomes. The new-style *nouveau riche* owes his position as a rule to the whims of an unpredictable technical turbulence. Against this is the fact that enterprises can rapidly start operating at a loss – in that respect the market mechanism is inexorable in a changing world. Only a widespread portfolio of investments offers sure guarantees against abrupt drops in income; in the world of the real entrepreneurs and capitalists actively concerned in special firms there is little security to be found.

Technical change can also provide other surprises. We have already seen that the drop in the share of capital could quite easily be turned round the other way if technology should begin to be capital-using to a major extent. True, this has not yet happened macro-economically – before the war technology offered only slight support to capital's share, and since the war it has perhaps offered no support at all – but it might very well happen in the unpredictable future, and then the top 1% profit. Without doing anything in return the rich will be able to take a greater bite out of income growth, and it is very difficult to take any action against this. The present sharp rise in the interest rate may point to this.

There is also a temporary side to this phenomenon (reaction of the investors to price increases), but perhaps it is the beginning of a new equilibrium and a new trend on the capital market from which the wealth-owners will lastingly profit. This doesn't make prediction any the easier.

And finally it is uncertain what the accelerated technical development will do with the concentration of firms. One possible hypothesis is that the profits of the giant concerns will grow in relative terms as a result. Because it is there that the money is to be found for large-scale research, there that the impressive staffs are available to search industriously for new products and working methods, there that the risk-absorbing financial stamina is located. The possibility of an invention is much more likely in a large concern than in a small firm. (If the chances of technical progress were in proportion to the profits, small firms would have no chance at all – but it doesn't work like that.) However, none of this guarantees that a changing technology cannot harm the giants' interests. In electronics and in chemistry, in cars and power supply, rapid shifts may occur and then profits at one place are accompanied by losses elsewhere. It is difficult to forecast exactly what influence that will have on the concentration of profits and personal incomes.

All in all, the downward trend in the share of the top 1% has been obvious so far; but it is less clear whether it will continue. My personal expectation is that a further levelling is in the offing for the top incomes from work, and perhaps also for pure interest. I would not venture to say this for the pure incomes from profit – they may very well disturb the picture of general levelling. This has only a limited effect on income distribution as a whole (the big profits are not more than 10% of national income, and only a small part of them go to the very rich), but this uncertainty operates precisely at the end of our parade, where the monstrously tall fellows are marching; it is profit that can suddenly place a person in the rear of the procession. But we may be sure that the men half a mile or several miles high will be with us for the time being. They avoid the general process of levelling, and obey the unpredictable laws of profit.

INCOME DISTRIBUTION

6. *Immutable Laws and Pliability*

Paretians and log-men, in their quest for the immutable laws of
income distribution, have considerably widened our insight into
income differentials, even though the only true formula has not
been found. They have indicated various forces at work in society
and leading to inequality. But they were not the only seekers of the
truth. The social critics and the general economists have also
contributed towards our knowledge. The social critics have shown
us how cumulative influences threaten to pull rich and poor ever-
further apart. Harrington in particular has pointed to the vicious
circles at the bottom of the ladder, and Lundberg to the tricks of
the super-top. In all this the economists have recalled a number of
underlying processes, such as the changing scarcity and the decreasing share of capital, and have constantly drawn attention to
the facts as shown by the Lorenz curve. The latter was necessary,
for on the strength of the cumulative forces one would expect an
increasing inequality – and for all the disagreement about the
subtlety of the figures it is indisputable that an ever-growing gap
between the top and bottom incomes and wealth is definitely not
the tendency that we observe in reality.

And further it has become clear that we have far too many
theories. Inequality, and its historical movement, is over-explained.
The reader who had hoped to be given one clear and hard-and-fast
theory of personal distribution will certainly be disappointed. He
has seen a display of varying views and contradictory explanatory
principles. It is difficult to make out from the preceding sections
who exactly is right, which forces have the most effect and which
prediction of things to come is the most effective. This impression
is as it should be: economics has not yet ascended to a level at
which we all bow down to the one view. Come to that, it is not
certain before the event that we ought to expect anything as odd as
one unique theory; income distribution has grown historically, a
resultant of complex causes, still daily subject to conflicting forces.
It is perhaps a very good thing that one self-contained model of
personal distribution does not exist; the diversity of the theories
should keep alive the realization that science is relative and life
complicated.

This does not alter the fact that in the above we have been able to discern a number of lines that are relevant to our practical view of society. It seems to me that the most important point to consider is this: what are the implications of the various hypotheses and views for the *pliability* of distribution? The Paretian and the lognormal distributions easily create the impression that they describe immutable relations, products of deep, natural forces that cannot be deflected by man and society. If this impression is correct, we could forget the pursuit of a different (for instance more equal) income distribution. If the determinism is half correct, in the sense that strong but not insuperable forces are at work in society that try to cancel out political intervention (like a sponge resists deformation), the political conclusion would have to be that policy must be doubly alert and doubly powerful to have any effect. I believe that the latter is in fact the case. Let us examine why.

In the first place we must recall that an algebraic relation such as the Pareto equation or the lognormal distribution does not point to an unchangeable distribution. Pareto himself drew attention to the changeableness of his constant α – this is not a contradiction or a paradox. As we saw above, the constant α means that an increase in the Selected Income Level brings about a fixed drop in the number of income recipients, whatever the Selected Income Level happens to be. (In fact this rule applies only to values of the Selected Income Level that are well above average.) But constant does not mean to say constant in time, or the same for different countries. On the contrary, almost all observers agree that α increases in the course of time, and in itself this need not stand in the way of Pareto's Law.* And the same applies to lognormal distribution; this may be more or less skew, the right-hand tail may be longer or shorter, and yet it can retain its lognormal character. In the language of mathematicians, the value of the parameters may change without Gibrat's Law going to rack and ruin.

And in addition the figures observed do not tally absolutely with the equations. Pareto's Law applies only to the top. Gibrat's Law does not entirely tally either; the empirical curve shows too many people at either end. By making the rich less rich and the poor less

---

* H. P. Miller misses this point when he asserts that Pareto's Law excludes changes in the income curve (*Rich Man, Poor Man*, 1964, p. 52).

poor we bring reality better into line with the algebra. Some will consider this to be a good piece of work.

Indeed, income distribution is anything but immutable. In the course of history the Lorenz curve has become flatter, despite the increase in the number of post-active persons. We see this flattening both at the top and at the bottom. That is particularly perceptible in countries with extensive systems of social policy, such as the United Kingdom and Sweden. The distributive shares have also shifted. Wage structure has been compressed a little. Wealth is less skew in its distribution than formerly. Although all these movements go relatively slowly, their overall net effect is clear: we have seen that inequality is decreasing.

Now this historical development is no evidence of deliberate pliability. It might be that the shifts from rich to poor and from capital to labour were the exclusive result of changed supply and demand relations, and that these fundamental processes took place without intervention. The fact that a natural sponge grows under water and in doing so changes shape does not mean to say that we can cause it to change shape by squeezing it. Through industrious study of intersecting curves many economists have retained the idea that it is these curves that fully determine income distribution. Their view implies that income distribution is a sponge. It opposes the other extreme: the naïve belief that income distribution is like putty. You squeeze it and it holds its new shape. A sponge always remembers its old shape; putty has no memory.

We have already seen that both views are one-sided. Wage structure is not exactly determined by scarcity; there is room for conventional and institutional wage-fixing, although this is not as large as the adherents of the putty theory believe. The nominal interest rate is probably very sponge-like in nature; its level cannot be influenced unless the authorities squeeze everywhere (i.e. start big-scale operations in the capital market themselves, ration demand, close the frontiers – and even then the success is dubious, as will be shown in Chapter VII, 3). The *level* of wages and prices, on the other hand, is putty, or rather an inflatable substance that can be increased to any volume. We saw above that the overall income structure in inflation is rather spongy; while the spiral is going on the old relations re-establish themselves to some extent. Not entirely; the sponge is slightly putty-like. Only some profits are pure sponge; they do not allow themselves to be compressed by the wage push, and they even may become larger through the income effect of wage increases on sales.

There is no doubt that factor price relations can be transformed to some extent by deliberate action. They are not only influenced by scarcity but also by institutional and conventional causes. And scarcity itself can be influenced; here the insights of the log-men help us to avoid exaggerated determinism.

Take for instance Roy's theory of the multiplicative effect. It deals with a fundamental process that can nevertheless be influenced. The theory entails that a person's earning capacity is determined by multiplying a number of his separate qualities, such as intelligence, ambition, leadership, etc. This multiplicative relation may easily lead to a highly skew distribution, especially if intercorrelation of the income-acquiring properties occurs. For a moment, it may look as if this skewness is rooted in natural circumstances beyond the grasp of deliberate intervention. But that is not as bad as it seems as soon as we realize that intelligence and leadership can be cultivated and that this may even apply to ambition. The way in which this cultivation is arranged depends on the educational system, on social mores, on the way we build our cities. These are pliable factors which can be planned in very different ways. It is not nature that immovably prescribes how children will develop; the loaded dice can be made into more honest playthings. Society can be changed. But that change works through to the deeper layers of the social structure. It cannot be achieved by superficial tinkering, and anyone who had thought that income distribution can be radically equalized by a few simple regulations realizes through Roy's theory that a more fundamental approach is called for. If people shrink from these fundamental changes on political grounds, income distribution stays as it is.

The same applies to the second important view of lognormal distribution: the proportional effect. Gibrat is of the opinion that the chances of percentage increases of existing incomes are normally distributed and that this leads to increasing skewness. But these chances are not immutable data. If *everybody* gets exactly the same percentage of extra income (and the spread of the chances is therefore nil), the skewing influence of the stochastic process does not operate, and the curve remains the same. This can be aimed at. It can even be arranged in such a way that the chances for poor people become more favourable and those for the more well-to-do relatively less favourable; to this end the privileges in education and environment must become negative. But this requires a tremendous effort. Schools for poor children must be *better* than those for the rich – the opposite of the 'natural' state of affairs. The drawbacks of slums must be overcompensated for. These are no small things, but they are at least conceivable.

Pliability is in principle also possible among the incomes that reflect hierarchy, status and prestige. However, this requires that the policy-makers revise their ideas on hierarchy, status and prestige, or that the power structure within firms changes. As long as these radical operations have not been performed in the socio-psychological and organizational situation, it remains difficult to change the conventional income structure. As has appeared in Israel, it sneaks in again through the back door (see Chapter V, 2). But, once again, the operation in the deeper layers of social tissue is conceivable, provided that the community as a whole calls for it. Income distribution is made by people, even though they do not always realize that. We shall return to this matter in the next chapter.

The fact that people, and not the man in the moon, make distribution also emerges from the low incomes that are the product of discrimination. Lower pay for women can easily be abolished, if people want this. They do not. Men don't, women hardly want it, and the unions, despite their propaganda, are not sufficiently interested either – otherwise unequal pay could not maintain its ground. The laws of lognormal distribution are also based in part on such unwillingness. To that extent income distribution is both pliable (*it could be different*) and unbelievably ponderous and immutable: what people want is ponderous and immutable. However, it is not economic laws that create this inflexibility, but the collective expression of an accepted scale of values. In the case of discrimination against women and racial minorities it is obviously not the scale of values and the power of a few corrupt capitalists or 'the system' but also and above all the ideas, the prejudices and the scale of values of the workers and their unions, who themselves are part of a discriminatory society.

What at any event can be countered by a deliberate policy are the cumulative forces of poverty. There is a strong natural tendency in this vicious circle, and income transfers plain and simple, though indispensable, are at the same time completely inadequate. The productive capacities of the underdogs must be increased, the social stratification has to be reduced. There is a lively realization that programmes directed towards this end have to be comprehensive. Improved education, collective and individual social work, urban renewal – these are tremendous tasks, and it is very much the question whether we are prepared to invest sufficient money and energy in them. But at least the direction that policy could take is clear.

Much less clear, particularly from an intellectual point of view, is the matter of the top incomes. Not a single theory has so far succeeded in sorting out how exactly the very high incomes come about. True, in principle every mechanism is known: the high remuneration for the super-specialist who combines talent and experience; the quick commercial wealth resulting from profit; and above all the top incomes from inherited wealth which led in our parade to figures miles in height. The cumulative forces can be listed, and the counterforces (including the declining share of capital) are known. There has been no lack of lists and inventories in the above. But none of that gives us a clear, quantitative picture. The multiplicative processes of Roy probably play a part, but perhaps a subordinate one. The dubious practices of the very rich, as described by the social critics (speculation with advance knowledge, financial manipulation, monopoly, coincidence of political and commercial activities) certainly occur – but would it make a substantial difference to the overall distribution if they were stopped? The influence of technical progress, to mention only the most important factor, on profits creates precisely with the top incomes a considerable weakness in the explanatory ability of the various theories.

This has its repercussions on the ideas about the pliability of the very high incomes, and in particular of profits. Some think that profits are too precarious and their importance to economic motivation too strategic for harsh intervention to be justified here. I am inclined to share this view. Action should be taken to suppress illegal, corrupt and harmful practices, but in the next chapter I will argue that the effect of this kind of intervention on income distribution cannot amount to much. I would add that a government really ought to try to restrict profits, by a kind of price policy, during an inflationary development, but this too has only a limited effect on distribution. Perhaps the best way to deal with this 'troublesome category' is not to interfere when profits are made but to arrange a different method of sharing them out. In such a way capitalism can be allowed to exist in full flower and yet the top incomes can be considerably reduced. This requires changes in the power structure of the firms – a subject to be discussed in Chapter VII, 6.

These remarks are meant as a transition to the following chapter, which is concerned with norms and policies. Such intervention would not be possible if the laws of personal distribution were rigid and successfully opposed any attempt at change. However, on the whole we have not encountered such laws. The equations of Pareto and Gibrat stimulate thought; they do not block action. And now more about this intervention.

CHAPTER VII

Norms and Policies

1. *Ideas on the Best Distribution: Twenty-one Varieties*

GOOD and evil do not speak for themselves. Many ethical systems exist side by side. Usually they do not bite one another, and there is little discussion between them. Followers of Christ and Mao-Tse-tung, Moslems and humanists, adherents of Nietzsche and of the Sufi movement live in their own world of ideas, usually self-contained systems which collide only when the practical measures come into conflict with each other. The number of ethical systems is large, but fortunately they do not all have something to say about income distribution, and so we can leave them for what they are. And yet it is as well to bear in mind that the standards for distribution described below are often founded in one *weltanschauung* or the other: the austerity of Calvinism, the solidarism of some Catholic interpretations, the strictness of Marxism, which rejects interest, land rent and profit, the bourgeois desire for comfort and security, the humanistic longing for freedom and development of personality, the romantic nostalgia for grandeur and splendour (which some think have vanished in this present age of levelling and sameness).

The great split on income distribution is that between left-wing egalitarianism, which starts from the fundamental equality of human beings, and the right-wing stress on the very special properties of very special individuals. This difference of outlook is of course rooted in deeper ideological differences: it is therefore connected in a systematic way with differences of opinion regarding the respectability of tradition and of authority, the desirability of co-partnership of workers, the best methods of education. The influence of heredity and milieu is differently appraised by Left and Right, and the correct level of death duties is assessed in varying ways. According to the Left, rich people are poor people with money; the Right considers their remarkable achievements, their function in society, their way of life. In the absence of proof to the contrary, the economic élite are owed respect on the strength of their riches. The Left believes, subject to proof of the contrary, that the rich probably came by their money in dubious fashion; every fortune conceals a crime. The unattractive side of the Left is its rancour and intolerance; hate of people who are better off and sometimes even of people who achieve more. The appealing side of the Left is its defence of the weak, its lack of unfounded respect and its confidence that society can be changed for the better. The Right is guilty of championing the interests of the strong and the powerful; it is inclined to blame the poor for their poverty and to turn a blind eye to the social mechanisms that perpetuate inequality. The Right often regards the poor as inferior. The worlds of ideas of Left and Right cannot be reconciled, but fortunately this *is* to some extent the case with the practical measures resulting from these two worlds. As experience shows, practical people can reach a measure of agreement on tax policy, death duties, social security, and sometimes even on an incomes policy on paper, even though they adhere to different ideologies.

It is not my intention to venture into ideological depths here. I shall remain at the surface and give a pragmatic survey of some ideas and norms in the field of distribution, with a few comments. Although ethical pronouncements are not very open to judgement from outside, it is nevertheless possible to establish a number of criteria. One of these is to see whether the reasoning is consistent. A person who objects to poverty, and in the name of this principle wants to make all incomes equal, soon gets tied up (because this might on occasion make the poor poorer), just as someone does who, in the name of freedom, wants to ban all private production. A following requirement – a somewhat weaker one – is feasibility. It is easy to think up unachievable desiderata with regard to distribution: a generous minimum income plus a pronounced vertical wage differential (cannot be reconciled with the limited nature of total income), or an income structure that is so fanciful that people rebel against it. Anything that does not stand up is not worth much as an ethical norm. And further norms may be inspired by manifestly incorrect conceptions: the pseudo-ethicist who believes that State ownership of the means of production is completely unworkable, or his opponent who condemns capitalism purely and simply because it reduces the share of labour or the standard of living, is evidently badly informed and his prescriptions and advice are things that we can do without.

I shall not refrain from saying whether a particular norm appeals to me or not. This is, of course, highly subjective, but the reader has the right to know what the author thinks of it. Only in this way can a discussion be furthered, and that is exactly the idea of the following list.

My starting point is egalitarian; income differentials are not necessarily wrong, but their justification must be proved. Very high incomes are wrong (but perhaps inevitable!). This view naturally makes itself felt in the following.

Here, then, comes a list of various, sometimes contradictory views. It is not meant to be exhaustive. Perhaps the reader will fail to find his favourite idea in it. What struck me most strongly is its length. To stress this, it has been numbered.

(1) *Distribution is irrelevant* because income is irrelevant. There is already much too much consumption of the wrong kind: soulless, artificial 'satisfaction' encouraged by advertising, which robs people of their freedom, makes them empty and unhappy. Property is theft, and 'income distribution' is the sort of expression that fits in with it. We ought to abandon the whole rotten production and consumption structure of industrial capitalism, we ought to live in communes, be directly supplied with simple, natural goods, and arrange distribution in direct consultation with one another. *Comments*: consistent and appealing recommendations, but hardly feasible in a world in which so many people still want cars, aircraft, cameras, expensive wrist watches, fast motor boats, etc. And in the case of some adherents it is not consistent either, to the extent that they themselves like to travel, read inexpensive books, engage in photography, enjoy records, and so on. There is scope for application on a small scale; the adherents can put their ideas into practice and, by their example, invite others to imitate them.

(2) *All to get the same*, with a slight differentiation according to size of family, age, or other elementary differences in wants. *Comments*: consistent, but hardly feasible. Nobody would be permitted to earn anything on his own account (and keep it him-

self), because that upsets the principle. The system therefore requires either a superhuman spirit of self-sacrifice or a good deal of compulsion. Practical application is possible within limited groups, (example: kibbutz) and (2) is really a variant of (1). The question is further whether some extra effort does not entitle one to some extra income. The sense of justice of most people demands this extra remuneration, but once you start with this bang goes the absolute equality.

(3) *Incomes from work only*. This is Marxism: all interest, land rent and profit is exploitation and must be done away with. In other words, capitalism must go. The norm is realized in quite a different society from our own. *Comments*: this can be done; indeed, it *is* being done in some countries. The pros and cons of those systems have been adequately described; we do not need to go into them here. However, even with this principle income distribution is anything but fixed. Just as under capitalism, it remains a problem as to how the total wage bill has to be divided up. Marx offered little to go on here! In practice the Lorenz curve in the Communist countries proves to be somewhat flatter than in the West, but not all that flat. It somewhat resembles the Civil Service curve, but their statistics are never cast in this provocative form – in fact they are hardly published.*

(4) *There is too much inequality because the rich are too rich*. Their wealth is the source of the poverty of the poor. The top x% (that has to be filled in later: 1%, 10%) should be stripped of their surplus, and the sources of that surplus must be drained: capital,

*The conference on distribution organized in Palermo by the International Economic Association in 1964 was also attended by delegates from Communist countries. Their contributions consisted of songs of praise about the situation in their home-countries without this situation even being described statistically, high-falutin normative reflections without it being checked whether these norms were satisfied in their own countries, and statistics on agriculture, the size of the government sector and much more, but not about income distribution. We do not get to see a parade of Communist workers, as described in Chapter III, 1. And even less a Lorenz curve. There is no reference to the fact that under Stalin egalitarianism was officially and vehemently condemned as 'petty bourgeois', whilst after 1956 this attitude seems to have been changed. It was a poor show. See the collection *The Distribution of National Income*, 1968.

power, monopoly, authority. A fundamental conflict exists between the rich (exploiters, capitalists, back-room schemers, power élite) and ordinary people. *Comments*: this norm is based on a factual analysis of our society which is not very plausible. The yarn about the usurpation of power is full of misunderstandings and gross exaggerations. The essential proposition that the poor are poor *because* the rich are rich is not correct; even under static conditions, i.e. with a given national income, this is barely true. The top 1% get less than 10% of national income; by reducing these people to the average a surplus of 9% becomes available for distribution among others. This is not very much, and in addition it implies that dentists, accountants, engineers and other more or less hard-working citizens have been cut down to the average. Of course, there *are* rich people who harm the poor (slum landlords), but high incomes are also earned from technical progress, from which many (including the poor) profit. The poor are often injured by people who are not too well-off themselves: small businessmen, landlords in a small way. Most of the rich become rich because they let the well-to-do pay. Most of the poor are poor for reasons that are not directly related to the wealth of the rich, and they would be no better off if the millionaires disappeared from the face of the earth. Establishing a causal connexion between the income of the top 1% and poverty is, in developed countries, arbitrary and not convincing.

(Of course one can put matters more generally and claim that a society that allows of excessive wealth and at the same time displays flagrant poverty is ethically objectionable. That is an obvious judgement, but it is not the same as making the rich responsible via a theory of combined force. See below under 5.)

Usually the adherents of the theory that the rich are responsible for the misery of the poor have a political connexion in mind. They are of the opinion that our social structure is maintained by a small élite exerting power and *en passant* enriching its members; they further believe that this structure inevitably entails great poverty. A particular proponent of this theory is the late C. Wright Mills, in *The Power Elite* (1956). He is of the opinion that power (in the United States) is exerted by three interlocking groups: the politicians, the 'Military High' and the 'Corporate Rich'. Their interests are interwoven, and they succeed in perpetuating all existing abuses and injustices. American imperialism, the decay of the cities, suppression, poverty everywhere; these are the results of the system.

This theory contains a sombre view of the functioning of democracy and the pluriform society. It is popular among many young people and those seeking a scapegoat for a series of abuses of a political and social nature. The criticism of society by Mills and others has the advantage that it opens our eyes to the secret mechanisms of power, to the semi-corruption of political life by the pressure groups and to the social abuses that continue to exist come what may; but as a theory of cause and effect élitism overlooks newspapers, unions, radio and television, and the universities. It ignores the influence of independent political judgement and also ignores its own influence. Politicians may act on the strength of their own ideas, which may turn out rational or bizarre, salutary or utterly destructive, but certainly not always in harmony with business interests as seen by the businessman.

It is true that the political mechanism functions laboriously, often because people do not know what they want, or because they want contradictory things. A right-wing policy cannot but prevail as long as the Left is entangled in internal squabbles and unrealistic analyses of capitalist society. The Left consists partly of people who first want to demolish society, and their activities get in the way of the evolutionary part of the Left. In many countries (France!) the Left is so fragmented and chaotic that it barely exists any longer. The power élite cannot be blamed for this – at most it exploits the ineffectiveness of the Left.

This is not the place to discuss the ramifications of the extreme leftist social criticism. It involves the whole of Latin America, and Vietnam and Biafra, the students' protest and the ideas of H. Marcuse on the addictive effect of consumption and on repressive tolerance. That is too much for a simple book on income distribution. I can only state my conviction that the abuses in the world cannot be linked together in simple fashion. The economic system in the West has less responsibility for good and evil than leftist critics think. The attraction of their view is that they seem to offer a key to truth: every door opens, everywhere the bright light of understanding shines. But that is an illusion. These theories lump everything together far too much. They speak of the United States and think that they have dealt with the whole of capitalism; in a political respect there is a great difference between Brazil, the United States and Sweden, all three 'capitalist' countries. International politics is far too complex to be captured by one theory which in addition is exaggeratedly economic in orientation. Biafra is not Vietnam, and a suggestive theory that explains the war in both countries by one principle – the consequences of capitalist exploitation – must be greatly distrusted. Nationalism, tribal wars, feudal and nineteenth-century legacies, ideological hatred, and further simple craving for power – these, plus the omnipresent blunders, are ingredients enough for a world full of escalating misery. It is true that free enterprise sometimes throws in a few extra conflicts, but the international concerns also create harmony, and the amount of the latter varies from country to country. Anyone who blindly blames the capitalist system for all conflicts exaggerates to a ridiculous extent, and is guilty of armchair determinism. The generalizations à la Marcuse are opium to left-wing intellectuals.*

(5) *High and medium-high incomes are immoral as long as impermissible poverty exists. Comments*: this is an obvious norm. It leaves behind it all the drawbacks of the political theories outlined above and takes as its direct starting point a solidarism of Christian or humanistic origin. This view is, I should think, fairly universally accepted, although it is not followed in practice. The main reason for the latter is that the misery in the world is so overwhelmingly great. Formerly – not only in the nineteenth century, but also in the Thirties – it was normal to have revolting poverty within the frontiers of one's own country; income transfers could not solve the problem, because it was too large. That is still so if one considers the world as a whole. Anyone who wants to adhere to this norm and does not wish to suffer from permanent disgust should

---

* What I dislike the most about books like *One Dimensional Man* is the absolute and total character of the reasoning. According to Marcuse manipulation under late capitalism is total. Power is total. Repression is total. The unbearableness is total. It seems to me more of a parody than a sensible theory.

concentrate his attention on his own country. (In addition he can advocate increased development aid, but this involves at most only a few per cent of national income. So we compromise between Utopia and reality.) Perhaps it is more respectable if we opt for permanent disgust. In that case this book is superfluous.

Within the countries of the West the concept 'impermissible poverty' can be interpreted in different ways. The minimum standard of living required is subjective – by referring to the plight of the beggars in Bombay you can reason all poverty in the developed countries out of existence. And yet there is a certain *communis opinio*. For the United States various calculations have been made, starting either from a minimum family income or from a series of other criteria (families in rural regions need somewhat less money than urban ones; family structure differs; the necessary pattern of expenditure differs from region to region as a result of climate). As a rule they arrive at the result that about 20% of American families and unattached individuals come below the poverty line. There are some lower estimates, but not much lower, and some higher ones.* One out of five families – that is no laughing matter. They are above all old people, families without a father or with a jobless, sick or disabled provider. They include many unattached individuals, with regular incomes – 44% of them were poor. And poverty among non-whites amounted to 42% – clear proof of the lasting racial discrimination. Among these groups there is thus an urgent task for a redistribution policy, as also emerges from the constant repetition of the expression 'war on poverty' – incidentally a very mild war, as some observers have remarked.

* cf., A. B. Batchelder, *The Economics of Poverty*, 1966. The pioneer in this field, R. J. Lampman, has pointed out in his *The Low Income Population and Economic Growth* (Study Paper 12 for the Joint Economic Committee, Congress of the U.S., 1959) that percentages for the United States 'reasonably range' between 16 and 36. Various close calculations by Molly Orshansky arrive at about 18%. (This is based on the Social Security Administration poverty index.) M. Harrington (*The Other America, Poverty in the U.S.*, 1962), finds that 20 to 25% are poor. F. Lundberg (*The Rich and the Super-Rich*, 1968) arrives at 70%; that is rather overdone. The figures for special groups given below are taken from Batchelder's book; they are based on calculations by the S S A.

For the countries of Europe, where the Welfare State is better constructed than in the United States, the presence of impermissible poverty is more controversial. Like Britain, most countries have a form of National Assistance by means of which the holes in social provisions are stopped up. However, a strange and little-known fact is that quite a number of people live below National Assistance level, even in Britain. National Assistance is available to those who are not in regular employment. But there are low-paid workers who earn less than the benefit. According to some observers their number is not large – it is estimated by J. M. Jackson at nearly 3% – but this does happen. Then there are families of self-employed, pensioned and disabled people who do not necessarily apply for National Assistance; that brings the percentage to about 4. It is higher in the group of the unattached individuals (nearly 6%) and among families with four or more children (over 6%). These figures relate to 1962.* But other students of the British poverty problem are much more pessimistic. According to an estimate by B. Abel-Smith and P. Townsend, in the Britain of 1960 there were still 7,500,000 persons, or 18% of the households, who lived below the level of National Assistance. A third of them had to live on pensions, nearly a quarter on other State benefits, and over 40% on earnings. These figures point to a situation that looks more or less like the American one. It is, however, to be remembered that most of these poor families got no assistance because they did not ask for it and also that the statistics relate to 1960.†

These figures for the United Kingdom are based on National Assistance benefit being identical with the poverty line. Of course, this is open to discussion. If a person has nothing else but this benefit, is he guaranteed against poverty? Hunger and physical distress are no longer the criteria in modern society; what we are concerned with are the 'underprivileged', people who cannot participate in life in the way that they may reasonably demand. This in itself makes it clear that money income gives insufficient information, and that other circumstances must be taken into account. In the slums a family needs more income to lead a reasonable

* 'Poverty, National Assistance and the Family', *Scottish Journal of Political Economy*, 1966.
† *The Poor and the Poorest*, 1965.

existence – not less, as many people seem to think. The squalor outside the front door must be compensated for inside the home, and the children must be able to get away from the area more frequently. The position of old people is also problematic – they can manage with less money because they do not buy any more new things, but they have extra expenditure (taxis) if they want to visit friends, children, the doctor. Old, lonely people who cannot leave their homes through lack of money are highly deprived.

There is no doubt that in this sense many people are unacceptably poor, even in the Welfare State, and that from an ethical point of view priority must be given to increasing their incomes. From a macro-economic point of view it must be possible to deal with this poverty. The lowest 20% of families get 7½% of national income in Britain (in the United States about 5%). If their incomes were to be increased by 50% this would require scarcely more than one year's growth of national production. And a 50% increase would help poor families along quite a bit, and eliminate the worst poverty for the time being. A more specific calculation of the 'poverty income deficit' does not come higher than 2% of national income even for the United States.* That amount, provided that it was carefully distributed, could alleviate the worst poverty.

To achieve the transfer of income well-thought-out measures would be required – it is no easy task to guide the redistribution in exactly the right paths! – but the well-to-do and the rich would not be seriously harmed in their possibilities of spending. If they are businessmen, they could even earn from the purchasing power injected into the ranks of the lower-income recipients. That is the characteristic harmony of the Welfare State – it attends to growing sales that are good for profits. Indeed, this harmony sometimes changes into conflict if total consumption becomes too great. That is inflation, and it is above all the poor who suffer from it. It is thus the danger of inflation that sets limits to the expansion of the Welfare State, and not the unbearable burden imposed on the middle classes.

(6) *The inequality is too great as long as the great mass of the workers are still not prosperous enough.* In other words, the steady worker

* According to A. B. Batchelder, *The Economics of Poverty*, 1966, p. 29.

must be able to support his family in suitable fashion. This is the language of the encyclical *Quadragesimo Anno* of Pius XI. *Comments*: as an ethical criterion this seems self-evident, but unfortunately it cannot always be achieved. In the poor countries the self-evident is impossible. When Pius XI published his encyclical (in the Thirties) there was no question of everyone having a decent minimum even in Western Europe; the Pope came dangerously close to revolutionary ideas.

Meanwhile the position of the average worker in the Western Europe of today has improved so much that many seriously doubt whether there are still compelling reasons for levelling in this respect. I believe that this is the most controversial point in the ethics of income distribution. Some say: the real income of the masses (the mode) is certainly open to improvement, but that must be left to economic growth. In this view it does not do deliberately to transfer income from the well-to-do to the workers, or consciously to compress the pay structure. Others think that the inequality between the average worker and the top 10% or 5% is still ethically unacceptable. The ordinary man has much too low a real income, and that must be improved not only through economic growth but also through deliberate levelling. And in fact there is not much that can be said about this difference of opinion that makes sense – *weltanschauung* and political preference get a free run here.

My own opinion would be that within the Western countries there is still some point to a degree of levelling between the higher-salary recipients and the modal-income recipients. Our parade includes employees of 20 feet and taller, while the working classes measure only 5 feet. That difference is too great, especially with a view to norm No. 10 below. But the urgency of reducing this differential is overshadowed by other requirements. These are the expansion of social provisions, the raising of the lowest wages (persons of 3 and 4 feet) and the enlarging of the collective sector. The last category also includes development aid. The average worker in the wealthy countries is still far from rich, but nevertheless he will have to help to pay towards the transfers of income on behalf of the poor countries. These transfers, plus those for the benefit of the really poor at home, limit the possibility of deliberate levelling between the mode of the income recipients and the well-to-do. We can't do everything at once. The general income structure must therefore be compressed carefully and gradually. Economic growth may certainly not be harmed as a result (see below, point 20) for only with a growing national income is an adequate growth of the collective sector achievable, and only with a sufficient growth of the collective sector (schooling, urban improvement) is an improvement of the earning capacities of the lowest-paid groups attainable. All this is further discussed below, but it is as well to establish this relationship right away.

(7) *High incomes should contribute more to the financing of State expenditure than low ones.* Or: taxation according to ability to pay. The well-off have less pleasure from their last pound than the low-income groups. This leads to progressive taxation. This is often further worked out on the principle of equal sacrifice of pleasure (so that the rich feel the same pain from taxes as the poor) or on the principle that the levying of taxation makes the total sacrifice of all taxpayers minimal. The latter principle leads to a progressive rate; so does the former, provided that the elasticity of the utility curve is less than unity. There is an abundant literature on this point.* *Comments*: creaming off the higher incomes is now not an end in itself (as with the earlier points), but a means of getting money for government expenditure. This makes the operation more acceptable to those who do not like levelling, and consequently progressive taxes are applied everywhere. Almost everyone is in agreement with this.† The point at issue is, of course, how high the progression should go. The two principles mentioned seem at first sight to offer something to go on for this, but that is not so. To apply them one ought to know the relationship between a person's income and the pleasure that he derives from it (or the displeasure at the money being taken away from him). These utility curves have not been

---

* See R. A. Musgrave, *The Theory of Public Finance*, 1959, Chapter 5.

† An exception is formed by a few adherents of the 'leave them as you find them' theory; see below, point 17.

measured and probably are not measurable either. Adding up the sacrifice made by two different individuals is not permitted, and even *comparison* between persons is regarded as impossible by most economists. Furthermore, it is not true that the satisfaction of wants yielded by an extra pound always works out lower with the higher incomes than with the lower ones. The middle classes are often less satisfied with their economic position than the manual workers. In sum, a firm foundation of the principle of ability to pay in objective, measurable relations is an illusion. Economics is not a referee; more's the pity, or perhaps not?

(8) *Money easily earned must be taxed more severely. Comments*: a consistent and appealing norm, but very difficult to put into practice. In real life one makes do with rough approaches, such as wealth tax and death duties. In Britain the Inland Revenue makes a distinction between earned and unearned income. At variance with this norm is the kind fiscal treatment of capital gains that occurs in many countries (see below, p. 346). A consistent application of this principle would mean that allowance was made for effort and the disutility of work, but that is not possible (I earn a small part of my income from writing books, easy and pleasant work, but the tax people do not succeed in taxing this income more severely than the money I earn by taking part in the cruel and repellent work of a board of examiners testing future teachers). Some people do their work with a song in their hearts and others hate every moment of it – perhaps it is only just that the latter should have tax advantages. Or not? It doesn't matter, because the tax authorities cannot make this distinction in any case.

(9) *Ill-gotten incomes have got to go.* We might think here of profits from monopoly and speculation, incomes from graft and crime. This norm is self-evident and for this very reason it is so disappointing that such incomes are so difficult to suppress. It is worth while devoting a special section to this subject (section 4 below).

(10) *Income distribution, and in particular the wage and salary structure, must be such as to be accepted by people.* This norm can be interestingly refined by the exchange principle put forward by J. Tinbergen. Justice between persons A and B is done when A, who

knows B's work and his income, would not change with him, nor B with A. Should A find the combination of work and income in B's case so attractive that he would like to swap places, then A's income must rise or B's fall until that wish vanishes. If the income correction meanwhile makes B want to change, it is clear that both of them should change places. Tinbergen says that in a society where income structure is such that people do not cast envious eyes on each other's incomes 'very pleasant relationships could exist'.* *Comments*: the exchange principle has the great advantage that it escapes one-sided subjectivism. Not you or I decide how the incomes have to be distributed, but those concerned themselves. Another attractive feature is that the central idea is based on mutual respect for one another's position. But the weak side of this norm is that it is not always possible to find an income structure that reconciles people to their situation. Dissatisfaction and rancour summon up the wish for permanent exchange, and thus for permanent change in the desired income relations. The exchange principle is therefore not logically consistent. Moreover, exchanging is not itself feasible: I may very well think that a surgeon earns too much, but all the same I cannot change jobs with him without serious harm being done to the patients. If he thinks that I earn too much money for the little that I do, he cannot change either. We both remain dissatisfied. In other words, the exchange principle is a guideline only if people are reasonably satisfied. They must be able to step mentally into the other man's shoes, and the information required for this must be available. They must also possess a certain degree of modesty. In brief, a society is required for this consisting of little Tinbergens. Reality is, unfortunately, quite different.

This does not alter the fact that we can keep the exchange principle in the back of our minds when we are pondering the right distribution. It offers a certain support in a chaotic world, and it condemns a series of income differentials that we observe in practice. It clearly shows how absurd some high incomes are. The idea of mutual respect also helps in the devising of harmonious wage systems based on job classification (section 2 below). Wage

* *Redelijke inkomensverdeling*, 1953. Tinbergen took the exchange principle from his teacher, the physicist P. Ehrenfest.

structure, which at present is rather arbitrary and messy, can be streamlined through it. And further this principle can serve as a guideline if firms are democratized and the firm parliament comes to talk about salaries (section 6 below).

(11) *Thou shalt not discriminate*: not between men and women, nor between white and non-white, nor between people doing the same work in different branches of industry. In brief: equal pay for equal work. *Comments*: where women and racial minorities are concerned, this seems to me a self-evident requirement, and it is shameful that it is not applied. Governments should make every anti-discriminatory law that they can think of.

However, discrimination between branches of industry forms a debatable point: by strictly observing equal pay you cut off some workers from higher wages, namely those in the flourishing branches of industry, and a number of workers in the branches of industry lagging behind will get higher wages than correspond to the rise in productivity. This contributes to the cost push and the inflationary spiral. These consequences of equal pay are open to discussion; so much so that the norm can be turned round: thou shalt not inflate (see No. 20 below). An anti-inflation policy and an equal pay policy may enter into conflict with each other; attempts are sometimes made to reconcile them by an incomes policy, but that remains a precarious matter, as will be discussed later.

A second difficulty is presented by young people. Strict non-discrimination means that young people's wages may not be lower than those of adults. But it may be argued that young people have fewer requirements. I do not know whether this is true. But I maintain that it is favourable towards a person's happiness in life if he starts off with little money and gradually sees his income improve somewhat.

(12) *To each according to his wants*. An old ethical principle, which, however, can be interpreted in different ways. It is certainly not the intention that every claim by every individual, no matter how fantastic, is honoured. The wants are evaluated in some fashion. The above principle should be distinguished from a strict variant which considers only primary differences in wants, connected with age, number of children, health. This is a consciously egalitarian

reasoning. A somewhat less strict variant allows for additional expenditure for one's work: someone who has a dirty job gets something extra to buy soap with. But this opens the door to much farther-reaching ideas, and then the principle suddenly becomes anti-egalitarian. A teacher has to buy books. If he teaches languages he has to travel. A step further, and the wants are detached from the specific job that someone does and are tied to the groups in society. The middle classes must be able to buy paintings and grand pianos; they must be able to visit the theatre and move about freely in a manner befitting their status. They should be able to educate their children by sending them to the best schools (see also the following point, No. 13).

One step further, and the want argument becomes a plea for the very rich. Now we're concerned with the upkeep of castles and country houses, living in style, keeping racehorses, being major patrons of the arts, including the building of museums and the supporting of ballet companies.

The latter reasoning tends to be developed by introducing into it the nature of society and contrasting the consumption of fish and chips with the grand manner, refined taste, superior culture. This is a plea for great inequality. And further one can support the argumentation by considering what we leave to posterity: castles and a cultural tradition or throw-away beer bottles. In this reasoning levelling is identical with low pleasures; a levelled society is a vulgar society. *Comments*: theoretically speaking, this is an interesting idea: instead of an optimum income structure derived from the productive contributions we get an optimum income structure derived from consumption patterns. A person's consumption also contributes to the Common Good, to the style of society. Old cultures are recalled by their patterns of consumption, their way of life, and these are not determined by the way in which the income is earned but by the manner in which it is spent. This might be called 'consumptivity'.

However, working out the norm yields a scale of possibilities on which opinions may differ. The sober variants of the norm have their repercussions on tax policy: reliefs and allowances. This technique differentiates between persons. The anti-egalitarian variants cannot be applied to individuals; they relate to groups or classes that claim to fulfil a social function. Incomes are thus allocated to individuals within the group who do not buy paintings but spend the money on low pleasures. It would be in conflict with the spirit of the reasoning to allow a person's income to depend on an appraisal of what he personally spends by some body or the other. It is instead an argument for a society with great inequality and low mass consumption. The masses are regarded as culturally inferior. But in our modern times scanty mass consumption is not attainable, because it is impossible to keep the income of the mode of income recipients so low that no more fish and chips are eaten. In this sense the anti-masses argument is a romantic antiquity. In practical politics it boils down to an argument for keeping the tax man's fingers off the highest incomes. If necessary the political conclusion can also be narrowed somewhat: one can advocate special reliefs for deserving expenditure. But then we are far removed from the real anti-levellers. They believe that the well-to-do have been wiped out by the tax authorities, by the Welfare State, by the unions, and so on. That is a misunderstanding about the facts. Plenty of rich people have survived, and their number is steadily growing. The reader will sense that I do not admire the whole view, however interesting the idea of consumptivity may be.

(13) *Everything connected with the family must be respected and supported.* That is to say, higher wages for married persons, family allowances; allowance for the *mère au foyer* (Belgium), i.e. the housewife who does not go out to work, and so loses income; unhampered inheritance with low death duties, and generous incomes for those sections of the population who allow their children to study because they did so themselves. The argument is that the family forms the tough thread of the social fabric, and that the natural responsibility for the clan makes people hard-working citizens. *Comments*: that married people get a higher income (or pay less tax) is acceptable to everyone, but this line of conduct can easily be exaggerated. A plea for generous incomes for the middle classes because the education of their children is expensive obviously comes into conflict with the norm of equal opportunity. Too rarely do the supporters of this theory realize the contradiction: a choice will have to be made between one or the other. Given the

cumulative forces that are already operating anyway in society, this choice does not seem difficult to me. In my opinion there is only very limited scope for saving the financial family traditions, but exactly on this point everyone must make his own normative choice.*

Family allowances are no less controversial. They can be defended in all kinds of ways: as a form of wage according to one's wants, as a method of safeguarding children against too poor a youth, as an application of the principle (to be found among some hard-shelled Christians, both Catholics and Protestants) that worries about money may not inhibit procreation, as a human measure in implementation of a divine intention (God will attend to there being bread on the table – but in large parts of the world God does not seem to be able to manage that), and as a cheap method of wage increase in countries that are too poor for a general improvement of income. The opponents point to the connexion between 'breeding bonus' and overpopulation and to the parents' own responsibility. Now that the pill has been discovered, the last argument is gaining ground. I believe that with a rising national income a drop in family allowances should be aimed at. To the extent that they are given I should like to confine them to the families that need them, for instance to the bottom 20%.

(14) *Wealth must be spread out more among people.* Just as a minimum income for everyone is called for, so is a certain minimum wealth. Wealth gives security, independence and a certain freedom. It makes real citizens of people. It is not good for haves and have-nots to exist side by side; spreading property is one way of making society more harmonious. There are various conceivable norms for the minimum: wealth to the value of a house of one's own, a percentage of one's annual income (e.g. 100% or 200%) or, less arbitrarily, a sum that is sufficient to finance one job, i.e. K/L. *Comments*: this idea forms the basis of various practical plans for paying frozen wages to workers, giving them shares in the profit or

* A strong plea for the family as the 'historical microcosm' through which the great cultural traditions are maintained is found in G. Morgan, 'Human Equality', *Ethics*, 1943. Morgan is not in favour of equal opportunity.

setting up collective capital-sharing systems. These systems are discussed below (section 5). Although profit sharing and capital sharing have enthusiastic proponents, the ethical side of the matter is still contested. Some critics see in this an incorrect way of converting workers into members of the bourgeoisie, into small capitalists, and of tying them to special firms. (However, the latter can also be avoided; in collective arrangements the workers do not invest in their own firm.) These plans are advocated above all by individual employers, by German Catholics, from time to time and with ups and downs by the German union movement, and by M. de Gaulle. As stated, we shall be coming back to them.

(15) *Deserving professions must be generously remunerated.* There is a scale of social values reflected in income distribution. These values relate in the first place to the professions, and in the second place to the manner in which someone practises his profession. An excellent violinist must be paid excellently. The surgeon who saves human lives daily too. The scientist who devises new farming techniques must receive an income that expresses his importance to mankind in terms of money. The manager of a big firm takes weighty decisions – only the best people belong in such jobs and their incomes must tie in with that. Great scholars whose names are still recalled centuries later must be remunerated in accordance with their importance *sub specie aeternatis*. The country that underpays its spiritual, intellectual and artistic élites undermines its culture. *Comments*: a consistent plea for the élite and against further levelling. In the background is a kind of job evaluation system that appraises the intrinsic merits of the work. That is no easy task for creative jobs, but it is not impossible. In this way we can come somewhat closer to an optimum wage and salary structure.

However, the principle can also be applied the other way round: no high incomes without special achievements, and that implies a radical levelling at the top! Babes in arms have achieved little and may therefore not be put in the possession of large sums of money via trust funds. Undeserving widows may not be rich. Every millionaire has to show that he is worth every penny of his fortune. And indeed the norm that deserving people should draw super-incomes is often encountered among people who at the same time presume that the very rich are people who think about nothing but making money. But it also happens that the supporters of this norm combine their view with the idea that the tax authorities (or anyone else) may not interfere with the wealth of families, that the right of succession is sacred (isn't a father entitled to work for his children?). Sometimes they hold the deferential view that wealth points to merit. The latter reversal of the onus of proof in particular makes the whole philosophy of generous remuneration an extremely suspect and apologetic system of values, an ideology in defence of top incomes without any moral basis. Hands off the rich is often the general conclusion. Anyone who wishes to invoke the norm must keep well away from such an uncritical application, and also subject millionaires to the rule: no merit, no money.

The argument of special achievements is often used to claim more income for the middle groups, such as teachers and doctors. It is then accompanied by lachrymose representations, unsupported by the facts, about the tight position of these people. It is often forgotten that these groups belong to the top 5% or the top 1% of the income pyramid. This misuse of the argument must, in my opinion, be avoided. Of course, I do not want to exclude the possibility that somewhere in the world of science and education there are people who are relatively underpaid. That could be dealt with, and a possible way of doing so is a comparison of salaries on the basis of job evaluation.

It is my personal belief that this norm finds its strongest application in the field of the arts: here the discrepancies between intrinsic merit and income are often flagrant ones. In the intellectual professions the market mechanism and the social conventions attend to decent incomes as a rule, but that is not the case with the artist. Even the regular workers with a contract of employment, such as members of an orchestra, lose out – in our society it is quite usual for the first flautist of the orchestra to earn only a fraction of the salary of an account executive with an advertising agency. That is conspicuously wrong; it suggests an indefensible scale of social values. It is even more wrong that creative artists as a rule earn still less than performing ones. Composers often barely earn an income, poets nothing at all and painters usually a dreadfully small one. If anywhere it is here that we find the proof that commercially remunerative is not identical with ethically correct. If, in spite of my egalitarian ideas, I adhere to norm No. 15 (in moderation), that is above all because of the abuses in the sector of the arts.

Bringing the incomes of artists into line with the others calls for radical measures which cannot be discussed here. The government must not only multiply its present subsidies and build up a solid artistic infrastructure – it should also cause new standards of value to be introduced. Art must leave its lofty pedestal. It must occupy the place at present taken by football. This is easier said than done.

(16) *Special effort must be specially rewarded.* We are therefore not concerned here, as in the preceding point, with the vertical pay differentials between professions, but with the personal performance in a given job. On ethical grounds it may be advocated that the hard-working and productive worker should earn more than the slow, lazy one. *Comments*: in practice this leads to payment by results and to merit rating – a highly technical matter because there are many systems, varying from simple piece rates to collective systems such as the Scanlon Plan (see below, VII, 5). The reason why payment by results is introduced is not primarily an ethical one; the management expects an increase in productivity from it. Now this is not immoral; ethical principles and more efficient production may very well go hand in hand. A conflict is born as soon as the piece rates tempt a worker to hustle and the rate fixer to increase his norms, and as soon as merit rating encourages permanent jockeying for a better position and the rat race. A sensible and limited use of the system is not only acceptable to people, but in line with their sense of what is right and proper. All the same, it would be wrong to view the connexion between more money and better work too directly and too simply; workers react favourably to the introduction of carefully thought-out systems of remuneration only if these are connected with more general improvements of the job situation and human relations in the firm.*

---

* This is argued by, among others, W. F. Whyte, *Money and Motivation*, 1955.

(17) *Leave them as you find them*. The government may not intervene in the primary distribution resulting from the market mechanism. The natural income structure reflects the consumers' preference. Supply and demand, or marginal productivity, is the most ethical distribution mechanism, which may at most be corrected by providing a minimum income to those who cannot participate in production. Taxation may remove incomes, but only in proportion. *Comments*: this non-intervention would be defensible only if the primary distribution were in fact optimum, but it is not. The confusion of ethics and the system of productive contributions occurs with J. B. Clark, and in the case of this pioneer of marginal productivity the misunderstanding was perhaps excusable; he had helped distribution theory out of the doldrums, and from theory to ethics is only one *faux pas*. Among later adherents of non-intervention (F. A. von Hayek, some members of the German Ordo group) it is not excusable. A person's marginal contribution may be small without that being his own fault, and certainly in a society of unequal opportunity and cumulative processes. The whole idea would not be worth mentioning if it were not fairly popular (though rarely voiced) among some people who have been successful themselves. And further a weakened form of the anti-intervention point of view is important to fiscal policy: a sense of justice opposes confiscation, or taxation that comes close to it. Although this is a highly watered-down variant, it nevertheless limits the practical room for steeply progressive tax rates, as discussed below in section 8.

(18) *Land rent must go*, then everything will be much better. Speculative profits on land must also be prevented. *Comments*: if carefully and partially applied, this may be a good idea. It becomes a cranky notion as soon as someone believes that nationalization of land would at a stroke transform income distribution into glorious perfection.

(19) *The wage-price spiral must be suppressed*. This is advocated not only on the strength of economic motives, such as the furthering of exports, but also with a view to distribution: the pensioner and the small rentier may not be harmed. For this purpose the increases in

income of each group must remain within the increase in productivity of that group. This line of conduct keeps the costs per unit of product constant. Exceptions to the norm are conceivable, namely in the case of very low wages, or wages that have got seriously out of line with pay for similar work, but such exceptions to the rule must be strongly argumented. Against these cost-increasing exceptions there must be other cases in which productivity rises more strongly than wages, so that price reductions are the consequence and the price level can remain stable. *Comments*: this norm is the sheet-anchor of incomes policy, or at least of the attempts at such a policy, in various countries. In Britain suppressing the spiral is the principal directive for the work of the National Board on Prices and Incomes. A familiar difficulty that frustrates practical policy is that the increase in productivity in some branches of industry can hardly be established, if at all (what are we to do with the fire services?). Furthermore, it must be borne in mind that the norm is of limited scope: it protects only the potential victims of inflation (rentiers and pensioners) and is not itself capable of improving the income structure. The latter – more equitable incomes – can be aimed at within an incomes policy, but then careful manoeuvring is called for. For improvements in the pay structure take place in the form of increases, and soon encourage the spiral. They are exceptions to the norm, about which more will be said in section 2.

(20) *Income distribution must be keyed to maximum economic growth* (or, in weaker form, income distribution may never be kneaded so much that growth is harmed). The ethical idea is that the growth of production offers advantages to all groups, while redistribution serves group interests only; if this means that growth is harmed, the group's interest is evidently in conflict with the general interest. The norm is elaborated by a number of more detailed rules, such as: incomes must palpably encourage the recipients to receive training, to make an effort to climb the ladder, to take risks, to save, to invest. There is a huge and in general highly sombre number of pronouncements on the extent to which the present economic policy, and in particular distribution policy, harms growth. We come across these pronouncements every day

in the form of editorials, speeches, meaningful hints; it is suggested that growth rate suffers from modern progressive taxes, modern social provisions, modern depreciation of the currency and modern levelling in general.

Comments: the norm seems sensible to me and even rather compelling. However, the same cannot be said of the way in which it is translated into specific policy measures. The opponents of more equality too easily claim that taxes, levelling, etc., inhibit growth. In modern society they see countless forces leading to enervation and slothfulness; once upon a time people worked harder, entrepreneurs showed more go, everything was livelier and more dynamic.

But that picture is contradicted by the facts. In all countries today taxes are higher than they were, social security greater and incomes less unequal; and yet almost everywhere the growth rate of production is tangibly higher than before. This applies not only to the United States and to the six countries of the E.E.C.; it also holds good for Sweden, which of all the Western countries has the most extensive social provisions and the flattest wage curve. True, Britain has to contend with economic disappointments (and therefore it is no wonder that the sombre theories proliferate exactly in that country), but all the same the expansion of production is not much lower than in the golden age of great inequality. Real income per head is growing by 2 to 3% a year in Britain. That is not less than before the war. It does, however, compare unfavourably with other European countries: there it is 3 to 5%. The distribution in those countries is not very different, and the taxes are not much lower. It is therefore not proven that the causes of the lagging growth in Britain – an extremely complex phenomenon! – lie in distribution. Further pronouncements on this matter would have to differentiate between the exact nature of the government measures that we are criticizing. An increase in death duties has a different effect from benefit paid to disabled persons or a bonus for low-cost housing. Some aspects of the Welfare State increase demand and thus production. Generalizing melancholy at the negative relation between equality and growth is misplaced.

This does not alter the fact that government intervention in income distribution should always be verified on its impact on growth. In this respect governments may not take any dangerous risks. This occurs above all with measures that could affect profits, investments and technical progress. If profitability threatens to become too small, expansion is endangered, and that sets limits to distribution policy. True, this often proves to work out all right in practice, since most profits react favourably to inflationary increases in demand; increases in wage costs are passed on in the prices, and taxes too are unloaded on to others. We have seen above that the share of profits in national income does not display any tendency to decrease. But we must remain aware that profit keeps the motor of progress running. This sets practical limits to government policy, and also to the extent to which the top incomes can be reduced. You may find this regrettable, but that does not make it any the less true.

(21) *Equal opportunity*. So far we have been talking about norms for the final distribution: the situation at the finish. Some observers place the ethical stress at the start. They are content if everyone has an equal chance. These observers consider the resultant incomes less relevant. (Corrections for cases of hardship, so that social security always remains possible. To continue to use the language of the racecourse, anyone who breaks a leg is assisted.)

An equal start calls for a radical application of death duties or, rather, abolition of the inheriting of material wealth; disappearance of privileges and compensation, as far as possible, for the inheritance of talent and milieu. This compensation can be given by education (schools in slums must be better than those in the suburbs), but it is not consistent until there are no slums left. Everyone then reaches the level that matches his intelligence; people can develop fully. *Comments*: equality of opportunity digs very deep, and was long regarded as a left-wing ideal *par excellence*. Until recently its drawbacks remained unnoticed. These consist in the fact that people of low intelligence lag behind in the course of their careers and can no longer attribute this to anything else but themselves. In a society full of barriers and privileges someone can claim that he never had a chance owing to the poverty and low status of his parents. But if personal merit is the only decisive factor, this personal merit (and its absence!) becomes plain for all

315

to see. A person's job and his income become the outward signs of his capacities, even if the latter are small. As a result, an unequal distribution of income becomes even more unbearable than it is now. This has been pointed out by M. Young in his evocative book *The Rise of the Meritocracy 1870–2033* (1958), in which he describes how the meritocratic society is swept away by a revolution in the year 2033. This revolution is caused by the frustration among the recipients of low incomes and by the protest against the rat race. If we give a free rein to the pursuit of careers and higher incomes it seems to me personally improbable that this rebellion can be postponed until 2033. Its first signs are already apparent among the students, and the protest will certainly spread to young workers.

The conclusion that we must draw from this is not that equal opportunity is an incorrect system, but that the open society is threatened if it displays an unacceptably skew income distribution. It has been argued from various quarters that equal opportunity automatically equalizes incomes, because the chances of promotion are no longer blocked off by handicaps for the lower classes, but that optimism seems unjustified to me. Innate talents may very well cause a skew distribution; that is the lesson of theories such as that of Roy (Chapter VI, 2). An increased vertical mobility does have a levelling effect, but we do not know how much of one (Chapter VI, 4); it may very well be that society demands so much more training that the net effect on distribution is slight.

We must therefore not confine our attention to the equal start but we must also keep the finish in mind, even in the meritocracy. With some exaggeration I would say: *precisely* a society with equal chances is obliged to take egalitarian measures en route *and* at the finish. The race must lose its character of a race.

In the above, twenty-one norms for distribution appear; a long list. They include a few radical desiderata, such as the abolition of all incomes from property, or complete equality; these can be realized only in societies run on completely different lines to ours. There is no point in going into this – this book is not concerned with communes or Communism, but with Western society and in what ways it can be improved. Manuals for the revolution have a different tone, as the reader had long realized.* The most interesting way of posing the problem is perhaps this: how much equality can we achieve in a society that in principle leaves decisions to produce to entrepreneurs and industrial managers, which respects private property in principle and which appreciates an increasing supply of goods and services? Moreover, we make the requirement that this society must be a democratic one, in the special sense that intervention in income distribution must be based on a certain degree of consensus.

Since both the norms and the interests of various people differ, the question is to what extent a few common principles may be discovered in the above. Perhaps it looks as if they are all in conflict with one another, but that is better than it seems. A reasonable compromise is not automatically out of the question, above all because the mechanism of industrial society makes all kinds of extreme intervention impossible or senseless. That is one of the themes of the following sections: life itself compels resigned acceptance of less desirable situations. Of course fundamental differences of opinion about the optimum degree of inequality remain, and every solution is therefore a compromise.

To achieve this the following numbers seem to me to be of particular importance: (5) minimum incomes for all, (7) progressive taxes, (8) more severe taxes on incomes easily acquired, (10) mutual acceptance of each other's income on the strength of job evaluation, (11) non-discrimination, (14) wealth spread out more widely, (15) special remuneration for special jobs, and no high incomes without corresponding achievements, (16) limited payment by results, (19) combating the spiral, (20) consideration for growth and (21) equal start. With a little give and take these eleven principles can perhaps be combined into a practical policy.

---

* Adherents of Marcuse will see this as a reinforcement of their view that neo-capitalism makes people into disheartened fellow-travellers. Utopia is nipped in the bud by the system. I agree with them that neo-capitalism, via increasing consumption, has this effect on many, but I should like to extend the proposition to other forms of society. Communism, feudalism, anarchism, primitive societies in the jungle can also tire the spirit and cause people to capitulate. Capitalism, if combined with democratic liberties and intense communication, is not the worst breeding ground for wild ideas.

INCOME DISTRIBUTION

2. *Harmonizing the Pay Structure*

Although the most spectacular inequality is caused by profits and
interest – they create the real giants at the end of the parade – it
would be wrong to ignore wages and salaries. For they form at
least 70% of national income. There too the inequality is great:
some top salaries are a hundred times as high as the lowest wages.
In our parade of income recipients we saw salaried characters
of a hundred and twenty yards in height and more.

Moreover, at practically all levels of the wage structure we
encounter inequities, unfairness and injustice. These perhaps
cause even more daily annoyance than the salary differentials with
distant persons. It appears that workers are inclined to compare
their pay with that of people whom they know and whose work
they can assess. If the 'wage relativities' (this is the rather heavy
expression popular with students of these problems) are, to those
who observe them, no good, this is a constant source of umbrage.
It annoys people, it undermines their confidence in the rationality
of the world in general. A person feels badly done by if a job comparable to his own is better paid. And if he also remembers how
much more the top dogs get, the basis is laid for bitterness. This
has all kinds of awkward consequences. His pleasure in his work
may be spoilt. Shop floor frictions are set up. Industrial conflict
breaks out more quickly. An irritated mood grows in the unions.
Political ideas turn sour. Moreover, this discord leads to inflation;
those who feel that they are lagging behind try to get themselves
higher wages, but then the old relativities often re-establish themselves, so that the process can begin anew. Frustration and
inflation go hand in hand.

Perhaps the reader thinks that I am exaggerating. But surely not
as regards the inadequacy of the British wage structure. There are
various reports on this matter by the National Board for Prices and
Incomes, hardly a body that has anything to gain from spreading
alarmist stories, and certainly not one composed of rebellious and
bitter critics of the capitalist system. The Board looks at wages
through the eyes of rationalists who would like to see some order
and harmony – but it describes what it sees as 'a confused pay
structure', 'a bewildering array of wage and salary rates'; differen-

tials are regarded as 'inequitable, irrational and arbitrary'; expressions like 'anomalous', 'unfair', 'inefficient' frequently occur; the structure is 'inexplicable', and often no other rules can be discovered than those of 'power politics and horse-dealing'. In brief, British pay relativities are a mess.*

There is therefore scope for improvement. But who has to undertake this? The unions have most to gain from doing so. It is their members who have to struggle with the irritation, and the messy wage structure leads to tension within the unions. The officials are also directly incommoded by all this: wage negotiations are long-winded and confused; it takes a great deal of trouble to keep on negotiating the irrational differentials. One would therefore expect that pressure would be exerted from this quarter to arrive at a more sensible structure. But then it is forgotten that the chaos came into being by precisely these wage negotiations by precisely these same union officials. They, or their predecessors, have helped to make the arbitrary structure. This is in part because the structure is repeatedly tinkered with, now here, then there. And it is also because jobs have changed – obsolete work is often still paid for by old standards. A further contributory factor to the chaos is that the British unions are traditionally too fragmented, and organized in accordance with antiquated craft demarcations. And in addition the confusion is worse confounded by the powers of the shop stewards, who influence the actual wages without the unions having a hold on their work. If no new forces are brought in, it is improbable that the unions will suddenly abandon this whole folklore.

The same applies to the employers. They too are inconvenienced by the inefficient wage structure, but nevertheless they have helped to create disorder. And yet it is a hopeful circumstance that the main architects of pay relativities, on both sides of the table, have what is fundamentally the same interest in rationalization. If some pressure is then exerted on the matter by an independent party – for instance the National Board, or a successor to this body – there is a chance that the situation will gradually improve. However, there

*Taken from Report No. 83: *Job Evaluation*, 1968, pp. 12–15. The same opinion is found in the report by the Royal Commission on Trade Unions and Employer's Associations (the Donovan Report), 1968. p. 40.

must be a technique for effectuating this improvement. This technique exists; it is job evaluation. It is no coincidence that this system is recommended by the National Board.

Job evaluation is not primarily a method of wage determination, but a means of establishing the intrinsic importance of a job. Once this has been found, and expressed by a number, a wage structure can be created that corresponds to the numbers thus calculated. You kill two birds with one stone: jobs are classified, which may be a useful auxiliary to the organization of the firm and to personnel policy, and remuneration is streamlined. The frustration emanating from underpaid and overpaid jobs is avoided. Moreover, in many cases the wage structure can be simplified: where an unnecessarily large number of differentiations had come about, and 'a bewildering array of wage and salary rates' had run wild, the superfluous and the complicated can be weeded out.

And finally wage negotiations can be conducted more efficiently; once a proper system of job evaluation has been introduced, the parties can concentrate the discussions about contract renewal on a broad adjustment of wage level. Essentials, such as a new contract, can be distinguished from side-issues, such as improved fitting-in of specific jobs. A real optimist can even expect a rationalization of the union division.

Now what exactly is this technique of job evaluation? Let us begin by establishing that this is not something that is brand new. The principle is long known, and indeed was described by Adam Smith: 'The wages of labour vary according to the small or great trust which must be reposed in the workman.' 'Trust' means the skill, the responsibility, the extent to which the customer's interests depend on the quality of the work. Adam Smith gives as an example goldsmiths and jewellers (if their honesty is doubted they are worthless); physicians, on whom our life depends; lawyers, whose work affects our fortune and our reputation.* These jobs make stringent requirements – their intrinsic qualities are such that they should be better paid than other jobs. According to the general sense of justice, a person carrying considerable responsibility deserves higher remuneration than someone who does not.

This way of comparing jobs can be elaborated in various

* *Wealth of Nations*, 1776 (Everyman's Library, pp. 93–4).

manners. An approximate method considers the length of training required for fulfilling the job. But this is not all. There are strenuous, responsible jobs with a short training: bus driver, soldiers in wartime. Now these are exceptions. A more serious objection to training as the sole criterion is that the quality of the training has to be taken into account – various courses inside and outside the firm ought to be reduced to one common denominator, and that requires careful comparison. We ought also to make allowance for experience, learning by doing. And then it is more effective for us to look right away at the job content – after all, that is what we are concerned with.

Another method, likewise a rough one, is ranking. Two jobs are put side by side and it is asked which of the two is harder, more responsible, requires more training and experience. By keeping this up long enough we get a ranking covering all jobs. The drawback of this is that we have not yet specified the properties of the job that we have to look out for, nor how we must weight these various properties. If we throw in this specification, we get the best method of job evaluation that there is, namely *points rating*.

It amounts to our analysing everyone's job on a number of properties. Is considerable physical strength required? Or stamina? Must the worker be quick-fingered? Must he have a feeling for machinery? More difficult to appraise, but not impossible: how much knowledge is required? Does he have to be able to express himself clearly and get on well with people? Is artistic talent essential? And judgement? Does the job entail responsibility in the sense that the man (or woman) must take his or her own decisions, or must he or she keep asking a superior what has to be done?* And further, if the work is done sloppily or wrongly, how great is the damage caused? By considering these subaspects a job can be analysed and evaluated. This evaluation boils down to a figure: the point rating.

This method involves a strategic artifice that is decisive for the result. It is the weighting of the various points of view. Everyone

* One particular method of job evaluation has the rating depend solely on the length of the period within which the employee may work on his own initiative. This is called the Time Span of Discretion. The method is fervently recommended by E. Jacques (e.g. in *Time Span Handbook*, 1964).

feels that the one property of a job is more important than the other. Feeling for machinery is less important than responsibility. But to what extent? We award points for each property; before these are added up they are first multiplied by a weighting factor. The choice of these weightings determines whether we shall presently find ratings that are close together or display a big spread. A person who attaches as much weight to knowledge and responsibility as to nimble fingers brings the female factory worker closer to the manager. Anyone who heavily weights responsibility and the power to make independent decisions will foster income inequality. This shows that the method is not strictly objective but has something arbitrary about it. We cannot avoid including evaluations of a social hierarchy in the appraisal.

If, then, the method does not produce objective results, what use is it to us? In the first place this: it can help us combat the chaos in pay structure. Suppose that the system of evaluation has been decided on and that the weighting factors have been chosen – employers and employees have reached agreement on that point. That proves possible in practice. One can then streamline the job classification and calculate the point ratings. By keying the wage relativities to the ratings the wage structure is ironed out somewhat. This need not be anything like ideal, but the underpaid workers are localized; they can be raised to the level to which they are entitled, given the remuneration of comparable jobs. The overpaid jobs have to be cut back in remuneration. The latter is a painful operation, but it can be delayed until the man doing the job leaves, or postponed until a general wage increase, so that no absolute reduction of the income in question occurs. This streamlining of wages is an obvious step forward. Old relativities based on tradition or arbitrariness are abandoned and rational relativities built up. It is a laborious, slow job, but it is worth the trouble, and there is reason to assume that employers and unions will collaborate.

There is yet another advantage. Special claims of special groups are admittedly not eliminated in advance, but job evaluation compels them to formulate their pleas rationally. If a group claims that it has been passed over it has to come forward with arguments relating to the job content. That makes the discussion more meaningful. Inflationary automatisms are interrupted; nobody may claim a wage increase just because the earnings have increased in a comparable occupation through a productivity agreement.* The technical reasoning incites people to think, and as a result the atmosphere may become less heated and more reasonable. Pretensions can be pricked like balloons, the blunt struggle for power can be checked. It all sounds slightly optimistic, but it is the only optimism that can hold its ground in the face of the chaotic facts of the British wage structure.

And perhaps it is not out of place to take the optimism a step further. We have seen that job evaluation in itself does not give unique answers to the question of how great the vertical differentials must be. The old problem of the salary relation between a primary-school teacher and a secondary-school one is not clarified – that happens only in appearance, as soon as we have chosen the weights of the various aspects of a job and come to regard these weights as sacrosanct figures. If we make the length of training and the degree of knowledge weigh lightly, we can very well arrive at a point rating for the secondary-school teacher that barely exceeds that of the primary-school man; they both teach at schools, and they must both be capable of explaining things in a manner that can be understood. The work of some police superintendents is no more difficult or strenuous than that of the detective sergeant on the spot, and it is very much open to doubt whether it requires so much more knowledge. But a superintendent is higher up the ladder, and the reader with much of a sense of hierarchy will find it a matter of course that the superintendent earns much more. He will invoke the responsibility of command and attach a heavy weight to these properties. If a person does not like authority and élitism, then with the job classification in his hand he will find that the superintendent needs only a slight additional remuneration for that command position, and should earn barely more than the detective sergeant.

A systematic discussion of this kind on the sense of the weights and on the sense of salary hierarchy has hardly taken place up to now. Vertical differentials that have always existed are accepted.

* Productivity agreements are possible exceptions to the standards of an incomes policy (see section 3). Crude comparability therefore spoils the game.

323

The opponents of greater equality are as a rule also opponents of a rational approach; they argue that the more senior posts cannot be analysed. These critics of job evaluation will invoke the immeasurable, the creative, the incalculable nature of management – and then fix highly measurable pecuniary salaries that reflect the situation of the highly placed incumbents of these positions. If no measurement and discussion take place, salaries emerge that reflect *somebody*'s social preference. These are then the preferences of the decision-makers – social groups whose size and exact location are not known, but which in any case form a selection from the population. Norms are used that are not explicit and not open to discussion. That is the present situation. In that case it seems better to me that the arguments for these differentials are examined from case to case. The method for doing so is job evaluation. And then the social conventions lying behind the weights automatically appear on the conference table.

The principal reason why such a procedure should be welcomed lies in the desideratum mentioned above (point 10) that people should respect each other's position in society and the corresponding incomes. We have seen that Tinbergen's exchange principle tries to give strict expression to the above, that this attempt may not have been entirely successful but that the fundamental idea, viz. mutual acceptance, is of importance to a harmonious society. If we want to give substance to this, the vertical differentials must be fixed in accordance with the preferences of the members of the community. That is not being done at present. Income differentials are left to the market, to tradition, to the power and self-interest of the decision-makers, who themselves belong to the economic élite. The whole procedure today is hush-hush and surrounded by taboos. A rational structure requires that the course of events be discussed in full frankness, and that certainly seems possible.

In Britain the National Board for Prices and Incomes has made a start with this frankness. It has published many reports on the payment of staff workers and top executives in various branches of industry, such as the gas industry, banks, insurance companies and the railways, and also on architects' fees, solicitors' remuneration and the salaries of university teachers. The tone of these reports is still highly cautious and the Board sets about the job so pragmatically that the rather radical nature of the new approach is not conspicuous, but the first steps have been taken.

Now a public discussion on these salary relations is desirable, but thinking, talking and writing are not enough. Ultimately reality will have to be brought into line with what emerges from the discussion. Power is needed for that. This is the moment to abandon optimism. For suppose – as may be expected – that a more egalitarian salary structure is desired by most people. How should this preference be realized?

A first prerequisite is that all income from work is regulated by collective agreements; they therefore apply not only to manual workers but also to top-flight employees of private firms. That is, of course, not inconceivable. Some of those involved will suggest that such an arrangement has something shocking and scandalous about it, but it is difficult to see why the income of a Permanent Secretary of the Treasury can be regulated in a generally accessible salary scale and that of a manager of ICI cannot.

Now suppose, for the sake of argument, that in the future all salaries are in fact fixed by collective bargaining and laid down in collective agreements. Will this automatically lead to a more egalitarian structure? I do not think so. That does not happen until these salaries have been fitted into rational scales reflecting the social conventions of society *as a whole*. Those directly involved, i.e. the decision-makers and those whose salaries are concerned, now negotiate among themselves. There are no representatives present of the general public, nor of the workers as a whole. The latter would change if a sectional union did not act on behalf of the workers, defending only the interests of its members, but its place was taken by a general trade union federation considering the whole wage structure. Thus architects are no longer represented by the institute of architects but by the general union of employees, the junior managers not by some association of junior managers but by the general union of employees. Salaries of top managers are fixed not by a handful of top managers but by the general union of employees. That sounds Utopian when it is borne in mind that this general union must try to restrain the sectional salary demands during the wage negotiations! It does not require an overcritical mind to consign this procedure to the realm of illusions. There is not a single sectional union that would tolerate such central interference in its affairs.

That even applies to the unions of manual workers, which represent exclusively small interests (and sometimes even sacrifice the long-term interest of their own members by countering technical progress and the increase in productivity). The groups of senior personnel are still more averse to interference by trade union federations. There is thus considerable opposition to an egalitarian settlement of all wages and salaries via one gigantic system of job classification. That is to say if it is left to free bargaining by free unions to bring it about. Via this method of traditional consultation wage and salary determination cannot be brought within the reach of democratic opinion-making.

Of course, there is an alternative: the salaries are no longer fixed in consultation between those concerned, but by the organization which, by definition, should express the social conventions of the whole people: the government. To some extent this is already happening, namely with the salaries of those in government service. They form about a fifth of the total. This is a substantial fraction, and it includes key jobs that influence remuneration in the private sector. And yet the government can hardly use its salary policy now as a lever for manipulating the whole pay structure. For an egalitarian policy would lead to the occurrence of wide salary gaps, especially at the top, between the private and the government sectors. Such gaps already exist. In Britain Permanent Secretaries, Second Secretaries and Deputy Secretaries earn less than people with a comparable post in business. In Britain it is a traditional doctrine that the rewards of the higher Civil Service cannot match the rewards in commercial employment. On the Continent civil servants are paid even less, relatively speaking. In most countries the horizontal differentials cannot become greater under penalty of a deterioration in the quality of the Civil Service. Consequently, indirect influencing of the total salary structure by the government via its own salary policy soon comes up against insuperable obstacles. The government can at most take care that it does not lead the field in creating too great inequality, but that is not the case in most countries.

The comprehensive solution is of course to have all wages and salaries fixed by the government, by law, as a result of the democratic procedure. It is difficult to keep a straight face even when suggesting this idea. Hardly anyone accepts such a system in the Western World. Liberals and socialists, industrial managers and unions, Mrs Barbara Castle and Mr Frank Cousins are in complete agreement that this would be going too far. Only dreamy idealists and academic scribblers perched in ivory towers are in favour.

All in all, then, things do not look so good. And I have not yet said anything about the purely economic forces that handicap control of the higher salaries. Scarcity and market relations doubtless play a part as well. True, they do not have such a compelling influence as is often assumed, but they do make themselves felt, and they form an extra complication. The fact, too, that in the higher echelons salaries are all mixed up with profits and income in kind stands in the way of effective control. However, there is only any point in going into that if it were an established fact that a formal control of all incomes from work were really desired, and that is not so.

The fairly negative result of the above discussion can be further underlined by recalling the Israeli experiment. Since its birth Israel has been pervaded by a highly egalitarian and socialist ideology, nurtured by the ideals of the kibbutz and the common fight. Zionism aims at a classless society, and at first the Histadruth also took the viewpoint of very modest differentials. The equality in income distribution was accepted as an ideal in large sectors of the new society, and many groups of specialists imposed voluntary limitations on themselves. When the Israeli Government inherited the British administration in 1948 they did not take over the salary scales; instead the much flatter scales of the Jewish Agency were introduced. The ratio between top salaries and lowest wages was then six to one (in the British administration ten to one).

In the second half of the Fifties opposition developed to this uniform structure. Senior civil servants, professionals and teachers exerted pressure. Every category spoke up for its own interests. Various sectional organizations were set up – the Israeli Doctors Organization, the Institute for Engineers and Architects, the Association of Teachers, the Association of Academic Workers.

These were directed above all against the policy of the Histadruth, which as a result was exposed to internal tensions. There were repeated strikes, especially by teachers. As a result, the vertical salary differentials grew, a trend that has continued since the middle of the Fifties. Although the inequality in Israel is now probably still less than that in most of the countries of Western Europe,* the difference is no longer spectacular. The egalitarian ideology of Zionism has not been achieved. In my opinion the main reason for that is that the higher-income recipients have not accepted this ideology on further consideration. They wanted their status to be expressed by their income. The lesson is this: in a free society acceptance of the egalitarian ideology by the economic élite and by the pressure groups is essential to an egalitarian policy.

In the light of this kind of experience it seems to me that for the time being we should not set our sights too high and too idealistically with regard to pay structure. But even then there is much that can be done. The measures may be divided into three groups. In the first place the very low wages should be raised. In Britain a small percentage of the workers get less than National Assistance benefit; this ridiculous state of affairs must be done away with by instituting general minimum wages. This wage floor should gradually be raised according as economic growth permits. This is primarily a task for the Government.

In the second place, the application of job evaluation should be extended. In Britain there are as yet few industry-wide schemes; they can be counted on the fingers of one hand. The Government can in this respect confine itself to publicizing and encouraging such schemes, because the interests of employers and employees are in harmony. In the long run nation-wide systems can perhaps be aimed at (as has been done in the Netherlands, though with limited success). In this way the wage structure can be cleaned up. In special cases overpayment and underpayment can be corrected. This work is going on. It is to be hoped that job classification will also be applied to a number of intellectual and above all artistic professions and that the blatant arrears in the incomes of a number

---

*The top 10% of urban families get less than 25% of total income. This suggests a somewhat flatter Lorenz curve than elsewhere, but the difference is not great. (Source: *Statistical Abstract of Israel*, 1968, p. 166.)

of painters, writers and orchestral musicians can be reduced.*

In the third place reduced vertical differentials between the top incomes and the average can gradually be aimed at, at least if this is desired. The natural development is already heading in this direction, but it can be accelerated by what might be called permanent discussion. The top incomes, too, prove to be sensitive to the general social and psychological climate (see p. 280). The minds of the decision-makers cannot escape prevailing views on what is right and fair. The way of thought of job classification, which unmasks false pretensions, plus a permanent criticism of exaggerated hierarchy, prestige and status, may contribute to a more uniform pay structure.

This development will certainly be a slow one, and for this reason it will not satisfy the strongly egalitarian-minded. For them another hope is dawning: perhaps before long the power structure within firms will change. That opens a much more radical prospect for reducing the gap between the top and the average incomes. We shall come back to that in section 6.

3. *Incomes Policy*

Incomes policy: the words sound promising. Just like penicillin and psychotherapy, they have about them an air of purposefulness, of 'everything is going to be all right now'. You can hear overtones of justice, rising productivity, balanced growth, the end of the bother with the balance of payments. There is a lot of talk about incomes policy, everywhere in Europe. (Not in the United States – there the expression has a rather exotic ring to it. The American language contains 'wage-price guideposts' but, to put it mildly, that inspires less confidence.) It is as well with such a conversational subject to see exactly what is meant by it.

Meanings vary. Some interpret it as all forms of economic, social

*I am aware that the latter is not only a matter of streamlining labour contracts, but that it also involves problems of subsidization. The market is not prepared to take a sufficient volume of artistic production. In the future this will probably become even more unfavourable, because labour productivity in the industrial sector is growing and that in artistic production is practically stationary.

and financial policy that influence income and income distribution. In that case it covers the whole of budgetary and tax policy, monetary policy, the furtherance of economic growth, intervention in labour disputes, the regulation of competition and above all the whole structure of social insurance and social services. In this sense incomes policy is as old as the hills; since Hammurabi governments have been concerning themselves with prices and incomes. In my opinion this definition is much too broad.

The other extreme interpretation is that incomes policy is identified with centralized wage policy. That is certainly too narrow. It is a well-known proposition that wage policy alone cannot hold its own; a one-sided intervention of this kind is not accepted by the unions. They feel, and rightly so, that wage control against the background of rising prices causes the share of labour in national income to fall. An at least formal attempt to control non-wage incomes is a condition for a centralized wage policy. Somewhere between the extremes of total economic policy and wage policy pure and simple lies a practical definition.

In my opinion this should be directed towards primary incomes, i.e. to factor prices (including profit). Income transfers, that is to say social insurance and social services, together with taxes, are not included. Nor is the budgetary and monetary influencing of national income. An incomes policy is concerned with wages, land rents, interest and profits, which are directly influenced by it. Indirect intervention (via employment, via the influencing of competition, via the rate of exchange) is not incomes policy in this definition. The only indirect form of influence which I do consider part of incomes policy is price policy; this aims at bringing profit margins within the grasp of the policy.

This definition shows which variables the authorities wish to influence. It does not yet tell us by what methods and for what purpose. The methods consist in general in giving guidelines, winning over pressure groups, fostering public agreement. Voluntary acceptance, gentle persuasion and sometimes somewhat more vigorous coercion come within the possibilities, and it depends on the political mood which are chosen. In Britain favourite terms are consultation and cooperation. Usually the choice is limited by what the pressure groups and national customs accept. If those concerned do not cooperate nothing comes of the whole system – that is the elementary truth over which governments have stumbled up to now.

There is considerable confusion about the objectives. What I have to say about this is, unlike the two preceding paragraphs, rather subjective. I am convinced that the incomes policies in various countries have been mainly inspired by the wish to damp down the cost push and the inflationary spiral. An improvement of the pay structure is not in the foreground; this is at most pursued as a secondary aim. The expression 'incomes policy' became fashionable as a result of the postwar disappointment at Keynesian policy. Governments had learnt how to avoid depressions: by keeping up the level of purchasing power. This proved a success. But the converse, the combating of inflation, proved a failure. Prices kept on rising, in all Western countries. Even without excess demand this continued to form an obstinate economic ill. Reducing purchasing power would theoretically have been a medicine, but governments rightly did not dare to apply this remedy; it summons up the danger of unacceptable unemployment and a reduction in the growth rate. This means that a Keynesian policy for curing rising prices is not feasible. Incomes policy was embraced as the way out of the dilemma. Its supporters hoped that direct intervention in factor prices would do away with the spiral of wages and prices and would reconcile full employment with economic stability. This hope is the *raison d'être* of incomes policy.

Of course there were other aims. A more just distribution of income is one of them. But anyone who places equity in the foreground has his hopes disappointed. For some governments – especially that of the United States – have in their eagerness to combat inflation done things that have given practically all observers the feeling that violence was being done to equal treatment of equal-income recipients. The reason is obvious. It is not possible to catch *all* inflation-makers. Many increases in incomes and prices take place in secret. Wage drift (rises in earnings exceeding the collective agreements) is elusive. So are most increases in profit margins. The authorities therefore catch who they can, and they are sometimes the weak or the most obvious offenders. Justice is not served by this, and anyone who puts justice before combating of inflation turns away in disgust.

If the reader wishes to see this disgust demonstrated, he must browse through the collection *Guidelines, Informal Controls and the Market Place* (1966). It is the report of a conference in Chicago, where various speakers expressed themselves in very unfriendly tones about the guideposts of the American Government. There was only one defender of the policy followed, and that was Gardner Ackley, the then chairman of the Council of Economic Advisers. He had thought up the guideposts himself and recommended them to the President, but his defence is a weak one. His story is in essence that the guideposts have contributed towards the combating of inflation; he admits that they are somewhat inequitable. Typical is the position of R. Solow, who was going to act as a kind of attorney for the defence; when his wife heard what he was going to say 'she muttered something to the effect that if those guideposts have you for a friend, they have no need for an enemy'.* That more or less represents the situation.

I do not mean to say that an incomes policy must inevitably lead to a worse distribution; one can, and one must, try to reconcile justice with the control of inflation (and one can try to do so, by leaning heavily on the techniques described in the preceding section); I merely want to say that the main aim of incomes policy is combating the spiral, and that one should not have too many illusions about the distribution aspect.

The principal norm for an incomes policy proceeds from the desire to avoid the cost push. It entails that the money income for a group of income recipients may not rise any more than the productivity. If wages rise more strongly than labour productivity (in the notation of the earlier chapters: if $w > h$) the labour costs per unit of product rise, and the passing-on process can begin. The interest rate may not rise more than the productivity of capital, which incidentally is fairly constant, viewed macro-economically. Land rent may not rise more than the productivity of an acre of land. The profit margin per unit of product may not rise at all. Once all these rules have been complied with (and import prices and turnover taxes are constant), the price level is stable. It is an effective medicine if it is swallowed.

Writing down these macro-economic prescriptions is one thing;

* The above collection, p. 62.

putting them into practice is another. The first stumbling block is translating the macro-guideline into a micro-economic indication for special groups. The decisions on wages and prices are taken by individual decision-makers; they have to know what to keep to. The best thing would be if everyone and every group knew how the productivity of his and its activity would develop in the coming year and kept to that carefully in the increase in income. That is how the authorities intend it too, and we are constantly enjoined to act in that way. If there are groups of wage-earners or others who cannot estimate their own rise in productivity, or if this concept is even pointless (a traffic policeman) they could adhere to the macro-economic average. The government works that out for us. It is often something like 2·8% or 3·2%; the exact figure is more or less immaterial, because the percentage calculated is always lower than what the pressure groups ask for. Governments are glad if after the event an average rise in income of not more than 4·1% or 4·9% results.

Note that we are not concerned here with the 'own contribution' of the factor of production, whatever that may be, but the average increase in productivity per unit of factor of production, *irrespective of the cause of this*. In the case of labour, therefore, an increase of Q/L (i.e. as a percentage $q - l$). If somebody thinks that the contribution of labour must be separated from that of management or of capital he is thoroughly confused.*

The micro-economic application of the norm tying each group to its own increase in productivity meets with three forms of opposition as far as wages are concerned. In the first place there are the notoriously low-paid jobs. These could be raised only if the

* It sometimes seems as if the National Board for Prices and Income falls prey to this confusion. In report No. 74 the Board went into the question whether employees of an assurance company had or had not made a direct contribution to the rise in productivity (the answer was yes) and in report No. 101 (on Workers in Agriculture) the answer was: it cannot be said. In fact here it is not 'the norm' that is under discussion but an exception. According to the British rules workers may get more wage than corresponds to the increase in productivity if they have cooperated in a special scheme ('productivity agreement'). To establish this exception the 'own contribution' of the workers must be estimated in specific cases. That is detached from the calculation of 'the norm', but it can confuse outsiders.

productivity were to rise by an extra amount, and this is usually not so. Then there are the industries with a low increase in productivity – in the event of a strict application of the micro-criterion these would get behindhand. In the third place, and this is a more general objection, the micro-economic application of the productivity norm would lead to horizontal wage differentials running counter to all wage relativities. For the same work more and more would be paid in the rapidly growing industries. These horizontal differentials are also completely at variance with job classification, for this considers the intrinsic job content and not the economic return of labour.

These three objections can be dealt with in various ways. In Britain the solution which has been followed in principle is that the national economic rise in productivity is decisive; this is *the* norm. Therefore $w = h$. For all sectors the same percentage increase applies, irrespective of the increase in productivity in the industry concerned. The macro-norm may be departed from if there are urgent reasons for doing so; this was the case from January to June 1967. With a view to the precarious situation of the balance of payments a macro-norm of 0% was proclaimed ('severe restraint'). But this is abnormal. While I write this (autumn 1969) the norm is $3-3\frac{1}{2}\%$ a year.

There are, however, exceptions to this general norm for special groups, viz. 'general recognition' that payment is too low 'to maintain a reasonable standard of living'; 'widespread recognition' that payment 'has fallen seriously out of line with pay for similar work' (there the streamlining of the wage structure thus enters into issue); 'more exacting work or a major change in working practices', 'directly leading to increasing productivity' (there the specific contribution of labour puts in an appearance!) and further an exception is made if a wage increase is necessary to attract additional labour to a branch of industry having to contend with a shortage.*

These exceptions allow of a flexible application of the norm, and if sensible use is made of them they can perhaps reconcile incomes policy with improvement of the pay structure. But the general norm brings us to another difficulty: by imposing it on industries

* These norms appear in the White Paper *Prices and Incomes Policy*, 1965.

with a low increase in productivity the costs rise there, as a result of which the spiral starts up again. This can be compensated for theoretically by the fact that the rapid growers may also pay out only the average rise in income, so that prices can fall there. The weakness of this is, of course, that it is dubious whether that drop in prices will actually take place; it is more likely that the profits of the fast growers will rise. The British system accepts these drawbacks. However, they have the annoying property of undermining the system. The divergent development of productivity remains a stumbling block for an incomes policy.

Now in addition to these micro-economic complications there is a much more serious pitfall for the norm $w = h$, which is of a macro-economic nature. It is this: if prices rise $w = h$ means that the share of labour falls. For a constant share of labour presupposes that $w = p + h$ (see Chapter IV, 9). In other words, wage policy is tenable only if the other incomes also remain within the norm, so that $p = O$. If they do not, the workers and the unions cannot be expected to cooperate. To put it yet another way, incomes policy must be an all-round success. If it starts to fail on some point or the other, it will also fail elsewhere. That is a characteristic of vicious circles.

It is therefore becoming time for us to see to what extent incomes other than wages and salaries can be subjected to the general norm of incomes policy. That is no problem as regards agricultural rents. They form only a small part of the national cost price, and in most countries the land rent contracts can be kept well in hand. Agricultural rent usually rises less than the yield per acre, if only through the fundamental forces that we described in the previous chapter. Urban rents, on the other hand, often increase in an objectionable way; this may annoy people and make the climate for an incomes policy worse. It is therefore self-evident that the authorities try to keep these rentals (and also house rents!) under control, so as to make a contribution to suppression of the spiral. This is possible in principle, although it often happens very incompletely in practice.

Profits are a bigger headache for the authorities. There are tens of thousands of products, each with its own quality. These qualities change. Packaging, types and brands also change. Try and find out whether the profit margins have in fact remained constant. Note that we are not concerned with constant prices; if the cost price falls (because the remuneration of the factors of production rises less quickly than productivity) the price must go down. If a price rises somewhere this does not prove that the profit margin has risen; a cost increase may be behind it. Upward and downward cost movements are going on all the time. Of course it is possible by close investigation to determine whether a profit margin has increased in a given case, but it takes a good deal of time and trouble.

In practice governments try to get out of this by picking on strategic prices. In the United States it is the custom (perhaps a good one) to bear down on the steel industry. In Britain the Board has published about sixty reports on prices, including those of obvious products like bread (everyone eats it) and soap and detergents (every housewife uses them, and everyone knows that the market for detergents is characterized by giant suppliers who spend a fortune on advertising). The Prices and Incomes Act of 1966 provides for an 'Early Warning System' under which price increases of certain goods must be communicated beforehand to the appropriate Government departments, and perhaps that has some psychological effect. We thus see that something is being done about prices, but it remains rather haphazard.

The index figures and daily experience show that prices are rising. Annual increases of 3% and 4% are quite ordinary. Now the public see in every price increase the hand of a profit-mad exploiter, and forget that cost increases may have gone before. The wage push as a cause of inflation is systematically overlooked. The annoyance and the pressure thus remain present – not a good atmosphere for general cooperation.

While the authorities occasionally have a small success in the battle for the profit margin, they are completely defeated when it comes to the interest rate. This really ought to come under incomes policy too, but little is ever said about that. For it just cannot be done. The interest rate hardly allows itself to be deliberately pushed down. The government can make special loans cheap, such as those for housing, for small businesses, but that is subsidization which cannot be applied to all borrowers because it would lead to great losses for the Treasury. Just after the war Mr Hugh Dalton followed a low-interest policy, which amounted to his borrowing money from the banks and using it to buy up Government bonds. The price of these bonds then goes up, and that is the same as a drop in interest. The awkward thing about this procedure is that borrowing from the banks involves the creation of money. That is most inopportune, because in this way the devil of cost inflation is cast out by the Beelzebub of monetary inflation. Dalton had to abandon this policy and a repetition is not required.

To the extent that deliberate interest policy is pursued today, it operates in the wrong direction. If the inflation becomes particularly frightening, and the lenders begin to incorporate this in the remuneration that they require (so that the interest rate goes up anyway), the central banks raise the official bank rate, as a result of which the interest rates creep up still further everywhere! That has the tendency to delay the creation of money, which is a good thing, but it increases the costs of production. True, this has only a slight effect on the cost price of the national product as a whole, but people still notice it. Borrowers are hit where it hurts. The high rate of interest makes itself felt in sensitive sectors, such as housebuilding, and may lead to substantial price increases there. This action by the central banks has nothing in common with incomes policy; on the contrary, monetary authorities run counter to the policy of members of the government who want to control wages and profits.

The income category that is thought about most is wage. But even there large sectors escape supervision. That applies above all to wage drift: the wage increase that exceeds the collective contracts. In some countries (Denmark, Sweden, Norway) this is a higher percentage than the rise in the conventional rates, and in the United Kingdom it is still some 3% a year. The causes vary. Sometimes employers pay their workers what they are not prepared to grant to the unions across the bargaining table. In addition there are automatic processes at work that translate a part of the increase in productivity into higher earnings: payment by results. Then there are various methods, such as simulated upgrading, for paying a given man or a given group more than is permitted in accordance with the norms. The tension on the labour market promotes this, and many employers reason: if you can't beat wage drift, join it.

This sliding increase in earnings has opposite effects on the workability of an incomes policy, but they are mainly unfavourable. On the one hand a certain flexibility is created by which the cooperation of the workers can be bought. If the norm is $w = h$ and prices rise, wage drift ensures that the share of labour does not fall, or not too much. Those are the positive sides. But on the other hand inequities are fostered. The one worker gets what is withheld from the other. The rehabilitation of the wage structure is rudely interrupted. Tension and frustration are created, which leads to new wage claims. The spiral goes merrily on its way. The credibility of incomes policy is undermined, especially when businessmen give the workers what they refuse the unions. This makes the union officials furious because it cuts the ground away from under their feet and is very suitable for thoroughly discrediting the whole of incomes policy. Wage drift is therefore at least as serious a pitfall as price drift and interest drift.

It is therefore no wonder that little comes of an incomes policy. It can function only if everyone keeps to it, but too many people have something to gain from evading it. That makes the others unwilling in their turn. We therefore see everywhere authorities who persevere with the courage of desperation, speaking encouraging and sometimes unctuous words (thereby laying themselves open to a charge of hypocrisy) and on the other hand critics who, unhampered by any responsibility for policy, speak clear or cynical language.* The final judgement on the policy followed so far lies in the degree of inflation control that it has yielded.

In this respect the record is not so hopeful. The countries that had an incomes policy, or claimed to have one, such as Austria, Denmark, Finland, the Netherlands, Norway and Sweden, have not displayed over the whole postwar period any lower price

---

* For instance, J. Corina (*The Development of Incomes Policy*, 1966, p. 54) says that 'despite all the declarations, speeches, resolutions, reports and machinery the truth is that Britain has no incomes policy'. One can in fact put it like that. However, one can also remark that the Board and Mrs Castle are doing their best and occasionally scoring a small success in the struggle against the spiral.

increases than the countries that had never heard of an incomes policy, such as Switzerland (there they have foreign workers: that is more effective). Even the wage increases are not lower in these countries.*

In Britain wages rose in the Sixties by annual percentages that exceeded 5% and sometimes came close to 10%. The wage push continued to have teeth. The annual price increase was in the neighbourhood of 4%, which is likewise nothing to write home about. But of course this is not the whole story; we ought to know what would have happened to the spiral if the authorities had not gone to all this trouble. That is difficult to estimate unless you know the situation in a country well. As regards the United Kingdom it is often said that only the short-run freezes have been effective – the national panic, usually about the balance of payments, keeps people in check for a while. That presents a dim view of the long-term prospects.†

As regards the Netherlands – the country with the most ramified incomes policy, which collapsed before everyone's eyes – I have the following opinion: in the Fifties there existed a laboriously constructed system of wage–land rent–price control that kept the spiral pretty well within bounds. Just as in Britain, it worked best in years of national panic about the balance of payments, but also over the years 1945 to 1960 as a whole the inflation was certainly less than it would have been otherwise. The Dutch competitive position on international markets became steadily better. The share of labour grew. However, the increase of prices could not be stopped, and that kept on giving new tensions. Under political pressure this system was gradually abandoned, and it was followed in the Sixties by several wage explosions of 15% a year and more. These were reactions to the modest increases of previous years. The price increase was higher than in the other countries of Europe. Viewed over the whole postwar period the result of the Dutch experiment has been minimal. It might have gone differently if

* For accurate calculations and nuanced conclusions see C. T. Saunders, 'Macro-economic Aspects of Incomes Policy', in: *The Labour Market and Inflation*, 1968.

† See for instance D. C. Smith, *Income Policies, Some Foreign Experiences and their Relevance for Canada*, 1966.

everyone had kept strictly to the rules, also after 1960, but that was not so. The lesson is that committees, boards and even draconic legal powers (of which there were plenty in the Netherlands) do not help ultimately if people do not cooperate.

Does this mean to say that we must give up the struggle against the spiral? I do not think so. Every damping of the price inflation is worth having, and so we have to persevere. And in addition we can try in the interim to smooth out the wage structure somewhat. This is the attractive aspect of British policy: it aims at a synthesis of inflation control and harmonization of wage relativities. True, as a result the British system is constantly balanced on a knife's edge. Combating the spiral is essentially maintenance of the status quo, and job evaluation means change. The two are not always easy to reconcile. But the effort must be applauded, and if those concerned display a little good will modest results are perhaps to be expected.

However, for our subject the stress must fall on the modest nature of these changes. An incomes policy, unlike the associations that the term evokes, is not a method of radically and thoroughly changing income distribution. At best it prevents fixed incomes being harmed by inflation, and here and there it can streamline. But that is no cure-all against disfiguring gross inequality. On the contrary, this is barely changed by it.

4. *Weeding Out Ill-gotten Incomes*

In an ideal society only useful, constructive activities should be remunerated. This in no way means to say that everyone would then regard income distribution as ideal – after all, it is possible that someone has so many scarce utilities to offer that the market mechanism rewards him with a lavish income, and that may be open to criticism from an ethical point of view. But we would be a good bit further if we could make sure that negative and destructive activities were no longer remunerated. In every decent society theft, blackmail and fraud are kept within bounds by criminal law. The success of this leaves much to be desired, but at least the intention is good. However, present-day capitalism contains methods of acquiring an income which do not necessarily come under the criminal code and yet look like theft. Instances that leap to mind are the exploiting of monopoly positions; the related deliberate increasing of scarcity by restraint of trade; and further speculation, especially when this is bound up with deliberate rigging of the market, advance knowledge and other unsavoury practices. In this way people manage to get high incomes without rendering society a service, and sometimes it is worse: in the case of contrived scarcity (in which production is deliberately limited or the lifetime of the product shortened) they damage overall prosperity. Concepts like 'productive contribution' and 'marginal productivity' are completely out of place here.

The combating of negative practices is generally regarded as a requirement of economic policy, even without one having income distribution particularly in mind. The ideology of free competition, free entry to the market, flexible prices and decentralized decision-making inspired in the United States the Sherman Anti-Trust Act (1890) and its successors; in the United Kingdom the Monopolies and Restrictive Practices Act (1948) and the Restrictive Trade Practices Act (1956) have the same aim. The distribution argument strengthens the desirability of such a policy, for from a distributive point of view too positions of power, contrived scarcity and specu-lation ought to be suppressed. It is particularly offensive if the un-scrupulous become wealthy through shady practices while masses of people get no further than a meagre wage by working hard.

Unfortunately the weeding-out is easier said than done. That applies right away to monopolistic power. Competition and monopoly are so subtly proportioned that sometimes you can hardly tell them apart. Every article with a special brand already has a touch of monopoly about it; on the other hand, some mono-polists compete with various substitute products; even rail trans-port can be partially replaced by road transport. Oligopoly – i.e. competition of the few – leads on some occasions to a fierce battle for the markets, and on others to inflexible prices and big profit margins. The profit that results from imperfect competition is often difficult to distinguish from the profit created by technical progress. Size and advanced technology are often closely connec-ted (the computer industry) while on the other hand size and monopoly are far from identical (cars, oil). A firm that deliberately keeps its volume of production small is difficult in practice to distinguish from the firm that understandably rejects orders showing a loss. Good and evil are sometimes tightly interwoven and if then in addition the government itself, by placing large orders (military equipment) and contracts, runs counter to competition, a vigorous and clear-cut anti-monopoly policy is hardly conceivable.

Now it is true that there are a few schools of economists (in Germany the Ordo group, in the United States a number of persons around the Chicago school) who believe that the government must promote competition ruthlessly, and that this will create freedom, fragmentation of economic power and the right income distribution everywhere. These neo-liberals regard monopoly as the capital sin of capitalism; if it is outlawed everything will go smoothly. Their prescription seems attractive, but it is extremely difficult to swallow. Breaking up big business requires such energetic intervention by the government that freedom seems to be harmed rather than fostered in the process. Large concerns would have to be chopped to pieces. Everywhere where the authorities suspect a restriction of competition they would have to take action. Entrepreneurs would no longer be certain of their legal existence. The marked reduction of patent rights, also advocated by this group, is a tricky business which hardly serves economic progress. A drastic policy as recommended by these neo-liberals seems worse than the malady and practically impossible.

In practice the government operates highly selectively and carefully seeks out the positions of economic power that it wants to tackle. Its strategy is very reticent. Only if the abuse is manifest does the government intervene, and then it often also considers the harm that a group of powerful firms do to their competitors. And indeed individual suppliers must be protected against the practices of cartels who try to put the independents out of business, for instance by exclusive trade agreements. The government must supply this protection. By so doing it also serves the interests of a just distribution of income, because smaller firms stay alive and newcomers get a chance.

Perhaps the government could be somewhat more active in protecting the consumers' interests. In its intervention the criterion should above all be the nature of the product and the income of the people who buy it. A semi-monopoly in Polaroid cameras may be a profitable business, but these profits are not earned at the expense of the poor. Anyone who buys such a camera can please himself; a transfer of income takes place from the well-off to Dr Land, who is a millionaire. Increasing inequality, admittedly, but nothing to get excited about all the same. An example of a more unfavourable situation is supplied by the pharmaceutical industry. Medicines with fantastic profit margins are bought by everyone, and above all by old people with small incomes. Monopolistic elements, price agreements and market domination come face to face with an inelastic demand; that can lead to unacceptable price determination. In Britain this is not so much of a problem because medicines are supplied by the National Health Service; the taxpayer foots the bill here. That is not pleasant, but at least it is better than when the patients are the victims; the latter happens in other countries. The pharmaceutical industry is constantly under heavy fire,* the matter being complicated by its research costs and by the undeniably positive effect of pharmaceuticals on human well-being. Come to that, these complications apply to the whole of the medical sector – no-one, especially the grateful patient, begrudges the doctors a good income, but it is not ethically sound for doctors and medical specialists to earn fantastic sums that come in part from poor people. Even if the burden is passed on to all and sundry by insurance a problem remains which, however, is difficult to solve for the free professions.

This example already shows that weeding out objectionable incomes need not be exclusively directed against big industrialists. In many cases the concerns can quietly keep out of harm's way, and it is precisely the individual small businessman or the professional who has to be aimed at. In the crafts, and especially in the repair business, suppliers are often confronted with an urgent and highly inelastic demand – a burst water pipe is the most vivid example. Abuses, also among small firms, must be countered here, and that does not make the task of the government any easier. It is not easy to make laws that put a stop to exploitation of positions of power, and once they have been made it is not easy to

---

* Well known are the publications of the late U.S. Senator E. Kefauver, such as *In a Few Hands*, 1965. This book deals not only with drugs but also with cars, steel, bakeries and other cases.

enforce these laws. There is the danger of a haphazard policy, in which the authorities seize on those whom they happen to be able to catch – the same objection that may be adduced against an incomes policy. The clumsy and the conspicuous get found out, while the smarter ones carry merrily on. That is not in the interests of legal security nor of income distribution.

This is not the place to discuss the anti-monopoly policy in the various countries, but the reader will agree with me that in this way income distribution can be improved only incidentally. The evil of ill-gotten monopoly profits is too diffuse and too closely bound up with the good of technical progress (even in the pharmaceutical industry!) for that. Profits are as a rule attributable to a complex of causes, and the unscrambling of the latter requires a thorough and time-consuming analysis, case for case. I do not say that the government does not have a task here, but it will have to act with great thought and reserve. Measures against monopolistic practices and restraint of trade are embedded in a much more general policy; governments must not only hamper industry and keep it in check, they must also encourage and further it. Monopolies are bad, but advanced firms that grow rapidly are good, and sometimes the two look alike. Weak firms must be spared for social reasons, even if this involves a slight restriction of competition (as happens in the retail trade and the crafts on occasion). Because of these limitations, the results of the policy are not spectacular. We must be satisfied if a number of telling cases can be weeded out from time to time. A radical improvement of income structure cannot be achieved like this. Even the most enthusiastic supporters of a vigorous anti-trust policy, as are to be found above all in the United States, will agree with me that the effect on distribution is minimal.

As regards speculation the situation is somewhat more favourable, though not much. True, speculation in goods can only be distinguished from more or less normal trade in exceptional cases but it is not there that the objectionable practices are to be found. These relate to land and financial manipulations.

Speculation in land is a source of easily earned incomes that serve no useful purpose and often are at the expense of people with modest incomes. Although limited sums are involved in total, such

344

profits are ethically unacceptable. Speculation is particularly open to criticism if it is based on advance knowledge of expected government decisions. An urban expansion can yield fat profits for unscrupulous persons, and if these people in addition possess information that should be secret we come close to corruption. In a decent country the government opposes this. This can be done for instance by expropriating urban building land at moderate prices, and better still by systematic government ownership of the land. The latter is practised by many municipal authorities, and it has the advantage that the plans for use of the land can be made effective and comprehensive. The primary reason for socialization of land thus lies in another field, but as a by-product speculation and the resultant ill-gotten incomes are prevented. Although it would be exaggerated to expect from this a general flattening of the Lorenz curve (as the disciples of Henry George do), this is all the same a policy that should have a high priority. In most countries the trend is indeed in this direction. There is still room for improvement, and for many it is not going quickly enough.

Speculation on the stock exchange is a different matter. For every shareholder and bondholder runs the risk of fluctuating market prices. The speculator who buys and sells short-term is difficult to distinguish from the normal investor, who also occasionally buys and sells a few shares so as to make his portfolio optimal. It is not always clear whom he harms, or whether his activities make income distribution more or less unequal. Either way, only indirect action is possible against this form of speculation: the monetary authorities can put the brakes on loans against securities. Such measures are usually taken for the primary purpose of checking the inflationary bullish market, but they can indirectly help somewhat against the acquisition of unearned incomes. However, the effect is not impressive.

While the buying and selling of shares, although profit is made in the process, is not a fishy activity, this cannot be said of transactions in which advance knowledge or manipulation is involved. Financial shrewdness and criminal activity merge here. At present there are in all countries huge fortunes in the hands of institutional investors – insurance companies, trust funds, investment funds – and when they buy or sell a certain share on a large scale the market price rises or falls. Of course there are officials of these organizations who know about that beforehand, and if they want to they can gain from it by making a pleasant little profit for themselves, perhaps via a figurehead. It is even not inconceivable that managers of large funds deliberately enter into transactions in one direction, and then in the other, to make their private speculation proceed a little more efficiently. It is a fact that such practices occur. To what extent is not known. Distribution definitely becomes more skew as a result, in the sense that small groups of unscrupulous persons make high incomes. There is almost no limit to the ill-gotten gains that a well-placed individual can make in this way, and the guilty persons can hardly be caught. It is a sad and unsavoury chapter from the financial chronicle which, moreover, remains largely unwritten.

Let us quickly return to normal things, and they include the steady rise in market prices. The government cannot prevent shareholders from becoming richer because the value of their investments rises. It is very much open to doubt whether it ought to try. If all prices rise, so do those of shares, houses and capital goods. If a firm becomes more profitable it is natural and legitimate that its assets and its shares become dearer. General measures to compensate for this enrichment may lie in the field of taxation. The increased wealth on the stock exchange is easily earned, if we forget about the incipient ulcers of some speculators, and may therefore very well be taxed at a somewhat higher rate. However, here we have the paradox that in many countries capital gains are more lightly taxed than wages and salaries. Sometimes they are entirely exempt, as in the United Kingdom up to 1962. This kind treatment may be upheld by regarding capital gains as something very special and not really income – an intellectually defensible position, but one that is ethically unsatisfactory. For it remains true that a rise in the market price causes a person's wealth to rise; the result is for the investor the same as if he had saved from his current income. In the latter case the Inland Revenue would have taken its usual share. The most resolute solution is therefore to regard capital gains as income and to tax them in accordance with the normal progressive income tax rate.

It is open to discussion whether this tax should apply only to realized capital gains or whether the rise in the market price of unsold securities must also be included. The latter occurs nowhere so far, but it could be advocated. In any case there seems to me no reason to perpetuate the preferential treatment of realized profits on speculation in respect of normal income, which is to be found in practically all the countries of the West. Because as long as these incomes are more lightly taxed than the ordinary man's wage, distrust is sown about the intentions and the resolution with which governments approach income distribution.* An incomes policy that demands sacrifices from some groups of workers does not have a leg to stand on as long as capital gains get the kid glove treatment.

And in fact both anti-monopoly policy and the combating of speculation and the taxing of capital gains should be related more than has happened so far to an incomes policy as described in the last section. If we consider in isolation the various measures directed towards the suppression of the spiral and the improvement of the pay structure, the drawbacks always prevail. Every pressure group, whether it is the unions who have to moderate their wage demands or the capitalists who are stripped of some of their capital gains, resists by bringing forward these isolated drawbacks with vigour and eloquence. The chances of a general consensus increase somewhat as soon as we realize that all these policy measures are interrelated. The government can then appeal to a group to make sacrifices by referring to the sacrifices made by another group. I do not say that this will make incomes policy a radiant success; on the contrary, I believe that it will still be a matter of floundering on and that the governments will at most achieve a modest success here and there. But by stressing the interrelation of the policy somewhat more collaboration and progress can perhaps be attained.

---

*In Britain the Inland Revenue makes a distinction between earned and unearned income. That is a good thing in this connexion, although that is not to say that a wealth tax and a special capital gains tax would not be preferable.

5. *Profit Sharing and Capital Sharing*

Profits and interest are the sources of the extremely high incomes. I do not say that in the general sense they are the great source of inequality – statistical research has shown that the variance of the total income curve is attributable for not more than 25% to these incomes, and that is understandable too, for their share in national income is a modest one (coincidentally also about 25%). But it is a fact that the financial giants who brought up the rear of our parade, the super-rich who stir our imagination, derive their huge incomes from capital, whereby profit and interest often merge. It therefore goes without saying that plans for greater equality also zero in on these income categories.

There is all the more reason for this because the distribution of profit, once it has been made, seems to be institutionally determined. When entrepreneurs were still independently operating private persons, risk-bearing 100% owners of their businesses who were responsible to nobody, it was more or less natural that profit accrued to them (after the tax people had first taken a bite). This situation still exists in part of business and in the free professions. But in the limited liability companies the risk-bearing ownership is separated from the managers who take the initiative. The entrepreneur has split into two (though in a number of cases the two halves have been fitted together again through personal unions). Profit is divided among four categories: first the tax authorities, who in most modern countries take nearly half; then the shareholders who, if possible, get enough to keep them happy, which on average amounts to their getting a quarter of the total; then the managers themselves, plus the echelons immediately below them, who draw a very small fraction in the form of bonuses: small though it may be, that fraction is large enough to supply very pleasant top incomes for that small category of employees. A quarter of the profit is then left, which remains in the firm, and that serves for financing expansion. Under the present legal regulations that last quarter accrues in principle to the shareholders. As a group they may not consume this share of the profit; individuals within the group can do so if they find another capital-holder willing to take over their share. This 50–25–25 formula (the managers' share having been left out of consideration) seems relatively arbitrary and therefore perhaps pliable; possibly it can be institutionally changed, and egalitarians of every country are casting their gaze on this formula. Let us see what possibilities it offers for a shift.

To do so we can tackle these profits in two ways. The first method is for us to give all employees the right to a distribution of profit; labour then joins the shareholders as a group with an entitlement to dividend. The employees are given their dividend, which they may spend or save; that is up to them. If they save they become small capitalists, but the same applies to saving from other incomes. This method is called profit sharing. The second way is called capital sharing; the employees get a title to the retained profits. They thus join the shareholders as a group of co-owners who cannot consume their property as a body.

These are the two methods discussed below. They must be distinguished from two other systems that resemble them to some extent, viz. gain sharing and investment wages. Gain sharing means a group of remuneration systems under which labour is paid in accordance with the performance of a group of workers or a department of the firm. The best known of the various systems is the Scanlon Plan, in which the organization of the work is delegated to the departments of the firm. Each department is entrusted with a task: so much has to be produced, productivity has to rise by so much, etc. If the group stays within this norm, part of the favourable difference between plan and plan implementation goes to the workers. The supporters of this scheme expect from it an enthusiastic participation by the workers which is also reflected in their incomes, and harmony between the various levels in the organization. But this is payment by results, not profit sharing. It does not bring about any fundamental change in the distribution of income, any more than piece rates do. The total profit of the capitalists becomes greater through it rather than smaller. Of course, some groups of workers can profit from it, and perhaps such plans are splendid in their way, but they are of very limited importance to our subject, and they may not be confused with profit sharing. A disadvantage of such systems is that they run counter to job evaluation and create horizontal differentials that offend the workers who do not get them. It is not the intention to go into such plans here.

Investment wages must be distinguished from capital sharing. Investment wages mean that the worker does not get a share of his wage paid out in money; it is frozen for him on an individual or collective account. This is therefore compulsory saving. In this way one does in fact make a small capitalist of the worker, but he could also have voluntarily performed that operation himself. If he does not do so he reveals a preference for consumption, and the arrangement is resolutely opposed to that. This compulsion is evidently an unattractive aspect of these investment wages. They have an unpleasant air of tutelage and 'we know better' about them, which is probably why they are not popular in the United Kingdom and the United States. They have been much discussed in Germany; a fervent supporter is O. von Nell-Breuning, operating in a Catholic world of ideas in which workers, furnishers of capital and management are viewed as equal partners in the firms. This view is consonant with the wish that the workers should get together a capital capable of financing one job.* Von Nell's ideas have been worked out in the Leber Plan (1964), under which employees had to pay 1·5% of their wages into a fund every year, which fund then became the property of the workers. The normal money wage then becomes correspondingly lower. The employers rejected the idea, understandably, because they feared that the unions would not in the long run accept the reduction of the normal money wage, so that the 1·5% would in fact be a cost increase. The Leber Plan was not implemented; it was replaced by a voluntary saving scheme, under which workers got a bonus on their savings. This obviates the drawback of compulsion, but all that remains of the plan is a bonus saving scheme – very nice, but quite different from a direct intervention in the distribution of wealth.

Back to profit sharing. It is an old system, applied a century ago in the coal mine of Messrs Briggs, in Yorkshire, and thereafter in various gas firms, shipyards, woollen mills, etc. There are still earlier examples in France (the *La Nationale* insurance company, dating back to 1823). In the United States an early instance is

* *Eigentumsbildung in Arbeiterhand*, 1955. *Vermögensbildung in Arbeiterhand; ein Programm und sein Echo*, 1964.

known from 1870 (Brewster & Co., cartwrights – the scheme was withdrawn two years later, after a strike). Although since then there have been many hundreds of firms where the system has been applied they are still exceptions; often they had a short life as well. In recent times there has been increasing interest. The practice is spreading to industrial giants, often in combination with employee ownership. A well-known example is I C I. The initiative for profit sharing in the Anglo-American countries is taken almost always by the management and the shareholders, rarely by the workers. The motives may be idealistic: more harmony, more widespread prosperity, recognition of the human rights of the worker. Sometimes the desire to increase productivity is involved. Formerly the motives were sometimes less altruistic: keeping the unions from the door. Sometimes the profit sharing is accompanied by a say of the workers in the firm; sometimes it is not. Unfortunately there have often been friction and displeasure; profits fluctuate and that may give rise to disappointment. It has happened that workers felt they were getting less than they were entitled to. Especially in bad times harmony is transformed into conflict. That leads in turn to understandable displeasure on the part of the management and to withdrawal of the scheme. A short lifetime is a rather common characteristic of profit sharing.

If we want to change society and income distribution radically, profit sharing must be stripped of this incidental and arbitrary character. Some therefore have that in mind. They want a general, obligatory scheme valid for all firms (perhaps above a certain size). In this way capitalism could be transformed into a society in which everyone participates in the fruits of progress. This *participation* was one of the hobbies of M. de Gaulle. Since 1968 all firms employing more than 100 persons have had to have profit-sharing schemes in France, and in fact many contracts have been introduced (at last count about 4,000). A number of Latin American countries, too, have introduced general compulsory schemes.

For the sake of discussion let us consider such a compulsory system and see what quantitative effects this would have on distribution. All limited liability companies therefore have to pay their workers a share in the profit which, let us say, is as large in total as the dividend that the shareholders get. (Of course, countless other ways of dividing the profits up are feasible. First 6% primary dividend can be deducted, the rest then being divided into the ratio of invested capital to total wage bill, but such variants are more or less irrelevant to our argument.) The 50–25–25 formula will therefore be changed. The question is, how is the workers' dividend paid? Or, in other words, who pays it?

We can only speculate on this matter, but some things are certain. The Inland Revenue probably suffers no harm. It is in a position to continue to demand its half. If it does not do so, the workers' share of the profit comes in part from the pockets of the taxpayers – not an obvious step forward. Nor is it to be expected that a government will introduce a compulsory profit-sharing scheme with the intention of suffering for it. The first of the three numbers therefore remains unchanged. What also seems fairly certain is that the small number (not included in the formula) indicating the bonuses for the top executives will remain constant. It can hardly be expected that the managers will lower their own incomes *because* a compulsory profit-sharing scheme for workers has been introduced. As has already been remarked many times above, the managers are in a position to fix their own share of the loot. This is governed by norms which they lay down themselves, perhaps in consultation with a few controlling shareholders. Profit sharing by workers probably has no substantial influence on this – unless the workers also get a say in the management, but that is another matter to be discussed below.

It is possible that the share of dividends drops as a result of profit sharing. But then not much. The great mass of anonymous shareholders as a rule get little more than they have to have to keep the prices of the shares up to the market level. It is conceivable that their requirements are somewhat modified by a compulsory scheme, but that is not certain. The shareholders have a simple way of demonstrating their lack of agreement: by forcing down the market price of the shares. This disapproval hits the managers where it hurts, for it means that new issues can be made only at a lower price. In other words, shareholders have their own weapons for keeping the number of 25% as it stands.

Then there is still the possibility that the new 25% of the workers is deducted from the retained profits. That would be most unfortunate, for the firm, and for the shareholders (who would react by lowering the market prices) and for the workers themselves, because the expansion of the firm, technical progress and the growth of employment depend on it. You can get too sentimental and timorous about this, but it remains a fact that growth is largely financed from retained profits; plans that sweep away this financing are not in the interests of the workers.

But I do not believe that in fact we need to fear or hope that one of the above-mentioned categories, especially internal financing, will suffer harm through profit sharing. The 50–25–25 formula will shift, and perhaps change into 50–14–18–18 or something of the kind, but at the same time the total profit, measured in terms of money, will increase. In other words, there is a good chance that the payment to workers will be passed on to the firm's customers. The burden will be spread out thinly over the whole of society. The ultimate distribution is regulated by a spiral in which labour tries to increase its share and capital defends itself. In this respect profit sharing resembles a general wage increase. It is probable that the economically strong will suffer less than the economically weak, so that a fundamental shift in income relations will not be achieved.

I admit that such a result is not certain. After all, we do not know for sure what determines the total share of profits in national income. In the view of those who regard profit as a purely passive residual item, it will not be possible to pass the burden on. More profit for labour then means less profit for the capitalist. And in fact they may be right if profit sharing is applied on a small scale, in isolated little islands, as it is today. In that case competition opposes increased profits. But this view becomes less likely as soon as the system is applied all along the line. It then includes large, strong suppliers, with a technical lead on their competitors, who will successfully raise their prices. Perhaps there will be weak firms that will go under and have to give up the struggle for existence. Their share of the market is added to that of the strong competitors, and that increases the possibility of the costs being passed on.

This makes the whole scheme less attractive. However, it is as well to continue the reasoning somewhat further, and to consider the additional income that accrues to the workers. It proves that this is in turn restricted. We have seen that in total profits form 20% of national income. But this includes incomes of independent professionals and small businessmen. Little can be done about these, and compulsory schemes are therefore intended as a rule for large firms. Their share of national income is about 10%. Of this part for instance 18% or, if we are improbably generous in our calculations, 25% would then accrue to the workers. This is therefore at most $2\frac{1}{2}$% of national income. This jump in the income of labour would occur only once, when the profit-sharing plan was introduced. Since the income of labour forms 70% of national income, the worker would experience this as a single wage increase of $3\frac{1}{2}$%. Note that this wage increase does not occur in successive years! The share of profit is incorporated in the income of labour, and gradually rises with the increase in national income. But we see the jump of $3\frac{1}{2}$% only when the plan is introduced.

That is the lot: an extra wage round of $3\frac{1}{2}$%. And this has to be borne by unknown, diffuse groups in society. Probably not by the strong ones, but by the weak. The above sample calculation, with all its assumptions, can be modified; if we put it most optimistically a macro-figure of 5% may result instead of $3\frac{1}{2}$%. That is one year's normal wage increase. A general plan for compulsory profit sharing would therefore raise the money income of the workers in 1975 to the level which it would otherwise have reached in 1976. Is it worth it?

If we now look at capital sharing we see a somewhat different picture.* It is a more favourable one. Here the 50–25–25 formula remains intact; no new distribution takes place. The workers acquire (individually or via intermediary funds – several variants are possible) a title according as the capital of the firm where they work grows through retention of profit. The operation is a painless one. At first sight no costs are incurred; nothing happens except that new owners are noiselessly added to the old ones. If that process continues long enough, the workers' property accumulates; they grow rich at work while the capitalists grow rich in their sleep. True, the total sum available is no larger here than in profit sharing, but the difference is that here the $3\cdot5$% is accumulated. After about

*This too is an old idea; it was already recommended in 1847 by P. F. Reichensbergen.

ten years a worker in an average profitable firm has built up about a third of his annual income, and through his total working life one to one and a half times his annual income. Not an awful lot, but still something, to which any normal savings from his income can then be added.

The matter can also be quantitatively approached as follows. Suppose that half of the retained profits accrues to the workers. That is then $12\frac{1}{2}\%$ of the annual profit, or $1\cdot2\%$ of national income. Over a generation that amounts to a capital sum equal to half of national income. If the national stock of capital goods (the K from the preceding chapter) is five times the size of national income, this means that after a generation the workers have acquired one tenth of the national wealth. Not bad.

Of course there are a few snakes in the grass. It is a fallacy that the operation costs nothing. In economics you don't get something for nothing. The property of the old shareholders takes quite a knock; the share capital is watered down. The shareholders can show their displeasure at this by demanding a higher return from new share issues (i.e. reducing the market price they are prepared to pay). As a result, the financing of the firm becomes more expensive, and this cost increase will be passed on, just as in profit sharing. In fact the same happens as with profits tax: the burden is borne by a diffuse group and not necessarily by the super-rich. To that extent profit sharing and capital sharing are birds of the same feather. But wealth relations do shift quite definitely through capital sharing. Not in a revolutionary manner, and the top 1% become no less rich, but the shift is still worth while.

Awkward problems occur in organization and legal set-up. Must the worker be assigned his share in the firm individually, or must trust companies, funds, etc., be interposed? Must he acquire a title only to the firm in which he works, or to the branch of industry, or to the national whole? How must he be able to transfer his title to others? What about small personal enterprises and firms? In such cases a system tailored to the impersonal limited liability company can lead to great difficulties. What are we to do about civil servants? Will capital sharing create disparities and inequities between workers in flourishing branches of industry and those in less flourishing ones? Does not the whole scheme run counter most undesirably to the streamlining of pay structures and job evaluation?

Depending on the system worked out, these questions can be answered differently. They can be dealt with as long as the capital-sharing schemes are applied individually, on a voluntary basis. As soon as we start thinking about broad compulsory systems these complications become most annoying. They lead to endless discussions and to opposition. The opponents have things made easy for them and the supporters become tired and discouraged.

This has been the typical experience in Germany, where a few concrete proposals have been worked out that were intended for the German economy as a whole. B. Gleitze, who is attached to the German federation of unions (the DGB, a kind of German TUC), and H. W. Büttner devised schemes in which special funds were set up per branch of industry. These were to act as intermediaries, and the workers would acquire claims on these funds. Nothing came of the whole business and the DGB is not wholeheartedly behind the schemes. In 1960 the *Sozialistische Partei Deutschland* thought up something similar (which provided for a national foundation), but the idea was abandoned at a later date.*

Such plans do in fact have the drawback that they can be pushed through on a large scale only if this is laid down by law. It is not easy to find a majority for this in the parliaments. The unions prefer to concentrate on day-to-day matters of wage policy and on social insurance. In the Anglo-American countries these plans are also regarded as attempts to tie the worker to small capitalist interests. As an American union leader once said to me: 'If a worker wants to save and invest he is man enough to do that himself. We'll make sure that he gets a decent wage, and how he spends it is his own business.'

This opinion seems too harsh a one to me. There are many fine examples of profit sharing and employee ownership. In Britain there is above all the John Lewis Partnership Ltd that attracts attention through its size (in 1964 16,500 employees, known as 'partners') and its generous scheme, and in addition firms like

---

* B. Gleitze, 'Lohnpolitik und Vermögensverteilung' in: *Sozialer Fortschritt*, 1957. H. W. Büttner, 'Eigentumsstreuung über Sozialkapital', in: *Sozialer Fortschritt*, 1958.

Kalamazoo Ltd, PA Management Consultants and Scott Bader & Co. Ltd.* The profit motive has not been weakened by these schemes, the shareholders are not up in arms, the power structure has not been revolutionized; but the income and ownership relations have gradually shifted. At Kalamazoo, the Birmingham business systems firm, the employees held half the share capital in the mid Sixties. These are interesting experiments worthy of encouragement and emulation. The government should treat them kindly and where possible take their interests into account. The least that must happen is that profit sharing and capital sharing should be given a fair chance, and preferably a little more. Everything that can improve income distribution and harm (almost) nobody must be encouraged.

6 Changing the Power Structure

Most economists dislike discussing the power structure. Their distaste is understandable. The term alone invokes associations with vague and unverifiable theories on income distribution, with empty words that are meant critically but cannot hold their ground against any counter-criticism. If someone talks about power structure he can be expected to speak the next moment about the authoritarian set-up of the universities in general and the London School of Economics in particular, about racial discrimination, Cuba and Vietnam, and about the total rottenness of the Western world – all these matters stir into a thick porridge, and I am entirely on the side of my fellow-economists when they want to avoid this kind of emotional discussion. But I do not agree with them when they claim that the power structure is a meaningless concept, nor when they maintain that power is one of the *data* of economic theory which we may not look into.

Now the concept of power naturally occurs in economic theory. As a rule it then relates to monopoly or oligopoly (a few big firms competing for the share of the market), and to the control that strong suppliers have over prices. Other groups, such as strong buyers or consumer organizations, can put up a fight against this –

* See a series of articles on these four firms in *Business*, September, October and November 1964 and January 1965.

that is called countervailing power, and since J. K. Galbraith it has been a popular idea, even among economists. And furthermore the union tends to be thought of in this connexion, even though some are inclined to consider the influence of these institutions on wage determination small and to regard the forces of the market as decisive (see Chapter IV, 3). All this is known and accepted; it is textbook stuff. But what is not textbook stuff and is quite wrongly left by the economists to critical young people with long hair and to uncritical business economists and accountants is the study of power relations *within* the large firm. Too infrequently do economics textbooks contain the proposition that has been repeated above to the point of boredom: inside the large firm remuneration is fixed by people who use it as a means of expressing their ideas of status and prestige. These income-setters are in a position to translate their ideas and their norms into reality. They have power, and this power imposes its stamp on income distribution.

The top executives in particular are in this position; they fix their own incomes. The shareholders, who ought to supervise this process, have little say in reining in the managers' claims. And they barely have a financial interest in this because these top incomes represent such a small fraction of the total costs. Very large shareholders who control their own company and are anything but weak or backward have a vested interest in staying friends with the top executives and buying their loyalty with high incomes. The resultant inequality is attributable to the firm's power structure. This is authoritarian and vertical; subordinates get orders from their superiors, who in turn have *their* superiors. Commands come down to the workers from above. They are entitled to say something in return, to make comments or suggestions, but superiors decide, and certainly where salaries are concerned. Anyone who wants to change income distribution will have to do something about this.

This approach to the problem seems imperative to me. Influencing the income relations for senior staff is doomed to failure if it happens from the outside. Incomes policy can do little about this. The unions can do nothing, because collective contracts are not concluded for senior staff. The pressure groups of qualified employees can even cause a central trade union all kinds of trouble, as the Histadruth found to its cost. Pushing up the lower wages is of little help – then the whole ladder moves up, with a slight compression at the lower rungs and perhaps in the middle, but barely at the top. The levelling of wage and salary structure that has taken place in the course of the years is attributable to the increased supply of candidates for more senior jobs and to the changed ideas about what a decent salary should be. This process will continue, but it goes slowly. Even the Inland Revenue can do little, for the higher salaries have a tendency to rise if taxes are increased, as a result of which taxes are passed on and the income after tax remains the same. The sponge resumes its original shape after being squeezed.

Until recently the authoritarian structure of the firms was regarded as the most natural and inevitable thing in the world. For most people it is self-evident that the boss is the boss, that he gives the orders and that anyone who does not agree with the orders simply resigns. We are also accustomed to the view that the owner of a commodity can do exactly what he wants with it, and the owner of a firm can thus by definition go his own sweet way with that firm. He is himself the top manager, or he appoints the top managers. They can then delegate power down the chain of command, set up committees, consult with their fellow-managers, listen to workers; they can put on a happy face and need in no way order people about like the army. A spirit of cooperation and comradeship may prevail; that is more pleasant for everyone and above all for productivity. It is known that workers have to be involved in the work as much as possible, that they should bear maximum responsibility; this improves their performance. The atmosphere in a firm may be amicable and jovial, but the command structure remains vertical. When it comes down to it, decisions are taken from above to below, and when it comes even further down to it there sometimes prove to be owners who have the last word. This is after all the basic legal pattern of our society. Law and order are directed towards maintaining this state of affairs, with cooperation from almost everyone.

The protest against these authoritarian organizations is confined to small groups. Historically anarchists, syndicalists, Fourier socialists have opposed it, but their point of view was too unpractical to be taken seriously. Somebody has to be in charge. And yet it is strange that in a society that keeps on talking in every key about democracy there are large islands where little or nothing can be seen of democracy and where the chains of command in principle run from above to below without any supervisory body in which those commanded are represented, and without any responsibility of the leaders towards the led. People know quite well that no democracy exists in business – they go to the factory or office five days a week, and they notice its absence there. In their leisure time they hear about the joys of democratic decisions.

Not only do these big undemocratic islands exist; they are accepted as well. This is certainly the case in the Anglo-American countries; even socialist quarters have never seriously tried to revamp business organization. Nationalization is of course a familiar alternative, but even then the set-up of the concerns remains vertical. Come to that, the national organizations that have been with us the longest – the armies – adhere to the most rigid principles of command conceivable. That is still so, and it is surprising that there are not more protests about it.

The union movement in Britain and the United States has at most nibbled away at the edges of this business power structure. Wage consultation enters into effect from outside, and changes nothing of the internal organization of a firm. At the lowest level of all, viz. the shop floor, the union can occasionally make its influence felt. There the worker is protected against incidental high-handedness and gross injustice. But that has little in common with changing the basic organization of the firms. Not a single union official will deny that control of the firm is at the top, and that at the bottom at most decisions from which specific individuals suffer are opposed.

In other countries attempts have been made to acquire influence at the top. In Germany in particular *Mitbestimmung* has been pursued: the large firms have directors who are supposed to represent the interests of the workers. This right of the workers to appoint directors is regulated by law. In some branches of industry – iron and steel, and mining – the workers are even represented on the board of directors on a fifty-fifty basis. That is a good thing, but it is not real democracy. For the *Arbeitsdirektor* is not directly responsible to the workers; he sits at the top as a new specialist, with perhaps another outlook and a different background, but the chains of command remain vertical. There is no firm parliament that supervises top management and exercises the ultimate say. In France too the *participation* of the workers is aimed at. These plans were a hobby of M. de Gaulle. However, the *comités d'entreprise* are simply consultative bodies; their representatives on the board of directors have only an advisory vote. Here too there is no fundamental change in the chains of command. Only in Yugoslavia are matters different; there workers' councils are said to determine the firms' policy. But in Yugoslavia the set-up of the whole of society is radically different; the firms are not the property of private capitalists, so that the situation can hardly be compared with ours.

I do not say that an authoritarian organization of the firms is wrong. On the contrary, it is probably most efficient. If everybody has a say not only does an expensive permanent discussion result, but there is absolutely no guarantee either that most decisions are so much 'better', whatever the word means. I even greatly doubt whether people are made that much happier by giving them consultation and participation in the management; democracy has its own frustrations. A group becomes enthusiastic about a plan, but the majority turns it down – that hurts more than when invisible authorities take decisions off their own bat. Nor is it undignified, as some people claim, to follow the instructions of others. It makes for peace and quiet, and you can lead quite a satisfactory existence in that way. I am therefore not unconditionally advocating a system under which the members of the firm get a greater say than they now have. But I do expect that people's wishes will go in this direction. The need for a greater voice is a need just like any other, though probably an expensive one. As national income grows, so will this luxury need. I do not know whether that is good or bad.

But I do claim that this is a method of getting income structure in a firm systematically under control. Or, to be more exact, I claim that if power remains concentrated at the top, the distribution of the firm's income among senior and junior employees will be a reflection of this command structure. Anyone who thinks that business, for the sake of efficiency, for the sake of existing law and order or to maintain existing differences in prestige, must retain vertical chains of command implies that top executives retain meritocratic top incomes, and the second echelon somewhat lower but still very high incomes, and so on, until finally the workers right at the bottom find in their wage packets a reflection of this hierarchy. I am not calling for a revolution, but I merely wish for the reader to see where the bottlenecks lie in our problem, so that he himself can decide what he prefers the firm of the future to be.

A democratic firm is possible. An essential requirement is a firm parliament that holds the ultimate power, hires and fires the management and approves or rejects the main lines of policy. These main lines relate not only to production plans and technology, but also to salaries, bonuses, fringe benefits, expense accounts, the use of the company planes. In that parliament capital and labour ought to be represented. It takes the place of the shareholders' meeting. One can argue about the exact arrangement – how many representatives of the personnel, how they are elected, what influence the unions are to have, what the ratio is between workers' votes and capital's votes, what rights of veto, if any, what position the management will assume, what the powers of the various bodies will be. In addition to a firm parliament one could also envisage department councils that elect the department heads and have a say in the performance of subtasks. One can imagine all kinds of things and weigh the advantages and disadvantages of such systems. The legal structure should certainly not be forgotten either, for without statutory compulsion this kind of thing will not come about.

A point that certainly deserves careful consideration is how the workers' power has to be limited with respect to that of the capitalists. Such a limitation is necessary because otherwise there is the danger that the workers will gobble up the firm. Growth and technical progress would be interrupted and employment would be endangered. In the long run this is certainly not in the interests of the workers, but short-sightedness or greed might cause them to follow their short-term interests. Guarantees must be created against this – a delicate problem. There is much that could be said about the exact arrangements. But that is not the intention here. It is my personal opinion that we shall be heading in that direction in the future – people will probably demand democracy in business, and their demand will be unstoppable. The events at the universities are a portent of this. Not being a prophet, I cannot say what turn development will exactly take, but the trend seems inescapable to me.

The question that interests us at this moment is simply this: what would be the influence of such a changed power structure on income distribution? And there is only one answer to that: if power within the firms is spread out more democratically and the fixing of salary scales becomes one of the prerogatives of the members of the firm as a whole, income distribution will acquire a more democratic look, in the formal sense that people's preferences will be better reflected than they are today. Tinbergen's exchange principle will describe reality better than it now does. It is highly probable that inequality will decrease and that the wages of manual workers will come closer to those of the senior employees and the top management. Perhaps the workers will find on closer consideration and after long discussion that the managers can rightfully and reasonably claim enormous salaries – that is then all right. Perhaps pronounced levelling will be the result – that is then all right too. Formally speaking, everything decided by the democratic bodies is an expression of the general will, and so all right.

Of course there are objections to all this. Some will deny that the remuneration structure is pliable and will invoke the market mechanism. Others will maintain that responsibility has to be rewarded, and refer to Lydall's Law: a person's income is proportionate to the total income of his immediate subordinates. I personally do not believe that the compulsion of the blind forces of the market is all that great. This is the case only if a firm wants to change income distribution on its own – that cannot be done.* It

* An example. In the firm of Kalamazoo Ltd, Birmingham, much of the power is vested in the Kalamazoo Workers' Alliance, to which about half the employees belong. But when profits were distributed in 1964, the operational grade got £54, the foreman grade £82, the divisional manager grade £936 and the general manager £3,120. That is a ratio of 1 to 60, not unlike the usual one between dwarfs and giants in firms. See *Business*, October 1964, p. 58.

can be done if the equalizing decisions are taken in the same way all along the line, i.e. in the majority of firms. By that simultaneous action of all firm parliaments the play would become much larger. I cannot prove this – that is the negative result of Chapter IV, 3, in which we were obliged to establish that the mix between the forces of the market and the forces of prestige and status cannot be exactly determined. However, there is definitely some pliability. Moreover, we are now concerned with the future, that is to say with an uncertain situation in which everything will be different: the income is higher, the K/L ratio has further increased, and so has training, and the technology is unpredictably different from what it is today. The systematic pressure by members of the same firm towards greater equality is being exercised in a dynamic world. That makes the chance of equalization greater. A number of fantastic salaries will disappear as a result of business democracy, if it comes; rationalization and streamlining will be the order of the day.

True, the advantage to be gained from that must not be over-estimated. Compressing the remuneration structure and cutting a number of top incomes down to size will not cause the material prosperity of the mass of workers to increase to any startling extent. Some naïve left-wing critics of the present income distribution are wrong about that. We must recall the figures: if we were to force the top 10% of *all* income recipients (who already begin at the senior supervisors, the technical staff, the department head) practically down to the average – and that is a fantastic operation that not a single firm parliament will be prepared to perform – only an increase in income of at most 15% would be gained for everyone. We can achieve the same result by some five years' undisturbed economic growth. If we were to curtail the real giants – 25 feet and more – to the average, that would yield – even before tax – little more than 5%, i.e. one extra annual wage round for everyone. If that increase in prosperity is our only motive we had better forget it. The reason for equalization must be that we aim at a more balanced society, without unreasonable exceptions, without exaggerated privileges. In such a society firms would be real partnerships which, for the sake of efficiency, display a certain hierarchy but which do not additionally rub in this hierarchy by striking differences in remuneration. Perhaps we can pluck the fruits of meritocracy without being constantly pricked by the thorns so richly produced by that system. (Perhaps. It may of course also happen that the partnerships degenerate into quarrelsome debating clubs, in which production takes a back seat, and in which the aggressive elements have their way and frustration grows at every hand. If we want to avoid that, we must wait for the human race to improve.)

7. *Give and Take: the Needy*

Up to now we have been talking about primary income distribution, that is to say the result of the distributive process that takes place at the same time as production. If this result does not please us, we can change it by transfers. This seems the most straightforward intervention conceivable: the government takes from the rich and gives to the poor until the secondary distribution tallies with our ethical norms. It can be imagined that in this way poverty is banished and inequality done away with.

In reality this does not happen. True, in modern society countless reallocations and massive transfers of income occur, but the ultimate distribution of income remains very skew. Many of the poor remain visibly poor, and in most Western countries (especially the United States) there are large groups below the poverty line. The very rich stay very rich, even after income tax. (In the following section we shall see that the share of the top 1% in national income is merely reduced by income tax from 8% to nearly 6%.) Even after the transfers have taken place, the bottom 20% of families in Britain do not get more than $7\frac{1}{2}$% of total income; in other countries, such as the United States, this is even less (5%). The question that forms the subject of this section is why we do not aim more resolutely at equalization, and more particularly why poverty is not tackled more radically by transfers. Are there perhaps economic laws that oppose this? Does the spongy character of distribution upset matters? Or is there something else at work?

When answering such questions we do well to recall the asymmetry between what happens at the bottom of the income scale and what happens with the rich and the well-to-do. We have seen above that the economic and social forces at the top and bottom of the income scale are not mirror images. Another reason for considering the transfers at the bottom and the top of the income ladder separately is that almost everyone believes that the deliberate allocation of incomes to poor people is admissible and desirable, while the removal of incomes, according to most people, requires special justification: it must serve a clear purpose, otherwise it is not permitted. That purpose is in part self-evident: the financing of State expenditure, but this sets limits to the amount that the Inland Revenue can take off someone. It is not a matter of decapitating incomes for the sake of financing. Complete confiscation must have a tremendously strong ethical argument behind it, and because such an argument cannot be easily found (most pleas for decapitation are inspired by rancour or by dubious views of economic power) the operation is not performed. But making up too low incomes is an aim in itself. It is with the latter that this section is concerned.

Transfers on behalf of special groups form the heart of the Welfare State.* They take place in all countries. The techniques vary, but the basic idea is always the same: if a person is unable to work, temporarily or permanently, he nevertheless gets an income. A distinction is often made between social insurance and social services. In the former case the participants pay a contribution while they work and receive benefit if they become jobless or sick; here the transfer of income is in the first instance one in time, or between the same groups. That is why those who profit from social insurance are not always poor. Salaried persons also come under it, and their benefit is coupled to their incomes.

The social services largely consist of income transfers too; the difference is that a contribution is paid towards insurance and not towards the social services. A second difference is that the social services are more closely aimed at the needy. National Assistance is a typical example. The money comes from the Exchequer and is

* Not to be confused with the Affluent Society. This expression relates to the average real income, which is assertedly so pleasantly high (though that proves to be a great disappointment). The Welfare State refers to distribution: it attempts to guarantee minima.

covered by taxation. (The latter is an older method than social insurance, as witness the Poor Laws.) In the social services greater attention is paid to vertical transfer than in social insurance, but this difference can easily be exaggerated. The difference often melts away when we look somewhat more closely at the way in which the burdens are shared. Contributions are passed on in wages, and so further in prices; the same happens with many taxes. It is therefore impossible to make a close distinction in the sharing of burdens between insurance and social services. The distinction is more of a technical and psychological nature: insurance experts explain to us that an insurance contract is quite different from a charitable donation, but since in the Welfare State the payments of benefit to the needy are made by law, and the recipients have rights, this difference is not very great either.

In some countries there is a tendency to insure everything that can be insured (sometimes on a compulsory basis), and to regard general benefit from the Exchequer as a final safeguard for border-line cases. Thus the United States has the OASDI programme, which insures 95% of all people in paid employment against old age, survivorship and disability. People who have had no fixed employment are not covered by it. In addition there is old age assistance, aid to dependent children, aid to the permanently disabled – social services paid from the Treasury, with General Assistance as the last resort. But the main thing is OASDI. In other countries, such as the United Kingdom, the greater part of benefit, viz. 60%, is paid out of taxes. There too National Assistance is meant as a final safeguard.* We saw before that this does not operate in-fallibly. Even in the Britain of the Sixties there were still many people who lived below the level of National Assistance. The reason why they got no assistance is mainly that they did not ask for it.

The social services have, of course, been greatly expanded in

---

* While the social security benefits in various European countries are at more or less the same level (15–20 % of personal income) the financing is different. Denmark and Ireland have the highest State contribution, nearly 70 %, followed immediately by the United Kingdom, with 60 %. The Netherlands is at the bottom of the list with 13 %. Source: *Incomes in Post-war Europe*, 1967, pp. 6,7.

recent decades. This has helped a number of genuine cases of necessity. However, elements have also crept in that tend to obscure the transfer character. A turning point in Britain was probably the Family Allowances Act of 1945. All parents with more than one child get an allowance irrespective of income. Including millionaires. Although in fact a special need exists here – children are expensive – the word 'needy' does not apply to the beneficiaries. The transfers are no longer specifically directed towards poor people. The middle classes, who sometimes take a bitter attitude towards the Welfare State, nevertheless profit from this. True, the State invites recipients who do not need the money not to draw the allowance, but this invitation is seldom heeded. These transfers are no longer vertical, but horizontal. This also applies, though to a lesser extent, to retirement pensions; in some countries (the Netherlands) that is also a general scheme, under which rich people have the same rights as the poor. In Britain a pensioner's own earnings are in part deducted from the pension.

In addition to the income transfers the Welfare State also has provisions in kind, of which the National Health Service is the characteristic example, then school milk, cod liver oil for babies, and so on. This too is usually considered part of the social services. Here the dividing line blurs with all kinds of other services rendered by the authorities to the citizens: education, street lighting, fire services. Some authors rack their brains to try and find the dividing line between social services and other government expenditure;* the criterion is whether the government activity is specially intended for people of modest means, but that is a slippery criterion. What are intentions? Was the National Health Service set up with the intention of benefiting the lower-income recipients, to expand the medical sector and make it more efficient, or to achieve deeper ideological goals? Do those intentions matter much after the event, and are not the actual effects much more important? It seems to me better simply to forget this philosophical distinction in government activities and to accept that the concept of Welfare State becomes rather vague by so doing.

The study of philosophical distinctions ought to be replaced by something else: a calculation of the benefits that the various social

* For instance D. C. Marsh, *The Future of the Welfare State*, 1964.

groups enjoy from the different government activities. These benefits are dissimilar. The fire services protect the interests of house-owners more than those of the tenants, to profit directly from motorways you have to have a car, Hyde Park is for everyone but anyone who himself has a beautiful garden or a house in the country has less need of it, the expenditure on universities benefits the middle classes and the rich more than the workers; in the case of scholarships the opposite applies. Subsidies to art, which are often recommended for allowing 'the people' to participate in artistic life, in actual fact benefit the higher income brackets. A cost-benefit analysis of this kind is occasionally made for special projects, but rarely for the whole mass of government expenditure.* The result is that nobody knows exactly what the redistributive effects of all expenditure are, and this uncertainty is a fertile breeding ground for numerous prejudices.

The most familiar one is that the Welfare State vigorously increases the below-average incomes and vigorously reduces the above-average ones. In other words, a marked vertical redistribution occurs. The opinion is a legacy from the days of the Poor Laws; you had to be completely down and out to profit from it. Now it is true that the present system still contains elements reminiscent of the Poor Laws, such as National Assistance. But a considerable part of social insurance and the social services, such as employment insurance and family allowances, is not confined to manual workers, let alone to poor people. The transfers are

* For the United States an interesting attempt has been made by W. I. Gillespie ('Effects of Public Expenditure on the Distribution of Income' in: R. A. Musgrave, *Essays in Fiscal Federalism*, 1965). His analysis, which necessarily involves numerous hypotheses (examples: two-thirds of the corporate tax is borne by the shareholders, excises and customs are borne 100% by the consumers, expenditure on education accrues to the students' parents) concludes that in 1960 the income brackets from $4,000 to $10,000 paid in tax what they got back from the Government (Federal, State and local); their net benefit was zero. The lower incomes had a positive surplus, the higher ones a negative one. An obvious objection to Gillespie's approach is that government services are evaluated in accordance with the cost price measured in money. Hence the apocryphal result that most people have no net pleasure from the government. If we were to apply this idea to the market economy nobody would derive any welfare from it – we all pay what the goods are 'worth'. But I could not say how to obviate this objection.

largely horizontal; they preserve incomes, but hardly do any levelling.

Now in some cases the government economy operates to the advantage of the rich. That is sometimes unavoidable, as in the case of the fire services, but sometimes it is especially curious, as in the case of agricultural subsidies in the United States; as the latter are often coupled to the farm's production or its acreage, the large farmers profit more from the subsidy than do the small ones. In that case the income transfers go against the grain; they switch money from the average taxpayer to the higher-income recipients. In many countries, such as the Netherlands, house-building subsidies can be seen to be benefiting the well-to-do. There are countries where recreation is subsidized – in itself an excellent aim – as a result of which vertical redistribution occurs from below to above: free parking, cheap yacht harbours. The Welfare State is often compared to Santa Claus, and that comparison is usually drawn by those who object to presents for poor people. But in fact the Welfare State resembles Santa Claus because he gives more to rich children than to poor ones.

And added to this is the fact that taxes and contributions have to be paid starting at very low incomes. That goes without saying in the case of indirect taxes – it is unavoidable that poor people pay purchase tax. But income tax too takes its toll of incomes barely above the poverty line (National Assistance benefit). The average tax rates are admittedly low in such cases, but the plight of such families is nevertheless intensified by the Inland Revenue, and a steady raising of the exemption levels is therefore an obvious measure.

These peculiarities must be borne in mind when it is asked why the Welfare State does so little to improve income inequality. Certainly it lays a floor beneath which nobody need drop. But this floor is low – even in Britain a family fully dependent on transfer income from National Assistance is on the borderline of the subsistence minimum. What happens above this floor is not exactly clear. Probably some vertical redistribution takes place, but not very much. In Gillespie's study mentioned above it is estimated that the overall system of transfer incomes, social security contributions and taxes in 1960 yielded a positive net effect for the lowest

14% of income recipients, while from then on a negative effect occurred, decreasing, however, above $5,000 – in other words, the burden is regressive. This regression is introduced by the social security contributions and the indirect taxes. For the United Kingdom Brown and Dawson, in their highly informative pamphlet on British taxes,* conclude that the combined effect of positive and negative cash transfers is 'pretty well proportional for most tax payers who pay a positive rate of tax'. (The progression is felt at the top, but that is a subject for the following section.)

The Welfare State is therefore something of a disappointment if viewed through the eyes of the egalitarian. It guards against calamities, it prevents the victims of illness or disablement – which can happen to us all – from slipping below the minimum limit, and it pushes the very lowest incomes up a little; but it does not change the general shape of income distribution much.

This also emerges from the following figures: the lowest 20% of families receive in Britain about $7\frac{1}{2}$% of national income. This is a relatively high percentage compared with the United States equivalent (less than 5% of the total), but it is very small compared with the total of income transfers. At the beginning of the Sixties they were already some 15% (in Germany, with its highly unequal primary income distribution, 20%). Since then they have risen everywhere, and most countries are heading for 20% of national income. That is a huge sum of money which is constantly churned through the economic system. Apparently a modest part of it clings to the lowest-income recipients, who despite this flow of money continue to get very limited percentages of the national income. Tom subsidizes Dick, and Dick subsidizes Harry, and Harry subsidizes Tom, and all three subsidize themselves. That is the way it must be, for otherwise the share of the lowest-income recipients would look more like the percentage of social security benefits.

If this reasoning is correct, it suggests two ways of improving the Welfare State. The first has already been mentioned: steadily raise the exemption levels of income tax. They have to be lifted more quickly than the rate of inflation and productivity together.

*C. V. Brown and D. A. Dawson, *Personal Taxation Incentives and Tax Reform*, 1969, p. 29.

The reason is that exemption should preferably rise more quickly than the wage level, while the latter already rises more quickly than $p + h$. Jacking up the exemption level is in fact a measure that left-wing politicians must constantly advocate. It has the additional advantage that an increasing number of taxpayers can be struck off the list, which reduces the costs of tax collection. Raising the exemption levels has the disadvantage that it costs the Exchequer a great deal of money, and that puts a brake on the speed with which this policy can be carried out, but the direction of the measure is certainly a desirable one.

Much more dubious is the second method of making the Welfare State more effective: ensure that the benefit does in fact accrue to those who need it. This is a tempting conclusion: select the recipients, and give as little as possible to the higher income brackets. The inequality will decrease, and that is the idea. Now paradoxically enough this approach is often recommended but, in particular, in Conservative quarters; in that case it is prompted by exactly the opposite wish, namely that of less redistribution. In a publication by I. MacLeod and E. Powell in 1951* it was already urged that benefit should be confined to those who really need it; the point of view of both gentlemen drew its inspiration from the thought that much too much equalization had already occurred, that the middle classes were being squeezed dry, and that most people received more from the general kitty than they put into it. The last point is an unproven and probably incorrect argument,† and the opinion about the middle classes being squeezed to death is a value judgement which is difficult to maintain after a glance at the Lorenz curve and at the middle-class giants in the parade of dwarfs. But it is rather odd that diametrically opposed objectives regarding equalization can lead to an identical policy!

This paradox begins to clear up when the reader realizes that the intention of the Conservatives is to save on expenditure on the Welfare State. By selective benefit they want to lighten the load on

* *The Social Services: Needs and Means*, 1951.

† It is probably the other way round; according to Brown and Dawson, 43% of households have their incomes increased while 57% have them reduced (p. 29). This estimate is highly uncertain, but what MacLeod and Powell claim is political prejudice, not a representation of facts.

372

the higher incomes. When they speak of people getting money without needing it or earning it they have workers in mind, I think, rather than people earning above-average incomes. My intention would be to use selective application to create room for a drastic increase of benefit at the base. If necessary the load on the middle classes and the top incomes could become greater (but preferably not, because I have other proposals that are going to cost the above-average income recipient money). But what, in my reasoning, may not happen is that the burden increases constantly at almost all income levels, and likewise the benefit at all income levels. Such a policy of increasing horizontal redistribution arouses the greatest opposition, because everybody feels that he is paying more than he gets. It has the same effect as inflation: although this barely changes general prosperity, everyone gets the feeling that he is in some way being cheated, and that it is *others* who profit from the Affluent Society (which is claimed to exist – it is described in books, and so there will be some truth in it, but most people don't notice it). The frustration of the general price increase, the frustration of the unselective Welfare State and the frustration of seeing nothing of affluence are brothers and sisters.

An illustration from the Netherlands. In the second half of the Sixties new social provisions were introduced (for the permanently disabled), and the benefit paid to old people increased. As a result, real wages rose only moderately, by 2·5% a year, while productivity rose by 4%. This gave rise to opposition from the workers. While the left-wing parties in Parliament, with union support, voted for the shift towards those not actively employed, and the distribution did in fact become somewhat more uniform, the unions protested against the low wage increases. This stirred up wage inflation, as a result of which the old people again felt they were being badly done by. Everybody complained, and it was generally forgotten that there were also people who gained from the shift. And this was a pretty selective extension of benefit. In the case of unselective increases the psychological opposition is even worse.

Selective application of social insurance and social services is easier said than done. The means test involves administrative costs and delay. Civil servants acquire positions of power. The discrimination, whereby applicants have to answer all kinds of awkward questions, is regarded as being aimed at the poor (while it is in fact aimed at helping those worse off!) Anyone who is turned down is really annoyed. In addition there is ideological opposition; people may point out that the Welfare State is for everybody, and that no exceptions may be made to that principle.

An even more serious drawback of selective benefit seems to me to be the following. Under the present system anyone from the middle income brackets who loses his job or falls ill is paid benefit coupled to his income. He loses on the deal, but his ties with the past are not broken. That is the reason why horizontal redistribution prevails. If this system is abandoned, middle-class people who fall ill have a chance of dropping back to the general minimum. That is levelling, but of a very rough kind. You have to be an egalitarian through and through to be consistently in favour of it. Personally I am against a rough reduction of income that claims innocent victims. A certain income maintenance for everyone is reasonable, but this cuts out a fair amount of selective application of the Welfare State.

The consequence of all this is that the Welfare State remains a very widespread affair, in which a great deal of money circulates that serves a respectable but not directly egalitarian purpose. The contribution to levelling remains limited. We could cautiously improve the system of income transfers somewhat by not only raising the exemption levels but also reducing here and there the benefit that does not serve a clearly egalitarian purpose. Family allowances could perhaps be done away with, at least for above-average incomes. Subsidies to institutions from which the well-to-do profit ought to be critically considered. But here too, just as in the revision of the wage structure by job classification, it is more a matter of streamlining than radical intervention.

An obvious, very radical, but impractical proposal is drastically to raise the benefit levels of the Welfare State. The most naïve variant is to give every adult a free minimum income from which he can live. He can then decide for himself whether he wants to earn anything on the side. The difficulty is, of course, that the whole body of adults not only gets this money but also has to supply it – a horizontal operation if ever there was one. But even an increase in specific benefit (e.g. National Assistance) has its drawbacks, for it must remain tangibly lower than the minimum wage. Otherwise odd situations occur in which some people prefer to live at the expense of the community rather than work. Even if the group that misuses the Welfare State is a small one, it offends morally and politically. The regulations may not be made in such a way that the parasitical group becomes too large, otherwise the resistance to the whole system becomes too great.

To obviate these drawbacks the idea has come to the fore in recent times of a negative income tax. The idea, which is rather fashionable, has been propagated above all by M. Friedman, an out and out anti-interventionist who believes that practically everything must be left to the free market mechanism; the book in which the idea is described is called *Capitalism and Freedom* (1962). The author, whom we encountered before on p. 242, where he explained inequality by natural risks, is against minimum wages, against the existing social insurance, against compulsory old age provision, against progressive income tax. In his opinion the load must be taken off the top brackets and the tax base broadened. To achieve this Friedman recommends a negative income tax (NIT), which works as follows. A guaranteed minimum income is fixed of, say, 300 units. If a person earns nothing he gets this from the tax people. Then an income is fixed at which no tax is paid: the exemption level of, say, 600 units. If a person earns less than the exemption level he gets money back; this sum is calculated by taking a fixed percentage (say 50) of the difference between the exemption level and the actual income. If, therefore, someone earns 250 units he gets in addition, in the form of NIT, half of 600–250, or 175 units; his total income is 250 + 175 = 425 units. He thus gets more than the minimum of 300: this is attributable to his own income which, however, has been partly deducted from the NIT. The NIT is nil at the exemption level, and above that level a proportional rate enters into effect (lower than 50%, of course). Other figures can be chosen for the minimum, the exemption level and the percentage, but the principle remains the same.

This principle amounts to the fact that the NIT smoothly decreases as income rises, but without complete confiscation of one's own income. An incentive to earn more remains. This is the difference between the NIT and the usual guaranteed minimum incomes. The subsidies are concentrated around the lowest incomes; in that way the system differs from the usual social insurances. The costs of the scheme are clear to see, no simultaneous flows of money in opposite directions are created, as under the present policy. Vertical redistribution is applied in pure form.

When passing judgement on the NIT it must be borne in mind that it was designed for the United States, where large groups of people live below an existence worthy of human beings. If the guaranteed NIT minimum is high enough, these groups are assisted. All over Europe there is National Assistance, as a result of which NIT is less urgent. In fact you have to compare National Assistance in its existing form and NIT, and see which works better. That is a fairly technical matter, whereby administrative aspects must also be examined. For instance, it seems to me that the officials of Inland Revenue would be required to have a different mentality from what they should possess today; in the case of NIT they must react quickly and generously and give the customer the benefit of the doubt. If they continue to operate slowly and punctiliously, seeking to justify every penny, the recipients of NIT will have died of starvation before they have got their money.

More important is the question whether NIT could replace other schemes besides National Assistance. We could envisage family allowances and retirement pensions. The advantage of NIT is that it operates more concentratedly and cuts out useless benefit which is in any case demanded back again later by positive income tax. Family allowances would largely disappear. Now perhaps that is a good thing, but we do not need NIT for that. General old age pensions would also cease to exist. But that would be an inconsiderate way of going about things; people with modest incomes would suffer, and that is the converse of what we want. We might also think about replacing National Insurance by NIT, but this is even more difficult. As stated, the traditional schemes couple benefit with the former income that has disappeared as a result of unemployment, illness or disablement, and under NIT such a link with the past does not exist. Anyone who is struck down by fate may then slip back badly to very low minima. In my opinion that is the principal point on which the possible change in policy must be assessed. Some people will consider such a steep fall from the middle classes to the minimum level of NIT an unacceptable form of levelling, and this point of view is certainly a respectable one.

If we accept the last objection to replacement of National Insurance by NIT, we opt for maintaining many of the existing arrangements. This makes NIT unsuitable for replacing the present system. For the negative tax does not lend itself to piecemeal application. It only has any point if it is introduced at one go, as a kind of revolution. And that does not seem to me to be a step forward, even for the United States. We must not expect that income distribution will be changed favourably by such novelties. In the system of the Welfare State improvements are indeed conceivable, but these are fairly technical matters, not magic charms. A better method than NIT is constantly to raise the benefit of the social services, and above all of National Assistance, so that this benefit keeps up with the general rise in productivity. The poor must not be allowed to lag behind as a result of inflation or economic growth. We must keep an eye on this, and not waste our energy on fashionable tricks.

Finally, it is often sought to improve equality by advocating expansion of the social services, i.e. not income transfers but the provision of free or partially free goods and services. True, the inequality of money incomes remains the same, but rich and poor increasingly enjoy the same consumption. This argument is often brought up with reference to the National Health Service and education: the consumption of these services may not be dependent on income.

And indeed society can be made better balanced in this way. But it is an expensive method because it is so unselective. The best proof of this is to take two wants as an example: one which is already fully satisfied by everyone (bread) and a luxury want (air travel). Free bread would involve enormous government expenditure from which the needy would profit only in proportion to their number. This helps, of course, but it is like filling the sky with shot to hit one single duck. This method is an extravagant one.* Free,

---

*This also applies to the Communist countries. Khruschev once announced that one fine day the Soviet citizens would be so well-off that they would get free food. I asked myself: why? If they're earning so much, surely

377

or almost free, air travel even has a rather negative effect: the rich profit from it above all because they have the resources for moving about easily in distant lands. Their expenditure would be subsidized by the mode of income recipients, and that has an opposite effect, in the same way that cultural subsidies affect distribution the wrong way round. Now one need not be put off by the latter; egalitarians will say that it is still worth while transporting rich and poor in one aircraft without distinguishing between class and money, and that argument is certainly a tenable one. But these operations are extremely costly, and that is a serious disadvantage at a time when it is already so difficult to finance normal government expenditure.

In practice the government will have to be selective. Priority must not be given to arbitrary free goods, such as bread or steak, but to wants that have some intrinsic merit or the other. Cod liver oil is to be recommended from a medical point of view, education for the development of the personality and to increase society's productivity, rehabilitation of the cities to improve the human climate and the quality of the community. These latter priorities are in themselves so expensive that little room is left for real expenditure with a purely redistributive effect, especially if we want to keep on raising the exemption level of income tax. The government can try to keep the interests of low-income recipients particularly in mind with reference to the intrinsically meritorious expenditure, and there in fact a fortunate harmony prevails: education and urban rehabilitation are in everyone's interests, but the low-income recipients can profit from them relatively more than the well-to-do, who have more possibilities of escape. In fact, education and city planning affect the fundamental forces which, in the last analysis, determine social stratification and income distribution. Thus, as regards real government expenditure, there is no reason for gloom, but the belief that a rapid and easy revolution in income distribution can be achieved via free provisions is an illusion.

---

they can buy their own meals. Free soup is more reminiscent of poverty than of affluence.

8. *Give and Take: the Top*

Suppose that we consider the rich too rich – an idea contained in practically every ethical study, and one which also pervades this chapter. What, then, is more effective and direct than simply taking their excessive income from them via taxation? And in fact this is the first thing that most people think of, and they then find that present tax policy apparently does not help much. The worst poverty may be a thing of the past, but skew distribution evidently is still with us, even after the Inland Revenue has taken its share. The outward characteristics of inequality live on. The shops are full of things that the man in the street cannot buy, the roads are populated by Rolls and Jaguars, the jets are always full of passengers, homes and neighbourhoods are strikingly unequal. The number of millionaires is on the increase.

But since, where tax is concerned, every opinion has its opposite opinion, we also hear it said that the tax authorities are responsible for repellent levelling. Income differentials have become too small, the incentives for effort and training have weakened and vanished, and everyone is being reduced to the same dreary denominator. Everything that gives colour and style to life has been excised by the hot hands of the tax man. On 23 May 1968, *The Times Literary Supplement* wrote in an unsigned leader that Britain places 'the heaviest fiscal load . . . upon the most constricted private sector among the leading industrial western nations. . . . On this showing, the frustrated, penalized, overburdened, increasingly hamstrung, diminishing private sector will grind to a halt.'

It is clearly necessary to take a look at the facts. But here we again encounter the fact that income distribution has different faces. It makes a tremendous difference whether we consider the burden of taxation as evidenced by the official income tax rates (and with the aid of our figures decapitate the giants in our parade) or whether we consider the income shares of the top groups before and after tax. The latter – the method of the Lorenz curve – conveys the impression of a much lower burden on high incomes than the former. We shall apply both methods, starting with that suggested by the Lorenz curve.

This is preceded by a theoretical remark which may be useful to the reader who wants to make similar calculations himself. There is a simple relation between four variables, viz. the income share of a group (e.g. the top 1%) before tax, the income share after tax, the average burden of taxation on the group (which we call τ) and the average burden of taxation on the whole population (which we call t). This relation may be derived as follows: call the income of the group before tax y and the total income Y. Then the share of the group before tax is y/Y. The share after tax is by definition $(1 - \tau)y/(1 - t)Y$. It follows that the relation between the after-tax share and the before-tax share is $(1 - \tau)/(1 - t)$.

Armed with this formula and the figures from the *111th Report of the Commissioners of Her Majesty's Inland Revenue for the Year Ended 31st March 1968* we find that the top 6% of British income recipients received about 20% of national income before tax and still retained 17% after tax. Only a small difference, as you see. The Lorenz curve has become only slightly flatter. Tax takes away from this group about one quarter of its members' income, which is twice the national average. If we consider the giants of the last 36 seconds of our parade (the top 1%) we see that before tax they got 8%, and after tax about 6%. The average burden on this group is over a third. That is quite a bite, but the lion's share of income remains in the hands of the income recipients: a rather surprising result. The flattening of the Lorenz curve, and the burden of taxation, is disappointing as regards the top 1%.

American figures give the same picture.* The effective tax rate of the top 1% is not more than 26%. As a result, their share of income falls from just under 8% to over 6%, and the equalization is therefore somewhat less than in Britain. The 4% of income recipients immediately below the top 1% pay only 14% of their income, as a result of which their share of 12% in total income is barely reduced: after tax it is still over 11%. When we realize that the average burden of income tax is about 10%, we see that this group therefore pays barely more than the average! And it should be borne in mind that the situation in the United States is not at all exceptional – as I have said, the overall picture does not differ from that of the United Kingdom or other Western countries with

*They apply to 1960 and are taken from the most authoritative book on this subject: R. Goode, *The Individual Income Tax*, 1964, p. 263.

a high rate of income tax, such as Sweden, the Netherlands and the German Federal Republic. This is highly disappointing for the egalitarian, and it is understandable that he cries: raise the rates!

But, strangely enough, these are already very high. Let us give a short survey of the British rates, if only because this system has a few peculiarities which can easily mislead the superficial observer.* What catches the eye above all is the standard rate of 8s. 3d., which seems to apply to all incomes. But take care. The flat rate is in reality not flat, and it applies to only a small fraction of incomes. This apparent paradox is caused by two things: 8s. 3d. applies to unearned income only. For 'earned income' a special relief applies, so that the actual rate becomes 6s. 5d. In the second place various other allowances and reliefs operate, such as those for low incomes, children, life assurance; the result is that the average rate drops quite a bit and becomes progressive. The marginal rate (i.e. the tax on an additional £) is in fact constant from £669 to £4,005; it is nearly a third of the additional income. Below £669 the actual marginal rate is lower, as a result of the reliefs and allowances; at £4,005 the latter cease to apply, and surtax takes an extra bite. The rate then becomes 7s. 4d., and above £9,945 it becomes 8s. 3d., i.e. the standard rate. The top marginal rate is reached at £18,550, and is then 18s. 3d., or more than 90%. For unearned income – a highly pregnant expression! – the marginal rate, as stated above, is 8s. 3d., and the average burden is likewise higher. But here other deductions enter into operation: favoured treatment for capital gains and gifts, for interest paid by the taxpayer. The latter deductions have a greater effect according as the income is higher: if a rich man borrows money he gets for the interest a deduction which makes a difference of over 90% in tax, and poor people cannot profit from that. They do buy on hire purchase, but they may not deduct the interest charges of that.

Misunderstandings about the British burden of taxation are born because the standard rate of 8s. 3d. is stated officially and

* Information on the British tax system may be found in the previously mentioned pamphlet by C. V. Brown and D. A. Dawson, *Personal Taxation Incentives and Tax Reform* (P.E.P. publication, 1969). Although I do not agree with all their recommendations (for instance on negative income tax), I regard this broadsheet as the best published on this subject in Britain.

widely published, while by far the majority of people pay the lower rate of 6s. 5d. But a more important source of misunderstanding is that the 6s. 5d. rate is actually a *marginal* one; the average burden is much lower. The accompanying graph in Fig. 7, taken from

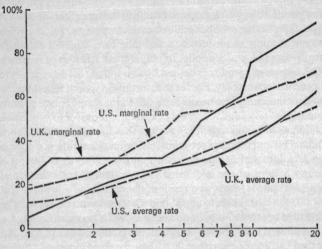

earned income in £ thousands (logarithmic scale)

Figure 7. *Income Tax Rates* (married man with 2 children)

Brown and Dawson, clearly shows this. The actual average percentage of income tax is not much above 10%. In other words two, at most three shillings! Because people talk about 8s. 3d. or 6s. 5d. almost everyone has the feeling that he pays more than he does. There is no better way of making people angry.

The very high marginal rates apply to only a very few people: in the mid Sixties the top rate of 18s. 3d. applied to half a *pro mille* of the taxpayers. However, their complaints ring out incessantly as a shrill overtone in all political discussions on income distribution, and that too gives an exaggerated picture of what is going on.

Other countries – like the United States – have a more rational trend of the marginal rate line. This too becomes clear from the graph, in which the jerky trend of the British marginal curve can be seen. The transition from horizontal to rising at £4,004, and the sudden onset of surtax, is a traumatic point; this is avoided by a flowing curve, like the American one, which also makes the double rate (standard rate *and* surtax) superfluous.

Moreover, the flowing line gives greater freedom in the choice of the gradient, i.e. the degree of progression. In the British system the last bit has to rise steeply if a high level is to be reached. In the American system that can go more gradually. Which is why the American Internal Revenue collects so much more, both average and marginal, than the British Inland Revenue as long as incomes around £5,000 are concerned. Against this the *marginal* top rates in the United States are lower than those in the United Kingdom; at £20,000 this rate is about 70% instead of 90%, while all the same the *average* rate for incomes between £10,000 and £20,000 does not differ much. That too is a consequence of the more flowing trend of the American marginal curve.

Given these properties of British income tax, we can regroup the facts of personal distribution. We again form the parade containing all income recipients; their height now corresponds to their income after tax. Everyone is shorter than in Chapter III. Suppose that we are all taxed as if we were the father of two children below the age of eleven. You and I, the spectators of average height, have then lost six inches. The mass of the workers, who measured barely five feet before tax, see themselves shrink by two or three inches. (If the standard rate for earned income were really equal to the average burden, these small people would be shortened eighteen inches!) Those who follow but do not reach average height – the highly skilled workers, a number of foremen, many primary-school teachers – lose four to five inches. Anyone who is taller than you and I, and so passes by in the last ten minutes, is considerably truncated. For instance, a lawyer who measured eighteen feet has now been reduced to thirteen feet six inches. Doctors, accountants and professors who first measured seven to eight yards now become five to six yards. We are now in the last minute. The Permanent Secretary becomes eight yards. These are still giants; the fiscal surgery makes them somewhat less frightening. This is made most clear by those who pass by in the last seconds. Mr David Barran, who at first was 120 yards high, now

T–N   383

becomes twenty yards. He was originally twice as tall as Prince Philip, but the latter has stayed as he was, namely sixty yards, because he pays no income tax, and as a result is three times the height of the best-paid managers of large firms. But Tom Jones, singing away, can continue to look down at the Prince; even after taxation he still measures some 200 yards. The last man in the procession, Mr Getty, if he were taxed at the British rate (and if that were also really applied, but that is not so) would no longer be ten miles high, but only a mile.

By watching this parade we get quite a different view of the facts of taxation than we did a few moments ago when we used the data of the Lorenz curve. We saw there that the effective tax rate of the top 1%, i.e. the last 36 seconds of the parade, is not higher than 33%. The Permanent Secretary, who is 13 yards high, already pays a higher percentage of his salary, and he is ahead of the very rich! In other words, something does not check, and indeed it would be misleading to shorten the last participants – supergiants a mile and more high – in accordance with the tax rates from the table. Ten miles is in fact not reduced to one mile. Blind application of the rates from the graph is mainly correct where salaries are concerned, but personal incomes derived from profit are treated in a different way in practice. They often get off more lightly.

That is, of course, due in the first place to the lack of exactitude with which the size of the profits is established. Deductible costs form an elastic concept. Profits can be spread out over a number of years. Depreciation is difficult to check. Then there is tax avoidance, rendered possible by loopholes in the law and by legal exceptions. Precisely among the top incomes parts of income escape taxation, or the rates are less high. Thus capital gains are taxed as normal income only if they are realized short-term; long-term gains are taxed at half the normal rate, unless the tax payer prefers a rate of 30%, and that is of course the case with those who are above a marginal rate of 60%, i.e. the very well-off. Moreover, that opens attractive prospects for the stock option, an arrangement under which executives are remunerated with shares that they acquire cheaply. If shares are not sold, the enhanced market value is not taxed at all. A percentage of trading profits is concealed as an increase in the value of assets, as a result of which the personal owners get off lightly.

High salaries, too, offer interesting possibilities for tax avoidance. These relate above all to the transferring of incomes to relatives and others. For instance, gifts are free (on condition that the donor remains alive for a further seven years – if not, the tax man claims his share after the funeral) and in particular recurrent gifts to which a person commits himself by a deed of covenant are tax-deductible. These covenants therefore lead a flourishing life in higher circles. Alimony for divorced wives costs little because the Exchequer subsidizes it – a privilege that the average and the modal taxpayers have to manage without. In addition, income can be shifted to the years in which one is pensioned and the rate is therefor lower. Insurance companies know these tricks and will be pleased to advise you. All this explains to some extent the moderate average burden on high incomes. (And then there are the untaxed fringe benefits – travel, hotels, entertainment – but these do not explain the low burden, for this income in kind has not been included in the height of the participants in our parade. The inequality is intensified as a result, however, precisely because the middle classes tend to spend a relatively large sum on holidays; the top groups can save on them.)

Things are certainly no better in other countries. In the United States in particular the loopholes for the top incomes are manifold and lucrative. Incomes of married persons can be divided into two and each part taxed separately, which can make an enormous difference in the rate. Many state and municipal bonds give tax-free interest. Research expenditure can be padded and is deductible. Trust funds are a rich source of tax avoidance: cultural, educational and charitable purposes are the conditions for freedom from tax, but it has happened that in particular the education of sons and daughters was served, and charity too can benefit a selected group. The Americans also have their depletion allowance, which enables oil millionaires to keep huge sums of money in their pockets. The parasitism of the rich many times exceeds the misuse that some unfortunate wretches make of unemployment benefit. In his study mentioned above, R. Goode comes to the shocking conclusion that the average burden of taxation borne by the richest

Americans is less than that on the well-to-do with somewhat lower incomes.* He attributes this to unjustifiable exclusions and deductions.

Complaints about this are general. *Newsweek* (of 24 February 1969) – anything but the voice of malcontent leftists – writes: 'in all too many cases the Federal tax regulations are nothing more than a happy hunting ground for individuals, industries and institutions with the expertise – or the money – to exploit them for private profit. It has been estimated that $50 billion a year in possible tax revenue slips out of the government's grasp through leaks in the present jerry-built Federal tax structure'. And in the same magazine (the number of 4 August 1969) Paul Samuelson, one of the best-known contemporary economists, points out there may be millionaires who, with a little ingenuity, pay no tax at all – everything goes in capital gains resulting from research, and the research expenditure may be enough to offset a nice big salary. If this picture is correct, the giants of for instance ten yards (the free professions) do get pruned by tax, but the super-giants of one mile or more do not. Samuelson champions above all the interests of ordinary people and the more modest giants (whom he calls 'middle classes'); in his opinion they are too heavily taxed. He advocates a minimum rate on gross income that cannot be avoided by sheltered income and deductions. He wants to combine this plugging of the loopholes with an increase in the levels of exemption and standard deductions at the lower end of the income scale. This alleviation at the base makes its effect felt further up the scale.

Such proposals are certainly sound and in the interests of equity. They will lead to higher effective rates for the top 1%, and especially for the top one *pro mille*. The reason why such a clean-up of the tax system goes so slowly, or not at all, lies in the piecemeal methods by means of which tax laws are enacted: the lawmakers pursue now this aim, and then the other. And so the loopholes stay open. The one time they have in mind the respectable interests served by the trust funds: education, the arts; and then they do not

---

* Goode produces a graph of the trend of nominal rates and effective rates (1960) which shows that at an income of a million dollars the nominal percentage of 95 is reduced by deductions and exclusions to about 30. The world of income tax is full of pretence and illusion.

consider the possibility that such institutions may serve very private interests of people making provision for their own families. The next time the lawmakers reflect that capital gains do after all have quite a different background from ordinary income, and they forget how the very rich can abuse these loopholes. In the United States the municipalities managed to arrange that the interest on their bonds would be tax-free – of course the granting of such a privilege is respectable in so far as it gives the municipal authorities cheaper access to the capital market, but the side-effect – tax avoidance for millionaires – was carelessly overlooked at the time. Of course the pressure groups are not backward, and plenty of lobbying goes on. What is required is a general revision of all these loopholes, in the interests of equity. That is no pushover. Doubtless special interests will be harmed occasionally, and a hard battle will have to be waged in the various parliaments.

It cannot be stated exactly how much this operation would yield. The estimate for the United States, cited above, would imply that more than 5% of national income would flow into the Treasury in the form of additional tax proceeds; the exemption limit could then be raised, so that the egalitarian knife would cut both ways. The figure quoted seems to me rather exaggerated – if we assume that this 5% is produced by the top 5% of income recipients, this would reduce their after-tax share from the present 17% to 12%, and that is very rough! – but even without large additional proceeds such a redistribution of the burden of taxation is urgent. The ethical gain cannot be measured in terms of money. However, it is to be doubted whether this would be a revolutionary intervention in the present system. I should think that it would be much more likely to amount to a certain streamlining, just as we saw before with the wage structure; the glaring inequities are smoothed out somewhat, the distribution of income becomes more rational, the after-tax Lorenz curve becomes flatter, but the general inequality is not fundamentally changed.

Nor can the latter be achieved by screwing up the marginal rates. The British rate is already very steep above £8,000, and a higher maximum than 90% is barely possible. One reason for this is that our sense of justice does not tolerate complete confiscation. Taxes serve primarily to cover State expenditure (or, according to more recent views, to check the overall expenditure of a country and avoid inflation) but not to cut down incomes, even if they are regarded as offensively high. It is equitable that the rich contribute towards the financing of State expenditure in accordance with their capacity – it is questionable whether tax may be used to decapitate the rich. And therefore a marginal rate rising to just above 90% is the most that egalitarians can get out of it. The marginal curve could be drawn tighter; instead of the kinks that it now displays it could come to look more like the American one. Thus one could increase the burden on incomes from £4,000 to £10,000 if one wanted to, but barely above the latter figure. This consequently does not have much to offer.

A further argument against pushing up the rate curve is that disincentives could possibly occur – a much-published scene, in which completely discouraged businessmen, non-working doctors, emigrating wealth-holders and time-killing workers play dramatic roles. Economists are inclined to reason as follows: high marginal rates shift the price ratio between work and leisure to the side of the latter, so that higher taxes will lead to shorter hours, earlier retirement, less effort. Evocative anecdotes may support such theoretical speculations. But all this can easily mislead us. Empirically, little has been seen of these disincentives so far. Studies have been made of lawyers and accountants in Britain, of people with incomes above $10,000 in the United States, of workers and managers in Scotland, by different investigators using different methods – the result was in all cases that the effect on taxes on work incentives was slight or could not be established.* (A funny byproduct of one of these studies was that 80% of the managers questioned – Scottish managers, of all people! – had a wrong idea about the marginal rate applicable to them – they estimated it too highly.)

The prediction at the beginning of this section: 'The ... private sector will grind to a halt' is not supported by much evidence. Capitalism is still alive and kicking, growth rates are higher than ever before in history. But despite all these results it may nevertheless be imagined that pronounced increases in the rates would lead in the long run to disincentives. The profit that creates the high

* See Brown and Dawson, p. 58.

incomes is after all a tender growth. I earlier suggested (Chapter V, 9) that the driving force behind capitalism is the two-way relation between profits and technical progress: profits lead to innovation, and innovation leads to profits. This sets certain limits to taxation.* It is better to avoid all too great risks to economic growth, and that makes drastic shifts in the rate curve all the less desirable.

And there is something else. Higher income taxes are partly ineffective because they are passed on to others. This does not apply to top incomes only. Many workers and salary-earners aim in the social process at a certain remuneration after tax, and they are partly successful in this endeavour too. Workers carefully note what they get in their wage packet, and the market supports this. Doctors and lawyers tend to increase their before-tax remuneration if taxes go up. In this respect after-tax distribution is less pliable than appears at first sight. Moreover, this passing-on leads to multiplicative processes that drive up prices. In highly exaggerated form this can be explained by means of the following extreme example. Suppose that a surgeon wants to pocket £100 net for a certain operation, and that his marginal rate is 90%; he must then charge the patient £1,000. Suppose that the patient is a rich manufacturer, who likewise goes bowed under a marginal rate of 90%; he must then earn £10,000 to pay the surgeon. Suppose that he manages to get this back from his firm, via his expense account. By then the original £100 has already multiplied by 100. If that goes on for a bit the result will be an immense increase in the price level, and in the end nobody knows any longer who ultimately pays.

This example is, of course, highly suggestive (for instance it makes no allowance for the deductibility of medical costs, and it uses improbable marginal rates), but it does illustrate an effect of taxes which is too often left out of consideration when we confine ourselves to the income tax tables. The process of passing-on is invisible. Workers do it to their firms, and they in turn to their customers. The one is handier at this game than the other, and the rich are perhaps the handiest of all. Sometimes the ball rolls on, sometimes it stops somewhere. Economists have occasionally assumed that it comes to a halt as soon as it encounters a surplus

* We can get out of this by nationalization. See section 9 below.

income somewhere, (see Chapter IV,6), but nobody knows whether this is true or not, because these rents are not measurable.

To find out exactly what is going on we would have to compare a world without taxes with a world with taxes – an impossible task. But one thing that is certain is that income distribution tends to oppose taxation, and this spongy character does not make it any the more attractive to screw up the progression further.

This is especially the case because at a higher level of the rate curve ever-increasing energy is invested in avoidance. The army of fiscal advisers grows. Not only the very rich but also the free professions seek the aid of experts who have to find the holes in the net. Evasion pure and simple is also increasing, and that hits at the heart of the tax system. Income tax is partially based on voluntary compliance – the taxpayer must cooperate. If he refuses to do so, the legal code is undermined on a sensitive point. All this means that a sharp increase in income tax rates which radically adapts income distribution to the theoretical norms of a highly egalitarian distribution is not practical.

Improvement of the tax structure in an egalitarian direction would therefore have to be sought elsewhere. We might envisage a reduction in indirect taxes. In many countries they form a relatively heavier burden on modest incomes. This regressive character has been established in particular for the United States,* where it overcompensates for the progression in income tax; the overall tax system is regressive. The situation in the United Kingdom is somewhat more favourable because purchase tax is concentrated on a narrow range of products; in some cases, such as cigarettes and beer, excise duties are added, so that a number of categories groan under the burden. And yet the whole tax system is barely more than proportional, and here too the indirect tax weighs down on the little man. From an egalitarian point of view it would be desirable to reduce these turnover taxes as much as possible.

But the trend is not in that direction, and that is understandable too. Governments everywhere are busy increasing the load on consumption. Here we encounter the difficulty that taxation must

* Especially by Gillespie (see p. 369 above). His figures confirm Goode's conclusions about the barely progressive nature of the effective rates of income tax.

keep private expenditure within bounds; this is necessary to suppress overspending, inflation and a deficit on the balance of payments. The last Labour Government, too, was not able to avoid this dire necessity. In Continental Europe the Value Added Tax has been introduced; a flat rate on all goods and services (with certain exceptions). That is an anti-egalitarian measure inspired by the desire for European unity. Were Britain to enter the Common Market, it would certainly be confronted with this trend towards turnover taxes. We can also put it this way: in an inflationary world (and an egalitarian world tends to be an inflationary one!) governments are after all obliged to levy taxes on a broad basis. Restricting the consumption of the rich does not keep the country's economy within the limits of productive capacity. And so, unfortunately, drastic reduction of indirect taxes is out of the question.

In our search for further egalitarian taxes we come across the wealth tax. This is not unusual on the Continent, the rates generally being modest; for Britain more vigorous proposals have been made by, among others, Brown and Dawson – in the framework of their radical revision of the whole system, in which surtax and the higher rate for unearned income disappear – and by O. Stutchbury.* The rate is envisaged as progressive: in the case of the former authors 1% on wealth in the range £50,000 to £100,000; 2% in the range £100,000 to £200,000 and 3% above that (the special rate for unearned income and surtax no longer apply). Stutchbury increases the rate to 4%, thus coming close to the real interest rate. At first sight this tax has a highly levelling effect. Its main problem is that it reduces the return on wealth – especially in combination with income tax – so that this return may easily become nil or even negative. The capitalists do not have to take that lying down. They have a weapon that no Chancellor of the Exchequer can ever take away from them: they can force down the market prices on the stock exchange. That amounts to a higher interest rate that has to be paid by the borrowers. These borrowers are the authorities and business. In both cases the burden of the wealth tax is partly passed on, either to the general taxpayers, who have to finance the interest on the National Debt, or to the consumers, who buy the products of industry. The avoidance cannot be complete; that is due *inter*

* *The Case for Capital Taxes* (Fabian Tract 388, 1968).

alia to the progressive rate, as a result of which the top wealth-holders will lose something. But a fair part of the wealth tax is paid by all and sundry. The capitalists have a position of power that allows of this passing-on; that is, after all, the mechanism of the capital market, as described in Chapter IV, 5.

The same applies to profits tax. In most countries this is a little under 50% (United Kingdom: 42·5%). A flat rate is more inclined to lead to passing-on than a differentiated one. As already stated above (p. 281), economists do not agree on how greatly profits tax is calculated into the price of the product; estimates vary from 40% to 100%. Here too the original distribution resists the impact of taxes, and the incidence is much more diffuse than the lawmakers had intended. It is a good tax for catching revenue, but a poor one for changing distribution. Come to that, it is perhaps as well that it is passed on; profits are an essential part of free enterprise society, and a draconic reduction of this vulnerable component of national income could have serious consequences for the investments in capital goods, for technical progress and for economic growth. In addition, higher rates would bring the tax authorities into conflict with the workers, who are trying to get a portion of this same income via profit sharing and capital sharing. The conclusion is that not much more can be wrung out of profits than the nearly 50% that the Inland Revenue already takes.

Finally, one of the most controversial forms of taxation: inheritance tax or death duties. Advocates of equal opportunity point out that the children of well-off parents have a lead in any case, partly through hereditary factors, and partly because their environment better prepares them for a social career. If they inherit wealth as well, opportunity becomes even less equal, and the handicap for the poor children still greater. In this reasoning the suppression of inheritance is a necessary measure for unloading the dice. This view is well summarized in the sarcastic caption to a cartoon showing Mr Barry Goldwater addressing two destitute paupers: 'If you showed any initiative at all you'd go out and inherit a couple of chain stores'.

Diametrically opposed to this is the view of those who regard care of the coming generation as a bounden duty and as the centre of a social ethic. In this view the family is the guarantee of continuity in time, of tradition and of social cohesion. Inheritance is a method for preventing society from disintegrating and being exposed to revolutionary disorder. In a somewhat watered-down form this ideology is shared by very many people; they feel that children are naturally entitled to take over their parents' savings at some time, and they feel that the tax man can interfere in this to a limited extent only. All too abrupt taxation is at variance with this sense of justice, and in practice that does in fact set limits to the extent to which the inheritance tax can be intensified. And then there are practical drawbacks to high rates: personal business firms can easily get into serious liquidity difficulties upon the death of the owner, and high rates encourage wealthy old people to throw their money around – this may yield an embarrassing sight. And, of course, the incentive to evade the tax becomes greater.

The rates in the United Kingdom are pretty steep as they are. On an inheritance of £20,000 the heir must pay 15%; on £50,000 this is 35%; on £100,000 the rate is 50% and on £1,000,000 it is 80%.* Against this, there are various ways of dodging the tax. The most legal one is the trust; it is said to lead to large-scale abuse. Settlements on a spouse also occur frequently. Gifts *inter vivos* are exempt only to a limited extent, but evasion is common practice. Consequently, the inheritance tax is often characterized as a tax on sudden death.

If we want to check inheritance there are other feasible ways besides stepping up the progression. In the first place one might envisage stopping up the loopholes, just as in the case of income tax. In the second place the rate can be differentiated in accordance with the wealth (or the income) that the heir already had; this progression does not occur at present, but would lead to rich people who receive legacies being more heavily taxed than poor ones. One method of achieving this is to regard legacies as income, and to apply the income tax rate (possibly moderated) to them. In the third place there is the proposal of E. Rignano,† under which self-saved wealth is taxed upon the death of the holder at a rate of $33\frac{1}{3}\%$, while wealth that the testator has himself inherited is subject to a tax of $66\frac{2}{3}\%$. In the third generation the rate would have to be

* In the United States a rate of 77% applies above $10 million.
† *The Social Significance of the Inheritance Tax*, 1924.

100% (but this confiscation could lead to strange things: huge parties, and the unrestrained spending of money). All in all, the inheritance tax can perhaps be improved, especially in countries where the rates are much lower than in Britain; but the tax authorities must nevertheless keep far enough away from confiscation if disturbing effects are not to occur and if the sense of justice of most people is not to be harmed.

Looking back on the above story of the taxes on high incomes and fortunes, we need not be defeatist. The agenda for improvements to the tax system is still a long one, and it includes various items operating towards greater equality. In the United Kingdom and the United States there are still many loopholes to plug up; in Britain in particular a rationalization of the rates of income tax can be aimed at; exemptions levels should be steadily and substantially raised; a wealth tax is probably a further step in the right direction; the inheritance tax can be levied more equitably. All this is anything but unimportant. But each of the proposals outlined above has its limitations. Passing-on partially restores the old situation. The large mass of families cannot be radically relieved of their burden because total consumption has after all to remain within the limits of total productive capacity. A sense of justice opposes too ruthless intervention, so that absolute decapitation of incomes is not feasible. It would consequently be wrong to expect a quick and rapid change in income structure from the reforms outlined. Fiscal influence operates gradually; it appeals to the patience and the good nature of the egalitarians. The latter must bear in mind that meanwhile the patience and the good nature of the taxpayers with high incomes are put severely to the test by the Inland Revenue.

9. Back to Fundamentals: Property

In the preceding sections measures were discussed that knead the structure of remuneration, change the distribution of the firm's income among the participants, stress vertical transfers and shift the burden of taxation. To a certain extent all these methods are superficial because they leave untouched the underlying distribution of the productive contributions. Economists and left-wing critics, this time brothers in arms, will remark that a more fundamental way of influencing distribution is to come to grips with property and the scarcity of the factors of production. A short survey of possible policy measures in this field follows.

When speaking about property we encounter in the first place land. We have seen above that agricultural and urban rent forms only an extremely small fraction of income but that it may be desirable, for reasons other than income distribution, for the government to own an increasing percentage of land. In so far as rent is then paid, it flows into the communal kitty and not into the pockets of the private landowner, who on average is richer than the average income recipient. In most countries this is in fact the development: roads, airfields and urban building land occupied by municipalities and towns are gradually covering a greater acreage. Supporters of equality would like to see this shift accelerated. But they must take care not to fall victim to an optical illusion: if the central government and local government buy this land with borrowed money (and that is the rule), the land rent that they receive passes in whole or in part through their hands to their creditors, and the net result for distribution may therefore be nil. Only if land prices rise (and if this rise was not allowed for in the price at which the government took the land over) does the community profit and income distribution become more uniform. Speculation in land and inflation are among the rational motives for an active policy of land acquisition. On the strength of the same motives private persons want to keep the land themselves, but the government possesses enough weapons to bring about a shift between private and public property in its own favour.

Something similar applies to the housing stock, but here it is uncertain in which direction the development is going. The community has the option: building by private persons or by public bodies. After the war Britain displayed a preference for the latter: at the beginning of the Fifties 80% of new dwellings were being built for the account of local housing authorities. But this percentage has steadily fallen; by the end of the Sixties it was about 50%, so that the public share in the housing stock is now constant. If the trend as evidenced by the falling percentage continues, privately owned housing will get the upper hand. Although it is possible that the small home-owner profits from this, egalitarians seem to prefer to see a reversal of this development. This is, of course, possible; the policy can set its sights at a higher priority for public house-building. But then a well-aimed effort is required; the authorities have to outbuild the eager private home-owners, whose number will swell progressively as national income increases.

More important than land purchases and house-building by the authorities is the distributive effect of the accumulation of capital in general. We have seen that a growing stock of capital tends to reduce the share of the capitalists in national income, and that this shift has led to greater equality in personal distribution. If we want to speed up this process we must further the growth of the stock of capital goods; this is, of course, also desirable for another reason: accelerating the growth of production. But this requires inegalitarian policy measures, for more is saved from large incomes than from small ones, and moreover big profits lead to large sums being invested; investments yield in part their own savings (see Chapter V, 4, on the Keynesian model). Egalitarians are confronted here with conflicting goals and so have to compromise.

This compromise can take the form of government policy giving priority to saving by low-income recipients, so that property is formed among those who as yet own nothing – which is the great majority of people. Fiscal relief can help in this to some extent, for instance by exempting savings from income tax up to a certain level. Such a system is in operation in Finland and the German Federal Republic. The addition *to a certain level* is essential, since otherwise the government is going to favour the rich too much.*
Another method of encouraging the small saver is to give bonuses

---

*That is the prohibitive disadvantage of the progressive consumption tax proposed by N. Kaldor (*An Expenditure Tax*, 1955). He proceeds from the sensible idea that it is better to tax someone on what he consumes than on what he produces. But abolition of income tax and its replacement by an expenditure tax would make no difference for many people who do not save anyway; it would only make a difference for higher incomes. So as to impose the same burden on the top incomes the progression of the expenditure tax must be very steep, much steeper than that of the present income tax. For the reasons explained in the preceding section, there are drawbacks to that. The expenditure tax fits effortlessly into the ideas of an anti-egalitarian, but Kaldor is not one of them.

on the interest. This is done in the Netherlands, among other countries. They are slow-working methods, they are rather fiddly because administrative conditions are often laid down for them (the money must be paid into a special account, if you draw it out you lose your bonus unless you buy a house, get married, etc.; evidence has to be presented of that special use) and they cost the Exchequer rather a lot of money. Cynics shrug their shoulders at this kind of messing about, and it may be imagined that a government which is perpetually short of money prefers not to embark on such plans.

But a somewhat more favourable light is cast on the bonus system if we reason it as follows: over the next twenty years national income per head will probably double. In that case the workers too have scope to save. But society today encourages consumption: window displays, advertising, emulation of the higher income brackets. It is the government's task to offer counter-incentives, and one such is the savings bonus. It need work to only a small extent and then the consequences over longer periods are already surprising. A pound saved today doubles at an interest rate of 10%, including the bonus, in seven years. Compound interest provides an automatic capital growth, and once the workers have got the taste for this, we shall be entering the realm of People's Capitalism within the foreseeable future.

True, so far little has come of all this, but the financial elbow-room of the workers has simply not been there, despite all the talk about affluence. Economic growth may change this, and then there is no reason why the workers could not become small capitalists. The Small Man's Capitalism is no Utopia, provided that consumption habits do not fascinate us to such an extent that we spend our last penny on perishable things. This prospect of a mass of small property-owners (contented citizens, the corner-stones of a stable society), busily saving, buying shares and above all houses, exerts a great attraction on some observers, while it fills the many left-wing critics of society with sheer disgust. Like everything, it is a matter of political preference.

An alternative and more spectacular method of fostering the accumulation of capital and at the same time reducing inequality is for the government itself to acquire property. The only way of doing that is to save; nationalization is another way only in appearance, unless the government takes over firms without compensating the owner, but that looks too much like theft. Saving by the government means that taxes are levied which are then partly invested. In other words, the total proceeds of taxation must exceed the current government consumption. To put it yet another way, the government must invest more in capital goods (roads, bridges, ports, hospitals, schools, railways, mines, oil companies, factories, airlines – everything that the British Government already owns plus what it would like to own) than it borrows, and the redemption of the National Debt must at least keep pace with the wear of the capital goods.

In this way the wealth of nations enters gradually into government hands. In so far as it earns interest, the latter goes not to private persons but to the community. True, only a small part of government wealth yields financial revenue; the lion's share is invested in production processes that are not paid for over the counter. But that could change if the government acquires more capital. The tax surpluses could be used for participation in private business. This can be done by direct financing, by buying shares or by setting up semi-public enterprises (that is how British Petroleum came about, and the man behind it was no socialist, but Winston Churchill). This investment of savings surpluses not only brings about a shift in income distribution; the government's say also grows and the left wing will welcome both aspects. We can help the government acquire part of the profit without needing to be afraid that we are removing the incentive for technical progress. For State concerns can very well operate in a technically advanced way.* Supporters of planning will moreover consider it a decisive advantage that technology is being used more for human goals – whatever they are supposed to be – and less for a maximum return. All this offers attractive prospects for egalitarians.

Indeed, the balance between the private and the public sector can be shifted in this way. But we must realize that the process of

---

* The typical example is the Italian E.N.I. (Ente Nazionale Idrocarburi), which has achieved the development and distribution of natural gas in Northern Italy at a great rate – probably more quickly than private companies would have done.

the accumulation of capital by the government is bound to be a slow one. For it is limited by taxation, and more particularly by the surplus of tax proceeds over current expenditure. The latter is inclined to increase very quickly. Proponents of greater equality are the first to think up new and expensive plans; before this book has come to an end I shall have made new proposals that involve additional expenditure. As growth continues more money is needed for environmental conservation like pollution control – an expensive business. And then the productivity in government administration and, come to that, in the service sector in general increases more slowly than in rapid-growing industry, so that government services become more expensive. On top of all that there is the desire to spend a greater part of national income on the developing countries.

Tax capacity can barely keep up with this growth in the budget, especially if, in the footsteps of section 7 above, we want to reduce the burden of taxation on the low incomes and raise the exemption levels. Placing a heavier burden on higher incomes likewise encounters numerous drawbacks (see section 8). Here we come up against the annoying problem to which economics owes its existence: we can't do everything at once. We can't lower the taxes on low incomes *and* raise current expenditure *and* allow the government to save.

Moreover, it must be borne in mind that it is not enough for the government to become richer. For the sake of equality it must accumulate more quickly than the private sector. A kind of race is going on. Private persons, and firms in particular, save out of self-earned salaries and profits; the government has to make use of taxes for this, and though these taxes flow in a larger volume than profits, they are also spent more easily. The government can hamper its opponent by wealth tax and death duties, and at first sight this puts it at an advantage. But this first sight is misleading. The race will probably be won by private accumulation.

The government can place itself in a more advantageous position by nationalizing firms and financing the take-over with borrowed money. Then the private owner is transformed into a creditor. The government gets profit and pays interest. That can be a favourable swap for it, especially if it fixes a low rate of interest for him, or pays him in dubious pieces of paper (blocked claims, inferior bonds with deferred interest). The financial advantage must not be overestimated, nor the effect on income distribution, for the former owners may invest their money in other things, perhaps abroad, and make profit again. Yet nationalization combined with government accumulation may, in the long run, lead to a slow but fundamental change in the structure of capitalism. If we, and our governments, really want to, we can work steadily in this (call it socialist) direction. From the purely economic (or call it bookkeeping) viewpoint the matter is simple. Politically the shift is less easy.

As I have stated, it is not my impression that in the Western world the governments are engaged in winning this race. For the United States and for the Netherlands some of the relevant facts are known. Developments in the U.S.A. are analysed by R. W. Goldsmith.* In his careful and highly documented study he reaches the conclusion that during the period 1945–58 no sharp change occurred in the share of government in civilian wealth. If military assets are included, the government's share shows a decline. As for the Netherlands, I suspect that the balance between public and private capital is steadily shifting in favour of the latter. True, the wealth of the central government has steadily grown. After the war it was negative, i.e. the public debt exceeded public assets. In 1965 a positive net value was achieved for the first time. At present the latter is rising by about 2,000 million guilders a year (provincial and local authorities borrow about as much as they invest). That is a tidy sum of money, but private firms invest more than 15,000 million guilders a year, and moreover dwellings to the value of nearly 6,000 million guilders a year (mainly private ones) are being built. Private accumulation is outdoing public accumulation; this is probably in accordance with the political preferences of most citizens (although at the same time there is a political preference

* *The National Wealth of the United States in the Post-war Period*, 1962. The book gives figures for the Government's share in some countries: U.S.A. 13%, Belgium 14%, the Netherlands 18%, Western Germany 10% (government-owned enterprises are excluded), France no less than 42%, Canada 15%, Australia 30%, Japan 22%. There is a good deal of variation, which points to the possibility of an option. The percentage is not a natural constant.

for more equality – people sometimes have contradictory wishes).

As far as Britain is concerned information is hard to come by. However, there are indications that the public sector accumulates at a slower rate than the private. In his *The Wealth of the Nation* (Cambridge, 1967) J. Revell gives figures for the composition of British capital over the period 1957–61. During these years the total wealth ('net worth') of Great Britain increased from £63·3 billion to £83·9 billion. The net worth (assets minus liabilities) of the public sector – central government, local authorities and public corporations – was negative. Though the various public authorities own rather more than a quarter of the nation's capital goods and rather more than one tenth of the nation's financial assets, the public debt, during those five years, exceeded these assets. The net worth was £ −7·8 billion in 1957; it increased to £ −5·8 billion in 1961. So the government accumulated only £2 billion of the total increase in Britain's wealth of £20 billion. If these figures are representative of what happens over longer periods then the public sector is clearly losing the race.

Now if they want to, statesmen can head in this direction or the other without quantitative information. But if they want vigorously to increase the wealth of the State, they can certainly expect political difficulties. An enormous effort is required to have the government win the race, and private accumulation has to be hampered. That encounters opposition. The Conservatives will become annoyed, and even mild middle-of-the-roaders will sharply criticize the heavy burden of taxation on almost all incomes. The argument that the State is exploiting its citizens will be heard. Left-wing critics will be dissatisfied at the hardships for the masses of workers – after all, the latter too will have to pay taxes to help make a capitalist out of the State, and if the process goes too slowly these critics will complain that capitalism cannot be changed because the capitalists are too strong. In the midst of the general disappointment a government will have difficulty in remaining in power. The shift from private to collective ownership may be a piece of cake from the book-keeping point of view, but politically even a left-wing government, backed by a somewhat leftist majority, can choke on it.

10. *Back to Fundamentals*: *Work and Life*

Although most people with an intense interest in politics and with
left-wing inclinations regard ownership of the means of production
and all that this involves as the strategic problem, from an egalitarian point of view another stress is also possible. Statistically, the
greater part of income inequality is attributable to the inequality
of incomes from work, and psychologically the comparison of
these remunerations summons up at least as much frustration. And
therefore an important question is what fundamental changes can
be achieved in the wage and salary structure. That is to say, not by
adjusting pay relations without an alteration in the underlying
factors, but by a different arrangement of productive contributions. Human relations interact with income relations. In the un-
sentimental language of the economist, the question is how supply
and demand on the labour market can be improved by a deliberate
policy.

Full employment continues to be a preliminary, somewhat
trivial but lastingly urgent objective. Anyone looking for work
must be able to find a decent job. Above all, unemployment
through deflation must be prevented, if possible with marginal
adjustments of government expenditure, tax rates and monetary
policy; if necessary with the aid of temporary massive tax reductions. Thanks to Keynesian insight, a serious recession can be
avoided; it is a matter of applying policy instruments purposefully
and effectively. This entails countless complications, too many to
discuss here.* Despite the benefit paid to those hit by it, unemployment creates a direct and unacceptable form of inequality. It is
sometimes argued that full employment is also needed to make
labour scarce and to improve its bargaining position *vis-à-vis* the
employers, but it should be borne in mind that keeping up the level
of sales is to the advantage not only of the workers but also of the
owners of the means of production, and that profits in particular
flourish when the market is easy. We have seen above that, against
expectations, the total share of labour is not affected by deflation,

* See my *Modern Economics*, 1965.

and consequently it cannot be maintained that the relative position of labour as a whole is spectacularly supported by a broad flow of purchasing power. However, the position of the weak groups is strengthened; older and less productive workers, who are the first to be laid off when the market is weak, have of course the most to gain from a Keynesian policy.

The avoidance of unemployment through deflation is not enough. The government must likewise counter unemployment through a shortage of capital. In the developed countries this is mainly a matter of regional policy. Every Western country has its grey or black spots on the map where there is too much labour and too little economic activity, and it is generally regarded as a task of the government to encourage these underdeveloped areas, which amounts to pouring capital into them. A better infrastructure by direct government investments or bonuses for industrial concerns that settle there are the usual methods. This does not always help too much, especially if the depressed areas have a long history of neglect and decline behind them, but the endeavour is praiseworthy.

The third form of unemployment – expulsion by mechanization and automation – can also be remedied. Here the government has the task of retraining the superfluous workers and making them mobile. Every worker who loses his job through technical progress must find in the government an ally who advises him on the direction in which he must seek new employment and who helps him, forthwith and unreservedly, to acquire the requisite capacities. This is the Active Manpower Policy, spoken of warmly in Sweden in particular. The supply of labour is actively adjusted to the demand, so that bottlenecks in growth are eliminated, wage inflation is countered, pockets of unemployment vanish and individuals are given an opportunity to develop to their fullest extent. If this policy of permanent deployment is to be a success, the government agencies must anticipate new developments in job structure. The coming technology and the corresponding requirement of labour must be predicted, and education must be based on this forecast. The schools must be in the van of technical development and serve the society of ten years hence.

This brings us on to stony ground. There is a tendency to take the easy way out and suggest that education can eliminate practically all the fundamental faults of our present society. If we have no idea of how to solve a problem, we refer it to schools, the teachers and the parents, and there is the answer as far as we are concerned. The failures of democracy, violence, juvenile delinquency, the lack of tolerance, the unsatisfactory place of art in the community, the shortage of creative activities, egotism, problems of war and peace – education has got to clean the mess up, and now we're going to do the same thing with income distribution. Unfortunately, the educators do not always know how to set about it; they are not *always* more intelligent, willing and forward-looking than other pillars of society. And they also have to contend with a number of internal problems: the schools have to handle a torrent of pupils, and they hear rumours about brand-new teaching techniques (programmed instruction, school television, learning by discussion); the universities too are labouring under the explosive increase in numbers, and they are confronted with new, not very efficient forms of administrative democracy, with rebellion and with the Great Refusal (Marcuse); and the parents are by definition Mr and Mrs Yesterday, who note with growing alarm the ideas and behaviour of their offspring. Education is reminiscent of an overburdened donkey which we, inspired by the desire for a better distribution, are about to saddle with a number of additional tasks. There are at least three.

First there is the familiar question of social selection. According as we look at higher levels of education, we encounter more children from the upper class; in Britain the percentage has already risen to above sixty at university level,* while the group from which these young people are recruited forms at most 5% of the population. There is little improvement in this over-representation. Almost everyone considers it wrong: talent remains dormant, social barriers continue to exist, opportunity is still unequal and distribution is, as always, more skew than it need be. The untapped reservoirs of talent in particular have been described, analysed and

* This figure is for Britain (1960) and is taken from an Organization for Economic Co-operation and Development study, *Social Disparities in Educational Participation*, 1970. For the United States the percentage was over fifty.

condemned in various reports.* The continued existence of these educational disparities is not just a matter of money; if that were so the government could remedy the situation by a generous allocation of scholarships. But the causes are more deeply seated. Workers' children go too infrequently to university because they go too infrequently to secondary school, and because they display too little ambition at the latter. The basis for the under-representation of workers' children at secondary school is laid at primary school; here the lower social strata are already at a disadvantage. And that is because these children have already lost ground even before they started attending school. Recent investigations attach decisive importance to what happens in the period from birth to four years. Social inequality is born in the pre-school age; it is the family, and in particular the mother, that gives the children a handicap that hampers their later life.

It seems above all to be a matter of command of language. Children from the lower classes learn fewer words, cannot express themselves as well, and this causes the development of their intelligence to lag behind. Command of language determines the capacity for abstract thought. Children who lag behind in this already have a more difficult time of it as soon as they go to school; they learn more slowly and in this way the process of selection is initiated of which the structure of the university population is only an ultimate reflection. Tinkering with the system does not help; a little more money for scholarships and the like is ineffective.

It is a discouraging thought that we have to go back to the pre-school age. The class system uses the parents as advance secret agents. The government can hardly attach to every mother a teacher and a social worker who help from birth to bring up the child. You can just see this couple entering the front door with the message: 'Madam, scientific research has shown that, thanks to your efforts, your toddler is bound to lag behind irreparably, especially in command of language; this leads to an undesirable social stratification and to unacceptable income inequality. That is why we have come to assist you with the child's upbringing. Kindly step aside, so that my colleague and I can undertake the elimination of class distinctions.'

* In Britain the Robbins *Report on Higher Education* in particular (1963).

One alternative is perhaps a lowering of the school age and an expansion of the number of crèches and similar institutions. The child is socialized at an earlier age. The government could make wider facilities available for this. It is not a wild idea; there are mothers who themselves organize these collective forms of upbringing of the toddlers by hiring a suitable room and taking turns to supervise. Up to now such initiatives have come mainly from middle-class families, the prevailing desire being to give the mothers more freedom. This goal is not at variance with a more effective upbringing of the children. The government could give more support, propagate the idea and could make available not only rooms and money, but also specialized assistants. An example of an incidental, massive campaign is Operation Headstart in the United States, in which more than half a million pre-school children, chiefly from underprivileged families, participated in the summer of 1965. There are countless beginnings of such things to be seen in modern society; they could be systematized. In this way the cumulative forces of environment are restrained.*

In the second place the schools in poorer neighbourhoods should be better than those in middle-class areas (come to that, the whole segregation in urban residential districts has to be done away with – I shall be coming back to this). Only on this condition can the comprehensive school really flourish. It has been found that children of lower intelligence are not really more stupid; they just need more time to learn the same things. In fact they now have less time allotted to them. Teachers must therefore concern themselves more patiently and more intensively with these pupils. The school must compensate for the handicaps of environment. The classes in the poorer districts must be smaller, the teachers better qualified. Here too command of language is a strategic factor; in the first school years possible arrears must be made up as well as possible. This applies very strongly to countries like Britain, where a person's accent is enough to bring him or her social downgrading. The schools, or specialized teachers in them, ought to be able to make children with a 'common' accent bilingual; young people

* Another method is widening and encouraging adoption. It is simply ridiculous that many children remain in families where they are barely welcome, while other parents would be delighted to rear them with love.

ought to be given the freedom to speak their own Cockney but, if desired, to master an Oxford accent too. The reader who raises his eyebrows at this line proves how deeply social stratification is still rooted in Britain, and how gigantic the task is that education has to perform. (You can also reason the other way round: we must try to reach a point where someone with a Cockney accent that you can cut with a knife can become a professor of Greek, a BBC newsreader or a High Court Judge. The question is, which way is the more difficult?)

In the third place the educational discrimination against young workers must be reduced. They enter the factories while their contemporaries are still attending school. This strengthens the class boundaries and young people find their possibilities of development blocked off. Young folk who continue their studies are subsidized by the State, while those who are already working have to pay tax. While the élite are being trained, the rest have the stamp of inferiority imposed on them. The government should counter this, and that is no simple task. But, according as society becomes richer and working hours shorten, there is room for continued education for the benefit of young factory workers; for instance, a few days a week could be freed for this, wage continuing to be paid. Such education may not be solely or even mainly of a technical nature, but must aim at general cultural skills, at active participation in the social process. Its purpose is to increase social mobility and, once again, to counter the natural distortive effect of the process of selection.

A consistent application of this principle is not confined to young workers. For older people, too, there must be a constant possibility of acquiring new technical, social and cultural proficiencies. That brings us to the idea of 'permanent education', a very fashionable term in France in particular. This is not a matter of the occasional refresher course, or of compensating for job obsolescence, but an unceasing process of intensive reorientation. Adults who did not have the opportunity before must be allowed to go back to school if they so desire. The open university is only a beginning; we need open secondary schools, without segregation, without class privileges.

It would not be difficult to write pages of glowing prose on this subject in which, at least on paper, the whole social stratification is abolished, with radical consequences for income distribution, human relations and the face of society in general. I could point out that permanent education implies a cultural revolution manifesting itself in every field of life. In support of such a rather exalted tale I could refer to Mao's China and Castro's Cuba, to new hopes of salvation and a new faith in the future, and I could pose the rhetorical question why these distant peoples are capable of a cultural leap forward and the nations of the West are not.

The trouble with such prose is that it does not have the ring of truth to it, and that the Communist examples suffer from intolerance, massive coercion and totalitarianism. Our pluralistic society tends to move in different directions at the same time. We read more and more books, we make more and more music, young people are freer and travel more than the parents; idealism is still alive and well and living among us. But at the same time we can point to many signs – passivity, encouraged by television and by spectator sport, boredom, escapism – at variance with a positive cultural development. Idealism assumes bizarre forms among us, and criticism of society is often based on dogmatic misunderstandings about capitalism and on a porridgy concoction of domestic and international problems. The protest by young people is only partially effective in the right direction; at the same time it invokes expensive friction, strengthens reaction and hampers evolution.

But such scepticism may not shake our confidence in education. A society with decreasing working hours should progressively make more room for a continuous educational process that can penetrate deeply into the social fabric. Learning, working and playing can merge, and moreover learning must not be regarded as an activity that is tied to a well-defined age, well-defined classrooms and well-defined chapters from textbooks. The government can make a major contribution to a change in the spirit of education by systematically drawing attention to these desiderata, by making the means available and by teaching the teachers. The allocation of national resources must gradually shift in this direction.

The principal intention of an educational system that is expanded and transformed along the above lines is that the individual freedoms of choice, especially at the foot of the social ladder, are increased. In economic terms this can lead to the supply of labour for the lower jobs declining, so that incomes in this category rise relatively. But this result is anything but certain. Roy's theory (p. 250) shows that a very skew income distribution may be the result of the multiplication of productive capacities; if we educate everyone to the limit of his capacities it may very well happen that this multiplicative effect stays with us in an intensified form, and that we walk straight into the arms of a meritocratic society. The untalented, the incorrigibly stupid, lag behind. We may hope that the jobs within their capabilities become scarcer than their numbers. This is not out of the question. Only it cannot be predicted with certainty, because we cannot foretell the job structure in the world of tomorrow.

Furthermore, the danger threatens that permanent education will lead to permanent stress on performance and achievement, to a concentrated pursuit of success and career, and so perhaps to permanent nervousness.* Those who speak complacently and naïvely about the joys of education should bear in mind that the schools are in fact advocated as the escape route from the working classes. Schoolteachers are the guides who show the social climbers the way up and regrettably leave behind those who cannot make it. Is it then surprising that fathers who are themselves workers gaze with lacklustre eyes upon this whole system, which condemns workers as a kind of social sediment?

Consequently, there is no point to an expansion of the educational system unless it nurtures at the same time a number of specific values: solidarity, responsibility, a sense of the relativity of social relations. Manual labour must acquire a new status, a new place in social values. That is a good thing in itself, and it will not fail to have its influence on income distribution.

Other values, from which a competitive society suffers, should

---

* And to permanent promotion in accordance with the principle: Every Employee Tends to Rise to His Level of Incompetence (R. Hull: *The Peter Principle, Why Things Always Go Wrong*, 1969). Although the book is meant as a joke, it has a serious undertone. Many people climb as long as they do their work well, and in this way arrive at places where they can no longer handle their problems. They get overworked, they lose their grip, and they make a mess of things. Moral: beware of too much promotion.

be discouraged: education must be anti-authoritarian, anti-élitist, anti-meritocratic. In this way the foundations may be laid for a new democracy and a more austere approach to the inevitable hierarchy. At the same time young people must be trained to bear responsibility, which may make it possible for them to participate actively in the running of the firms where they work – an effective means of changing income distribution.

The reader who is of the opinion that the influencing of personal incomes is now being moved all too far into an imaginary future is right. For him a further remark follows on a more sober aspect of permanent education. It is beyond dispute that in the coming decades working hours will be further shortened and that we are heading for a four-day working week. It is also predictable that the division of labour will be refined, in the sense that the number of specified jobs will grow; some will demand long training, others a short period. It will therefore become attractive for many people to work in different kinds of jobs in succession or perhaps simultaneously. It is the task of the government to offer the necessary skills to all who ask for them when they want them. Once education is no longer a prerogative of youth, people are enabled to get a second and a third chance if their start has been disappointing. Moreover, it enables them to adapt their income to their preferences; leisure time and money can be exchanged for one another. Men and women who want to can have two jobs side by side. In a world in which moonlighting is no longer a curiosity but a normal weave in the social pattern, income distribution at once comes a good deal closer to the optimum. That this will happen in the near future is pretty certain; much more certain than the realization of all those spiritual requirements I enumerated before.

A final fundamental factor is the city as a way of life. The population of the future will live almost entirely in metropolises, and the nature of these places of residence will be largely influenced by public policy. Here there are strategic possibilities for a collective choice. Laissez faire will lead to situations that stress social stratification and perpetuate income inequality. Neighbourhoods for poor people will continue to exist, and so will middle-class districts and areas for the wealthy. Transport and changing technology will, it is true, effect quick shifts in where people live, so that some

neighbourhoods decline, and others advance – but this technological dynamism easily gives rise to new slums and new ghettoes.
Their inhabitants, and particularly the young people who live
there, have a more than normal chance of belonging to the lowest
20% of income recipients. If we do not intervene consciously, most
vigorously and in a well-planned manner in urban development,
houses will collapse and car parks proliferate. The mechanisms
that keep skew distribution alive – described in Chapter VI – will
continue to exist and perhaps intensify. The environment, the
street, the vacant lot will add an extra handicap to the situation of
the low-income groups.

But the choice may also be another one: the government can
upset the social segregation. In the Fifties the Cutteslowe Walls in
Oxford were demolished. Their former purpose was to protect the
middle classes against the social infection of the adjoining working-
class neighbourhood. Pulling down walls is a symbol, but as an
actual decision it is not enough. The aim must be new, radiant
cities. The metropolis can be restored to its function as the focal
point of a civilization in which all share. This requires social investments, the keys being schools, open museums, creative workshops,
sports fields, community centres. Service facilities and perhaps
industrial production firms have to be locally integrated with the
residential function and not banished, as in the nineteenth century,
to dreadful parts of town where the proletariat was also sent to
follow them. The traditional dividing lines on which Cairness
based his non-competing groups can be deliberately expunged in
the new metropolises. A special responsibility rests on the architects and city planners, but when all is said and done political
decisions are vital. The old saying 'city air liberates' could be given
new substance.

I have used the picture of the city not to hazard a visionary
depiction of the New Jerusalem but to show that income distribution is rooted in the way in which we organize the community.
If you read an economics textbook it is as if marginal productivities,
collective wage negotiations, the degree of monopoly, profit
sharing, social security and the burden of taxation form the
apparatus with which the problem can be fully understood. And
indeed these categories are important, but the ultimate determi-

nants lie much deeper. The city is comparable to Kapteyn's device: its construction influences the grains of sand in their fall, which symbolizes the course of human lives. If we want to influence this process, we must be aware of the fact that numerous decisions by individuals and collective bodies, firms and authorities help to determine the development of the community. Budgetary policy but also education and town planning are of strategic importance to our subject. A policy directed towards better distribution requires not only the constant rethinking of the very incomplete theory as outlined in this book, but above all social imagination and the will to push through conscious priorities. In a democratic society that can succeed only if as many people as possible are aware of the complex relations. This book has been written as a contribution to that awareness. It is, as I see it, part of the permanent debate on income distribution.

Postscript to the Pelican Edition

Now that a sufficient number of people (among them, I hope, many housewives) have bought this book to justify a Pelican edition, the author is confronted with the awkward question of which changes ought to be made to the text. It was written in 1970, and many things have happened since then. Great Britain acquired a new Government, with a slightly different jargon, and there was a minor shift in policy, but it seems improbable that the impact of the Conservatives on the distribution of incomes has been substantial. There were, of course, the strikes of 1973, but they did not bring about the income revolution. The wage structure remained as messy as it has been depicted on page 318 of this book. In the United States an incomes policy, or rather an incomes freeze, was imposed on the startled public in 1971; the upshot was to save the floating dollar from sinking, and as such the outcome was doubtful. Price increases slowed down under the freeze (Phase I); they remained modest under a somewhat more flexible system called Phase II, but the rate of inflation became disquieting in Phase III, the period of 'voluntary moderation'. The success of the whole operation, if any, was of a temporary nature; in the first half of 1973, when prices rose at an annual rate of 9%, the Administration decided to reinstitute the price freeze. There is, however, no reason to assume that income relationships were deeply affected by the whole operation. Of course, a number of speculators profited greatly from the floating dollar and the enormous increase in gold prices. These gainers are difficult to locate. Some of them are just plain ordinary multinational corporations who handle their money matters with somewhat more than common intelligence and foresight. The speculative profits on their holdings of international currency may have neutralized part of the profit squeeze.

This latter phenomenon was an intriguing and rather hotly debated reality, particularly in Europe. At the end of the sixties

413

the British saw a further decline in the rate of profit per unit of invested capital.* This gave rise to pessimistic speculations. It might signal the beginning of a long and deep depression; it might be the final result of the process of wage inflation; it might signify the structural decline of capitalism. But since then the level of profits has proved its ability to make a comeback – as it always did in the past. There is no reason to believe that the macro-economic distribution of income has changed so much over the last three years that I have to rewrite this book. This is, from an author's viewpoint, a reassuring idea.

However, in the meantime there has been a substantial output of new literature on our subject. Incorporation of the new ideas in the old text might break up chapters, paragraphs and page numbers – a possibility that did not appeal to the publisher. So we decided to limit the alterations in the main text to correction of errors and minor revisions,† and to review a few recent developments of the literature in this postscript. The books and articles I have in mind are by Bronfenbrenner (on general distribution theory), Kregel (on macro-economics), Tinbergen (on human happiness), and Jackson (on poverty). It is, of course, a rather arbitrary selection, but it serves a purpose: to underline a conclusion drawn in every chapter of this book, namely that the analysis of income distribution is not an unruffled pool. Turbulence seems a more appropriate description.

In the same year in which my book came out, Martin Bronfenbrenner published his *Income Distribution Theory* (1971). There is reason to compare the two volumes, because they cover about the same field and are about the same size. The main difference is that

---

* Cf. Aubrey Jones, *The New Inflation* (Penguin Books, 1973). The existence of such a continuous and dramatic decline is denied by M. Panic and R. E. Close ('Profitability of British Manufacturing Industry', *Lloyds Bank Review*, 1973); they believe that most of the observed deterioration in the rate of profit took place in the fifties.

† I am indebted to Professor F. J. de Jong of Groningen University and Professor R. A. Musgrave of Harvard who drew my attention to several errors. I hope I have succeeded in correcting these. Frits de Jong and I agreed to disagree on the interpretation of Kaldor's theory. I might have formulated my criticism of Kaldor in a more friendly way, and I would if I had to write the text again.

Bronfenbrenner writes for professional economists and I profess to write for a wide, wide circle; his book is much more sophisticated than mine. Though Bronfenbrenner reviews modern and fashionable developments, he says (p. xi): 'This is an old fashioned income distribution book'* – in the sense that the author adheres to the neo-classical school: the Good Old Theory, as he calls it, or GOT for short. This means that he explains income relationships by the scarcity of productive contributions, marginal productivity, substitution between labour and capital; he makes extensive use of a 'production function' (as described in Chapter IV of the preceding pages). This is not to say that Bronfenbrenner sweeps all criticisms of the Good Old Theory under the carpet – on the contrary, he deals with it at some length, and improves the GOT in the process (taking account of various forms of monopolistic competition – in this he goes much farther than my book does). But he is impatient with the so-called 'Cambridge Criticism' – he deals with this heavy attack on the GOT in an offhand manner and needs exactly eight lines to rebut it (p. 397). (I will need about eight pages of this postscript to inform the reader that he is, according to me, entitled to his own opinion.) Bronfenbrenner is prepared to defend the core and the tradition of the GOT, and he firmly rejects its rivals, whether they are of neo-Keynesian, neo-Marxist, institutional or sociological origin. These alternative theories suffer (p. 439) 'from dependence on highly specialized assumptions, tautological characteristics, confusions of cause and effect, shaky microfoundations, and/or general formlessness'. I am afraid that here our positions differ slightly. Though I am a cautious partisan of the GOT† and, like

---

* Compare Pen, p. 22: 'This book is characterized by a lack of originality'.

† More cautious than some reviewers of my book have suggested. Professor E. J. Nell for instance (*Journal of Economic Literature*, June 1972, p. 442) underrates, I think, the mental reservations I make in this book. One of these reservations – marginal productivity does not explain profits – is crucial. On the other hand Nell believes that only three or four per cent of the labour force fall under marginal productivity theory – this is not what I think. Nell excludes non-direct labour, probably on the strength of the argument that its marginal productive contribution is difficult or impossible to ascertain, but is this true for salesmen, tax consultants, etc.? I don't think so. The demand for these kinds of 'non-direct' labour certainly depends on what employers think that their marginal revenue product might be.

Bronfenbrenner, I reject the views of Kalecki, Kaldor and Weintraub, I find myself more in sympathy with sociology than Bronfenbrenner does, and I notice in my own book a tendency, probably deplorable in Bronfenbrenner's eyes, towards eclecticism. He discusses various endeavours to fit pieces of several theories together (by Joan Robinson, Melvin Reder, Sydney Weintraub and others) and he does not like them one bit. My own position would be that there is simply no single coherent theory of income distribution available, and so to explain the facts of life we have to combine elements of various theoretical approaches.

Bronfenbrenner has the advantage that his book is centred around one consistent system of micro- and macro-economics: the GOT. My own macro-economics, being pieced together from various elements, is sometimes found confusing; one reviewer says that it reminded him of 'the conversation of a witty sociologist at a sherry party'.* This pejorative description certainly does not apply to Bronfenbrenner; he writes rather wittily, I think, but it's not the way sociologists actually express themselves, either at sherry parties or elsewhere. His is strong neo-classical economics, with a lot of highly informative comment on rival approaches. Perhaps I may recommend Bronfenbrenner's book to those who want to go beyond the limits of my simple treatise. But I modestly claim that I have, in this book, somewhat more to offer when it comes to ethical norms and to incomes policies. Bronfenbrenner adds his chapter on guidelines, etc. as 'something of an after-thought' (his own words, p. xi). He hardly deals with other policy measures, like profit sharing, education, nationalization; and I do.

A second book, also published in 1971, is J. A. Kregel's *Rate of Profit, Distribution and Growth: Two Views*. The theme here is that the distribution of income influences the rate of growth of an economy, whilst the rate of growth influences distribution. This two-way relationship (which is dealt with in my book in several places, like p. 227 ff, but in a rather loose way) lends itself beautifully to rigorous model-building, and that is what Kregel does. Like Bronfenbrenner, he confronts neo-classical and neo-Keynesian thought, but unlike Bronfenbrenner he leans in the

* D. G. Champernowne in a review article, *Economic Journal*, March 1972, p. 243.

Keynesian direction. His book is very formal. Nobody would associate it with witty talk at whatever kind of party, and even less with a sociologist's conversation. As a matter of fact, Kregel does not seem to write about human beings and their incomes; his book is all about the blind mechanisms that determine aggregate income levels. It is a very cool report on one of the fiercest battles ever fought in theoretical economics, the Battle Between the Two Cambridges, where the Cambridge, England, brigade is headed by Mrs Joan Robinson (it includes Kaldor, Pasinetti, Bhaduri; the high priest of the school is Piero Sraffa) and the Cambridge, Mass., band by R. M. Solow and P. A. Samuelson, who defend the neo-classical position. In my own book this heroic struggle was not mentioned, mainly because I thought that the reader would be sufficiently confused by the text as it is; but I believe now that he, or she, is at least entitled to a few remarks on this utterly complex and unsettling subject. The following paragraphs intend to fill the gap, but are no more ambitious than that. They reflect my own rather unsure opinion and Dr Kregel is only responsible for them to the extent that his book made it clear to me that I should not have avoided the subject. My conclusions are certainly different from his.

Neo-classical theory, or the GOT, explains wages and the rate of interest by introducing the concept of marginal productivity. The marginal product of capital is the additional output one gets by adding one unit of capital to the existing stock. To formalize this idea, the production function $Q = F(L, K)$ was invented. Here Q represents the volume of production, L is the labour force and K is the existing stock of capital. The wage rate and the rate of interest are the partial derivatives of this function. (Those readers who find this difficult are referred to Chapter IV, where the same idea is explained somewhat more slowly.) Now in Cambridge, England, it was pointed out that the stock of physical capital is a heterogeneous mass of things like machines of different types, buildings, etc.; so the quantity K makes sense only if we measure it in money terms. But this value of the stock of capital is, as Piero Sraffa has shown,* not independent of the rate of profit. Therefore

* *Production of Commodities by Means of Commodities: Prelude to a Critique of Economic Theory*, Cambridge, England, 1960.

neo-classical theory gets into the vicious circle of explaining capitalists' incomes by assuming a given value of capital which can only be explained if capitalists' incomes are known. This weakness had already been spotted by Mrs Joan Robinson in the fifties;* she called the production function 'a powerful instrument of miseducation'. So the core of the Cambridge Criticism is either that the capital stock does not exist or that it cannot be evaluated if income distribution is not already given.

There came a reply from over the ocean when Robert Solow defended the neo-classical approach,† but the discussion remained rather calm for a number of years. It flared up in the sixties, after the publication of Sraffa's book, and it was mixed with a number of related issues. Is it true that neo-classical theory depicts capital as 'malleable', as a kind of jelly? Should we, instead of paying attention to the whole stock of capital, concentrate on the rate of return of this year's investment and thus escape the circulatory criticism?‡ Could we drop the notion of a stock of capital altogether and rely on 'a complete analysis of a great variety of heterogenous physical capital goods and processes through time'?§ The discussion gained in confusion when 'double-switching' and 'capital reversion' came to the fore. The former means that the same technique of production is the most profitable at two different rates of profit, but not at the rates of profit in-between; the latter means that a lower value of the rate of profit, instead of leading to a higher capital intensity, may lead entrepreneurs to a lower capital intensity. The question is: are these funny and unexpected happenings just curiosa, exceptions to the general neo-classical

* 'The Production Function and the Theory of Capital', *Review of Economic Studies*, 1953–4.

† 'The Production Function and the Theory of Capital', *Review of Economic Studies*, 1955–6.

‡ This is Solow's solution (*Capital Theory and the Rate of Return*, 1963). But Mrs Robinson replied ('Solow on the Rate of Return', *Economic Journal*, 1964) that the rate of return on investment implies a guess about prices and wages – that is about the rate of profit.

§ Samuelson's recommendation to rescue neo-classical theory, in 'Parable and Realism in Capital Theory; the Surrogate Production Function', *Review of Economic Studies*, 1962 (dedicated to Joan Robinson on the occasion of her visit to the Massachusetts Institute of Technology).

rules, perversities of badly behaving production functions, or are they devastating to the whole neo-classical mode of thinking?*

These are all highly technical matters; they are usually dealt with in terms of algebra and in a jargon that is difficult to follow even for economists. But in the background lurks the more ideological question of whether labour and capital ought to be treated alike. Because this is what neo-classical distribution theory does: labour and capital are both 'factors of production' or 'inputs'. They are both productive and scarce, they are both bought and sold in a market, they both command a price, and this price, whether it's the wage rate or the rate of interest, can be understood in much the same way. It is this symmetry that is under attack by the neo-Keynesians, because they believe that investment is determined in such a macro-economic context that the equilibrating forces of the capital market do not work (investment leads to saving, not the other way round). The symmetry between labour and capital is even more shocking to the neo-Marxists because, in their view, capital exploits labour and, in a capitalist society, the two can never be on the same footing.

And even among non-Marxists there seems to be a suspicion that the GOT is an ideological weapon in favour of raw capitalism and *laissez faire*; these people fear that once we accept the notion that capital is scarce and productive, we are committed to the view that the capitalists are *entitled* to whatever income the market will bring their way. Low wages will be morally justified by the worker's low contribution to the value of output. I think it is the supposed moral overtones of the whole business that makes Joan Robinson say that the production function is not only a swindle, but a harmful swindle at that.

Now the reader may ask where I stand in the Battle Between the Two Cambridges. The answer could be distilled from the main body of the book, but it seems better to formulate it more explicitly.

---

* The latter opinion is held by L. Pasinetti: 'The Rate of Profit and Income Distribution in Relation to the Rate of Economic Growth', *Review of Economic Studies*, 1962; A. Bhaduri: 'On the Significance of Recent Controversies on Capital Theory: a Marxist View', *Economic Journal*, 1969; and P. Garegnani: 'Heterogeneous Capital, the Production Function and the Theory of Capital', *Review of Economic Studies*, 1970.

I think that neo-classical theory has so much common sense behind it that we should try to defend its main positions. It can help us to understand certain remarkable developments; for instance, while capital becomes more and more important in the production process, capital gets a diminishing share of the national income. It has no ethical or reactionary implications. One may use certain elements of the GOT and still end up with egalitarian conclusions (Tinbergen is a case in point, see below, pp. 424 ff). Of course there are reactionary people who abuse the GOT for their own purposes (the 'leave them as you find them' school, see p. 312 above); but we should not reject the GOT for that reason. Moreover, in the field of distribution the neo-Keynesians have little to offer in its place, and the Marxists almost nothing.

The common sense of the neo-classical view is that the main part of the factors of production is bought or hired in markets by businessmen who are out for a profit; this motive makes them susceptible to the productive contributions of these factors. The marginal productivities do matter for the demand side of the labour market and the capital market. This is certainly true from the micro-economic viewpoint; it would be a pity if we had to give up this kind of common sense in macro-economics. To formalize these macro-relationships the production function is a useful instrument. To use it we must suppose that a thing like capital exists; it is of course a complex and heterogeneous quantity, but the same is true of other macro-economic quantities like output, the labour force, the export volume, etc. If we abandon capital as a measurable variable, we should not stop there, and then macro-economics goes down the drain. This will save us a lot of trouble. A more constructive approach is: how to value this thing called capital? Can we avoid the circular reasoning in which we explain the remuneration of capital by the value of capital and the value of capital by the income capitalists get?

Now there is one method of valuing the capital stock K that we should refrain from using. It is this: capitalizing the value of the expected future income stream. Though perfectly sound in a micro-economic sense, this method cannot be used in the context of a macro-economic theory of income distribution. It obviously falls victim to precisely the Cambridge Criticism: we derive capitalists' incomes from a value which is nothing but the discounted present worth of capitalists' incomes. Moreover, if we discount this income stream we let K crucially depend on future profits – and marginal productivity does not explain this specific kind of income. So, if Joan Robinson tries to push the adherents of the GOT in the direction of this method of valuation, they should firmly resist her.

That leaves us with the alternative valuation: the value of capital K should be measured by its cost of production.* This is a figure from the past. It should be corrected for general price movements (we try to measure *a volume*!) and, more complicated, for wear and tear. Now this method does not save us from the influence of profits (and rents of land, and interest) insofar as these elements enter into the past prices of capital goods. In fact, all history is embodied in the capital stock; not only the level of wages, profits, etc., but also productivity, the old state of technology and even institutional and legal arrangements (taxation, for instance, may affect the number of windows in houses). The capital stock is the link between the past and the future, and we cannot extract income relativities from this sequence. What the neo-classical theory cannot avoid is assuming that the old income distribution is still with us in the frozen value of capital – but is that a reason to reject the whole reasoning as fraudulent? I don't think so.

This way of looking at the problem seems helpful, but unfortunately it does not answer all criticisms. The value of a given capital stock is not only determined by past costs, but also by the rate at which old equipment has been scrapped. This rate is not just a matter of physical wear and tear; it is influenced by the speed at which technically sound equipment becomes obsolete. But this speed depends on present and future cost and price relationships; in other words, on income distribution. So we cannot escape the

---

* There seem to be other possibilities, for instance the one favoured by Marxists: capital is measured by accumulated labour time. I do not recommend this. The background of the idea is the labour theory of value – a highly scholastic construction. Even more scholastic is Sraffa's idea of using a Standard Commodity as the yardstick. Sraffa is looking for the Absolute Standard of Value; he reminds me of Hegel.

conclusion that the value of capital is in some way determined by the very variables we want to explain.

In this sense the Cambridge Criticism of the GOT is certainly justified. But is that decisive? A century ago the Lausanne School showed that in economics everything depends on everything else. This contains a warning against oversimplification; we may leave certain relationships out of account, but only if they are sufficiently non-strategic to the problem in hand. In this particular debate on income distribution everybody has to answer the question for himself whether he or she thinks it admissible to forget (temporarily) about the income relationships that are implied in the value of capital. My own answer is affirmative, but this a matter of taste. I am not a firm believer.* If the reader prefers to accept the Cambridge Criticisms, I cannot stop him.

Unfortunately, my position towards neo-classical theory is even more cautious than this. The neo-classical school, as I see it, can explain a good deal of wages, the rate of interest and rent of land. But it cannot explain profits. Genuine residual profits remain 'the troublesome category' (Chapter IV, 7). We know the causal factors that determine profits – they are neatly enumerated in this book – but we don't know the mix of these determining factors; there is no rigorous model of profit determination in existence, at least not macro-economically. Now this is a crucial point. Neo-classical theory is a strictly closed system on the condition that there are no profits. So it does not explain one hundred per cent of reality. My guess would be that this unexplained residual, as far as profits are concerned, constitutes about ten per cent of the national income.

Now there are two possible opinions, both legitimate. On the one hand we may follow Piero Sraffa's theoretical pureness, and say: if this neo-classical system leaves us with such a gap it is no system at all. A bucket with a hole in it is no bucket. Everything depends on everything else; leave profits unexplained, and your

---

* But I firmly believe that the double-switching and capital-reversion issues ought to be dealt with in a vermiform appendix. The fact that these funny anomalies are magnified by Bhaduri *et al.* until these authors believe that they have defeated neo-classical theory makes one think that there is something wrong with their sense of proportion.

rate of interest is in the air; you can't say what determines wages, your macro-economics is simply nowhere at all. On the other hand one may deplore, as I do, the fact that we have no consistent, all-embracing system and still believe that neo-classical theory can be useful for systematizing and explaining certain facts of life. A bucket with a hole in it is not a practical device to carry quicksilver in; but perhaps it is useful for the transportation of a few bricks. This cautious belief, mixed with scepticism, is the foundation of much that is written in the chapters of this book. The recipe will not appeal to those who look for rigorous, radiating Truth, for Absolute Standards and for perfectly closed systems.

Before I leave the reader to his own conscience (and to the extensive literature on capital theory*), one more word of warning. If he decides against the GOT he will be left in a barren world, where income distribution is determined, if by anything at all, by blind mechanisms. Sraffa, the deepest thinker of the Cambridge School, has no theory of distribution. Though the wage rate and the rate of profit are vital to his system of values, they are exogenously given. Of course, some neo-Keynesians have theories about wages and profits, but they are not commendable. A most funny construction, but not untypical of a whole group of economists, is the so-called Widow's Cruse. We divide the national income, first into wages and profits, and next into consumption and investment. Then we suppose that workers do not save; they consume their wages. It follows, with strict logic, that profits equal investments. Now we take one big step and start telling people that we have discovered the laws of distribution. The proportion of wages and profits is determined by the entrepreneurs; they decide the level of investments, and therefore their own total sum of profits. What they invest comes back to them. This is the Cruse. The idea is summarized in the beautiful adage: 'Workers spend what they get, capitalists get what they spend'. It's a good joke but it does not illuminate the world we live in. In practice it

* For instance the Penguin Reader, *Capital and Growth*, 1971, edited by the neo-Keynesian G. C. Harcourt and the neo-classicist N. F. Laing. Learned stuff – intellectually fascinating but rather remote from what most people would expect when they are curious about income distribution. Yet the book is relevant to our subject.

may so happen (and it does happen nowadays) that investment creates tensions in the labour market; this drives up wages, profits are squeezed, the Widow's Cruse is emptied. Of course, investments may go down in the course of the profit squeeze, but that does not save the theory; for in the meantime distribution is not explained by the level of investment but by, *inter alia*, supply and demand in the labour market. Variations on this barren theme are found in Mrs Robinson's *Accumulation of Capital* (1956) where, as I understand it, the case is discussed in which entrepreneurs decide to increase their level of investment *when money wages are given* – to nobody's surprise this act of investment leads to increased profits. The same story is told by a scholar called Föhl, whose work is discussed on p. 181 above. The most popular theory among neo-Keynesians is Kaldor's, but unfortunately in his view the causal chains run backwards; given distribution a certain saving ratio results, but there is one and only one saving ratio that is consistent with a given level of investment. So if investment is fixed at a pre-determined level, and if workers and capitalists have different saving habits, distribution is determined. The reader who does not understand this quick summary of Kaldorian economics is referred to p. 186 above.

I sometimes think that my main ideological objection to this type of neo-Keynesian distribution theory is that distribution is severed from what happens in the markets for productive factors. The neo-Keynesian mechanisms do away with the influence of human capabilities on macro-distribution. Education cannot improve the share of labour in the national income. The human-capital approach becomes fruitless. There is no *raison-d'être* for trade unions. Minimum wages are of no avail. All the important things happen behind people's backs, by widow's cruses, differential saving ratios, 'structures' and blind mechanisms. If you always believed that people are powerless, the victims of capitalist society, then this is your school. It is not mine.

I am glad to mention a specimen of the opposite way of thinking. It is Tinbergen's deeply humanistic research into the actual and the optimal wage and salary relationships. This is all about human beings, their personal capacities and their happiness. Though this approach remains within an existing tradition – the 'human-capital' theory – there are a number of marked differences. One technical point (also discussed on p. 251 above) is that Tinbergen does not only take the supply side of the labour market into account, but also the demand for certain human capabilities. In this way one may estimate the influence of an expansion of education on wage and salary differentials. In his more recent work the scope of the theory has widened; Tinbergen not only wants to explain the existing income distribution but he also tries to provide a scientific help to answering normative questions such as: what is the optimal or just degree of inequality? And the most ambitious question: what does all this mean to human welfare?* Of course, speculative thoughts about these matters are not new, but Tinbergen tries to formulate the answers in a quantitative way. It is precisely the combination of ethics and econometrics which makes Tinbergen's contribution so fascinating.

The method is roughly as follows. The labour market is divided into a number of compartments (about twenty – the number differs in various publications) each characterized by the level of required schooling, called s, and the level of actual schooling, called v. These variables are measured in years of schooling. For each compartment the number of workers in it, their average pre- and post-tax income, and the divergence between actual and required level of schooling are estimated. This difference $s-v$ is important because it influences income distribution, but it is even more important because it influences human welfare. A worker will be unhappy when his work is too difficult for him, but also when he feels that his capacities are insufficiently made use of. Income is explained in terms of s and v, and in certain cases also by a person's capacity to make independent decisions. To determine the specific scarcity element in the income scale a Cobb-Douglas production function is used† and wages are equated to marginal products. Scarcity incomes are interpreted by Tinbergen

* J. Tinbergen, *An Interdisciplinary Approach to the Measurement of Utility or Welfare*, Fifth Geary Lecture, 1972. Published by the Economic and Social Research Institute, Dublin, 1972. Also: 'A Positive and a Normative Theory of Income Distribution', *Review of Income and Wealth*, 1970.

† See p. 191 above.

as 'exploitation' by human capital.* A person's utility (that is, the happiness he or she derives from his job and the income that goes with it) is assumed to depend on the logarithm of his consumable income y, corrected for the (in)conveniences of higher job requirements s, and for the square of the deviation between the required and the actual level of schooling $s-v$. This utility function is estimated; the result (a highly experimental result, and only ascertained for the Netherlands in the sixties) is ln† $[y - 0.45s + 0.32 (s-v)^2]$. Tinbergen's ethical starting point is the fundamental equality of human beings; people are assumed to be equal until empirical proof of the contrary is given. This basic idea leads him to the opinion that, under certain assumptions, incomes are justly distributed if all individual utilities are equal.‡ From this it follows that a person's income ought to be $0.45s + 0.32 (s-v)^2$, plus a constant. The capacity to make independent decisions does not enter into this normative income, because Tinbergen suggests that this may be an innate characteristic; in the strictly egalitarian creed innate properties are no justification for income differentials. For similar reasons, there is no direct connection between one's level of schooling and the just wage. Only the required level of education and the tension factor $s-v$ enter into the distributive ethics. These just incomes are calculated and compared with actual post-tax incomes; the result is that upper-middle-class salaries should be decreased by 30 to 40 per cent, whilst the lowest wages should be increased by 25 per cent. In Tinbergen's train of thought this levelling could partly be achieved by a massive injection of education. This would change the relative scarcities of different kinds of labour. Another quantitative but very tentative conclusion (for the Netherlands, 1960) is that doubling the number of university graduates would halve income inequality, the latter

* *An Interdisciplinary Approach*, p. 15.

† *ln* is the sign for the natural logarithm; see p. 26.

‡ This ethical position differs from the Ehrenfest-Tinbergen principle of exchange, discussed on p. 303 of this book. Equality of individual utilities comes closer to the strict egalitarianism of John Rawls (*A Theory of Justice*, 1971). Tinbergen leaves open the possibility that people have quite different needs; this may, of course, lead to a different shape of the optimal distribution, but this issue is not considered in the publications discussed here.

in the specific sense of the ratio between the average income of the top decile and average income.*

Tinbergen sees his recent research as a first step; it is meant as a challenge to more refined work. He indicates a number of refinements, such as the use of job-classification data for estimating s and $s-v$. It is obvious that a number of criticisms can be made to this line of work. The econometrics is ingenious but sometimes rather reckless; in particular the measurement of the tension between required and actual education is a thorny affair.† The utility function is necessarily arbitrary and some will feel that it is primitive. The strong egalitarian coffee will not be to everybody's taste, and in particular anti-egalitarians will disagree with the notion that an official's responsibility and his capacity to make decisions should not at all enter into the salary he is entitled to. The main recommendation – a heavy dose of additional education to reduce income differentials – raises uneasy questions, such as the capability of sufficient numbers of children and young people to be educated; an elitist view would deny this possibility.‡ Also the process of intensified education might produce more complicated technologies and a more complicated sort of society generally, which results in an undesired byproduct: the shifting of demand for highly qualified labour to the right. This shift might partly neutralize the levelling effect on the income structure. Until

* J. Tinbergen 'The Impact of Education on Income Distribution', *Review of Income and Wealth*, 1972.

† In fact, Tinbergen measures s by the schooling level of the best-educated 25 % of the people in a given labour-market compartment. This implies that he assumes that 75 % of all Dutch workers are not qualified for their jobs.

‡ And some observers even deny that education makes a difference. One sometimes hears hardboiled businessmen say that they don't care what a boy has learned in the classroom; what matters is whether he has a sense of purpose, the ability to look a man in the face without seeming to stare, the right outlook on life generally, the right accent, etc. This school has recently received unexpected support from Christopher Jencks in his book *Inequality, A Reassessment of the Effect of Family and Schooling in America*, 1972. His position seems to be that if all people had the same schooling, income differences would still be the same; employers would just look for other capacities in their employees to justify income inequality. Jencks's reasoning is hardly convincing, if only because he does not make clear why employers

now, the effect of increased schooling has not been impressive.*
Tinbergen would be the first to accept that his starting points and
his methods are imperfect but his reply would be that his research
is meant to be improved.

One more recent book should be mentioned: Dudley Jackson's
Poverty (1972). This is an analytical approach, centred around the
distinction between want and deprivation; both are forms of
poverty. Want is defined as a failure of a person's or family's
income flow; this may lead to insufficient nutrition, poor health
and a low life expectancy. Deprivation is a matter of stocks:
assets, liabilities and their balance, called net worth. Examples of
a person's assets are: physical health, education, abilities (human
capital), housing and equipment (physical capital), family life
(cultural capital), social security (social capital). Liabilities are
defined as stocks that impair one's social functioning, like illness,
insufficient intelligence, old age, living in a slum. These distinctions
are important to an understanding of the dynamics of poverty:
flows change the level of stocks, and stocks carry the situation
forward from one period to the next. What Jackson has in mind
is a dynamic stock-flow model of want and deprivation. Though
he does not formalize this model into a quantitative system of
equations, and in his book there is no endeavour to estimate the
net worth of individuals or groups, this conceptual framework
lends precision to the more impressionistic accounts of the
vicious circles of poverty by authors like Michael Harrington
(whose *The Other America* is discussed above, p. 261). Moreover,
the 'Social Welfare Matrix', as described by Jackson in his final
chapter (a kind of input–output table for the British social services), obviously invites work in a quantitative direction. If this
kind of research is to be really fruitful it should be inter-disciplinary;
sociology and economics must go hand in hand. The 'net worth'

---

are so keen on stabilizing the salary structure, and because he does not seem
to be aware of the forces of the market.

* Cf. Zwi Griliches, who studied an enormous mass of statistical evidence:
'The puzzling thing is that these large differentials and rates of return
should change so little in the face of very large shifts in the number of
educated workers' (*Education, Income and Human Capital*, 1970, p. 104).

of a Puerto Rican family in New York City should be ascertained and compared over a number of years; rates of return on investment in its housing, its education, its neighbourhood could be estimated, so as to determine the best social policies. Basically, this approach is consistent with the human-capital approach and even with neo-classical theory.

There is one important aspect of inequality that has not been systematically discussed in the literature. Suppose it is true what the new Club-of-Rome doomsday philosophy says, that the rate of growth of real income will slow down in the near future, either because energy and raw materials will become bottlenecks to a further increase in production, or because governments will follow a deliberate policy of putting brakes on growth to protect the environment. In that case distribution will probably get a new and vicious political edge. It is often alleged that society can cope with such an unprecedented situation only if inequality is drastically diminished. If the burdens of zero-growth cannot be shared equally, tension about distribution will run so high that any policy aiming at a more stable kind of production will necessarily fail. But neither the harsh measures aiming at zero-growth nor the corresponding methods to reduce inequality have been studied by economic theory. There appears to be a gap in our knowledge and our imagination which deserves the attention of a profession that has, for a long time, been taking economic growth for granted and that has been studying income distribution in the context of continuous growth.

This quick and somewhat haphazard review of developments since 1971 shows one thing: the theory of income distribution has not yet come to a standstill. What is needed is not just refinement, some more computer work or a settling of minor squabbles. There are fundamental differences of opinion about the most fruitful approach; in the meantime in the field of quantitative research quite new directions are being opened. There is still a lot of work to be done.

A Glossary of Technical Terms and Symbols

Production function: the way in which the level of output (Q) depends on the input of productive factors, mostly labour (L) and capital (K); in symbols $Q = F(L,K)$.

Cobb-Douglas Function: special form of the production function, e.g. $Q = AL^\alpha K^{1-\alpha}$. Special properties: $\alpha = \lambda$, $1-\alpha = \kappa$, $\sigma = 1$ (see below, at Elasticity of Substitution, Labour's Share, Capital's Share).

Solow Function: another special form of the production function,

e.g. $Q = (L^\alpha + K^\alpha)^{1/\alpha}$. In this case $\sigma = \dfrac{1}{1-\alpha}$.

Marginal Product of Labour (or Capital): the additional amount of product δQ which results from one additional unit of labour δL (or capital δK). Also the partial derivative of the production function $\delta Q/\delta L$ for labour and $\delta Q/\delta K$ for capital.

Labour Productivity: amount of output divided by amount of labour. In symbols: Q/L.

Capital Productivity: amount of output divided by amount of capital. In symbols: Q/K.

Capital Intensity: amount of capital per worker, K/L.

Elasticity of Production with regard to Labour: the percentage increase in production which follows from an increase in the amount of labour by 1%.

Elasticity of Production with regard to Capital: same as for Labour (see above).

Elasticity of Substitution: the percentage increase in the capital intensity (K/L) which follows from an increase in the price ratio of labour and capital by 1%. Symbol: σ.

Demand (Curve) for Labour: the way in which the amount of labour demanded by employers depends on wage rate.

Demand for Capital: same as for Labour (see above).

Supply of Labour: the way in which the amount of labour supplied by workers depends on the wage rate.

Supply of Capital: same as for Labour (see above).

Elasticity of Demand for Labour (or Capital): the percentage increase in the quantity demanded which follows from a decrease in the wage rate (interest rate) by 1%.

Elasticity of Supply of Labour (or Capital): the percentage increase in the amount supplied by workers (capitalists) which follows from an increase in the wage rate (interest rate) by 1%.

Inelastic Demand (or Supply): demand (supply) with an elasticity smaller than 1.

Phillips Curve: the way in which an increase (w) in the wage level (W), expressed as a percentage ($\triangle W/W \times 100$), depends on unemployment as a percentage of the total labour force (U).

Degree of Monopoly: price minus marginal cost as a fraction of the price ($\frac{P-M}{P}$).

Logarithm of a Number: the power to which a given base number (often 10) must be raised to obtain that number.

Labour's Share (λ): total wage bill as a fraction of national income. In symbols: $\frac{WL}{Y}$.

Capital's Share (κ): total of interest as a fraction of national income. In symbols: $\frac{RK}{Y}$. Sometimes the share of capital also includes profits and rents; in that case $\lambda + \kappa = 1$. If the share of capital is limited to pure interest ('Pure Share of Capital') this is obviously not so.

Hicks's Law: if the elasticity of substitution is smaller than 1, the fastest-growing factor of production sees its income share diminished.

Lorenz Curve: shows how the income share of a group of income recipients (measured as a percentage of the total and ranked from the poorest upwards) depends on the percentage of the group in the total number of income recipients (also measured as a percentage).

Pareto's Law: the number of income recipients (N_y) earning a given Selected Income (y) or more decreases by a fixed percentage (α) if we raise the Selected Income Level by 1%. In symbols $N_y = A.y^{-\alpha}$.

Gini's Law: if we lower the Selected Income Level (y) by such an amount that the total income (Y) earned by income recipients who get that Selected Income or more increases by 1%, then the number of income recipients increases by a fixed percentage (β). In symbols: $N_y = B.Y^{\beta}$.

Van der Wijk's Law: the average income of all income recipients above a Selected Income Level is proportionate to that Selected Income Level. In symbols: $\dfrac{Y}{N_y} = \gamma.y$. Pareto's Law, Gini's Law and Van der Wijk's Law can be transposed into each other.

Gibrat's Law: the logarithms of personal incomes are distributed normally.

Lydall's Law: each Selected Income Level is proportionate to the total of the incomes of the job-holders just below it.

Index of Persons

MORE ABOUT PENGUINS
AND PELICANS

Penguinews, which appears every month, contains details of all the new books issued by Penguins as they are published. From time to time it is supplemented by *Penguins in Print*, which is a complete list of all titles available (There are some five thousand of these.)

A specimen copy of *Penguinews* will be sent to you free on request. For a year's issues (including the complete lists) please send 50p if you live in the British Isles, or 75p if you live elsewhere. Just write to Dept EP, Penguin Books Ltd, Harmondsworth, Middlesex, enclosing a cheque or postal order, and your name will be added to the mailing list.

In the U.S.A.: For a complete list of books available from Penguin in the United States write to Dept CS, Penguin Books Inc., 7110 Ambassador Road, Baltimore, Maryland 21207.

In Canada: For a complete list of books available from Penguin in Canada write to Penguin Books Canada Ltd, 41 Steelcase Road West, Markham, Ontario.

BRITAIN IN FIGURES

A HANDBOOK OF SOCIAL STATISTICS

Alan F. Sillitoe

Second Edition

This handbook of statistical graphs and diagrams, with explanatory texts, has been prepared by a sociologist to illustrate recent and current social trends in Britain (with foreign figures for comparison). It makes the perfect tool for quick reference on the desk and for settling arguments in the home.

Population – Growth, ages, expectation of life, deaths, density, immigration

Social Data – Marriage, divorce, pensions, house-building, religion

Education – Numbers at schools and universities, examination passes, expenditure

Labour – Hours worked, Trade Unions, strikes, unemployment

The Economy – Public and private expenditure, prices, incomes, taxation, inflation, exports and imports

Transport & Communications – Cars, telephones etc., road deaths, road-building

Mass Media – Newspapers, radio, television, cinemas and their audiences

POVERTY: THE FORGOTTEN ENGLISHMEN

Ken Coates and Richard Silburn

Is poverty in Britain a thing of the past? Too many of our countrymen regularly do without the minimum considered necessary for a healthy diet; they live in houses that are overcrowded, insanitary and ludicrously expensive to keep warm and comfortable; their children attend schools in which teaching is a near-impossibility.

Ken Coates and Richard Silburn look again at what is meant by the word 'poverty'. They conclude that vast numbers of Englishmen, living in slums throughout the country, are, for most of their lives, living in acute poverty. What this actually involves is spelled out by means of a detailed survey of one slum – St Ann's, an area of Nottingham which has now been cleared but remains typical of hundreds of such districts.

The book continues with a study of welfare services and why they fail to alleviate or remove poverty, and finally there is an analysis of the frequent failure of slum-clearance schemes.

Originally published as a Penguin Special, this Pelican attacks a problem – that of modern urban poverty – neglected by western society.

'Writing with compassion, style, wit and an almost complete lack of jargon, (they) present us with inescapable facts which must remould our thinking and our actions' – *The Times*

POVERTY AND EQUALITY IN BRITAIN

A STUDY OF SOCIAL SECURITY AND TAXATION

J. C. Kincaid

If you are complacently satisfied that the British system of social security is the finest in the world, this important book by Dr Kincaid may shake you.

Quoting estimates that suggest that 2,000,000 people in Britain are living in acute poverty, he argues that their poverty is a direct consequence of inadequate social-security schemes, that the Welfare State does nothing effective to iron out inequality, and that the services offered are far less egalitarian and more punitive than is generally supposed.

In the belief that poverty and inequality are integral components of a competitive social order, the author urges us to re-think our ideas about the poor. Working-class militancy, in his view, lacks political expression: if the unions were prepared to take action over the sores that fester in our society 'neither a Labour nor a Conservative Government would dare treat the old, the sick and the unemployed as they do at present'.

GUIDE TO THE BRITISH ECONOMY

Peter Donaldson

Third Edition – Revised

Guide to the British Economy is intended for the general reader who would like to have some grasp of what economics is about and what makes the economy tick, but who may find the textbook approach unpalatably abstract. Economic ideas, therefore, are presented here within the real context of the British economy. The aim is both to give an impression of the working of the different elements in the economy, and to illustrate the extent to which economic analysis can be helpful in solving the problems which face policy-makers.

In the first part of this introductory guide Peter Donaldson is mainly concerned with matters of finance, including the stockmarket. After a full examination of industry, labour, and trade he goes on, in the final section of the book, to a general discussion of economic theories, their scope, and limitations.

'This highly readable text raises and discusses sensibly and constructively the large and controversial economic arguments that rumble on day after day in our newspapers and in front of the television cameras' – *The Times Educational Supplement*.

'An excellent little book. It provides a most lucid and absorbing survey of the British Economy for the intelligent layman or for the beginning student of economics. It really cannot be faulted in either its scope or its exposition' – Professor Lomax in the *Economic Journal*

ECONOMICS OF THE REAL WORLD

Peter Donaldson

A sense of economic failure is in the air. The British economy may be working better than ever ... without booms and slumps, without mass unemployment: yet government after government fails to achieve simultaneously full employment, stable prices, and economic growth.

Explaining why this is so, the author of *A Guide to the British Economy* describes here how a mixed economy is managed and (given the underlying market mechanisms) what can and what cannot be the subject of economic policy. More basically he argues that economics itself is strangely remote from the urgent problems of ordinary people and that policy-makers confuse ends and means. What matters, in his view, is not growth, but growth of what, for whom and at what cost; not full employment but the nature of work; not just more wealth, but its more equitable distribution.

For *this* is the real world – a world of values and people – neglected by orthodox economics and evaded by policy-makers. Why? Because, suggests Peter Donaldson, if the real issues are to be tackled, there has to be a revolution in our whole outlook on economics and society.

MODERN ECONOMICS

J. Pen

In 1936 Keynes published his famous *General Theory of Employment, Interest and Money*, and the science of economics has never been the same since. Gone is the comfortable 'classical' belief in a self-adjusting balance between supply and demand; moreover, allied to Keynesian theory, the growth of exact quantitative economics has tended to produce a distinct 'modern economics'. A silent revolution has occurred.

It is widely held that Keynesian theories can only be comprehended by the expert, and this in itself delays the application of modern ideas, since every citizen, when he shops, works, or votes, is a practising economist. Professor Pen, the well-known Dutch economist, challenges this assumption in this Pelican, in which he sets out to explain to the non-expert the meaning of Keynes's ideas and the findings of modern statistical methods.

His book provides a clear (and frequently humorous and hard-hitting) introduction to modern theories regarding international trade, national budgets, the function of money inflation and deflation, wages, economic growth, and many other economic topics in daily discussion.